In Nature's Ha

Also by Louise Riotte

Carrots Love Tomatoes
Roses Love Garlic
Sleeping with a Sunflower
Astrological Gardening

in NATURE's HANDS

An Organic Gardening Potpourri,
from Armadillos
to Zucchini

LOUISE RIOTTE

With Illustrations by the Author

Taylor Publishing Company
Dallas, Texas

Published by   Taylor Publishing Company
               1550 West Mockingbird Lane
               Dallas, Texas 75235

Designed by Barbara Whitehead

Library of Congress Cataloging-in-Publication Data

Riotte, Louise.
    In nature's hands : an organic gardening pot-
  pourri, from armadillos to zucchini / Louise Riotte.
      p.   cm.
    Includes index.
    ISBN 0-87833-787-3 : $13.95
    1. Organic gardening—Miscellanea.
  2. Gardening—Miscellanea.
  I. Title
  SB453.5.R54   1992
  635'.0484—dc20   91-46772
                                              CIP

Printed in the United States of America
10 9 8 7 6 5 4 3 2 1

CONTENTS

Introduction: The *Possible* Dream   1
A to Z Hints For Those Who Would "Take it Easy"   5

Layering: A Healthy Way To Grow   200
Harvest When The Time Is Right!   202
Use Your Garden Fence   206
Conserving Energy—Yours!   208

Sources of Supply   211
Bibliography   213
Index   215

I dedicate this book to
My lovely granddaughter—
Laura Elizabeth Riotte,
Who grows in beauty of mind and spirit
With each passing day.

North, South, East or West,
Hope springs eternal in the gardener's breast;
His dream is something he holds most dear
That this will be the perfect year
Onions will bulb, and corn grow tall
The orchard will give a great windfall;
He'll have the garden of his dreams
And he falls right in with Nature's schemes.
We've tickled the earth through countless years,
And she's laughed with a harvest through her tears;
We've worked with her as she commands
And placed our trust in Nature's hands.

Louise Riotte

INTRODUCTION:
The *Possible* Dream

This used to be among my prayers—a piece of land
not so very large, which would contain a garden, and
near the house a spring of ever-flowing water, and
beyond these a bit of wood.

HORACE

Ah yet, ere I descend to the grave
May I a small house and large garden have;
And a few friends, and many books, both true,
Both wise, and both delightful too!

ABRAHAM COWLEY (1618–1667)

To own a bit of ground, to scratch it with a hoe, to
plant seeds, and watch the renewal of life—this
is the commonest delight of the race, the most
satisfactory thing a man can do.

My Summer in a Garden (1870)
CHARLES DUDLEY WARNER (1829–1900)

Why garden at all? When I ask my readers why they garden I receive a surprising number of different answers. Lots of people make a vegetable garden, even a flower garden, to save money. However, just as many tell me they enjoy their garden as recreation, a change of pace after a day of desk work or the stress of talking to clients, seeing patients, or working with complicated machinery. Others feel that their gardens provide them with a better product: organically grown, clean, unsprayed fruits and vegetables that may be allowed to ripen on the plant to a finer degree of taste and succulence than those picked partially unripe (so they will withstand shipping without spoilage).

Taking any or all of these reasons into consideration I believe that gardening also should be *fun*. To this end I have written *In Nature's Hands* with the idea that gardening should be made as easy as possible, that you should be able to achieve all these things in a pleasant and profitable way. However, just as "there is no such thing as a free lunch," there is no such thing as a "no-work garden." But the work should be as light as possible, as interesting as possible, and as productive as possible—and this book will give you plenty of labor-saving tips.

Of course it is desirable that gardeners obtain all possible scientific background for their garden work; such a background is highly valuable, but it cannot take the place of practice and experience. And a gardener's best source of information is often the reliable authority nearest home—someone in your own area who is familiar with the climate and soil. There is no better way of learning about gardens than watching and talking to a good gardener. "Ask the man who grows one," and you will probably receive a treasure-trove of valuable information which will see you well on your way to achievement.

In writing this book I have drawn upon not only my own experience but also that of many of my friends and readers who have generously shared with me tips, tricks, and shortcuts that they have found useful and time-saving. Most of us do not have a large acreage on which to garden, but even a city backyard or vacant lot garden can supply an important proportion of the fresh vegetables a family needs. Sometimes it can even furnish a surplus for storing, canning, or drying, depending on how much good land is available and how well the garden is managed— using interplanting, succession planting, companion planting, and any available fences or trellises. A well-handled home garden in a suitable place should consistently yield produce with a money value considerably greater than the cost of seeds, fertilizer, lime, manure, insect controls, and tools needed for the garden. The health values of the produce and the outdoor exercise are of particular interest to many. And, since cut flowers have become increasingly costly, there is growing interest in these as well.

As our concern over the use of pesticides grows each year we become more intensely interested in ways to overcome their use. Pollution of the soil is long range and may take many years to eradicate. In some instances our soil may never be healed again and become fit for human occupancy—certainly

not for the growth of plants intended for consumption as foods. Companion planting is emerging more and more as a safe way to keep crops pest-free without the use of harmful chemicals. And companion planting and organic gardening go hand in hand, its practitioners endeavoring to create harmonious interactions in their garden plots.

Nature abhors idle ground. Left to her own way she will always have roots hanging into the topsoil to prevent erosion. And she almost never leaves wide, unplanted, unmulched areas between growing plants. Furthermore, her plants, in most instances, grow very closely together. And she is totally realistic in the matter of checks and balances. Instead of isolating particular kinds or varieties, she often places them "shoulder to shoulder" with each other. Thus they become—in her plan—a source of needed shade, a climbing support, or a provider of mulch and soil-conditioning food. They may even repel other plants, preventing a sturdy too-aggressive species from completely taking over.

Even so, when fertile soil is left uncultivated, it is likely to host a tangled diversity of plants. But you, as a gardener, don't have to let a jungle spring up in your backyard in order to bring natural integration into your garden. Companion planting, practiced with care and thought and a knowledge of plant relationships, is an orderly way to create natural diversity. This *controlled* diversity permits you to maximize your gardening area's use of water, sun, and soil nutrients. And, of course, the use of "companions" is one of your most valuable weapons in pest and weed control.

Interplanting is another way to increase your production, especially valuable for the small garden where space is at a premium. I like to keep a succession of lettuce plants coming up to use for transplants between broccoli, cauliflower or cabbage. As the *Brassicas* grow and need more room, the lettuce is pulled. It is crisp and sweet right into hot weather because it has grown in the shade of the larger plants. Another way to utilize space is to pop a lettuce plant into the onion row as young onions are used for the table. With this type of planning it is possible to get nearly twice as much production from a given garden area. You also get all the mileage possible out of your compost or fertilizer.

Knowledge about and practicing garden tricks and tips makes everything a lot more fun and helps ensure success. Who wants an aching back when you can do things the easy way? And who wants skinny, anemic-looking fruits and vegetables when it is just as easy and a lot more rewarding to have them plump and succulent? The best gardening methods are creations of Mother Nature—not clever gardeners—so look, learn, and adopt!

All that in this delightful garden grows,
Should happy be, and have immortal bliss.
EDMUND SPENSER

A-FRAMES Vegetables, once considered space wasters in the small garden, can now take off skyward! Designed with vining vegetables in mind, the A-frame is actually an extension of the trellis idea. A-frames are especially suited to the small fruited watermelon, winter squash, melons, cucumbers, small sugar pumpkins, and just about anything that vines can be vertically trained on. A-frames have several advantages over the vertical trellis. You can position them to take advantage of maximum sunlight and heat on one side, leaving the other for growing crops needing a cooler environment. Supporting itself, an A-frame does not need heavy permanent posts. And, when no longer needed, it can be hinged to fold flat for storage. An A-frame can be converted into a tent for early spring frost protection by covering it with plastic.

Pole beans and cucumbers are easier to see when the "trellis" is on a 45- to 70-degree slant. And cukes, when hanging down, grow straighter. If the frame is latticed on one side and open on the other, vegetables then hang down and may be harvested more easily.

ADDER'S TONGUE OINTMENTS
Don't sell the fernlike adder's tongue (*Ophioglossum valgatum*) of fields and waste places short; it's a supreme wound herb. According to Juliette de Bairacli Levy in her *Herbal Handbook for Farm and Stable*, the general preparation is by infusing the leaf and spike in warm olive oil, brewing gently, not boiling. A fine balsam of a brilliant green color is thus produced.

French gypsies make adder's tongue ointment by using equal parts of olive oil, white wax (beeswax), and fat (preferably the nut fat sold in vegetarian or health food shops). In general, herbivorous animals instinctively dislike the fat of other dead animals being used on their bodies. The fat is melted over a slow fire until fully dissolved, resulting in about one pint of melted fat into which is put as much finely chopped adder's tongue as will be absorbed. Stir for about 10 minutes. Pour into jars, keeping uncovered until well set. Helpful when applied to all wounds, sores, bruises, ulcers, etc. or horses, cows, sheep, goats, dogs, etc.

AFRICAN VIOLET (*Saintpaulia* spp.)
African violets seem to be constantly increasing in popularity. If you have never grown them before, take a tip from thrifty Louise and buy one of the inexpensive older varieties for your first adventure into a

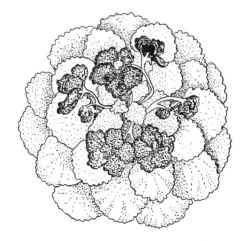

hobby that may well become in time almost a religious experience!

In 1892, Walter von Saint Paul Illaire, the German governor of East Africa, found specimens of African violets growing in Tanga Province. He sent plants to his father, Ulrich, who turned them over to a well-known botanist, Herman Wendland of Herrenhausen, the director of the Botanic Gardens. Wendland described the specimen as *Saintpauli ioantha* in the June 19, 1893 issue of *Gartenflora*.

Despite the fact that these beauties are old favorites, they are *not* one of the easiest houseplants to grow. They have very firm likes and dislikes, are quite "set in their ways," hate sudden change, and absolutely loathe to be moved around. Here are some hints for those who would like to enjoy growing them. Once you understand the African violet, you can move on to some of the gorgeous beauties like Burpee's "Blueberry Muffin." Becoming an aficionado may take a little time but it will be worth the effort.

African violets do not like extremes. The temperature they thrive in can range between 60° F and 85° F—but no lower or higher than that. Only mild winter sun should ever be allowed to shine on them directly, for they can be burned to a fatal crisp by the hot blaze of summer rays.

They just *love* humidity. Never let them dry out between waterings. But even here they have a dislike for extremes; damp, yes, dripping, *no*. Water with lukewarm or room temperature water—your plant will be grateful for extra care in watering. Not only must you try to avoid splashing or wetting the leaves, but you should also think in the terms of the best water available. Save rainwater or use melted snow, particularly if your "city water" is hard. Your African violet may wilt just at the thought of hard water.

They prefer small, neat pots. And they just love being cleaned and groomed; use a soft watercolor brush to flick dust off the leaves. Sit the pots in a gravel- or pebble-lined container and keep water at pebble level. This will also help maintain the gentle humidity and genteel atmosphere that keeps them in a good humor. Once you graduate in African violet care you can "go for broke" and treat yourself to 'Raspberry Rose,' 'Spots and Dots,' 'Snowkist Haven,' 'Creole Royale,' 'Grand Duchess,' or 'Peach Jubilee.'

> **African Violet Tip:** You can buy seeds for all the plants you want for less than the cost of a single plant. Just sow the tiny seeds on top of a moist growing medium (such as Park's Grow Mix), keep moist, and provide light. You'll have blooming 4-inch plants in just five to six months!

AIR LAYERING   Propagating new plants by air layering is a method of vegetative propagation convenient to use when stems or branches do not lend themselves to ground layering. To do this girdle the stem or branch by removing a narrow strip of bark all around it at a point some 8 to 12 inches from the top of the shoot; or, at about the same distance from the tip of the shoot, make a cut in the stem about an inch long and extending one third of the way through the shoot. Make this cut upwards, towards the tip of the shoot. Peg the cut open with a thin sliver of wood. Around the incision wrap a rather large bundle of sphagnum moss and tie it securely in position with string. Keep the moss moist by wrapping it tightly in polyethylene film and keep the roots of the old plant rather dry. New roots will soon appear at the incision, penetrate the moss ball and be visible on its outside. Separate the new plant from the old one by cutting it off below the moss ball. It should then be potted and kept in a close, moist atmosphere until it has become reestablished. (See "Layering: A Healthy Way To Grow" in the appendices.)

AMARANTH According to *The Great American Food Almanac*, amaranth was a basic food in the New World before Christopher Columbus arrived. On thousands of acres of Aztec and Inca farmland grew this grain, and 20,000 tons of it were sent annually to Moctezuma's palace in what is now Mexico City. Aztec women ground the seed, mixed it with honey (or human blood), and patted it into the shapes of snakes, birds, deer, or gods to be eaten during ceremonies at the Aztec temples.

This truly wonderful and nourishing grain is becoming popular again through the efforts of Rodale, the food and environmental wizards of Emmaus, Pennsylvania. I grow it in my own garden and it is a magnificent producer.

ANIMALS AND ORGANIC PESTICIDES Fun-loving gardeners are also highly intelligent and keep informed. They know that even the new organic pesticides may harm warm-blooded animals (that's us as well as dogs and cats!) when they are swallowed, when they come in contact with skin and are absorbed, or when they are inhaled. A list of commonly used insecticides from the least to the most dangerous is as follows: pyrethrum, allethrin, rotenone, methoxychlor, malathion, chlorthion, chlordane, lindane, toxaphene, aldrin, dieldrin, nicotine, endrin, parathion, demeton. The fungicides, except the organic mercuries, are not highly toxic and are safe to use with ordinary precautions. It is very important to follow all label directions carefully with regard to dosages, crops to protect, safe interval between last spray and harvest, and precautions. Best of all is to garden without pesticides using protective garden companions.

APHIDS LOUSING UP YOUR GARDEN? Entomologists recognize at least 2,000 more-or-less distinct species of aphids, making it difficult for the gardener to distinguish between even a small portion of them—nearly every plant in the garden being a potential candidate for an aphid feast!

I'm not one to tell you that biological controls always work—they can help—but with a species so diverse, the right control may not always be present and, even if obtainable, the gardener may not know which one to select. Some control insects, however, are likely to be already present and quietly going about their work. A good example is the tiny parasite wasp of the *Broconid* family, which lays eggs in the aphids' bodies. One such wasp, *Aphelinus mali*, has proven quite successful in controlling woolly apple aphid. A better known aphid predator (but unfortunately a less effective one) is the ladybug beetle. Helping ladybugs demolish corn leaf aphids are other insect predators such as the goldeneye lacewing and its larva, the aphids' lion of the *Chrysopidae* family, and certain species of syrphus flies.

Plant resistant varieties, aided on your part by cultivation and mulching for aphid control. Another aphid defense is to use a miscible oil or plant-derived spray only when parasites and predators aren't as active, mainly in spring and fall. Early in spring, before budding and leafing out take place, dormant oil on fruit trees can and will kill aphid eggs overwintering on the bark. Rotenone and pyrethrum will kill hatched aphids and can be applied heavily in the fall when cool weather limits predator activity and aphids continue to proliferate.

To control root aphids, especially the corn root aphid, you must control the cornfield ant. Cultivation and rotation destroy their nests. Cultivate around your ornamentals, too, if corn root aphids present a problem.

Many species of aphids (or plant lice) are kept by ants because they produce a sweet fluid called *honeydew*. The ant licks up the honeydew as it pours out of the tip of the aphid's body. Ants even move some species of aphids from one plant to another in order to have a good supply, and in this way may infest an entire garden, as aphids multiply very rapidly.

APHRODISIACS IN THE GARDEN

In the good life all things must be considered, and it has been known for centuries that vegetables, while promoting good health and vitality, also promote virility—but some are more potent than others. Let us approach this listing with a light touch and a light heart.

French beans (or dwarf kidney), according to Charles Connell, writing in "Aphrodisiacs in Your Garden (and Your Window Box)," are definitely stimulating, also the succulent broad bean. Both should be picked when they are young. The haricot, a type of French bean, and the scarlet runner are also candidates. Their effectiveness is vouched for in the old West Country tag:

> When runners be podding,
> Summer's a-nodding:
> When runners be shedded,
> Winter's warm-bedded.

Celery, though a bit difficult to cultivate, is an aphrodisiac par excellence. The tomato was once known as the Love Apple and it has been eaten both as an aphrodisiac and for its succulence ever since it was introduced into Europe in the sixteenth century. Not especially stimulating on its own, it does make a contribution toward the general effect by making soups and salads tastier. Stuffed with a variety of goodies and baked, the tomato does add to the amatory urge created by the whole. The easily grown shallot, sometimes called scallion, says Connell, has long been considered a "contributory crop," probably by the Greeks and certainly by the Romans. Martial stoutly declares:

> If envious age relax the nuptial knot,
> Thy food be scallions and thy feast shallot.

The onion's reputation as an aphrodisiac is legendary. The Arabs boil them with spices, fry them in oil, and add egg yolks in the firm belief that this dish taken on successive days is a powerful amatory aid. In *The Perfumed Garden*, Sheikh Nefzawi recommends a broth of onion juices and purified honey. The famous erotologist says this brew should be taken at bedtime and *for one day only*.

The garden pea has a long and well-deserved reputation for contributing to virility and consideration should be given to its culture. Again Nefzawi gives a recipe: "Boil with onions, powder with ginger, cardamoms, and cinnamon." In France peas are simply made into a delicious pea soup.

Carrot varieties have all developed from the wild carrot which still thrives in rural England and also in parts of southern Europe. According to the Spaniard Juan Ruiz, who wrote the *Book of Good Love*, the carrot was first introduced into Europe by the Arabs. Connell rates it higher than the tomato but lower than onions and celery.

The radish's popularity goes way back—to the days of the ancient Egyptians and Greeks. They were often served at marriage feasts. Heliodorus is quoted as saying, "Great deeds need great preparations." The best radishes, crisp and sweet, are those developed quickly in a warm rich soil.

Asparagus should not be neglected, for the ancients knew it well both as a vegetable and an aphrodisiac. It is a luxurious food, served with melted butter and a sprinkling of parsley. Parsley, just chock-full of vitamin E, has a reputation all its own for imparting vigor and vitality. It also contains vitamins A and B_1.

Spinach, with its rich iron content and possession of vitamins A, K, E, B_2, B_1, and C, has a justifiably good reputation as an amatory stimulant and fortunately it is available at practically all seasons of the year. You can even grow it in most Southern gardens during the winter for it resists cold.

Gayelord Hauser in his "Treasury of Secrets," speaks glowingly of pumpkin seeds, "a secret handed down from father to son for countless generations," and beloved of the Hungarian gypsy, the mountain-dwelling Bulgarian, the Anatolian Turk, the Ukrainian, and the Translyvanian German, "who all knew that pumpkin seeds preserve the prostate gland and thereby, also, male potency." He goes on to say, "In these countries pumpkin seeds are eaten just as sunflower seeds are devoured in Russia, as an inexhaustible source of vigor offered by nature."

There really is no mystery about it: good, organically grown vegetables contribute to our health and thereby to the "good life."

APPLE (*Malus pumila*)   *Cyclamen elegans*, in the primrose family, is useful in killing parasites on apple trees. Saponin, a principle found in its bulbs, is effective fresh or dried. Bags of sumac leaves buried around the base of apple trees infested with woolly aphids are effective. Tannin is the active principle in sumac leaves. Ground oystershell placed around the roots is helpful in reducing insect damage. Ryania speciosa is effective against apple aphid. The red-banded leaf roller, a major apple pest in the Northeast, is susceptible to a virus, granulosis. In field tests, spraying of the virus over apple foliage resulted in total destruction of the insects. It is, however, slow acting.

A few sound apples, stored with potatoes, give good keeping qualities to the potatoes and retard their sprouting. It has been said that the reason old-fashioned apples bloomed only every other year was to interrupt the life cycles of their pests, and that modern breeding to produce annual bloomers has also produced immense pest problems.

Apples, especially dwarf varieties, may be pruned in late summer. After some of the new and some of the one-year shoots are re-

moved, more light will penetrate to the tree center, improving quality and fruit color.

APPLE MAGGOTS ON THE RUN
Here is a brew that will trap one of the worst enemies of your apple crop: the apple maggot that spoils apples from inside out. Mix one part molasses with nine parts water, then add yeast to produce fermentation. Pour this mixture into wide mouth jars and hang in nearby trees.

APRICOTS (*Prunus armenica*)   The raw fruit is an exceptional source of vitamin A, providing about 2,700 International Units of that nutrient in an average serving. Apricots are promoted as the "beauty fruit" because of vitamin A's beneficial effects on skin and hair. Fresh apricots are also a good source of potassium (281 milligrams per 100-gram portion) and vitamin C (10 mg.).

In sun-dried form, apricots become a truly outstanding source of vitamin A with 10,900 I.U. per 100-gram serving. They are also an excellent source of iron (5.5 mg.) and potassium (979 mg.). The Apollo astronauts ate pure apricot bars similar to the fruit rolls enjoyed for centuries by people in the Middle East. Apricots can be made into a thirst-quenching, nutritious beverage called apricot nectar. The Hunzas use apricot oil, squeezed from the kernel of the fruit, as their cooking oil. The bitter, almondlike seeds of apricots contain cyanide.

Laetrile, the cancer-fighting substance (vitamin B-17), is made from defatting and crystallizing apricot and peach kernels. By means of refinement Laetrile becomes chemotherapy—in the same way foxglove is turned into digitalis for heart medicine.

ARMADILLOS   Are armadillos common garden pests? Just ask my son! Eugene has spent a young fortune making wire cages for his young pine trees, only to find that the armadillos dig under them! They are, however, digging for insects, not the pines.

The Texas armadillo, which has moved steadily northward (they even show up in my hometown of Ardmore), differs from other members of the family in that its litters run from four to ten, whereas members of other species bear but one or two young at a time.

Through cactus, coarse grass, scrub oak, and tangled brush the active armadillo, dangling its long tail, trots about in search of insects. It often stops to poke its pointed nose into holes and, when lucky, draws out a meal of ants on its sticky tongue. Perhaps a fleet of armadillos could be useful in controlling the dreaded fire ant? Armadillos aren't terribly bright: intent on securing a meal of insects they've been known to bump against the legs of a man standing still.

An armadillo kills small snakes by rolling on them and pressing them against the earth with its armored back. Its jerky movements sandpaper the serpents into a helpless state and, softened, they are ready to be eaten. However, in spite of its usual diet, the armadillo in captivity enjoys a repast of beaten eggs.

The armadillo is quite harmless and is organized more for self-defense than aggression. When alarmed it can run with considerable speed; cornered it will roll up into a tight ball, relying on its pliable segmented shell for protection.

The armadillo's lair may consist of a hole in a limestone ledge or a burrow in the ground, depending on the region, and they can dig into sandy soil with startling rapidity, using the well-developed claws of their forelegs.

The Seminole Indians of Oklahoma and Texas, according to *American Wild Life*, compiled by the Writer's Program of the Work Projects Administration of the City of New York, hunted armadillos for their meat and hides with specially trained dogs. The hides were made into baskets by cutting off the animal's legs and stuffing them in the mouth; the tail formed the handle.

ARRANGING YOUR GARDEN   There is no one "right" plan for a home garden, but you can develop many good plans for any

one locality. Consider your own preferences, your climate, and your own particular garden spot in planning and arranging your garden. But one tip I would give you here: in a garden that is much longer than wide, it is generally more convenient to work with wheeled tools if the rows run the long way. It matters little whether the rows run north and south or east and west, but on a sloping area it is important that the rows run across the slope, not up and down. Running the rows across the slope, or on the contour, helps hold the rainfall on or in the soil instead of letting it rush down the sloping rows and carry away the soil.

ASPARAGUS (*Asparagus officinalis*)   Delicious and possible nearly anywhere in the United States—and a well-kept bed will last for twenty years. Dig a 1-foot deep trench and half-fill with compost mixed with 1/4 cup of bone meal per 1 foot of trench. Set roots 18 inches apart and gradually fill the trench with earth as the roots sprout. With this planting plan you can harvest a crop in two years, while seed will take at least three years. A good, established bed will yield for ten weeks each year, generally starting in mid-April. Do not put salt on your asparagus bed. In warm climates do not cut the plants back until late fall—they go dormant during the heat of summer and cutting back throws them into growth, usually spindly spears that spoil the spring crop. After cutting back, a top dressing of well-decomposed manure is very helpful. If this is not available use compost. Asparagus has few insect enemies; Ryania has been found useful against the asparagus beetle.

Asparagus Purée: Don't throw away the stem portion of your asparagus. Keep the clean, tender portion and boil it down, purée it in the blender, mix it with butter (or margarine), milk, seasonings, and you will have a delicious asparagus soup.

ASPARAGUS BEANS (*Phaseolus multiflorus*)   If you want to grow "bragging beans" try asparagus beans, sometimes called "yard long." Two feet is actually about as long as they get but even that is rather spectacular. Shell pods when just showing a yellow tinge. The seeds, usually dark, are best cooked with ham or bacon. Snap a few tender long pods and add them to the pot.

Asparagus bean vines climb high. One home gardener reported that he ran the vines up an eight-foot tripod. They hit the top and cascaded back after waving about frantically trying to find something taller to climb. Asparagus beans do best in the South, the lower Midwest, and the warmer Southwest—wherever their close relatives the Southern peas (black-eyes, crowders, purple hull, knucklehull, cream peas, silver peas, or clay peas) do well.

ATTRACTING HUMMINGBIRDS

My friend and fellow newspaper columnist, Bugs Barringer, once told me that his column about hummingbirds produced more than six hundred letters. I had much the same reaction myself when I wrote such a column—I thought the phone would never stop ringing. So let's talk about the hummers.

To begin, Plants of the Southwest (see "Sources") has some great ideas for providing food by planting "Hummingbird Flowers." Fifteen different species of tiny iridescent hummingbirds flash through Western gardens (the ruby-throated hummingbird is the only hummingbird widespread in the East). They are easily attracted by planting bright red flowers which they home in on from great distances (like most birds they have excellent color vision), but, once in your garden, they will visit flowers of any color in search of nectar and small insects.

Hummingbird flowers have much in common. They are long and tubular, often borne sideways or drooping rather than upright, and contain abundant nectar. The hummingbirds hover before the flowers, insert their long bills and tongues for the nectar, all the while whirring their wings more than 3,000 times a minute.

Good flower choices also providing season-long color are: red columbine (*Aquilegia elegantula*) and Indian paintbrush (*Castilleja*

integra), which bloom in the spring; scarlet bugler (*Penstemon barbatus*), other penstemons, and skyrocket (*Ipomopsis aggregata*), in the summer; and hummingbird trumpet (*Zauschneria latifolia*) in the fall. Some species, such as Indian paintbrush, scarlet hedge-nettle (*Stachys coccinea*), and autumn sage (*Salvia greggii*), begin blooming in early spring and are stopped only by fall frosts.

The ruby-throat in particular likes monarda (or bee-balm), coral honeysuckle, jewel-weed, and cardinal flower as well as the wild columbine's five inverted horns of plenty. Canna, nasturtium, phlox, trumpet-flower, salvia, and a host of others will also delight his eye and his palate.

This hummer is wonderfully neighborly, coming to the flower beds or window boxes for small insects as well as nectar, with undaunted familiarity in the presence of the family. This cheery audacity makes him a favorite with the housebound or disabled who can enjoy watching him close-up without going outdoors.

You may know a male by the brilliant metallic-red feathers on his throat. His mate lacks these, but her brilliancy has another outlet, for she is one of the most expert nest builders in the world. An exquisitely dainty little cup of plant down, felted into a compact cradle and stuccoed with bits of lichen bound on by spider webs, can scarcely be told from a knot on the limb to which it is fastened. Two eggs, not larger than beans, in time give place to two downy hummers about the size of honeybees. The presence of the young is frequently betrayed by the father, who will dash angrily at any intruder near.

Have you ever seen pigeons pump food down the throats of their squabs? Baby hummers are fed the same way. After about three weeks in the nest they are ready to fly; but need to rest on perches the first month of independence more than at any time afterward. No weak-footed relative of the swift could live long off the wing. It is good-bye to summer when the last hummingbird forsakes our frost-nipped northern gardens for happier hunting grounds far away.

Which brings me to a question I am often asked: "When should I take in my hummingbird feeder?" The migrations of the ruby-throat occur in May in the spring and October in the fall, so there is your clue for putting out and taking in.

When I was a little girl my father promised me a quarter (big money in those days!), if I would catch a hummingbird. I was notably unsuccessful and couldn't understand why they eluded me. I did not know then as I do now that the tiny hummer is the only bird known to fly backward as well as forward. It hovers motionless, poised in midair before a flower, its wings whirring rapidly, so rapidly indeed as to be almost invisible.

The smallest hummer, indeed the smallest bird of all, is the bee hummingbird, a native of Cuba. It is about two inches long and weighs about one-tenth of an ounce. The nest of the bee hummingbird is the size of half a walnut shell.

ATTRACTING SONGBIRDS is of prime interest to many gardeners. And just because they delight us with their lovely songs doesn't mean they can't be useful as well in holding down insect populations. Birds vary in their food requirements and when you know what they like to eat and the type of nesting they require, you'll have a head start in inviting them.

- The **cardinal** likes autumn-olive, corn, dogwood, sunflower, and various berries.
- The **mockingbird**: autumn-olive, elderberry, firethorn, highbush cranberry, holly.
- The **robin**: cherry, cotoneaster, dogwood, Russian-olive, various berries.
- The **eastern bluebird**: dogwood, honeysuckle, mountain-ash, red cedar, various berries.
- The **Baltimore oriole**: apple, cherry, elderberry, mountain-ash, various berries.
- The **American goldfinch**: mulberry, sunflower, seeds of garden flowers, weeds and conifers.
- Some of us *do* like the **blue jay**, so let's include him, too, and plan for acorns, cherry, sunflower, wild plum, and cultivated grains.
- Another bird you might want to attract is the **slate-colored junco**, who dotes on sunflowers, wheat, and seeds of grasses, weeds, and conifers.

Birds like variety, so mix and blend plants—create a varied pattern with an intermingling of species, sizes, and shapes. Give birds a choice of places for their activities—from the tops of tall trees down to low-growing flowers and grasses. A choice of food sources also helps—seeds, nuts, fruits, berries, and flower nectar. Many songbirds combine these plant foods with animal foods like insects, worms, and spiders.

Choose plants of wildlife value. Yards and grounds that have only deciduous trees and shrubs can be improved by adding junipers, cedars, yews, and other evergreens that provide winter shelter for birds. The plants mentioned here are adapted and useful in the Midwest from Michigan and Indiana west to the Dakotas and Kansas, many also doing well in the central and southern states.

Most birds need open water of some kind. A small pool with stones in the shallow edges draws them to drink or bathe. Landscape the area with conifers, clumps of shrubs, and hedges for resting, nesting, and feeding. Encourage some aquatic growth but control its spread.

Wade H. Hamor, biologist, SCS, suggests using living screens such as hedges and rows of trees to screen off unpleasant views and reduce noise from highways. In crowded neighborhoods they offer privacy for both the birds and you. And they attract birds year after year. Living fences such as hedges or rows of honeysuckle, dogwood, or autumn-olive can replace a wire fence between fields, and can protect the house area. Cardinals, brown thrashers, and mockingbirds find living fences much to their liking.

But you need some open areas too. Meadowlarks, bobolinks, and several kinds of desirable sparrows favor open stretches of lawn and fields with few, if any, trees and shrubs. In such open areas you might try planting a variety of native grasses, thereby protecting the soil and adding variety.

A windbreak for winter protection consisting of cedars, spruce, or pines, with maybe a crabapple tree tucked in on the sheltered side, will give birds a warm, safe place to rest when the snow is deep. A food plot or feeder nearby helps keep the birds with you through the winter months.

Plant food plots. "Seedeaters," such as goldfinches, cardinals, juncos, and sparrows, come to food plots of millets, grain sorghum, corn, or sunflowers. Wild bristlegrasses and ragweeds are also attractive. Plots can be large or small according to your space and inclination.

In general, trees and shrubs that attract birds grow satisfactorily on well-drained, fairly fertile soil, somewhat loamy soils not particularly suited for vegetables and flowers. When planting for birds, consider such things as soil, slope, drainage, exposure aspects, and climate as well as your personal wishes. Added benefits occur where plantings help provide shade, stabilize soil, and control potentially damaging water runoff.

AWAY WITH THAT ACHING BACK!
Gardening isn't fun if you hurt from stooping to plant seeds. Go to a sporting goods store and buy a golf shaft protector—they're very inexpensive and just the right length, at about three feet. Place one end of the tube on the ground in the row; then drop the seeds down the other end.

AZTEC FARMING   Did the Aztecs make gardens? Indeed they did, and by a very unique method. Farming formed the basis of the economy of this colorful, interesting, and somewhat mysterious people. They even had a god of agriculture, Tepoztecatl, who in religious ceremonies was resplendently costumed.

Corn was their most important crop, but they also grew beans, squash, peppers, avocadoes, tobacco, and hemp. The Aztecs had no plows, draft animals (dogs and turkeys were the Aztecs' only domesticated animals), or iron tools, cultivating the soil only with simple digging sticks. But, even with nothing but this primitive equipment they were able to produce enough food, not only to supply their own needs, but also those of the craftsmen and government officials in the city.

Much of their success came from the way they used shallow lakes in a skillful way for raising crops. Aztec farmers heaped up the very rich soil from the lake bottom to form small islands of moist, fertile earth. These islands were called *chinampas*. In time, roots from trees and plants on these islands interlaced and attached the chinampas to the lake bottoms. They made canoes from logs hollowed out by burning, and used them to travel about their "islands" as well as for religious ceremonies. A few of these so-called "floating islands" still exist near Mexico City.

AZTEC LILY (*Sprekelia formoissima*), sometimes called Jacobean lily, is a tender plant belonging to the *Amaryllidaceae* family. It has a roundish bulb and six petaled flowers with the uppermost petal standing upright, each stout stalk bearing a cluster of large crimson flowers. Aztec lily flowers in June and July. Although native to Mexico, its botanical name commemorates J.H. Von Sprekelsen, of Hamburg, Germany, who sent the plant to Linnaeus. They make excellent plants of the greenhouse but may be grown outdoors in the South. They should be lifted before frost and fully dried. Then remove dried foliage and store in perlite or vermiculite through the winter at a steady 55 to 60 degrees.

AZTEC MARIGOLD (*Tagetes erecta*), sometimes called African, is the tallest one, 18 inches to 3 feet tall, and has many flower types, some resembling chrysanthemums. All garden marigolds are descended from the wild Mexican species.

With their bright colors, varieties and heights, marigolds serve all garden purposes—beds, borders, terrace pots, mixed with other flowers or massed alone. According to James Underwood Crockett, writing in *Annuals* (Time-Life Books), their versatility extends far beyond garden uses. In Mexico, acres of orange-flowered marigolds are grown for chicken feed; when the blossoms are fed to hens, the eggs have dark yellow yolks, a quality in great demand there. Elsewhere I have mentioned that they also impart a golden color to the skin of the dressed fowl.

Marigolds are easy to grow, may be started in the house and set out when weather is suitable. They flourish in ordinary garden soil in sunny locations. The W. Atlee Burpee Company has developed many types and now even has a white one. Others are scentless. Not for me. I like their "funny" smell!

Broad acres are a patent of nobility and no man but
feels more of a man in the world if he have a bit of
ground that he can call his own. However small it is
on the surface, it is four thousand miles deep;
and that is a very handsome property.

CHARLES DUDLEY WARNER

BALDNESS Garlic has been widely acclaimed for many of the ills that afflict mankind. But this use found in *Kitchen Medicines* by Ben Charles Harris, may be new to many. Garlic, as an effective remedy for baldness is not new, having been so employed for centuries. Harris recommends cutting one third of a clove and rubbing in the juice. An hour later, after drying, massage in a few drops of a mixture of Bay rum and olive oil. This practice should be followed morning and night. Kelp, a product of seaweed, when taken internally is also believed to be helpful in influencing hair growth.

BAMBOO A cry for help! Bamboo is taking over my yard! Most of the books I've researched speak joyfully of bamboo and all its various uses. But sometimes there can be too much of a good thing. However, the *New Encyclopedia of Gardening* does mention that bamboo will self-destruct, dying after flowering, and cautions that seeds should be always looked for on flowering plants. A curious phenomenon is that species flower, and

die, simultaneously over a wide area in the wild, and also, though not quite as simultaneously, under cultivation. Cutting may help if done in August when the moon is old, third and fourth quarters, under the barren signs of Leo, Aries, Virgo, Aquarius, Gemini, and Sagittarius, listed according to the degree of nonproductive qualities.

In the meantime, if your bamboo is the edible type, why not eat and enjoy? *The Rodale Encyclopedia of Gardening* says that gourmets recommend cutting them into one-eighth-inch thick slices, after peeling off the outer covering. Virtually all varieties, with the exception of 'Sweetshoot,' have a more or less bitter taste, so it is best to parboil them for 6 to 8 minutes, then change the water. Further cooking for about 20 minutes will bring out their delicate flavor while retaining the firm, crispy texture. Cooked like this, bamboo shoots taste very much like young field corn. You can serve them as a vegetable hot with butter (or margarine), cold as a salad or in mixed salads, or use them in meat stews. An interesting bamboo is the fascinating

"Buddha's belly" (*Bambusa ventricosa*), so called because the portions between the nodes swell out oddly. This variety grows 40 feet tall outdoors, but will stay in miniature for years when potted.

BANANA PEELS Not generally known, the inner surface of the skin is blessed with healing properties and may be applied as a poultice directly on burns and boils. The skin is also useful to alleviate the suffering caused by poison ivy and will stop the itching almost immediately. The inside of the peel is good against warts, used for several days.

Save your banana peels, chop them up, and incorporate a handful in the soil when you transplant tomatoes and green peppers. This will ensure very strong trunks and stems. Banana peels contain 3.25 percent phosphorous and 41.76 percent potash. They're also an excellent fertilizer for roses, but use them sparingly; 2 or 3 peels per bush at a time is about right.

BANANA TREES MADE EASY If you live in the southern states and grow banana trees, you may not need to dig them up and store them in your basement. Instead, cut the plant off at ground level. Cover cut stems with a layer of leaves or grass clippings, then top with a sheet of plastic or other waterproof material, anchoring the edges. Remove plastic in the spring. When the new shoots emerge they will be stronger and grow better.

BARGAINS are fun. Did you know there is a way to get a lot of cheap (but good) seed without spending a lot of money? Black-eyed peas and all sorts of beans—limas, pintos, red beans, etc.—cost very little if you buy them packaged. Just a few days ago I bought a package of black-eyed peas (enough to plant my whole garden) for 43 cents. Just look in the dried foods section of your favorite supermarket.

You can do the same thing by going to the spice section. Most of the seeds you find there will grow also: caraway, mustard, dill, and lots more.

Now, go the fresh vegetable section. At certain seasons of the year you will find leeks with their roots still attached. Plant these and they will split their bulbs and you can quickly increase your stock. Jerusalem artichokes can also be found in this section and they will grow well in your garden, giving you a quick, easy, and cheap start. Buy them even if they are a bit shriveled—they're hard to kill! You may find gingerroot displayed—this, too, is viable.

Dried garlic will root quickly if planted. Just separate the cloves and poke them in wherever you want them to grow. This is particularly useful to know about when you are planting young fruit trees. Garlic, put around the trunk when the trees are planted, will help to keep out borers.

BATS IN THE BELFRY! We, as gardeners, have been praising birds as insect predators but we haven't been giving much credit to bats—the night patrollers of the insect world. They begin early, about dusk, and range far and wide in their nocturnal flights. Bat colonies have been known to destroy tons of insects in their foraging flights, using their radarlike sense to locate insects as well as to avoid obstacles. They pursue night-flying insects such as moths who lay their eggs on plants where their larvae can be very harmful. And, by the way, one of the bat's favorite foods is mosquitoes. The amount of insects consumed sometimes triples with varying conditions, as when a mother bat is nursing her young. Studies have shown that the little brown bat can devour as many as 600 or more mosquitoes in the space of an hour. Bats were used successfully by an apple grower in the Yakima Valley in controlling an infestation of codling moths. A colony of some 500 was established.

James Poling, writing in *Marvels and Mysteries of Our Animal World*, says that bats are the only mammals with the true power of flight. Bats actually fly with their fingers.

Simple Bat House

Use a four-foot-long 1" x 8" board. Cut as shown on the cutting diagram, using a fitting circular or jigsaw to cut the bevel between the backboard and roof pieces. The smaller angled ends of the triangular sides must be cut off to allow an opening of about one inch at the bottom of the bat house, as shown in the side view. The cutting angle for this will be approximately 62 degrees, but you will need to adjust it to suit the thickness of your wood.

Assemble the box with nails or screws and glue. The glue will provide some weather sealing and help retain heat. If desired, apply caulk to all joints.

The front door pivots at the bottom on two nails. Drill a hole high up on one side and into the side of the door. A loose fitting nail placed into these holes will hold the door in place. Provide additional weatherproofing by attaching narrow strips (½" x ½") of wood to the inner sides of the house to act as door stops. Attach a small screw to the front of the door to use as a doorknob. The house may also be built with a fixed instead of hinging door, but this will make it more difficult to clean should birds nest in it before it is inhabited by bats. Apply a coat of polyurethane to the outside of the house only.

Place at least 10 feet up on side of building or tree. Use rough sawn lumber or make many small dents in back board for bats to cling to.

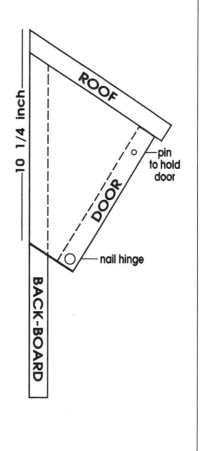

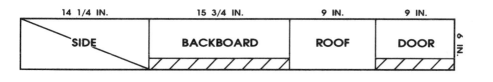

Their wings are the anatomical equivalent to a human hand with a membrane stretched between the fingers. Not as fast in flight as birds, they have the edge on even swifts and hummingbirds in their maneuverability. Even at full speed a right-angle turn can be made in little more than their own length.

Once believed to catch their prey in their mouths, high-speed photographs have shown that they scoop up flying insects in the membrane stretching between their hind legs, cupping it like a pouch. Reaching in they eat their meal in full flight.

You may be shocked at the unusual idea of building a "bat house" but Peter T. Bromley (USDA-EA, Department of Fisheries & Wildlife, Virginia Polytechnic Institute and State University, Blacksburg, Virginia 24061-0321) has designed just such a house for the purpose of giving bats a place for daytime rest and breeding purposes, or even to live in year-round. They are harmless creatures and do not "try to get into your hair," though this has happened occasionally when they are trying to escape by flying low from an enclosed area such as an attic.

> My garden will never make me famous,
> I'm a horticultural ignoramus,
> I can't tell a stringbean from a soybean,
> Or even a girl bean from a boy bean.
> —Ogden Nash

BEANS ARE MIGHTY CHOLESTEROL FIGHTERS! Beans were once believed to have magical qualities. According to Scott Cunningham in *Magical Herbalism*, a small dried bean rubbed against warts, pimples, blemishes, and other growths during the waning moon would remove such imperfections. But the true magic of beans lies in their nutritional value. Dr. Benjamin S. Frank in his famous book, *Dr. Frank's No-Aging Diet — Eat and Grow Younger*, recommends beans with grains, nuts, and seeds. The American Heart Association tells us we can increase our iron intake by eating more peas and beans, both fresh and dried. The Indians grew beans, squash, and corn to form a nearly perfect vegetable protein.

I plant both bush and pole beans in my garden but in the heavy rains of the spring of 1991, my bush beans wilted and died after setting one heavy crop. Not so the pole beans. Park's new introduction Early Riser continued to rise and flourish, as did Shepherd's Serbo and Emerite, and Burpee's old favorite Kentucky Wonder. And, as an added bonus, I could pick standing up. A great boon to an elderly lady!

So much for green beans, now let's take a look at shell beans. One morning, working in my backyard, I notice an enticing fragrance wafting across the hedge from the backyard of Al Hilliard, my next-door neighbor. Al is a great cook so I knew something good was happening. Following my nose I was soon sitting on his back steps gazing with fascination into a bubbling bean pot. The bean pot, Al told me, was cooking on canned heat and was a utensil he had often used when he was driving the big semis and parking was a problem. I finally tore myself

away upon his promise to bring me a "taste." Those were the best beans I ever tasted and I begged for the recipe which he shared with me and I will now give to you.

Al's Stormy Weather Bean Soup

To get the desired result you must follow the directions exactly and you can enjoy these delicious beans without "inconvenient" consequences.

In large pot place 3 chopped onions, one smoked ham hock, and 1 to 2 finely chopped jalapeno peppers. Add water, cover, and bring to a rolling boil.

Slowly, so boiling continues, add one pound of Great Northern beans. It is important to keep the mixture boiling *uncovered*— so that gases will escape. Add boiling water as necessary. Cook 1½ to 2 hours or until beans have softened. Cut up ham hock and add to beans. Al adds no salt: the ham hock does the seasoning.

This bean soup freezes well and you can use limas, pintos, or any favorite shell bean in this recipe. It's really great!

Bush beans, such as Tenderdrop and Golden Wax are easy to grow and require no support, simply plant after danger of frost is past. (The Vermont Seed Company has beans in practically endless supply. See "Sources.") Pole beans are something else again, and if you don't have a fence try making a bean "Tee-Pee": simply set six 10-foot poles in a circle and bind them together at the top. Then tie mesh or string between the poles (for vine support) all the way up to the top, leaving room for a "doorway." Plant vining beans around the outside every 4 inches except where the doorway is to be located and soon the vines will cover the tee-pee. Particularly pretty if planted with scarlet runner beans. Children love this and if they are interested in their own garden it makes an ideal project.

Pick beans while young to keep plants productive. Pick when they are pencil width and seeds barely visible. Letting beans grow past this stage puts the plant's energy into seed rather the flower production and it is the flowers that give you more "bean."

BEES—MY CLOSE ENCOUNTER
My husband had kept bees as a young boy in New York and when we married he brought his equipment to our new home. When we decided to keep bees again we bought a queen and a small colony to get started, but unfortunately they did not live. But the hive was still out in the garden when I went out one morning and found a fine swarm clustering on a small fruit tree. I knew very little about bees but I wanted to capture them so I rushed back into the house, donned bee veil and gloves and bravely sallied forth. I did know that I was in little danger of being stung for swarming bees are gentle, being literally "drunk" on honey.

I took the hive and set it under the tree carefully and gently shook the bees down into it where they appeared to settle quite contentedly. When my husband came home for lunch I proudly took him into the garden to get a look at "my" bees. Alas, the hive was completely empty! He then explained to me that I should have moved the hive, that the bee scouts had returned and led the swarm away. I cried.

But sometimes life gives us a second chance. A few days later history repeated itself and a second swarm showed up on another small tree. I repeated again my little routine, but being three days wiser this time I moved the hive and set it up under some big shade trees at the south end of the garden. Evidently the scouts didn't find them for they remained and prospered. Oh how they prospered! We put on "super" after super and when extracting time came we had jars and jars of delicious golden honey. Some of which we mixed with ground up roasted peanuts we had grown ourselves. Of course we did not take all the honey, leaving plenty for the bees to winter over. In time we had swarms of our own and added more hives.

Bees can be as interesting as butterflies and the butterfly feeder described in "Butterfly Gardening" later may also be attractive to bees. If this occurs a close-up observation of bee-feeding habits may also be carried out and could give much pleasure to someone who is housebound. But children should be advised to keep a respectful distance between themselves and the bee—preferably with a pane of glass between them if the child is a bit nervous.

We hear a lot these days about the so-called **killer bees** and, perhaps, fear and hate them without understanding the nature of the bee. Juliette de Bairacli Levy has this to say in her *Herbal Handbook for Farm and Stable*:

"The biggest crime of the bee-keeper is the killing off of the chosen Queen of the hive. The heart, the love and inspiration of the hive then dies, and the very tragic shock brings sickness. . . . The reason for such killings is that the bee-keeper wants to possess docile bees which he can rob without any of the famed bee warfare. The true Queen is removed and killed and a Queen of a quieter strain is put in her place. The quiet Queen then produces a strain of weak fighters. But the core of the hive's power is the fighting fury which protects the kingdom from such enemies as hornets, rodents, ants—and man. Better to keep the hives strong in warfare and for the bee-keeper to wear more protective clothing against bee stings."

She then goes on to tell of the island of Rhodes, where she is writing her notes, of the fury of the bees when the honey is being taken from the hives. This is so great she says that homes near the beehives have to be shuttered up for several days to protect the people from the fighting bees. Yet no one even considers trying to subdue this natural protective fury.

Favored bee herbs according to Levy are all aromatics, such as lavender, rosemary, thyme, santolina, sage, bee-balm, basil, marjoram, and many more; bitters such as southernwood, wormwood, and rue; all mints, especially peppermint; all the rose family, especially wild roses, blackberry and hawthorn; most of the borage family, especially borage, alkanet, viper's bugloss and anchusa; the heaths, especially ling and bell heather; scabious of all kinds; and the carnation family, especially clove pinks. Of the trees, especially lime (linden blossom), acacia, carob, tupelo and olive, and the rose family, apple, pear, cherry and others.

BEES DO IT—BUT ONLY OUT-DOORS
Bees, butterflies, wasps, and other insects pollinate your plants outside. In-doors, it's up to you. When they bloom, take a cotton swab or a fine paintbrush (a soft one as for watercolors), and transfer the pollen from flower to flower. As you make like a bee, swirl the brush lightly inside each flower, one after the other. Best to repeat the process again the next day to make sure you catch the flowers when they're ready.

Not all will produce fruit. Success will show up in tiny fruits as the flowers wilt. Don't wait too long after the blossoms appear to pollinate—they may wilt before you have a chance. Your best chance of success is to do your "bee act" a day after the blossoms open.

BEER AS BAIT
Evidently the codling moth is a heavy drinker! Fermenting carbohydrates such as beer, sugars, molasses, and yeast will attract the codling moth, Oriental fruit moth, fruit fly, and borer. Sometimes it is even more attractive after a few days fermentation. Fill a small bowl with beer, then sink it in your soil so that the lip of the bowl comes even to the soil. The pest falls in and can't get out.

And be sure to save the plastic can holders you get on some six packs. Staple them together (an office stapler can be used) and when you get the desired size, use them as a support for climbing vegetables. Quite decorative, they do not rust or rot, and may be made into different designs.

BEAUTY AIDS FOR SKIN
My mother, who learned her herbal lore in the Kentucky hills, set great store by chamomile. She made a tea by bringing one pint of water to a boil,

removing it from the heat and adding two teaspoons of dried flowers. It was then covered and allowed to steep for 45 minutes, strained, and used when lukewarm as a face wash several times a week. The tea may also be used as a hair conditioner, especially for blond hair. Chamomile tea, taken warm with a few drops of honey, was to her a sovereign headache remedy.

Our grandmothers liked to use lemon juice as a skin lightener and brightener. The Ponderosa lemon can be grown indoors as a container plant and the large lemons will make two or three lemon pies. And give serious consideration to cleavers or bedstraw (*Galium aparine, G. verum*) if you have tired skin. Cleavers makes an excellent face wash as it tightens the skin, helping erase the sags and bags that come with age.

Honey as an ingredient enters into the composition of so many old-time recipes for beautiful skin that I researched it in Deborah Chase's *Medically Based No-Nonsense Beauty Book.* She says, "Honey is composed primarily of sugar and wax. It has no special properties for the skin. However, masks that contain honey create a watertight film on the face and permit the skin to rehydrate itself."

BEAUTY BATHS
Our old family doctor used to say, "It's good for you to sweat, helps the body to get rid of poisons." Whether this is true or not, it's a fact that fun-loving gardeners do sweat when they are wielding that hoe vigorously or digging with that spade. What could be nicer after a stint in the garden than to take a beauty bath, fragrant with herbs you have grown yourself?

No less a personage than lovely Marie Antoinette had a favorite bath which consisted of wild thyme, marjoram, and a handful of coarse salt. Ninon de Lenclos, a beauty of the old French court, preferred a bath of thyme, mint, rosemary, and lavender flowers, mixed together, then tied up loosely in a muslin bag. The bag of herbs was covered with boiling water and after standing 5 or 10 minutes the bag and infusion were added to the bath water.

Another simple bath mixture was made with sodium bicarbonate (baking soda) sprinkled liberally with oils of lavender, rosemary, and eucalyptus. Mix well and keep in a glass jar, well corked. Countless variations may be made with essential and floral oils. (Indiana Botanic Gardens has many flower oils—see "Sources.")

Beauty baths with vinegar: You can make a delightful rose vinegar by drying a quantity of rose petals in the sun. Just put them in a closely-stoppered jar or bottle in the sun and let it stand for three weeks. The proportion of petals is an ounce to a quart of white vinegar. Elder flower, carnation, and orange flower vinegar is made the same way, except that for the latter the flowers must not be dried.

You may also purchase such essential oils as those of lavender, rose compound and oil of rosemary to use with white vinegar. Always store vinegars in glass containers.

BEDDING VINE CROPS! Here is a
spring suggestion that's easy and cheap. At second-hand shops, or even the city dump, you can often find old bed springs. Tie two at the top, spread the bottoms 3 or 4 feet apart and you have a garden trellis. Easy to put up and take down, you can grow vine crops on the springs and lettuce in the shade underneath.

BEETS Beets have never really had a good
press, nobody seems to care much one way or another. However, a very interesting fact is given to us by Dr. Benjamin S. Frank, author of the *No-Aging Diet.* Dr. Frank says: "Although beets, like most vegetables, are not high in nucleic acids [which he believes help to promote a healthy, youthful appearance], they are an important part of my diet. They contain an amino acid which the body uses to create its own nucleic acid, plus another nutrient important to brain function."

Beet seeds, which are actually clusters of seeds, should be sown *thinly,* about six or seven seeds per foot. Cover with peat moss to avoid soil crusting. Thin early, allowing only one seedling to grow. You can make sure that your soil will have enough for beets to make a good growth if you will incorporate ½ pound table salt per 100 square feet.

BELLS-OF-IRELAND (*Molucella laevis*)
Now how many green flowers do you ever see? An unusual plant beloved of flower arrangers, bells-of-Ireland grows to about 24 inches with charming "bells." Sow in a carefully prepared seed frame in May when soil has warmed up. Keep constantly moist until germination. Transplant to garden beds in late June. Flower arrangers sometimes "groom" the plants by removing all the foliage, leaving only the belllike bracts with the little flower "clappers" in the center of each.

BENEFICIAL BARK Composted bark,
according to Professor H.A.J. Hoitnik of the Ohio Agricultural Research and Development Center, as a soil ingredient in potting mixes produces superior growth and controls root rot and other soil-borne pathogens.

In three years of tests, rhododendrons grown in containers in a mix of two parts composted hammermilled bark and one part sand showed "considerably superior" growth and no occurrence of Phytophora root rot, compared to slow growth and losses due to root rot in a peat-sand mix.

Certain diseases caused by nematodes are also reduced by bark media; barksoil mixes "greatly reduced the incidence of root-knot on tomato and population levels of plant-parasitic nematodes on forsythia." In Oregon, fields in which bark composted with ammonium nitrate was incorporated grew larger and more productive strawberry plants, and the incidence of red stele disease was far lower for two following years than in untreated fields.

BENEFICIAL INSECTS Many times bio-
logical controls are present, so quietly, that we gardeners are unaware of them—often

arriving "on a wing and a prayer" when needed. I have observed in my own garden that lady bugs will increase in numbers when aphids are present on okra, spinach, or other plants. The larvae of lacewings destroy many garden pests, Trichogramma wasps kill eggs of more than 200 insects, fly parasites attack the eggs and larvae of flies, praying mantis will stalk and eat moths, beetles, cutworms, and other insects, grasshopper spore is an effective way to control grasshoppers. All of these beneficial insects are easily obtainable. Usually worms will arrive when you build up the organic matter in your soil, but if you wish to help things along order a supply of hybrid red worms. I know of no source of supply for garden spiders, but if you have them don't kill them: they kill and eat many insects, including grasshoppers which they often catch in their nets or on the ground floor.

BERRY BASKETS   Berry baskets, like the openwork plastic type you buy in grocery stores, make ideal covers for tiny seedlings, providing protection from small animals, heavy rains, or hail. They also filter strong sunlight, giving the seedlings the dappled light which they seem to like best. Plastic baskets, with covers, may be used as "greenhouses" to raise seedlings.

BIRDS   Birds, which are entirely innocent of wrongdoing, may be both friend and foe to the gardener, depending on the crops planted and their relative numbers in a given locality. Given a choice, birds usually will prefer their natural wild food to our cultivated crops. For instance, it has been observed that birds will eat tart wild berries before coming to the milder domesticated ones. Offering a substitute crop such as sunflowers may be at least a partial answer to their depredations. An oldtime farmer found that a bucketful of shelled corn, soaked overnight and scattered in the field where corn was just beginning to come up, induced the resident crows to leave the standing corn alone. Netting seems to offer one of the best

safeguards in the home garden to protect berries, small fruit trees and young seedlings.

BIRDS SHARE NATURE'S SECRET

There's magic in the song of a bird—
More than the song that is often heard—
Birds sing in spring more loudly and long,
Because that's the way to coax Nature along.
There's more in their song than exhaltation,
Their singing is at a rate of vibration,
That causes the leaves to bud
out and turn green
We hear only the song, but
the leaves are seen.
—Louise Riotte

According to Linda Goodman, writing in her book, *Star Signs,* there's a magical reason for this little-known phenomenon of nature. The singing of the birds sets up a particular sound vibration that promotes the growth of the young leaves of trees, plants and flowers, so the birdsong is fairly constant all day long in the spring while the new growth is occurring. In summer the birdsong ceases, except at dawn and twilight and sometimes, if not quite all of the leaves are full, also during the early morning hours of summer. After the leaves are full, the chemical activities of the trees, plants and flowers change every day in the summer—at dawn and at twilight.

BIRTH CONTROL PILLS   This should probably come under the heading of "weird ways that work." A year or so ago I was a guest at a garden club meeting where the principal speaker was a woman who was noted for being phenomenally successful in growing roses. Her most unusual suggestion was to place birth control pills in the hole when she planted a new rose bush—and dig additional pills into the soil at six-month intervals later on!

BLACKBIRDS   Flocks of blackbirds sometimes strip the ears from sweet corn when it is in the milk stage, often making their depredations at dawn and dusk. A workable solution is the use of waxed paper softdrink cups, obtainable from paper wholesalers. Measuring about 7 inches long they are large enough to cover sufficiently even the huski-est ears. As soon as the corn is pollinated slip a cup over each ear and the birds will be unable to strip the ears. As the ears mature remove the cups and place them over the less mature ones and eventually to rows of later plantings. At the season's end gather and store the cups for the following year.

BLACK-EYED PEAS This mainstay of Southern gardens is well worth growing as a second or summer crop. If cornstalks are left standing after harvest, vining types of black-eyes will climb right up. They need warm days and warm nights to develop properly. Excellent fresh at the green stage, or dried for winter. It is traditional to serve black-eyed peas and ham hocks at New Year's to bring good luck for the coming year.

BLOSSOM-END ROT This puzzling con-dition often occurs when tomatoes are in full bloom with many good-sized tomatoes. They become black-spotted at the bottom for no apparent reason. Blossom-end rot is a physio-logical condition and is most prevalent with plants that have had abundant water during the early part of the season, and are then sub-jected to hot, dry weather and a shortage of moisture. Prevalence of this condition can be reduced by watering, mulching to con-serve moisture, and thorough preparation of the soil before planting. Also avoid giving plants excessive supplies of nitrogen. Cal-cium deficiency may also be a cause of blossom-end rot. To correct add lime. Do not, however, mulch tomatoes until after they start blooming—the plants need the sun-warmed soil on their roots to enable them to flower well.

BLUEBERRIES Blueberries, often a free-for-the-asking product of Nature's own vast garden, are more than just a delicious des-sert. The leaves and twigs possess medicinal properties, containing myrtillin, a substance now known to reduce blood sugar as does insulin. The fruits tend to act as a new-fashioned blood purifier, such action depending upon the blood-fortifying miner-

als as calcium, iron, phosphorous, and one other, just as important as these three, man-ganese, this last acting as a catalyzing agent. For best results eat the fresh fruits uncooked and without sugar.

If blueberries don't grow wild in your neighborhood, the cultivated, large-fruit hy-brids are easy to grow. They like a moist soil and plenty of water while the fruits are devel-oping. Soil must be of acid reaction, pH 4.5 to 6.0, with a good amount of humus. Grow in full sun, planted 4 feet apart with 8 feet between rows. Roots are close to the surface so avoid cultivating. The new, named hy-brids are self-infertile. By growing three or more plants of different varieties close to-gether, perfect fertilization takes place. Be careful to choose varieties for the north or south, depending on your locality. Wayside Gardens suggests named varieties of *Vaccin-ium corymbosum* for the northern states, and for the South, selected varieties of the Rab-biteye Blueberry, *V. ashei.*

During hot, dry weather, put containers of water in your berry patch. If you don't, the birds will eat the berries to get water from the juice.

BLUEBONNETS (*Lupinus texensis*) I hate to admit defeat! Having run out of space on my own premises I persuaded my son to let me plant bluebonnets on one of the mead-ows adjacent to his home where several plants of purple lupines already grew. I had fallen in love with bluebonnets one spring when I saw them growing in a yard about three blocks from my home. The corner lot was a solid mass of bright blue and I never forgot how lovely it looked that spring. I wanted to see them growing again. To this end I spent well over twenty dollars for seed, buying from three different sources, taking care to buy scored seed and soaking them in boiling water and allowing them to stand for 24 hours. Then I planted in the fall as recom-mended.

Alas, not one single, solitary bluebonnet came up! Since lupines already grew in the meadow and bluebonnets are also lupines I don't know what went wrong. Then I read an article in *The Dallas Morning News* on bluebonnets and it put me in the mood to try again. It seems that now Texans are growing bluebonnets in flower beds and patio pots. After only three years of commercial availability they are becoming as popular as pansies and violets as fall-planted annuals.

Commercial production of the state flower became possible as a result of germination techniques developed by Texas Agricultural Extension Service specialists. Because the seed coat is very hard, only a small percentage of seeds sprout, according to Dr. Don Wilkerson, an extension service horticulturist. In fact, they may lie dormant in fields for years (maybe there's hope yet!) before the tough coating cracks so the seed can grow.

The process developed at Texas A & M University involves soaking the seed in a sulfuric acid bath, which produces 80 to 90 percent germination, as required for commercial production. These cultivated bluebonnets should be considered annuals as they are unlikely to come up on their own the following spring. There are now also white, light-blue, and pink versions of bluebonnets.

BLUEJAYS   These attractive but often noisy birds are often disliked, yet over 80 percent of their food is estimated to come from weed seeds, grasshoppers, beetles, and other insects.

BOIL TWENTY MINUTES AND LIVE
Home canning is a precise science and variations from recommended procedures, which sometimes occur when inexperienced canners begin to preserve the produce of home gardens, could result in botulism poisoning. If, upon opening, the liquid is cloudy or the food doesn't smell quite right, observe the rule of boiling for 20 minutes before tasting.

BORAGE   Borage is a hardy annual herb that grows from 1 to 3 feet tall. Sow seeds in well-drained, moist soil, after frost date where they are to grow. Borage leaves are 6 to 8 inches long, gray-blue in color, and covered with fine hairs. The young, immature rosettes of leaves are excellent for the salad bowl, but become too sticky for use as they mature. The beautiful, sky blue flowers may be dipped in slightly beaten egg whites, then sugar, and allowed to dry. Store in a dry place, well covered, until used.

BOTTOMLESS JUGS   There's an easy, inexpensive way to make your own mini-greenhouses for setting out plants in the early garden. Large bottles or glass jugs keep plants warm and admit sunlight. To remove the bottom tie a heavy string soaked in gasoline or lighter fluid around the bottom of the jug. Light the string and when the jug gets hot, lower it into cold water and the bottom will fall off.

Presto! An insect-proof glasshouse!

BOTTOMS UP!   Here's a practical tip for seed starting time. If you have access to foam plastic cups with lids, here's an excellent use for them. Rinse cups if they have been previously used. Place the cup lid on and make some small holes in the lid and around the lip of the cup with an ice pick. Turn the cup upside down and cut about one inch off the bottom.

Fill the cup with a good soil mix and plant the seeds or transplant in the soil. Place the cup in a pan of water and remove it when the soil surface becomes moist. Set aside and drain. You can do this again when the soil becomes dry.

When it's time to set the plants out, moisten the soil and remove the lid from the bottom of the cup. The plant will pop out easily. Plant according to variety. Then you can use the cup as a cutworm guard by placing it over the plant and pressing it about one inch into the soil.

Note: If you are planting tomatoes dig a fairly deep hole and place in it several dry, broken-up corn cobs. Cover with soil and then put in your transplant. The corncobs will help to hold moisture and will also provide some nutrients when the roots grow down and find them. When transplanting large plants you may find a post hole digger more practical than a shovel.

BOX TURTLE (*Testudinidea*) These slow wanderers will work long hours for low pay. Though they may occasionally nibble a lettuce leaf or take a bite out of a tomato they do consume lots of worms, slugs, snails, and insects in their leisurely travel through your garden. However, while they do make efficient predators there's no guarantee they will become permanent guests unless your garden is fenced—they are inveterate nomads and like to see the world.

BROCCOLI (*Brassica oleracea*) I find broccoli easier to grow than cabbage. A cool-season vegetable, it may be grown in either early spring or late fall. Cut when florets are in tight bud—yellow blossoms on the head indicate overmaturity. After harvesting the central sprout, side sprouts will give you a second crop for several weeks. A side dressing of compost when plants are half-grown is helpful. If troubled with green cabbage worms use Bacillus thuringiensis, sold under various trade names such as Dipel, Biotrol, Thuricide, etc. High in vitamins A, B, C, E, and K—broccoli is a sprout with clout.

BROMELIADS (*Bromeliaceae*) These members of the pineapple family can be stunning houseplants and the long-lasting inflorescences are not difficult to maintain. And, as a result of sporting, many new forms are appearing—variegation consists of longitudinal striping of a brilliant white, yellow, pink, red, or purple, such as exists in no other plant family.

Bromelain and papain (found in pineapple and papaya, respectively) have long been used as meat tenderizers. Now there is an interesting new discovery. Recently they have been found to enhance the collagen/elastin (the fibers that hold skin firmly in place) regrowth technique. The enzymes bromelain and papain actually dissolve old fibers and accelerate the rate at which they are replaced by new and youthful fibers. It is believed that along with increasing your intake of these two enzymes, it is also helpful to step up your daily allotment of vitamin C, zinc, selenium, and protein. These nutrients are what youthful skin fibers are made of.

BRUSSELS SPROUTS (*Brassica oleracea*) The miniature, bite-sized cabbages grow up and down the stalk rather than in a large head at the top. They are considered upper-class members of the cabbage family. A well grown single plant may produce as many as a hundred sprouts. Brussels sprouts are indifferent to freezing weather and, like kale, gain in flavor from a freeze. Often they will pull through a northern winter with a straw mulch.

Plant seed indoors in early spring and transplant to the garden in compost-enriched soil about six weeks later. When sprouts lower down the stalk near harvesting size, pinch out the plant's growing tip at the top, thus throwing strength into sprout development. Harvest lower sprouts first, breaking off the leaf under each as you harvest it.

Both nasturtium and mustard contain mustard oil and may be used as trap crops to lure insects away from brussels sprouts and other garden members of the cole family.

BULBS and MULCHES Don't mulch in the fall where you have bulbs until the ground has frozen. Early mulching often provides a warm home for rodents who will feast on the bulbs. If you wait a while, the little pests will have gone somewhere else.

BURNET (*Poterium sanguisorba*) Usually called "salad burnet." We may not think of this herb as a healer, yet in Revolutionary days it was made into a tea to stanch the flow of blood. The styptic attributes of this bushy plant are indicated in its generic name: *sanguis* meaning blood, and *sorbere* meaning absorbing. *Poterium* is from the Greek drinking cup, the Poterium. Salad burnet was used in olden times for the "cool tankard," popular with the Pennsylvania Germans, the leaves being steeped in tankards to make a drink called "cool cup." Burnet is used in green butters, or sauces, cream cheese, and dips and may be used as a change from parsley as a garnish. To salads it imparts something of the taste and flavor of cucumbers. It also makes a fine herb vinegar that facilitates salad making.

The plant's ability to remain green on poor soil throughout the winter adds to its value in the salad garden, particularly in the Northwest, where few greens are available year-round. It is a long-lasting source of fresh greens.

BUTTERCUPS (*Ranunculus*)   The buttercup tribe are the villains of the garden, giving nothing and taking all the good things available, seriously depleting the ground of potassium and other elements. The secretions from their roots poison the precious nitrogen bacteria in the soil so that other plants suffer from their deficiency. When weed varieties, such as the bulbous or creeping buttercups get into a strawberry, pea, or bean bed, they will throw them into a panic and cause them to produce small, premature fruits. Even the lovely and desirable garden subjects such as delphinium, peony, anemone, clematis, and others share this incompatibility with other plants, so that their beds and their neighbors must have constant feeding and replenishing.

BUTTERFLY GARDENING   Butterflies among the insects are what birds are among the higher animals: the most attractive and beautiful members of the great group to which they belong. They are primarily day fliers and are remarkable for the delicacy and beauty of their membranous wings, covered with myriads of tiny scales that overlap one another like the shingles on a house and show an infinite variety of hue through the coloring of the scales and their arrangement upon the translucent membrane running between the wing veins. This is the characteristic that gives to the great order of

butterflies and moths its name *Lepidoptera*, meaning scale-winged.

Butterfly Bush   (*Buddleia davidii*)   For those who don't have much room but want to attract butterflies, simply planting the butterfly bush will fill your need. This lovely woody shrub attracts over 20 American species of butterflies. It thrives in full sun, tolerates almost any kind of soil and blooms all through the summer in hardiness Zones 4–9. The shrubs grow about 6 to 7 feet tall, spreading to 5 or 6 feet. It may die back in winter in cold areas, but comes up in spring.

Butterfly Plants   If you are truly "into butterflies" you should consider planning for a wild garden in some out-of-the-way spot on your property to give them a breeding ground (butterflies feed on some plants but breed on others). Besides the butterfly bush try planting butterfly weed (*Asclepias tuberosa*), globe thistle (*Echinops*), milkweed (*Asclepias speciosa*)—the Monarch's host plant, or verbena (*Verbena*). (Gardens Alive and Plants of the Southwest have even more suggestions.) Butterflies are attracted to flowers in the red, scarlet, and blue range. These finicky eaters will dine only on highly specific plants, most species of which are not usually found in gardens. Butterflies like to lay their eggs on stinging nettles. Your little butterfly garden is one that must not be tamed, just place it at the edge of your property in full sunlight, and let it find its own wild, natural look. Most butterfly plants are perennial or self-seeding and will be a permanent sanctuary for butterfly caterpillars.

But what of the housebound, elderly, or disabled—how can they enjoy butterflies? Julia Percivall and Pixie Burger, in their book, *Household Ecology*, give us a suggestion. "Often you can persuade them to settle and feed on a sunny windowsill if offered the right confection. This confection is simple, half a teaspoon of honey and half a teaspoon of sugar mixed in a cup of warm water will make an adequate butterfly nectar.

"To make a feeder, use a saucer and a wad of cotton. Butterflies taste through their feet, so they need an island of cotton in the middle of the nectar sea. The cotton will absorb the honey-water so that the butterfly, when it lands on the cotton, will taste the food through its feet and then it will stand on the island and lower its thin rolled tongue and suck the nectar up."

BUTTERFLY TRAP Butterflies seldom exist in large enough numbers to be of much importance as either harmful (in the caterpillar stage) or helpful (as pollinators) to plants. Only one, the cabbage worm butterfly, is really a garden nuisance. Look for its pale yellow eggs (which hatch into voracious green worms) on the leaves of cole plants— broccoli, brussels sprouts, cabbage, etc. Treat with Bacillus thuringiensis (B.t.) which is sold under various trade names: Dipel, Fertilome, etc. Or try this trap:

Mount a flat board of scrap lumber on a stick and paint the board bright yellow on both sides (a butterfly-attracting color). After the paint is dry, spread heavy motor oil on both sides with a paint brush. The yellow will attract the white cabbage butterflies that lay their eggs on plants of the *Brassica* family and they will stick to the oil. Remove the insects as often as necessary and add new oil. It works!

Come forth into the light of things,
Let Nature be your teacher.
WILLIAM WORDSWORTH

CABBAGES (*Brassica oleracea*)   These plants are really the backbone of any vegetable garden. Decorative and nutritious, they do well under a wide range of conditions. The cabbages (or coleworts) developed a head about the time that Charlemagne was crowned king of the Franks. Every time the peasants would see a cole that had formed a head they would point and say "cabouche" (head or noggin). In no time at all, people were calling the coles with round, pointed, flat, or hard heads—CABBAGE!

Cabbages that get too much cold, too much heat or not enough water may go directly to seed without bothering to form a head at all. This is called bolting. Cabbage heads split if the plant gets too much fertilizer, water, or heat. Splitting can be reduced by withholding water as the heads are reaching maturity. If there is lots of rain, cut the roots on one side of the plant with a spade or twist the whole plant a quarter turn while it is still in the ground. When harvesting, cut off the head but leave the stalk with a couple of leaves. Often a few heads the size of a fist will regrow on the stalk.

CABBAGE WORMS   To kill, mix one quart of wood ashes together with one quart of flour and one small cup of fine table salt and use to dust plants.

CACTUS   Who needs it? Maybe you do! Even that great plant wizard Luther Burbank thought cactus was so important that he spent a lot of time developing a spineless form that has proved to be a useful source of food for both men and animals.

Picture this scenario: you are lost in the desert, your car has conked out, or your plane has gone down—and there you would be. In deep heat. Along with other survivors, without food or water. Providing other matters were not too serious, a knowledge of cactus would assure you of instant social success.

First things first—the barrel cactus is a reservoir of liquid. If you slice off the top and then mash the pulp inside, you'll get several quarts of sticky juice. This knowledge has saved the lives of many a thirsty traveler lost in the desert. It doesn't taste all that great but it's wet and will keep you from drying out.

Next in importance is the flat-leaved type called *opuntia*, or prickly pear. Several kinds grow in the southwestern part of the United States, but cactus is not limited to this area;

several varieties grow as far north as Canada. These can be eaten boiled or fried, with spines removed, of course, and the beautiful flowers made into salads. The seeds may be ground up into meal and made into cakes.

According to Anne Lindsay Greer in *Cuisine of the American Southwest, nopales* (cactus pads), are "delicious and succulent, somewhat similar in taste to green beans." But how do you go about defrocking a flat pad of opuntia? Peeling is a must. Cactus sold in the supermarkets today have been mechanically de-prickled, but, even so, there often remain some stinging, invisible hairs to irritate the unwary. Avoid them by jabbing a fork into the fruit and, while holding the cactus pad steady, slice ½ inch from each end, then cut a lengthwise slit about ¼ inch deep. Slip the tip of the knife under the cut, beneath the thick underlayer and skin. Pull off the outer and under layers of skin by holding them down on the work surface with the knife blade as you roll the fruit with the fork—or, more easily, with your hand, as the exposed pad may be grasped at this point. This sounds complicated but, after you have done a few, you get better at it and faster.

And, by the way, there are nutritional reasons for cooking with cactus. Cactus is low in calories, about 45 per pad, and it is rich in fiber (a cholesterol fighting aid), supplies vitamin C and potassium (good for the heart), and is very low in sodium. Cactus is even romantic; how could they have made all those cowboy movies without it?

CALLING ALL CHOCOLATE LOVERS!

The *Great American Food Almanac* observes that Linnaeus, the Swedish botanist who spent his lifetime giving Latin names to plants, chose an especially apt one for the cacao tree. He called it *Theobroma*, "food of the gods." Chocolate has been praised as an aphrodisiac, denounced as a narcotic and was once viewed with indifference by the Spanish court upon Columbus's fourth return from the New World. It was dumped as worthless cargo by pirates, rejoiced in by Quakers who regarded it as a substitute for gin, and in recent years touted as a replacement for the feeling of being in love. One of its compounds is phenylethylanine, the same chemical produced by the human brain when it considers itself in love. Now some say that chocolate causes high cholesterol.

So, if you must eschew chocolate for health reasons (and to save your teeth), you might like to consider carob (*Ceratonia siliqua*), a tree that has flourished for thousands of years in countries bordering the Mediterranean Sea. It bears large, brown pods containing 40 percent sugar and 6 percent protein. According to John Heinerman, the pods are the so-called "locusts" consumed by John the Baptist during his wilderness residency, hence the common name of "St. John's Bread." Seeds were used in ancient times as weight units for goods from which the term "carat" is reportedly derived.

You can use carob as a substitute for either chocolate or cocoa in any recipe and get equal taste without paying for it in calories, since there are only 180 calories in 3½ ounces. Compare that to cocoa's 295 calories and to the whopping 528 calories in the same amount of sweet chocolate. In addition, carob is also rich in calcium, phosphorus, and potassium, with traces of sodium and iron. Not related to cocoa or chocolate, it has no caffeine or theobromine. People who are allergic to chocolate can safely enjoy carob dishes. Carob—unlike chocolate—contains no oxalic acid to interfere with the body's ability to assimilate calcium.

Because carob powder is sweet, it can be used instead of sugar in bread and pastry products, including bread, waffles, cakes, pies, pancakes, cereals (hot or cold), crepes, muffins, etc. The color will be chocolaty-brown. Commercial powders are finer but Southern Californians often make their own by gathering, drying and grinding the pods themselves.

Carob pods also have medicinal properties and have been used as a medicine for the prevention and treatment of diarrhea in livestock. It has been advocated for the prevention and cure of human dysentery, especially in children. The pectin and lignin in carob also help digestion, combining with harmful elements—even radioactive fallout—in digested food and carry them safely out of the body. Carob is indigenous in the Mediterranean region but can be grown in the States in hot climates such as Southern California or Arizona where it is often planted as a street or park tree. These showy evergreens are drought-resistant with long roots that reach deep for underground water. I found, upon planting some seeds sent to me by a friend, that I could grow them in southern Oklahoma, if given winter protection. (If interested in growing carob trees write to Survival Shop, P.O. Box 42216, Los Angeles, California 90042, and ask for prices on whole carob pods.)

If you can't have chocolate and don't care too much for carob—but you are still a chocolate lover—you might enjoy smelling the chocolate flower (Plants of the Southwest). They say "it's a must for chocolate lovers"! The fragrance of chocolate fills the air in the early morning when *Berlandiera lyrata* is at its best. The blossoms are pale yellow with maroon centers, the undersides of the petals having bright red veins. Enjoy chocolate flower in the morning for it nods in the heat of afternoon. It's nice to know you can still smell chocolate even if you can't indulge! It's one of life's minor pleasures—and it's not addictive!

CANNA (*Canna* × *generalis*)   Cannas give! They have beautiful and luxuriant foliage and their bright colors put on an unequalled show from July until frost. And they bloom year after year, the bulbs increasing steadily. Give them a moist, sunny spot and they will be a traffic-stopping spectacular. Northern gardeners may need to dig and store the bulbs in the fall, but in the South they may be safely left in the ground if planted about 6 to 8 inches deep. Cannas come in red, yellow, coral, pink, and bi-color. "Cleopatra," a

multicolored charmer, is a combination of bright red and yellow. Strangely, solid reds and yellows may appear among the bi-colors, often all on the same plant. Cannas are also called Indian shot because of their large dark seeds.

Carefree gardeners in Southern and Western states can also plant cannas: On July 20, 1986, in a temperature of 107 degrees this bed of red cannas, grown in full sunlight, stood up in blazing red glory and did not wilt!

CANTALOUPES (*Cucumis melo*)   There's no taste thrill quite like that of a vine-ripened cantaloupe, a privilege enjoyed by few other than home gardeners. Treat yourself to this pleasure! Sow melons directly into the garden after the soil is warm, or start indoors in pots and transplant. Give them room: 18 inches apart and 4 feet between rows. Ripe melons are distinguished by their fragrance. Harvest when the stem slips easily from the fruit with slight pressure. Honeydews turn pale yellow or tan when ripe, even though stems may not slip. Place aluminum foil or wax paper under melons to prevent insect damage. Rich in vitamin A, they also contain B and C, iron, calcium, and phosphorous.

CARDOON (*Cynara cardunculus*)   This thistle-flowered, spiny-leafed herb resembles a huge tropical fern with leaves that are grayish green above and white and woolly on the underside. A relative of the globe artichoke, it will also produce similar but smaller heads, but it is for its blanched stem, and not for its heads, that the cardoon is grown. In the South of Europe it is grown for its roots, which are thick and fleshy. This plant is very attractive in the gray garden or as an accent plant. It likes a rich soil and plenty of moisture, the culture being much the same as for the artichoke. The thickened (and blanched) leafstalk is boiled and served like spinach or eaten fresh like celery. Space plants 3 feet apart.

CARPENTER BEES (*Xylocopa*)   Also known as leaf-cutter bees. These bees range in size from ¼ of an inch long to as large as a bumblebee. They sometimes bore out the pith of rose canes to cause wilting. Control by pruning canes below the infested section whenever wilted canes are noticed. To prevent bees from entering cut canes, insert a flat-headed tack in the end or plug the hole with grafting wax, putty or paraffin. An insect called the bee assassin makes a specialty of feeding on bees that it catches in flowers.

Eat your carrots if you would be,
Clear of eye, and quick to see!
Louise Riotte

CARROTS (*Carota*) With four older brothers to spoil me I was truly a rotten little kid. And I never "showed out" to more naughtiness than in church, finding the long hours tedious and boring. One particular Sunday morning I had behaved more badly than usual; the fire and brimstone sermon delivered in a raucous, thundering bellow had truly unnerved me. I had started crying and begging to go home—to my mother's intense embarrassment. When the family went out to get in the car my oldest brother, under the pretense of buttoning my coat, whispered, "Stay in the car," hugged me and picked me up to sit beside him. Arriving home my mother walked toward the house, grimly determined to improve on the unimprovable. When she reached the steps she turned just in time to see my brother driving off with me. He kept me out for about an hour, returned me home by the back door and slipped me quietly into my room clutching a new coloring book and a box of crayons. I stayed there until time for Sunday night supper.

I remember that supper very well because it was the first time I, not wanting to call attention to myself, accepted a large helping of detested carrots without making a fuss. To my surprise I liked them and when I asked for more all heads turned toward me in pleased amazement. That evening I began a love affair with carrots that was to last a lifetime. . . .

Carrots like to grow in loose, sandy soil and if you have clay soil you will find carrots very challenging and likely to be small and misshapen. Denny McKeown, in his book *Midwest Gardening*, has an excellent solution: "Simply dig a trench 12 inches deep and the width of your shovel. Mix sand and peat humus with some of the existing soil (about half and half), and backfill the trench. Then plant your carrot seeds." To this I would add a hint of my own. After preparing the soil as suggested sprinkle the seeds thinly on the surface and cover with an inch or so of peat moss. Then water carefully with a sprinkling can if weather is dry. The peat moss will hold the moisture and the carrots will sprout quickly. Be ruthless when they sprout and thin them to one every 3 inches or so. When carrots are mature the orange crown will appear at the soil line. When you harvest carrots clip the fern tops at once so they will not draw moisture from the carrots.

Plant in early spring. Carrots are easy to grow and seldom subject to insect attack. Watch them if a prolonged rainy spell is followed by warm, humid weather for they may rot in the ground if nearing maturity.

Carrots eaten as an uncooked vegetable are a wonderfully all-purpose protective food. A glassful of carrot juice should be considered a *complete meal*. Sip it slowly and swish it around in your mouth to ensure complete digestion and assimilation. The saliva is actually the first stomach enzyme that all food must encounter, and is called ptyalin. Caution: one glass is good but do not overdrink in the mistaken belief that two glasses will be twice as beneficial. This may lead to a condition known as "carotinemia," in which the skin assumes a distinctly yellowish hue resembling jaundice. Carrots contain lots of vitamin A, the "eye" vitamin.

CARROT STORAGE If you don't have a cellar, try this. Use a jar, tub, or similar container, and line the bottom with crumpled newspaper. Cut the tops off freshly dug carrots (preferably from a fall planting). Leave about ¼ to ½ inch of stem on the carrot, but do not wash the carrots. Alternate layers of carrots and crumpled newspapers. Store the container in the coolest area of the house. In the spring carrots stored like this will taste as good as fresh ones.

> At the first sound of whippoorwill
> in the spring, the Indian knew it was
> time for planting.
>   Indian Wisdom

CATALOGS Looking at all those picture-perfect visions of fruits and vegetables displayed in living color, do you feel inspired or intimidated? Working your hesitating way through "best," "finest," "latest," do you feel like you need a map? Seedsmen and nurserymen always put their best foot forward and you have to stay alert. It's like the word "enhanced" that's frequently used by the government when speaking of raising taxes. Take "naturalizes well," for instance. While the plant may be beautiful and worthwhile, it may also take over the place! "Once established" is another phrase to watch—this one may take years before you even notice it's there!

Even so all this feast for the eyes does contain, here and there, useful bits of information on the same page for planting, cultivation, and harvesting. Some catalogs even give you recipes.

January is the month when catalogs usually begin to arrive. Gather as many as you can and have fun. Lots of varieties are available and no one seed company has them all. Pay particular attention to the catalogs that are applicable to your region. The varieties offered have been tested to perform well under the growing conditions found in a specific geographical area.

Varieties that meet the specific challenges of your garden are most likely to succeed. So determine your garden's profile. What adverse conditions, such as heat, drought, and cooler-than-normal temperatures are likely to be present? How long is your growing season? How much space is available? What disease have you noticed in your garden? Once analyzed, you can single out varieties with characteristics such as tolerance to heat, drought, and frost and times to maturity that match your growing season. You may want to choose plants of bush or dwarf growth. Remember these are not inferior to standard-size ones and in fact may be even more productive and carry good disease resistance. A great many veggies are now available as "dwarf."

"Days to maturity" may be another puzzler. They are seldom the same in any two or three catalogs. Be guided by your own experience: after several seasons of growing the same variety and keeping record, you should get the feel for how long that variety takes to mature in your own garden. Also note if the maturity date is given from transplant size, for you may need to figure in the time from germination to the time it takes to raise seedlings to transplant size.

CATNIP (*Nepeta cataria*) Catnip has proven its therapeutic worth for several hundred years as an antispasmodic, carminative, and diaphoretic. For nervousness, insomnia, and nervous headache, a mixture of ½ teaspoon each of valerian root, skullcap, and catnip is steeped to prepare a warm infusion. This preparation is most helpful if a cupful is drunk three times a day, one hour after meals and about a half-hour before retiring.

"Set it and the cats will get it, sow it and the cats won't know it!" My cats still don't know it, they simply turn up their respective noses and walk away. So I eat it. And chopped for salad and mixed with other greens it's absolutely delicious. My guests always comment on it and wonder what that interesting and different flavor is.

Nepeta cataria is common catnip, but there is also *Nepeta* 'Six Hills Giant,' *Nepeta macrantha*, *Nepeta mussiniix faasenii*, (a latter-day hybrid with lovely mauve-blue flowers), and a new arrival in this country, *Nepeta citrodora*, bearing blue-gray flowers and having a musky melon fragrance.

CAULIFLOWER (*Brassica oleracea*) "The cabbage with a college education," according to Mark Twain, gets its name from the

Latin, *cauliflora* (flowered cole). The edible flower buds that form the tight solid head are called curds. In a few varieties this head may be green or purple but is usually a creamy white. To give your cauliflower this lovely complexion, tie leaves over the curd when it is about the size of an egg and harvest about two weeks later. Two toothpicks, in the form of an "X" are handy for securing the leaves. To keep track of cauliflowers tied up at different times, use different colored yarn or rubber bands. Some of the new varieties do not need tying. Self-blanching, their leaves curl over and protect the heads, except in hot weather. Do not tie until heads are about 2½ inches in diameter and never tie too tightly or too closely over the head. Grow cauliflower in soil that is deep and rich, cultivate constantly, and side-dress with a high nitrogen fertilizer.

CECROPIA MOTH (*Hyalophora cecropia*) This beautiful North American native is a member of the silkworm family, and is a familiar sight to most Midwesterners and Easterners. It is actually the largest moth found in all North America, having a wingspan of 5 to 6 inches!

The female lays 200 to 300 white eggs in small batches on the underside of apple tree leaves. Cecropia caterpillars are also fond of cherry, lilac, elm, maple, willow, and walnut trees. The bizarre-looking bright, pea-green caterpillars are studded with thorny yellow spikes and little red club-shaped protrusions in two rows down the back, with blue spikes and yellow "eyes" along the sides. After spending all summer eating, the larvae select a likely-looking twig and spin a brown silk cocoon length-wise along the stick, secure from the wind.

They may be controlled by late season sanitation. Seek out the cocoons and destroy them. Oil sprays applied in early spring before trees leaf out will also be of help.

CELERIAC (*Apium graveolens* var. *rapaceum*) This vegetable, which is truly a celery, deserves a better press agent. Looking a little like a turnip it has, when both raw

and cooked, the authentic celery taste. The texture is different, and it is used for the swollen base and not the stalks . Even so, the celerylike tops can be eaten: the leaves themselves as celery-flavored spinach and the leaf stalks as celery flavored seakale.

Celeriac likes ample fertilizer and should have as much sun as possible. It needs a long growing season so start seeds indoors. After hardening off the seedlings, plant in the garden from the end of May to early June, making sure that the little bulbous swelling at the base of the plant stays at the soil level. Water gently. Unlike kohlrabi the celeriac root should be allowed to swell to a decent size before harvesting. Harvest in late fall, covering remaining roots with straw for winter protection. In very cold climates it is safer to lift them for storing.

Varieties include 'Large Smooth Prague' (120 days), 'Alabaster,' 'Apple,' 'Globus,' 'Snowball,' and 'Early Paris.'

CELERY (*Apium graveolens* var. *dulce*) Celery likes fertilizer and thrives on plenty of organic matter, best added in the form of leaf mold, compost, or well-decomposed manure, otherwise you may not have much luck with this particular vegetable.

Start seeds indoors and transplant when plants are about two inches high. Removing some of the leaves will make the roots stronger in relation to the top of the plant; also, the plant is less apt to wilt. Pinch off all but the center sprays. If hilling celery seems a bit much, you can use boards to blanch it. When plants are about 10 inches tall prop a 1-by-10 inch board up against either side of the row, fastening the tops of the planks together with wire so they won't blow over on a windy day. Celery needs lots of cultivation but the roots are near the surface so don't go too deep. Celery, though somewhat fussy about growing conditions, has practically no insect enemies.

Fresh celery juice contains much needed organic sodium, which helps to maintain calcium in solution at a 4-1 ratio and therefore the proper fluidity of the blood (and lymph) and to prevent it from becoming too thick. Fresh juice also has a high percentage of magnesium and iron. Eat celery uncooked, either alone or with other vegetables or simple protein, not with fruits. Do not discard the pale green leaves of your own garden-grown produce, they are a must ingredient in salads and even more tasty and nourishing than the familiar stalks.

CELERY MADE EASY   Here is an alternative to growing celery from seed. Buy a stalk of celery at the supermarket and cut off the bottom 2 or 3 inches. Use the top as usual. Plant the bottom and it will usually make 2 or 3 sprouts. Again cut the bottom so each part contains a sprout and plant with the bottom just below the ground, allowing plants to grow to maturity.

CHEMICAL WARFARE   David L. Rhoades, a zoologist and chemist at the University of Washington in Seattle, conducted studies on willow and red-alder trees indicating that when they are attacked by webworms and tent caterpillars, they give off a chemical that somehow alerts every other tree of their kind within several yards to brace themselves for an attack. These trees respond by changing their internal chemistry and, as more tannin is pumped into their leaves and tissues, the defense deters the hungry insects. Still other trees are known to produce insect-growth hormones, which disrupts the reproductive cycle of their enemies.

The so-called soft chaparral, a unique association of broadleaf evergreens and stunted shrubs and trees, have the startling ability to invade grassland and encircle themselves with bare soil "moats" several feet wide. Scientists explain this as the release of chemical compounds called terpenes from their leaves into the surrounding air, creating a characteristic fragrance.

And who would have thought cucumbers could be deadly! Seeking to test the theory in the laboratory, Michigan State horticulturist Alan Putnam and Cornell agronomist William Duke pitted two weedlike plants—millet and mustard—against 41 varieties of

wild cucumber. Their findings indicated that about three percent of the cucumbers inhibited weed growth by more than 75 percent.

And it has long been known that the roots of certain species of marigolds exude a substance that will kill nematodes. The active ingredients are sulphur-containing substances known as thiophenes, isolated by Dutch scientists from the roots of the African marigold. It has also been discovered that the beneficial effects of sowing marigolds lasts about three years.

NUTS TO CHICKENS!   Are your layers suffering from midwinter seasonal slump? And just when eggs are the highest priced! There's a way to keep them on the job. Oatmeal, widely touted for human consumption, is good for hens too. Just soak some oats or oatmeal in warm water and give it in addition to their regular ration. Clean, lukewarm drinking water helps as well: it gets them to drink more. Give the henhouse plenty of litter, being sure it's thick, warm, and *dry*. Chickens too, get discouraged if they have wet, cold feet. A bit of extra insulation in ceiling and walls around nest boxes pays off as well. Use doubled sheets of cardboard from large cartons—the kind used for furniture and appliances—for the insulation.

But what was the remark I made about nuts? Here in the southern and southwestern

states there are some years when we have an abundance of pecans, walnuts (black), very nutritious, or hickory nuts. Just crack the shells and let the hens have the fun of picking out the nutmeats. Keeps 'em busy, gives 'em exercise, and keeps 'em healthy. It's a secret oldtimers knew to keep layers laying. You don't have to give them your best pecans either. There are a lot of small, nutritious, natives that simply are not worth the trouble for us humans to pick out that will serve the purpose and make the hens just as happy.

Truly an egg in January may be worth two in June, and with a little extra care and forethought you can keep your hens contented and busy—laying.

CHIGGER (*Trombidiidae alfreddugesi*) The chigger, or harvest mite, is a tiny red creature with a body divided into two parts. It creeps into skin pores and hair follicles to feed, and causes a rash and instant itching. While it is merely a nuisance in North America, it is far more serious in Oriental countries because it carries a typhuslike disease called Japanese river fever. Harvest mites are common in the Midwest and South and you may wish to take measures against them when they occur in great numbers.

Clearing your garden of brush and cutting your grass close to the ground will help control chiggers. A dusting of diatomaceous earth has been found helpful. Trichogramma wasps may be used for control of chiggers in the egg stage and lacewing has proven effective for chiggers when they are grown mites.

CHINESE CABBAGE Often called celery cabbage, this plant is really a member of the mustard family and not in the cole group. Burpee's Hybrid is fun to grow in the cool days of fall, making giant cylindrical heads, 13 inches high and 8 inches across. The leaves are heavily savoyed, thick, succulent and nicely folded over the top. The inner leaves blanch nearly white and it is an excellent keeper. Don't sow too early or the plants may bolt. Marvelous for salads or stir-frying in a wok. Bugs rarely bother Chinese cabbage when sown in the autumn.

CHIVE (*Allium Schoenoprasum*) A must for every garden. Perennials, once planted they are yours practically forever. Chives add a zesty flavor to almost everything. Put them where they can remain undisturbed—they are pretty enough to be planted in a border along with the flowers and are almost completely disease free. After a year or two, you can separate the plant clusters and expand your stock. To use, clip off tops as needed.

CHIVE COMPANION Put an earthworm into the pot you're using to grow chives during the winter. Earthworms favor chives over all plants and the chives will respond with abundant leaves and bulblets that quickly reach a large size.

CHRISTMAS WREATHES Wed fun to thrift and make your own with easily come-by materials. With the future in mind start collecting materials throughout the fall season. Take a hike in the country or down a country road and gather attractive weeds and dried grasses here and there. When storing these materials I've found that just giving them a coat of inexpensive hair spray works about as well as anything. Magnolia leaves, placed in a mixture of glycerine and water, will become soft and pliable and these you may wish to save for future use—so treated they are not likely to shatter.

Decorations made of natural materials reflect the flavor of the region and the plants that grow there. Many like to start with a grapevine base, but you might try inexpensive chicken wire bent into shape or even heavy cardboard.

Yarrow, artemisia, and oakleaf hydrangea, which bloomed in the summer, remind us of the garden, now lying dormant—but we know it will bloom again. Prickly pear cactus, abundant in my region is unusual for wreath-making, but used judiciously, lends itself particularly well and gives a "flavor" of the Southwest. And where would we be without the time-honored pine cones, both large and small? And sprays of cedar, having the very scent of Christmas, are abundant everywhere, are pliable, and make a nice background for other materials of contrasting color.

A field or roadside holds many treasures—the seedheads of Queen Anne's lace, the pods of milkweed, and the plumes of wild grasses, teasel, broomsedge, and cattails. Burpee's catalog has a section on lovely grasses you can grow in your own garden to enjoy in the summer and use at Christmas.

Don't forget okra pods. Red okra is particularly effective combined with the tiny ears of strawberry popcorn (also good to pop), giving you something truly unusual in natural colors.

Because of the vine base, materials are easy to fix in place with wire or a hot-glue gun. Attach the leaves, pods, grass, and flowers so they appear to flow in one direction on the wreath. If you fall in love with your wreath and just can't bear to take it down—well, it's yours—leave it up if you like and enjoy it until spring's fresh flowers come again!

CHRYSANTHEMUM TIP   You, too, can have big, bushy chrysanthemums in your garden this fall—and you need not sacrifice a lot of space this summer. Plant your new divisions or rooted cuttings in one-gallon plastic pots in May or June. Stretch black plastic over the ground in a sunny, out-of-the-way place with access to water. Set pots atop the plastic, spacing so the plants have room to become bushy. The plastic will keep the roots from growing into the soil. When the mums start to show color in the fall move them to a prominent spot, group them according to the color desired, and astonish the neighbors who will wonder where you've been hiding them.

CLEAR THE AIR   You can remove onion odor from your breath and the taste from your mouth by chewing parsley for a few minutes.

CLOSE ENCOUNTERS   A small mirror mounted on a pancake turner makes it easy to inspect the underside of leaves for insects such as red spider.

COLEUS (*Coleus*)   Native to the African and Indian tropics, coleus are really members of the mint family: the square stem and leaves that are equal and opposite are a dead giveaway to the relationship. Coleus, with their flamboyant foliage, are so easily raised from seed, so undemanding as to the quality of soil, that they're often a mainstay of public and park plantings. But, though they like the sun, they will also do well in semishade. One of the cleverest uses is to plant coleus as a filler between small, newly planted shrubbery—taking advantage of its fast growth and easy culture.

Mealy bugs seem to be the worst pests to bother them, but spraying at the first sign of these tiny, soft, white sapsuckers should solve the problem. A spray solution of soap and water is easy to prepare and usually will suffocate the little beasties. Coleus are very adaptable and often can be carried through the winter as an attractive houseplant. Cuttings made in later summer and early fall will pot up nicely and, if kept pinched back in an attractive shape, will bring good color and form to your inside planters and hanging baskets.

This plant shows promise against glaucoma, the buildup of fluid pressure in the eye, that affects 2 million Americans and can lead to blindness unless promptly treated. According to a report on 10 volunteers in the British journal *Lancet*, doctors at Yale University School of Medicine were able to lower significantly fluid pressure in the eye with a substance called forskolin obtained from the coleus plant.

COLLARD   The oldest coleworts are the kales and the collards. Primitive types, they are representative of an ancestral form. Collard is a contraction of colewort, the name also being given to young plants harvested as greens before they have headed. In the South collards are highly regarded as "soul food," being especially relished when cooked with a ham hock. The tolerant collard will take more heat than cabbages, more cold than cauliflower.

THE COLOR PURPLE

My mother used to say, "no fools no fun." Some spring when your "funnybone" is working overtime why not astonish the neighbors and plant your yard or garden in a riot of reds and purples? Most of which are edible, entertaining, and useful. You could be the talk of the town!

Amaranth—Hinn Choy, red leaved amaranth (Good Earth Seeds)

Asparagus—Most varieties have purple-tinged tips but Waltham is the "top"

Basil—Opal basil; Thai basil; 'Purple Ruffles'

Beans, bush—Royal Burgundy Purple Pod, hyacinth bean, lilac blossoms, violet pods

Beans, lima—Speckled Calico

Beans, pole—Purple Pod

Beans, runner—Red Knight has beautiful red edible flowers

Beet—Lutz Greenleaf, purple-red; Red Ace Hybrid, Ruby Queen, many varieties

Black-eyed pea—Cowpea Purple Hull, Field Pea Hercules

Borage—Blue-purple flowers, used for flavoring, attracts bees

Brussels sprouts—Rubine

Cabbage—Red Acre, dark reddish purple; Red Rookie Hybrid, Scarlet O'Hara

Carrot—Japanese Scarlet Wonder, a deep scarlet color

Chicory—Radicchio, Red Verona, Red Marina

Chives—Lavender flower heads, delicate, onion-flavored foliage

Corn, broom—makes a feathery fence, seedheads attract birds

Corn, popping—Strawberry

Eggplant—Wide choice in purples; Rose Bianca is a rosy-lavender (Shepherd's)

Gow choy—Chinese chives, mild garlic flavor, hint of onion, lavender flowers

Grass, ornamental—'Imperata Red Baron,' at its best in full sun (Park)

Jicama—delicate light purple flowers, edible root

Kale, ornamental—red on green, Peacock (Park)

Kohlrabi—Early Purple Vienna, Rapid, deep purple

Lavender Vera—lilac flowers, delightfully scented

Lettuce—Ruby, Red Sails, Red Salad Bowl, Pirat (heat-resistant), Marveille des Quatres Saisons, red-tinged (Shepherd's)

Mustard—Red Giant

Nankinensis perilla—red-leaved, aromatic peppery taste, distinctive flavor

Okra—burgundy

Onions—Red Mac, Red Torpedo, Red Hamburger, many other varieties

Onions, fall scallions—Red Beard, a red "green" onion (Shepherd's)

Oregano—lavender-pink flowers, strongly scented

Pak choy—flowering purple (Good Earth Seeds)

Peppers, hot—many mature to red and purple; Mexi Bell Hybrid, Super Cayenne Hybrid, Super Chili Hybrid, etc.

Peppers, sweet—Lorelei, Purple Belle Hybrid, Purple Beauty; many varieties red when mature

Potato—Red Pontiac, Dark Red Norland, Cherries Jubilee (Shepherd's) is red inside as well as outside

Purple leaf plum

(Most of these varieties are listed in several catalogs, which you will find under "Sources." Purple and red varieties of vegetables, grasses, and fruits require no special culture and will grow in ordinary, organically enriched garden soil. They are just as tasty as the green varieties and indeed many, like burgundy okra, turn green upon cooking. Others, like strawberry popcorn, may be dried for winter decorations. Red okra pods are also candidates for winter bouquets.

Radish—Easter Egg, Cherry Belle, etc.; many red varieties, Crimson Giant, French Breakfast

Red-leaved perilla—peppery aromatic herb with delicious flavor

Rosemary—blue to purple flowers

Spinach, summer—Basella Malabar Red Stem (Burpee)

Strawberries—edible, decorative grown in strawberry jar

Swiss chard—rhubard chard, bright red stems, red-tinged leaves, very decorative

Thymus serpyllum—fragrant foliage, purple flowers, ideal to plant between flagstones

Tomatoes—wide choice, many red varieties both large and small, early and late

Turnip—Purple top, Scarlet Queen entirely red

The strawberry grows underneath the nettle,
And wholesome berries thrive and ripen best
Neighbour'd by fruit of baser quality.
            Henry V
            William Shakespeare

COMPANION PLANTING   Is it worthwhile? Shakespeare certainly thought so. And before him the Roman agriculturist Marcus Varro observed more than 2,000 years ago that certain plants did not do well when planted near walnut trees. Recent studies have confirmed this. The roots of black walnut secrete a toxin that inhibits plant growth in the immediate area such as alfalfa, beans, blackberries, peas, peppers, potatoes, and tomatoes. But it does not inhibit iris; I have lovely iris growing almost up to the trunk of my black walnut tree, also daffodils and daylilies.

There is an old saying: "Sow fennel, sow trouble." It's true, bush beans, caraway, kohlrabi and tomatoes are especially hindered by its presence. Peas and beans grow well with carrots, turnips, radishes, cucumbers, corn, potatoes, and many aromatic herbs, but they heartily dislike being companioned by onions, garlic, and gladiolus. On the other hand, as set forth in my book *Carrots Love Tomatoes, Secrets of Companion Planting*, there are dozens, perhaps even hundreds, of happy companionships to be observed among vegetables, herbs, flowers, and other plants. Some of these, such as aromatic herbs, protect other plants from insect ene-

mies; some, such as nettles, help other plants to grow; others, such as carrots and tomatoes, beets and kohlrabi, onions and lettuce, occupy different levels.

COMPANION PLANTS

Plant	Companions and Effects
Anise	Germinates better in the presence of coriander
Asparagus	Tomatoes, parsley, basil
Basil	Tomatoes (improves growth and flavor); said to dislike rue; repels flies and mosquitoes
Beans	Potatoes, carrots, cucumbers, cauliflower, cabbage, summer savory, most other vegetables and herbs; good around houseplants when set outside. Enemies: garlic, onion, shallot, gladiolus.
Beans (bush)	Sunflowers (beans like partial shade, sunflowers attract birds and bees), cucumbers (combination of heavy and light feeders), potatoes, corn, celery, summer savory. Dislike: garlic, onions, shallots, gladiolus.
Beebalm	Improves growth and flavor of tomatoes.
Beets	Onions, kohlrabi, bush beans, cabbage family, lettuce Dislikes: pole beans
Blackthorn	Will revive an old appletree if planted nearby.
Borage	Tomatoes (attracts bees, deters tomato worm, improves growth and flavor), squash, strawberries
Buttercup family	Delphiniums, peonies, columbine, etc. are inimical to clover.
Cabbage family	Potatoes, celery, dill, chamomile, sage, thyme, mint pennyroyal, rosemary, lavender, beets, onions. Aromatic plants deter cabbage worms. Enemies: Kohlrabi and tomatoes stunt each other's growth.
Carrots	Peas, lettuce, chives, onions, leeks, rosemary, sage, tomatoes. Enemy: Dill retards growth.

Catnip	Plant in borders: protects against flea beetles
Celery	Leeks, tomatoes, bush beans, cauliflower, cabbage
Chamomile	Cabbage, onions. Chamomile placed near sickly plants will help them to recover, but use in very small portions. A good spray against damp-off. Improves heavy, wet soil.
Chervil	Radishes (improves growth and flavor)
Chives	Carrots: plant around base of fruit trees to discourage insects from climbing trunk. Use spray against apple scab, powdery and downy mildew.
Coriander	Repels aphids; helps anise germinate; hinders seed formation of fennel. Aids germination of anise.
Corn	Potatoes, peas, beans, cucumbers, pumpkin, squash. Do not plant corn and tomatoes close together as they are attacked by the same worm.
Cosmos	Reported to repel corn earworm.
Cucumbers	Beans, corn, peas, radishes, sunflowers Dislikes: sage.
Datura	Poisonous to animals and people, but repels Japanese beetles. Aids pumpkin growth.
Dill	Cabbage (improves growth and health). Hinders carrots and tomatoes.
Eggplant	Beans
Fennel	Most plants are supposed to dislike it.
Flax	Carrots, potatoes
Garlic	Roses and raspberries (deters Japanese beetle); with herbs to enhance their production of essential oils; plant liberally throughout garden to deter pests. Aids vetch. Inhibits growth of peas and beans.
Gladiolus	Inhibits growth of peas and beans
Henbane	Poisonous to animals, people, birds, and clover.

Horseradish	Potatoes (deters potato beetles); around plum trees to discourage curculios
Horsetail	As a spray fungicide.
Lamb's-quarters	Nutritious edible weed; allow to grow in modest amounts in corn. Good as groundcover.
Larkspur	Good against Japanese beetle.
Lavender	Good against ticks and as a moth repellent.
Leek	Onions, celery, carrots.
Lettuce	Carrots and radishes (lettuce, carrots and radishes make a strong companion team), strawberries, cucumbers.
Lovage	Plant here and there in the garden. Improves health of its neighbors.
Marigolds	Workhorse of pest deterrents. Keeps soil free of nematodes; good against bean beetles; discourages many insects; plant freely throughout garden. Can be used as a spray.
Marjoram	Here and there in the garden.
Melons	Helped by morning glories.
Milkweed	Attracts aphids away from tomatoes.
Mint	Cabbage family; tomatoes, deters cabbage moth. Repels ants, black flea beetles, and cabbage worm butterflies.
Mole plant	Deters moles and mice if planted here and there in the garden.
Morning glories	Stimulates melon germination, beneficial to corn.
Nasturtium	Tomatoes, radishes, cabbage, cucumbers; plant under fruit trees. Deters aphids and pests of cucurbits.
Nettles	Increases essential oil in neighbors; reduces spoilage.
Onion	Beets, strawberries, tomato, lettuce (protects against slugs), summer savory. Stunts growth of peas and beans.
Oregano	Plant with squash and cucumbers to repel beetles.
Parsley	Tomato, asparagus, roses.

Nettle

Rosemary — Carrots, beans, cabbage, sage; deters cabbage moth, bean beetles and carrot fly.

Rue — Roses and raspberries; deters Japanese beetle. Keep rue away from basil.

Sage — Rosemary, carrots, cabbage, peas, beans; deters some insects.

Skunk cabbage — Crush and place around garden to repel raccoons.

Southernwood — Cabbage; plant here and there in garden.

Soybeans — Grows with anything; helps everything.

Spinach — Strawberries.

Squash — Nasturtium, corn, radish, hindered by potatoes.

Strawberries — Bush beans, spinach, borage, lettuce (as a border). Dislikes cabbage.

Summer savory — Beans, onions. Deters bean beetles.

Sunflower — Cucumbers, beans. Improves soil. Hinders potatoes.

Sweet basil — Good companion for tomatoes.

Tansy — Plant under fruit trees; deters pests of roses and raspberries; deters flying insects; also Japanese beetles, striped cucumber beetles, squash bugs. Plant around doorways against ants.

Tarragon — Good throughout garden.

Thyme — Here and there in garden; deters cabbage worm.

Tomato — Chives, onion, parsley, asparagus, marigold, nasturtium, carrot, limas. Dislikes dill and kohlrabi. Do not plant near potatoes as both are attacked by the same blight. Tomatoes are good planted with roses.

Turnip — Peas.

Valerian — Good anywhere in garden.

Wormwood — As a border; helps to keep animals from garden. Poisonous.

Yarrow — Plant along borders, near paths, near aromatic herbs; enhances essential oil production of herbs.

Peas — Squash (when squash follows peas up trellis). Peas grow well with almost any vegetable (except onions), and add nitrogen to the soil.

Petunia — Protects beans, beneficial throughout garden.

Pigweed — Brings nutrients to topsoil; beneficial growing with potatoes, onions and corn; keep well thinned. Brings up nutrients from subsoil.

Potato — Horseradish, beans, corn, cabbage, marigold, limas, eggplant (as trap crop from potato beetle). Do not plant potatoes and tomatoes near each other as they are attacked by the same blight).

Pot marigold — Helps tomato, but plant throughout garden as deterrent to asparagus beetle, tomato worm and many other garden pests.

Pumpkin — Good to plant with corn against raccoons. Datura helps pumpkins.

Purslane — Small succulent which provides good groundcover.

Radish — Peas, nasturtium, lettuce, cucumbers, squash; a general aid in repelling insects. Dislikes hyssop.

Rhubarb — Use spray made of leaves boiled in water on roses against greenfly.

COMPOST IN A HURRY Do it the easy way! Alfalfa meal, high in nitrogen and protein, makes a great activator and is relatively inexpensive. Leaves, stored in a bin may take literally years to break down, but if you mix a layer of alfalfa meal between four-inch layers of leaves and keep the pile moist, you'll have rich, crumbly leaf mold in a hurry. If you can't get anything else, a big bag of high protein dogfood will work as an activator. So will barnyard manure, blood meal, or even a layer of good, rich garden soil. Of course, the more chopped up your material the quicker it will be to decompose and become compost.

CONTROLLING ALGAE If your brick walks or patio become green and slick with algae, mix a solution of one-half liquid chlorine bleach and one-half water in a large sprinkling can. Thoroughly wet the area—hopefully choosing a warm, sunny day. If the algae buildup is heavy, you may have to scrub with a brush. This will also help control weeds in between bricks.

CORN Nothing beats the taste of sweet corn—five minutes from garden to cookpot—if you haven't eaten it like this, you just haven't lived! For many, corn is their favorite vegetable.

Northern gardeners can have it too. A balance has to be struck between giving the corn as long a season as possible for growing, yet not exposing it to any danger of frost. You can sow in a greenhouse, or in a cold frame in late April or early May and harden off the young shoots ready for planting out in late May or early June. Unfortunately, sweet corn hates to be disturbed by transplanting. To get around this use peat pots. Sow two seeds in each pot, 1 inch deep. If both seeds grow, reject the weaker—cut it off, don't yank it out.

Don't plant corn until the weather is really warm, then it will take off and grow unbelievably fast. A friend of mine claims he can actually hear it growing on warm nights! Sow your earliest plantings 1½ inch deep and do not fertilize until it is well up. It is

good to make successive plantings of one or two preferred varieties rather than planting several with different maturities that are not of equal quality. Corn is wind-pollinated so should be planted in blocks rather than in a long straight row. Corn with a long, tight husk (such as Washington, Farmer Seed & Nursery Co.) is helpful in protecting ear tips.

Roots are shallow, so practice light cultivation. You can find out if corn is ready for harvesting by the "spurt test." Slit husk slightly while still on the stalk and prick and exposed kernel with your fingernail. If it's ready it will react just like a grapefruit. Have your water boiling and hurry it into the house—you never tasted anything so good as just-fresh-picked corn!

Foil the corn ear worm by applying several drops of mineral oil to silks at tip of ear as silks begin to dry and turn brown—not before or pollination will be insufficient and you will get undeveloped kernels.

Be sure to chew your corn thoroughly to insure complete digestion for it is a starchy food. Fresh corn has vitamins C, A, and B_1, in that order, and these depreciate as it ages. A wonder drug, nitrofurazone, better known as furacin, is made from corn cobs and is a powerful antibiotic. It is successful as a germ killer in treating various skin infections and wounds, in destroying disease-causing fungus and as an antihistamine in the treatment of the common cold and certain allergies.

CORN SALAD (*Valerianella olitoria*) If you have a problem with lettuce, discover corn salad—an old favorite among gourmet salad lovers. Stokes has a special strain imported from Holland that produces nice broad leaves during the summer and early spring if sown the previous September. The upright plants have a compact growth making it easy to harvest the outer leaves. The taste is mild and it combines well with more flavorful greens and crisp roots like radishes or carrots. Though it is not as crisp as lettuce, this is not displeasing. It retains its flavor even after maturity and, unlike lettuce, does not become bitter. Best sown directly into the garden but will survive careful transplanting if sown indoors. Some other names for corn salad are fetticus or lamb's lettuce and *maches* in France where it is very popular.

CORN SMUT   This is a common fungus disease, appearing as large, irregularly shaped galls on all parts of the plant. At first grayish white, the galls darken as the season progresses until they burst to release masses of black fungus spores. These masses have an oily appearance. Preventive measures include a three-year crop rotation, use of disease-resistant varieties, turning under of garden trash or manure, and removal of old stalks in the fall. Once the galls occur, spraying is of no help. The galls should be removed and burned.

In Mexico, however, a different view of corn smut is taken. The smut, called "huitlacoche," is regarded as a delicacy and sells in the markets at fancy prices. The name, an Aztec word, shows how long it has been appreciated as a food. Mexicans prepare it by sautéing it lightly, often with chili peppers. It is also regarded as one of Mexico's healing plants, and is considered useful in treating internal hemorrhage caused by gastric ulcer or inflamed hemorrhoids.

COTTON (*Gossypium herbaceum*)   Collodium is prepared from the root of the cotton plant. A syrup of the flowers is a good cure for hypochondrasis. The seeds are used as an aphrodisiac, the oil as a lubricant and liniment to rheumatic joints. Malays use the cotton plant in the treatment of fevers. The seeds are woolly and yield a short stapled cotton. The plant is biennial and has flowers with yellow petals and a purple center. The capsules when ripe split open, revealing a white tuft around the seeds. Gurney's has a lovely ornamental cotton which produces large, fluffy white balls and the plant will grow well in the north central states. Collodium (or collodion) is a heavy, colorless clear liquid and is used for covering burns or wounds. Painted on the skin it dries rapidly,

forming a thin covering which protects the wound.

COVER UPS   Wouldn't you like to pick crisp green lettuce or zesty radishes after a heavy frost, maybe until Thanksgiving? You can, if you sow seeds toward late summer and grow the plants under cloches (row covers) or in a cold frame. Before cold weather comes, and even afterwards on warm sunny days, you will need to raise the cold frame lid, or open the cloches to let in ventilation. You can even improvise row covers if you have access to bales of hay. Put the bales on either side of the rows of lettuce and radishes, covering the plants on cold nights with burlap, sheets, or other material stretched across the top of the bales. When winter finally ends the growing season, use the hay to mulch borders of perennials or bulbs.

CRABGRASS   At last I have found a use for crabgrass! The Dakota Indians gather the seeds and cook them like rice for a good breakfast cereal.

CREAM OF THE CROP   Variously called cowpeas, stock peas, Southern peas, or cream peas, these very different peas are well worth knowing about. Not all of them are "black-eyed." Mississippi Silver (64 days, Vermont Bean Seed Co.), for instance, has smooth, silvery colored pods occasionally streaked with rose. The peas are large, light green to cream and flattened or "crowned" at the ends. They are also some of the easiest to shell. These peas (*Vigna siensis* cvs.) were introduced from Africa by slave traders and have become a favorite food crop of the South, being considered "soul food" along with many types of greens, and are great served with Southern corn bread. They may be cooked with some form of pork, usually ham hock, and, like black-eyes, may be served for good luck on New Year's Day. To save space you can plant them among sweet corn and let the vines grow up the corn stalks. Sow seed after the soil is above 70°F; they love warmth, otherwise their culture is like that of garden peas. But they will produce well in less fertile soil than garden peas require. Great for a second crop. My mother made succotash with cream peas (or black-eyes), corn cut from the cob, chopped onions, and green peppers and seasoned all with "chunk bacon." We practically lived on this dish most summers.

Succotash

2 cups shelled cream peas or black-eye peas
6 cobs of sweet corn, corn cut from cob
2 medium onions, chopped
2 green peppers, chopped
1–2 jalapeño peppers, seeds removed, chopped (optional)
¼ to ½ pound slab bacon, cut in ½ inch chunks
Salt and pepper to taste

Cook all together, and serve with hot cornbread and iced tea with a slice of lemon and a sprig of mint.

CRESS The sharp-flavored leaves of cress add a tangy taste to salads. Use young leaves as the mature plant is practically inedible. Plant cress early and grow during cool weather. Sow thickly and cover with ¼ inch of soil. It will be ready in 6 to 8 weeks after planting and you may make successive crops until hot weather when it will go quickly to seed.

CROP ROTATION The heavy feeders such as cabbage, cauliflower, kohlrabi, broccoli, brussels sprouts, tomato, celeriac, leek, cucumber, squash, sweet corn, spinach, celery, and leafy vegetables such as chard, head lettuce, and endive, should be followed by the light feeders which include root crops such as carrot, beet, radish, turnip, and rutabaga. Knowing this helps to make the most efficient use of compost. The light-feeding vegetables favor compost greatly, especially when mixed with finely pulverized raw rocks.

CUCUMBER Cucumbers, like squash, do not set fruit from the first blossoms. Cucumbers come only from female flowers and the first ten to twenty are male. The scientists have tamed the space-hogging cucumber and we now have excellent bush varieties such as Park's Bush Whopper Hybrid. These grow on dwarf, mounded plants. Whopping big cucumbers 6 to 8 inches long are produced on short vines, and the plant bears profusely.

If you want one of the vining types try a cucumber tower made of concrete reinforcing wire, easy to reach through if fruits grow inside the ring. Cukes are heavy feeders so fill your enclosure with grass clippings, decomposed manure, etc., which will feed the plants as it decomposes. Also plan to give plants plenty of water during the growing season as the fruits are about 96 percent water. Keeping the plants well mulched is also helpful. Picking regularly will keep plants producing.

> Cucumber skins and fresh bay leaves are effective in repelling cockroaches and ants.

When cucumbers become bitter under stress, such as drought, they may be made edible. Cut a small slice, about ¼ inch, from the stem end of the cuke. Rotate the two cut edges vigorously against each other, for 10 to 20 seconds. A white foam will form a ring around the cucumber, as thick as the cucumber is bitter. Then slice below the white line, discarding that part of the cucumber. The rest should then be palatable.

CUCUMBER BEETLES Cucumber beetles spread disease that may prove to be a bigger problem than their insatiable appetites. To control, a handful of wood ashes and hydrated lime are diluted in two gallons of water. Spray mixture on upper and lower sides of cucurbit leaves. Garlic juice used in a spray is effective against diseases that damage cucumbers. Try planting a few radish seeds in every cucumber, squash, or pumpkin hill. Beetles will devour the radish leaves and, hopefully, leave your other crops alone.

CUT FLOWERS WILT? Try putting an aspirin in the water. Also, flowers take up water better if the stem is cut on a slant or mashed a little.

CUTTING COMMENTS One of the easiest and most effective methods of propagating plants is by cuttings. Green or softwood cuttings are generally rooted in greenhouses or coldframes. Leaf cuttings, such as a mature leaf of the Rex begonia can be cut from a plant, slashed at each point where two large veins unite, placed flat on wet sand and weighted down with pebbles or pegs, and tiny new plants will develop at many of the points where cuts were made. Hardwood cuttings are made from the ripe wood of the past season's growth or older wood. Such cuttings are often placed directly in the earth and kept moist in a shaded location until roots form. Most hardwood cuttings take a longer time to root than do softwood cuttings.

CUTTING DOWN CUTWORMS This nocturnal marauder, with a destructive period lasting from 17 to 21 days, is the larvae of the brown, night-flying moth. It does its dastardly deeds by night, creeping from beneath your surface soil. With a scissorlike motion it chews through the stems of your newly planted tomatoes, peppers, eggplant, brussels sprouts, or broccoli. There are several hundred species with differing life cycles and feeding habits; some have a lifestyle that keeps them below ground feeding on roots and stems.

Cutworms win no beauty contests—they have fat, smooth, soft bodies, scantily covered with coarse bristles or hair—and come in a variety of colors: dull shades of gray, brown, black, greenish gray, greenish white, or even red. If it coils itself into a ball when you touch it—it's a cutworm.

Certain sites and situations are more vulnerable than others. Gardens started on soil previously covered with grass, weeds, or a cover crop, will be particularly susceptible to cutworm infestation.

There is no sure-fire way of control, so experiment with several. One way is to slip a piece of stiff paper or thin cardboard, three inches wide, around the stem of each seedling. It should clear the stem by ½ inch with 1 inch extending into the soil. Used matches, toothpicks, sticks, or nails stuck into the soil alongside the emerging stem are also useful in stopping cutworms.

One gardener ties thin onion stalks to seedlings, another uses garlic leaves in the holes in which he sets his plants, tied around the plants and scattered around their bases. Tansy is effective in some instances. Or you can place compact handfuls of elder sprouts, milkweed, clover, or mullein in every fifth row or hill and tamp down. Cutworms gather in this material and can be collected and disposed of. They can also be immobilized with a mixture of equal parts of molasses, hardwood sawdust, and wheat bran, moistened and scattered around each plant at dusk: lured by the molasses they get caught in its stickiness and the bait clings and hardens. Chicken manure for fertilizing has been reported as an effective control. So has interplanting with onions. Eggshells, crushed, scattered and covered with a thin layer of soil, have been used. Also dampened wood ashes or sharp builders' sand. When I lose a plant I always dig down around its base and I usually find the culprit. Always try to do this before replanting.

There is also help from above—meadowlarks and the fledgling redwing blackbird will prey on cutworms—and below from toads, shrews, and moles. If you have chickens or hogs, send them on a search-and-destroy mission through your freshly plowed plot in the spring before planting.

And even the firefly can be a friend. In their larval stage they will prey on cutworms underground or in rotting wood. Furthermore, good garden practices of mulching, adding compost, organic fertilizers and minerals to your soil will go a long way toward helping you cut down on cutworms.

Dear common flower that grow'st beside the way,
Fringing the dusty road with harmless gold,
First pledge of blithesome May,
Which children pluck, and full of pride uphold . . .
"To the Dandelion"
JAMES RUSSELL LOWELL

DADDY LONGLEGS (*Arachnida*) This harmless, longlegged creature is related to the spider. Its legs are bent and its body hangs close to the ground. Although eight legs are characteristic, you may see daddy longlegs with fewer legs because the legs break easily and do not regenerate. Most active at night, daddy longlegs (also known as harvestmen), prey on aphids, mites, leafhoppers, and other garden insects.

DAMIANA (*Damiana aphrodisiaca*) Damiana is a small mintlike plant found growing wild in California and Mexico, particularly along Mexico's western coast. It has fragrant yellowish flowers. It is considered a nerve tonic to the brain and to the organs of reproduction. It overcomes exhaustion and is a good remedy for nerves. It is much used as an aphrodisiac,

Damiana

either alone, or in combination with other herbs. The plant is believed to contain phosphorus. As a general tonic it overcomes cerebral lassitude, loss of nervous energy, and tendency of power loss in the limbs. It is said to be much used, as a tea, by Mexican women an hour or two before intercourse. It is considered most effective when used in combination with saw palmetto berries (*Serenoa repens*) in a 1-to-1 ratio. The marijuanalike euphoria lasts about 1½ hours.

DAMPING-OFF With the present emphasis on organic gardening most seeds are no longer treated with fungicides. In the past these chemicals prevented the fungus that caused damping-off from getting to the seeds and destroying them before they germinated. Captan, which may be purchased at most gardening centers, is an effective fungus killer. Take a toothpick or paper match and dip about one-fourth of it in the Captan. Put in seed packet and shake vigorously before planting and you are not likely to have damping-off.

DANDELION (*Taraxacum officinale*)

Many people go slightly mad when they see a dandelion, uprooting them with an enthusiasm worthy of a better cause. I *eat* mine! Since I regard dandelions with a friendly attitude I have plenty of wild ones, but if you want a really superior dandelion try Burpee's 'Thick-Leaved.' It has large, thick, dark green leaves that may be used as greens for boiling. The hearts may be eaten raw if the leaves are tied together and the hearts blanched.

For dandelion "coffee," dig up the long taproot, clean it and roast in an oven until brown. Then grind it in a coffee mill and brew. You'll be surprised at just how much it looks and tastes like coffee—but it doesn't contain any caffeine.

To make dandelion tea, select dark green leaves from an older plant, put them in a brown paper bag and leave them out in the sun to dry. I clip the bag to the clothesline for a few days. Then crumble the dry leaves and steep them in boiling water (a heaping teaspoonful per cup). The tea has a mild, herbal taste.

DATURA (*Datura stramonium*)

According to Levy this is a plant of dry ground and waste places, distinguished by its showy appearance, broad, glossy leaves of an unpleasant narcotic odor, and big white, solitary trumpet-shaped flowers. These flowers, though a bit coarse, are beautiful, and

there is also a lovely white double datura. The seed vessel resembles a small round prickly cucumber.

The plant yields valuable narcotic drugs, especially atropine and hyocine. Datura is a semipoisonous plant of the Belladonna group. The American Indians burned the dried fruits and foliage and used it as a smoke treatment in chronic asthma conditions. The Arabs used the pulped fruits in jaundice treatment, pushing the fruits up the nostrils and also making poultice bags of the fruits and placing them over the stomach regions. The fruits are brewed, and a narcotic extracted.

Datura is one of the ingredients of the voodoo zombie potion used in Haiti. Fumes have always played a prominent part in the magical arts and the narcotic fumes of datura smoke are said to have been a part of witchcraft ceremonies in the Middle Ages as well, sometimes thought to have induced the "flying dream." Datura yields a valuable medicine, but it should never be used unless prescribed by a physician.

Algonkian Indians of eastern North America made a drink called "wysoccan," which contained Jimson weed and was given to young boys being initiated into manhood. It is said a type of violent madness would occur lasting 20 days and resulting in a total loss of memory of their former life. Thus the boy

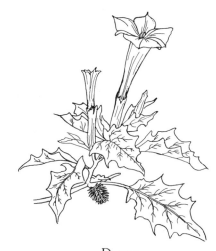

Datura

would start adulthood forgetting that he was ever a child.

Datura was used in India, whence, presumably came its name *Datura*. It is also called Jamestown weed, jimson weed, apple of Peru, thorn apple, stink weed, devil's trumpet, angel's trumpet, and dewtry.

DEEP CULTIVATION? Inexperienced gardeners often feel that deep cultivation is desirable. Actually it is not, for often it brings more weed seeds to the surface where they germinate. Eliminating the need for hoeing altogether through the use of mulches cuts down on the work of garden-keeping, keeps the soil from washing, conserves moisture, and keeps fruits cleaner.

DEER Beautiful as they are deer can sometimes be a serious problem to the farmer and gardener. You can use fencing, but it must be at least seven feet high or they will jump it. Electric fencing has been used more successfully. Soybeans and corn planted as trap crops at the edge of the garden will lure the deer to them. Foxglove and castor beans have been used as repellents. A few pails of human urine, placed at the corners of the garden, as well as in the middle, deter deer.

DEER'S TONGUE Native to Louisiana and Florida, this herb is found growing in the low pinelands. Slave herbalists gathered bunches and hung them in their cabins to make bitters to take when prostrated by fever. The fresh plant is scentless, but when dried emits a pleasant vanillalike odor. It imparts a pleasant fragrance to tobacco when mixed with it.

DESERT GARDENING is a constant challenge. Temperatures of 100°F and 15- to 20-mile-per-hour winds blowing all day long act as a dehumidifier taking all the moisture out of the soil. The answer is constant composting, replacing what the sun and wind burns away. Ground temperature may be as high as 125°F in the sun and the decomposition process is speeded up. Never water in the heat of the day, but watering daily, often several times, may be necessary. Spreading hay or other mulching material around the plants is helpful to retain moisture and keep down weeds.

DESERT PLANTS Since desert plants must endure long periods of extreme drought, desert vegetation is made up of plants having various specialized body structures that enable them to survive conditions of severe drought. But a desert is not necessarily a place of shifting sand dunes: our Southwestern deserts in particular are characterized by rich and diversified plant cover. And many of these plants are edible, or otherwise useful.

- Crested pricklepoppy (*Argemone platyceras*): Seeds are reported to contain a narcotic more potent than opium.
- Desertlily ajo (*Hesperocallis undulata*): Papago Indians eat the bulbs, which have an onionlike flavor.
- Joshua tree (*Yucca brevifolia*): Indians use the smallest roots, which are red, for patterns in their baskets.
- Spanish bayonet (*Yucca arizonica*): Roots of the yuccas have saponifying properties and are still gathered by some tribes and used as soap, particularly for washing the hair. Also said to keep hair dark well into old age.
- Beargrass (*Nolina*): Indians use the very young flower stalks for food and the leaves are browsed on by livestock in times of drought.
- Spoonplant (*Dasylirion*): Rounded heads are high in sugar, which is dissolved in the sap of the bud stalk. The sap, when fermented, produces a strong beverage called "sotol"—the "bootleg" of northern Mexico.
- Common reed (*Phragmites communis*): Used by the Indians for making arrow shafts, prayer sticks, pipestems, and loom rods. Mats, screens, nets and cordage, as well as thatching, are made from the leaves.
- Seepwillow baccharis (*Baccharis*): Among some Indians, the stems of this plant are chewed as a toothache remedy.

- Tree tobacco (*Nicotiana glauca*): In addition to nicotine, tree tobacco contains an alkaloid, anabasine. Leaves are smoked by the Yuma and Havasupai Indians during ceremonies.
- Catclaw acacia (*Acacia greggii*): Seeds were at one time widely used as food by Indians of Arizona and Mexican tribes.
- Mormon tea (*Ephedra*): Stems and flowers were used to make a palatable brew by the Utah pioneers, hence the name "Mormon tea." The beverage was also used by Indians and settlers in treating syphilis and other afflictions, as it contains tannin and certain alkaloids.
- Evening primrose (*Oenothers*): The oil of this plant is presently much in favor as a treatment for arthritis, obesity, mental illness, heart disease, and postdrinking depression.
- Mesquite (*Prosopis juliflora*): During pioneer days mesquite was important as fuel, in building corrals, and in making furniture and utensils. A meal, called Pinole, may be made by grinding the long sweet pods. When fermented it is used as an intoxicating drink by the Pimas. The gum, which exudes through the bark, is eaten as a candy.
- Incienso (*Encelia jarinosa*): A gum, exuded by the stems, was prized as incense by early-day Catholic priests. Indians heated the gum and used it for relief of pain.
- Prickly pear (*Opuntia*): The large, red to purple and mahogany, juicy, pear-shaped fruits are known as *tunas*. Both native peoples and animals eat them.
- Barrelcactus (*Ferocactus*): Cooked in sugar, the flesh of the barrelcactus forms a base of cactus candy.
- Agave (*Agave*): A coarse fabric is woven by the Mexicans from the leaf fibers. The sap of the young stalks, fermented, forms a highly intoxicating beverage. Among these are mescal, pulque, and tequila.
- Devil's claws (*Proboscidea*): Young pods are eaten as a vegetable or pickled.

- Thistle (*Cirsium*): Thistle is used by the Navajo and Hopi Indians for medicinal purposes.
- Strawberry cactus (*Echinocereus*): Red, juicy fruits are rich in sugar and may be eaten like strawberries. Pima Indians consider them a delicacy.
- Desert sage (*Salvia*): Seeds of California chia (sage) were once an important item in the diet of the desert Indians and are still used today.

DEVIL'S-BACKBONE (*Pedilanthus tithymaloides variegatus*) or Jacob's-ladder. A great plant for outdoors in the South or for container growing in the North. A succulent, devil's-backbone should be grown in porous, well-drained soil, and placed where it will receive bright, indirect light. Easily propagated from cuttings: let them dry overnight and then insert in moist soil. Handle cuttings with care, however, as the white sap may be caustic. The name "pedilanthus" is derived from *pedilon*, a shoe, and *anthos*, a flower, and refers to the shape of the latter. The foliage is a delightful combination of green, white, and pink.

DILL (*Anethum graveolens*) Dill is used primarily in making pickles, but it is also delicious in soups, salads, and breads. Dill seed is slow to germinate, sometimes taking as long as two weeks to come up, but once you have it in your garden it self-sows year after year. If you want to save the seed heads, cut them just before they turn dark brown. Hang the heads up to dry and they can be used throughout the winter.

Dill is medicinal and is considered aromatic and carminative. Dill water was a favorite in "grandmother's day" for nausea and stomach distress. For colic and flatulence of infants and the elderly, a mixture of equal amounts of dill, anise and fennel in a warm infusion is recommended. Place one-half teaspoonful of mixture in a cup of hot water.

DISABLED GARDENERS CAN PLAY TOO! Yes, even those confined to

wheelchairs. If you can't get down to the garden, bring it up to you. Many people, young
as well as senior citizens, have back problems
and find bending over difficult. The trick is
to build boxes, preferably using redwood lumber, two feet wide by four feet long, placing
them on sturdy two-by-four legs at the
height most comfortable for work. Depths
should vary according to what is planted,
some being 8 inches deep, others 12, and
so on.

There's an added advantage to raised
beds—they can be placed anywhere most
convenient for work or the planting's best location—out from the shade of large trees. I
consider near a southern wall the best spot.

Of course, to produce well the soil must be
fertile, such as a sandy loam with plenty of
organic matter (compost or well-decomposed manure). Perhaps you can get
someone to deliver a truckload of fairly good
soil that can gradually be built to a higher
state of fertility for your concentrated garden, or try buying it from a florist or garden
store.

Before putting the soil into your boxes,
half-inch holes should be drilled in the bottoms for drainage and covered with copper
screening. Uniform and gentle watering can
be provided by setting the hose nozzle deep
in a tall glass jar buried in the soil, its top
just level with the surface. As water flows up
and out of the jar in a gentle stream it
spreads evenly throughout the bed. Don't
waste it when it begins to seep through the
bottom of the boxes, just set a plant or two
below to use what soaks through.

An extra bonus of this type of gardening is
being eye-to-eye with any invading insect
pests. Weeds quickly spotted are just as
quickly pulled from the loose, friable soil.
And no-stoop harvesting is a real joy!

DISCOURAGING DOGS   Plant injury
from dog urine often resembles brown patch
or dollar spot. Grass turns brown or straw-
colored and usually dies. Such injured areas
are often bordered by a ring of lush, dark
green grass. If soluble salts from dog urine

enter the soil, tree roots may be killed. A
metal collar on the trunk protects only the
bark, not the roots, and the entire planting
may have to be screened off from dogs. Moth
balls and naphtha flakes have been shown to
discourage dogs. Some experiments have
also been made with ultrasonics, and practical controls may be developed to keep these
animals away from valued flower beds and
gardens. Fencing, though expensive and not
always practical, is the best way of keeping
unwanted animals away from your premises.

DISEASES AND ROTATION   Controlling diseases by rotation of crops is excellent
advice but hard to follow if you happen to be
working in a ten-foot-square garden! Here's
a simple system: Divide the garden into quarters. Plant what was in quarter number 1 this
year in quarter number 2 next year, etc. Tomatoes, however, are one crop that don't
mind being planted in the same place each
year provided they are given plenty of
fertilizer.

DISEASE PREVENTION   These basic
steps are helpful in preventing disease in
your garden:

- Stay out of the garden when plants are
  wet: water is often the carrier of diseases.
- Rotate crops to avoid soil-borne diseases.
- Select disease-resistant seed varieties. Buy
  seed from a reputable company. Seed
  protectants are also helpful.
- Well-drained soil is important to almost
  all crops. If soil stays wet, raised beds may
  be a solution. Soil is warmer at planting
  time in raised beds, and the seedbed will
  drain better. Raised beds are also good for
  heavy soil, because it doesn't pack down
  as much.
- Use mulch in the walkways and wide-row
  growing to prevent raindrops from
  splashing soil and disease spores up onto
  plants.

DITTANY, AMERICAN (*Cunila mariana*)   Sheep are sometimes poisoned by
eating common laurel (*Kalmia latifolia*). If
this is suspected, a strong tea made of Ameri-

can dittany, moderately warm, should be given. Even sheep in the last stages of this disorder have been known to recover when so treated.

American dittany is an attractive native plant with a fragrant odor resembling marjoram. Covered in late summer with small, pink flowers, it is attractive to bees. In pioneer days the dried herb was often used to make a tea for treating colds and to excite gentle perspiration.

DOLOMITE In addition to the commonly used organic materials for weed control there are others that may be used, such as ground dolomite rock which orchardists have found useful. Similar to limestone, dolomite is a mineral composed of carbonates of calcium and magnesium. These minerals are essential to plant nutrition.

DON'TS In planning your gardening procedures do's are important but so are *don'ts*. It takes years of study and experience to become an expert gardener, but a reasonable amount of study and careful attention to simple instructions will give you a head start in avoiding disastrous or humorous errors and get you some gratifying results. These don'ts will help keep you out of some of the commonest troubles.

DON'T try to grow vegetables on a lot that is
too poor to make a good growth of weeds, or grass.
made up mostly of rubble or unweathered subsoil "fill."
contaminated with coal-, chemical-, or oil-product wastes.
so wet that it grows weeds common to marshy or poorly drained soils.
likely to be flooded often by stream overflow.
located so that it receives much storm damage or surface water from above.
shaded by large trees more than a few hours a day.
DON'T spade, plow, or cultivate soil that is too wet.
DON'T apply too much lime.

DON'T run the row up and down a slope.
DON'T plant seeds, roots, or tubers too deeply.
DON'T sow seeds too thickly, and
DON'T fail to thin out plants to the proper distance.
DON'T guess at the amounts of fertilizer or strong manure to apply per unit acre of land.
DON'T let fertilizer or manure come in contact with seeds or plants.
DON'T cultivate deeply enough to injure the shallow roots of the vegetables.
DON'T let the weeds get big before you try to destroy them.
DON'T apply water in numerous light sprinklings. (Instead, water thoroughly about once a week if rainfall is deficient).
DON'T let the vegetables become too old before harvesting them, thereby losing high quality.
DON'T let any vegetables go to waste. Use fresh or can, dry, or freeze.
DON'T leave any land idle during the growing season.
DON'T leave the soil in such condition that it will wash or blow away during the winter.

DO PLANTS HAVE SEX? Yes, indeed, and they were having it for thousands of years before we humans discovered the fact. Certain garden plants such as squash and cucumbers form male flowers first. Every year readers of my column in *The Daily Ardmoreite* become quite upset and start calling or writing me to complain that their squash vines are blooming "like mad" but not forming fruit. The patient gardener knows the fruit will form and is distinguishable by a small bulb at the base of the female flower. Hollies must be sold in pairs, or you can use one male to about seven females so the lovely red berries will be pollinated. And, of course, in the fruit tree orchard you must plan for pollinators for certain varieties.

DO PLANTS SLEEP? Yes, plants sleep the same as human beings do during a period called "dormancy." They are affected by the cycles of winter, spring, summer, and autumn, as well as wet, dry, cold, and hot seasons. A plant discovered growing wild in a climate that is cold and dry in the winter will require the same conditions in cultivation. The length and time of the dormant season varies depending on the natural habitat of the plant and whether it needs the long-light days of spring and summer or the short-light days of fall and winter to trigger growth.

Plants accustomed for untold centuries to a period of darkness at night are also adversely affected by night lighting, or so-called "safety lights." They become less vigorous and more susceptible to air pollution. Trees get confused and often continue growing on into the fall when they should be stopping to rest for winter. This succulent growth is often killed by winter cold, resulting in unsightly dieback in the spring. Many people, unaware of the needs of plants, find it difficult to understand what has happened. Perhaps if your garden isn't doing well, it simply needs its nightly rest.

DOUBLING UP   Here's a tip for small-space gardeners who want to get extra crops. When you plant your potatoes in spring, plant peas right on top of them. When the peas are ready for harvest, pull the whole plant, using what you wish and shelling and freezing the rest. Use the vines for mulch or put them in the compost heap. Depending upon planting conditions, this harvesting occurs once a week for about a month, leaving the space to be occupied by the potatoes.

This form of companion planting works well for other vegetables—peas can also go on top of carrots, beets in with onions, beets with kohlrabi, lettuce with onions, and carrots with tomatoes. Jerry Baker advocates growing potatoes and tomatoes together in the same container for the apartment gardener.

DRAGONFLY (*Odonata*) is a beautiful water insect. It has four large, fragile wings that look like fine gauze. They shimmer and gleam in the sunlight when the insect flies. Its long slender body is either green, blue, or brown. Its enormous compound eyes, covering most of its head, search in all directions at once during its speedy flight. The dragonfly can see motionless objects six feet away, and moving objects two or three times that distance. It can use its legs to perch on a limb, but it cannot walk. As it flies through the air, the dragonfly holds its legs together to form a basket in which to capture insects. Grasping prey with its legs or jaws, it eats while flying and consumes enormous numbers of insects—particularly mosquitoes.

Dragonflies are beneficial even in the nymph stage. A mother dragonfly may lay as many as a hundred thousand eggs. Many are eaten by fish but others hatch into nymphs. The pencil-thin nymph eats mosquito larvae and other insects. The nymph molts several times as it grows to be a dragonfly. Strange names have been given to the dragonfly, such as devil's darning needle, snake doctor, snake feeder, horse stinger, and mule killer.

DRAINAGE   Why is "good drainage" constantly emphasized? Because roots suffocate when water replaces the air in the soil. Roots simply will not develop without a constant supply of oxygen and a constant removal of carbon dioxide. In a well-drained soil water moves through quickly, never completely shutting off the movement of air through the soil. A heavy clay is not a good gardening soil, neither is sandy soil, which may be well drained but dries out quickly. You can quickly change either one through the addition of organic matter—not just a little—enough means at least one-third of the final mix. This need not necessarily be expensive; use whatever desirable waste products are abundant in your locality: sawdust, bark, manure, grape pomace, nut shells, leaves, grass clippings, small prunings, straw, spoiled hay, green weeds, dry weeds, vegetable harvest refuse, coffee grounds, eggshells, shredded paper, wood ashes. Compost made of any or all of these materials will improve an unfavorable soil quickly, making it possible to grow truly succulent vegetables or beautiful flowers.

DRESSED TO TILL   Entire books have been written telling the corporate executive how to dress for success, but what about the gardener? If you want to knock your corn on its ear, dress for comfort. Wear clothes that bend where you do, stretch where you do, and maybe even wrinkle where you do. Perhaps even more important, your clothes should provide protection from the sun, from annoying bugs, and from poisonous plants. In climates of intense sun a good pair of dark glasses is helpful.

Sartorially correct gardeners include in their wardrobe a hat, a long-sleeved blouse or shirt, long pants, sturdy shoes, and cotton work gloves for the head-to-toe look. A fairly wide-brimmed hat will protect you from sunburn, sunstroke, and heatstroke. For the ladies, nothing beats the old-fashioned sunbonnet, which also protects the neck. For the fellows, the best kind of hat is made of straw, which will allow air to circulate around your scalp. The sun is the worst enemy of good skin. Even on cloudy days, as much as eighty percent of the ultraviolet rays that burn the skin can reach the earth's surface—and yours. Spending long hours in the sun can also cause the development of skin cancer—fair-skinned people, especially those who freckle, are the most susceptible.

Wear a long-sleeved shirt or blouse. This should be of cotton, not synthetic material, so that perspiration can be carried away from the skin and evaporated into the air. Pick a light color that will reflect the sun's rays and keep you cooler. Insects, too, seem less interested in investigating light colors than bright colors or flowered fabrics. Avoid any form of perfume, including suntan lotion, hair spray, deodorant, or after-shave lotion: if you smell like a flower you may be treated like one! Be sure to wear long pants, even on warm days; they'll keep you from getting sunburned and protect you from poisonous plants. Good solid, flat-heeled shoes are a must—you need them for balance and pro-

tection when you are spading. You will be less tired if you have the support of good shoes. Don't wear fancy gloves, a pair of cotton work gloves protects hand from dirt, helps prevent blisters, and usually launders sweet and clean. So suit up and enjoy your gardening even more!

DRIP, TRICKLE, AND OOZE   Water grows increasingly precious—and expensive. Ways to make a little go a long way—to give the root system, and only the root system, what it needs for growth—are especially welcome to the home gardener. With drip irrigation, the water drops onto the soil surface without disturbing the soil structure, so that it can seep between the soil particles. In drip irrigation the water is replenished on an almost daily basis, the amount being equal to the water used by the plant since the last irrigation. These are not really new techniques, the home gardener has been doing much the same thing with coffee cans, draintiles, and such for a long time. What is new is the more convenient equipment now available. The basic components of a drip irrigation system consist of the head, laterals, emitters, and hose lines. If you find watering a chore, time-consuming, and inconvenient you might like to investigate these new possibilities at your local garden center.

DROUGHT-RESISTANT VEGETA-BLES   Let's face it, most vegetables are not prime candidates for a waterless garden—there ain't no such thing! For taste and succulence they depend on copious supplies of H_2O administered as a regular routine. Even so there are all sorts of little tricks we can avail ourselves of—and I should know. I've been battling our hot, dry, southern Oklahoma climate for the last fifty years—and doing pretty well at it.

There is mulching, of course, always to be thought of as a means of conserving scanty water supplies. Here's a trick I use for **okra**. I plant two rows, fairly close together, dig a trench between them, and fill the trench with grass clippings, leaves, or whatever light materials are available. In hot, dry, windy weather I fill the trench with water. The mulch floats to the surface and as the water sinks into the soil the mulch also sinks back down, holding the moisture. There is no law I am aware of that would prevent using this idea for other veggies.

Then there are vegetables that actually are known to do reasonably well in hot weather. Bloomsdale Long-Standing Spinach is slow to bolt and will give a longer cutting season. Follow it with Basella Malabar Red Stem Summer Spinach, heat tolerant and vigorous (Park's).

Tomatoes are ninety percent water, but according to an article in the August 1990 issue of *Smithsonian* magazine, the easiest and most productive variety to grow is the tiny cherry tomato (try Baxter's Bush Cherry, Gardener's Delight, Sweet 100 Hybrid, or Tiny Tim—Burpee's). An early spring variety of tomato that beats the heat may also be grown in the fall; try Burpee's Early Girl Hybrid.

For **broccoli** try Shogun (Shepherd's), a Japanese variety that gives an early spring harvest. **Brussels sprouts**, withstanding cold, may give you a late fall crop when summer's heat is over and fall rains arrive. Ditto **turnips. Beets** withstand hot weather well, especially Shepherd's Bolthardy, particularly well-suited for early spring or late summer planting.

For **corn** borrow the Indian strategy of planting the cornstalks farther apart. In semidesert regions they've been doing this for centuries and making good crops, on the theory that each stalk will avail itself of the water in its root area without too much competition.

The American **cucumber** The Duke (Shepherd's) is recommended as a heavy-yielding variety that thrives in hot weather climates. I grow them successfully in semi-shady areas. **Eggplant** Little Fingers (Shepherd's) is very, very early—"It keeps pumping out dark little eggplants in glossy clusters of three or four from every fruiting node of the vigorous plants."

I find the pretty, tasty, savoy-type **cabbage** easier to grow than the smooth-leaved kind and also, for me, it retains good quality longer in hot weather. For **lettuce** try the loose-leaf types and forget about "icebergs." Park's Cos or Romaine lettuce Rosalita holds up well under early spring heat and is also tolerant to frost burn. Black-seeded Simpson, Oakleaf, and Slo-Bolt are also good looseleaf types. Butterhead Little Gem can even be grown in a windowbox.

Burpee's Fordhook Giant **Chard** is a heavy yielder even in hot weather.

Onions must have some water but they actually like heat and sunshine, bulb-forming being determined by the amount of daylight the plant receives and not because of the maturity of the plant. **Garlic** grows larger in good, moist, organic soil, but will grow practically anywhere—though making smaller bulbs—under adverse conditions.

Celery is a difficult plant for me to grow but Celery Dinant from Nichols Garden Nursery, an unusual type that sends out a multitude of narrow thin stalks, has a fuller flavor than common celery and is marvelous for seasoning soups, stews, salads, and dressings. It withstands heat well and can even be dried for winter use. You might also like to try celeriac, the round roots being the part used.

Black-eyed peas and several varieties of so-called "field peas" do well in my garden, taking the heat of summer in stride and producing bountifully. **Sweet potatoes** are another warm-weather crop that is easy to grow. Shepherd's Carib potatoes "produce big tubers . . . are very early maturing and heat and drought tolerant." This is true; I've grown them. And don't forget **peanuts**— they make a great second crop to grow after beets.

In my garden **jalapeño** and other hot pepper varieties are not as fussy as bell peppers, withstanding both heat and cold more successfully.

Jicama, a newcomer to many gardeners, has also done well for me in summer's heat. I know I must cut the beautiful purple sweet-pealike flowers so the "strength" will go into the bulb—but I always let one plant flower.

Jerusalem artichokes or "sun chokes" are another of my favorite plants (but you must watch them or they will take over the place), and they grow easily for me along my fence where I can tie them back for support. Used raw in salads they taste a bit like water chestnuts, being crisp and tasty. They keep well in the ground, but not in the refrigerator, so dig them as they are used.

The Indians also managed to grow a lot of **beans,** even in arid regions, mostly favoring the drying types that could be stored for winter use. The Vermont Bean Seed Company has a multitude of choices. **Squash,** another hot-weather plant, with infinite varieties, does need ample moisture but grows well with warm days and nights. I mulch mine heavily.

If the drought gets bad enough you may be "willing to try anything." So, even if you don't "believe in astroorganic gardening" consider Rudolph Steiner's recommendation to plant in the sign of Taurus which promotes excellent root growth with "short nodes and strength of plant intensified," enabling plants to withstand heat and drought.

DUTCHMAN'S-BREECHES (*Dicentra Cucullaria*) Bleeding heart, or squirrel corn, sometimes also called dielytra. This beautiful spring-flowering plant grows wild in Japan and China. It bears dainty, heart-shaped, drooping, pink and white flowers on arching stems in May. Dutchman's-breeches is an eastern North American native that is suitable for rich, reasonably moist soils in woodland gardens and shaded rock gardens. Easily propagated by seeds sown in a cold frame by dividing the clumps of roots of clusters of tubers, and by root cuttings made from thick, thonglike roots in fall.

DWARF FRUIT TREES How big do they grow? Here is a generalized comparison. Standard trees, 20 feet; semi-dwarf, 18 feet; dwarf, 14 feet; genetic dwarf, 9 feet.

Every little pine needle expanded and swelled with sympathy
and befriended me. I was so distinctly made aware of the
presence of something kindred to me . . .

Walden

HENRY DAVID THOREAU

EARTH WISE! Compost is the very "heart" of the organic garden. And just about anything can be used. I once heard a very funny story about an ardent composter who, having accidentally cut his finger, ran over to the compost heap so he could "bleed on it"! And most of us have heard about the Indians who "planted" a fish in their corn hills. E.L. Whitehead, Extension Horticulturist, Stillwater, Oklahoma, now retired, wrote the following recipe for making compost from fallen leaves.

Directions for making compost rank with other favorite recipes because many homemakers are enthusiastic gardeners.

1. Start with a layer of leaves about 6 inches deep.
2. Sprinkle 3 cups of compost starter (such as Burpee's "Brown Leaf Compost Flakes")
3. Add 1 cup of lime (agricultural lime)
4. Water and layer well.
5. Spread about 1 inch of garden soil on top.
6. Keep adding leaves, additional flakes (about 1 cup), lime, water and soil in alternate layers until the pile is about 4 feet high.

7. In 60 to 90 days the composted leaves and other wastes should be broken down and ready for use.

The soil, water, and compost maker aid in the decay of the leaves, dried grass clippings, and other waste organic matter to make good compost. Leaving the top layer saucer-shaped will help to hold additional water which soaks into the compost and speeds up the aging process. Add extra water to the pile during dry periods to keep it from drying.

The size or dimensions of the pile would depend upon the amount of composting materials available. It need not be exact; usually four feet by four feet is recommended. Neat compost bins are available but boards or concrete blocks can also be used if you happen to have them handy and are far less expensive. A pit can be used instead of a pile if located so that excess rain water will not run into it. Pits are very satisfactory during the dry season of the year.

Compost may be spaded or tilled into the soil, spread on top, used in the row at planting time, or used as a mulch after plants start to grow. It is a good soil conditioner, helping to hold moisture as well as provide nutrients.

EARTHWORMS are a fun gardener's best friend because they do a lot of your work for you. Give him plenty of organic matter and he will happily tunnel around under the soil, digesting and fertilizing as he goes, and turning the compost into food for plants that they can use, the nutrients that they need to produce those succulent vegetables and beautiful flowers that make gardening so much fun. You will attract earthworms to your garden when you begin to provide plenty of organic matter in the form of humus. The castings they leave behind are far richer than what they take in. Their tunneling through the soil also permits the passage of air and water. They are our best garden friends and they work "for free"!

EDELWEISS (*Leontopodium*) This famous plant can be cultivated in cool regions of America and Europe. It thrives best in a well-drained, limy soil, full sun in spring, semishade in summer, and light protection in winter. Either evergreen boughs or salt hay should be used, as leaves pack too hard and keep the plant waterlogged, which may result in rotting. From seed they should bloom well the second year. Carry the plants over in a cold frame, in pots, the first year.

In its native countries the edelweiss is considered a rare plant, because it grows wild in high regions and is difficult to obtain. The edelweiss plant has long, narrow, sage-green leaves, and grows from 4 to 12 inches tall. From the leaves grow white, star-shaped flowers. It is an attractive plant for the rock garden.

EDIBLE BAMBOO Easy to grow, bamboo will thrive even when the temperature dips down into the teens. Just give it an acid soil and good drainage, cover the rhizomes with about an inch of soil and work in some organic fertilizer. The following year an application of high-nitrogen fertilizer, such as blood meal, is helpful.

Moso (*Phyllostachys moso*), an excellent edible variety, should be spaced 10 to 15 feet apart, as it may attain a height of 80 feet. The shoots are delicately flavored. The sprouting buds that are not cut develop into canes and, though it's hard to believe, are able to grow at the fantastic rate of two inches an hour.

'**Sweet-shoot**' (*P. dulcis*), an early sprouting bamboo, is medium-large and is said to be the common vegetable bamboo grown throughout China.

'**Green Sulphur**' (*P. sulphurea viridis*) is still another bamboo of edible quality, especially distinguished for its delicate fragrance.

Shoots should be cooked for about twenty minutes to eliminate any bitter taste with one change of water after the first ten minutes. Some varieties are entirely free of bitterness even in the raw state. Sprouts are a good source of phosphorus. Tender bamboo shoots can be eaten as a vegetable, pickled, candied, or incorporated in various dishes, such as potato-bamboo salad. When preparing bamboo for cooking, cut off a small portion of the base of the shoot and discard. Peel the outer covering and cut into slices about one-eighth of an inch thick.

EGGPLANT (*Solanum Melongena*) Wild eggplant occurs in India and was first cultivated there. The Arabs took it to Spain, the Spaniards to the Americas, and the Persians to Africa. By 1806, both the purple and white ornamentals were growing in American gardens.

Yes, there is a secret to growing eggplant successfully. First, buy young, healthy plants or grow your own from seed. Don't grow the young plants too fast until the fruit is set. Grow them on well-aerated soil that is amply supplied with lime. Use plenty of compost in the holes when setting out and keep the plants well watered. Set them out when the ground has thoroughly warmed up. Set 2 feet apart in rows 2½ to 3 feet apart. Cultivate often.

Eggplants are even more tender than tomatoes, being particularly susceptible to low-temperature injury on cold nights. Don't set them out until temperatures are in the 70-degree range, for once stunted they seldom make the rapid growth necessary for quality fruit.

If blossoms drop off there could be several reasons. You may be growing your plants too soft with manure. Grow them slower with less nitrogen. High temperatures when the flowers are open will cause the flowers to abort. Watch for insect pests that may get into the flowers. The use of Blossom-Set is helpful. Dust with rotenone if bugs eat the foliage, or spray with nicotine spray if plant lice are present.

Plants heavy with fruit may need support, and watch out for flea beetles and Colorado potato beetles. Harvest when the fruit has a high gloss. If upon opening the fruit seeds are brown, the best eating stage is past. When harvesting cut the woody stem with pruning shears—don't try to twist off or you will leave ragged edges.

EGGSHELLS Not only do these add lime to the soil, plus nitrogen and phosphorus, but crushed and sprinkled around seedlings they will help to foil cutworms.

EGYPTIAN ONION (*Allium cepa*) Sometimes called "walking onions" or "top multipliers" because small, edible bulbs are produced at the top of the hollow stalk. These eventually fall over and the small onions take root and grow, forming new plants. Planted in the fall, in early spring they may be used as green or bunching onions. With a distinctive flavor, they are a bit stronger than chives but milder than garlic. In southern states they may be harvested during the winter and used in cooking or salads.

ELDERBERRY (*Sambucus nigra*) An old proverb says, "He who cultivates the elderberry will die in his own bed." Amazing properties have long been attributed to the wine and other products made from *Sambucus nigra*. Medicinal values are said to be in leaves, bark, and berries, but the most common use is in the making of wines and jellies. Elderberry has also been used as an aphid pesticide, the crushed leaves against maggots and branches employed as a mole repellent when placed in their tunnels.

ENDIVE (*Cichorium Endivia*),   Brussels Chicory. You may know this plant as an herb, the leaves of which are used as a salad, or as endive escarole (*C. intybus*), a variety of chicory. Endive is considered valuable in a salad, its bitter flavor stimulating the secretion of saliva; and its rich mineral content, especially potassium, sodium, calcium and phosphorus, making it very nourishing to the optic system. It is said the leaves should not be washed as this tends to increase bitterness; instead, wipe away any dirt with a paper towel. Endive goes brown if exposed to the air, so leaves should be dressed and served at once. For hors d'oeuvres, leaves may be stuffed with roquefort cheese or cottage cheese with French dressing.

Here's a tip for Northern gardeners: Endives are thought to flourish only in rather warm soil (if planted in earth that's too cool, they will bolt instead of producing leaves), so seed is generally sown in early June. However, if endive is planted sometime in August or September, and then cut back before winter (but being careful not to snip out the heart), the roots can be left in the soil and little bunches of endive can be harvested in April and May.

ESSENTIAL OILS Increasingly we are returning to natural products for treating problems of skin and hair. Using essential oils of flowers and plants is a centuries' old method again returning to favor. Essential oils are odorous and highly volatile (readily evaporating in the air). Differing from fatty oils, they have a consistency more like water than oil. Their chemistry is complex, but they generally contain alcohols, esters, ketones, aldehydes, and terpenes. Some contain hormones, and these are the ones of special value in skin care and rejuvenation. Essential oils are the personality of the plant and there is little doubt that they are of practical use. Animals (and probably humans) are sexually attracted by aromatic substances called pheromones. Many plants, through odor, attract the insects needed to bring about fertilization.

Lavender oil has long had a justifiable reputation as a healer of burns. Another healing agent is oil of neroli (orange-scented). Hormone creams have a reputation for rejuvenating the skin. Fennel oil, which contains estrogens, has a reputation as an antiwrinkle agent. Other oils, such as rose and jasmine, contain phytohormones, or have a hormonal action, which are of benefit in helping to rejuvenate the skin. Such oils benefit both dry and oily skins and also bring about a remarkable firming of the skin, stimulating the metabolism of the dermal cells. Essential oils, according to Robert B. Tisserand in his book, *The Art of Aromatheraphy*, are natural organic substances, and work in harmony with the natural forces of the body. Neat essences, however, should never be used on the skin as they may cause irritation. It is best to dilute them with a bland oil or incorporate them in a face cream. The emollient, cooling effects of oils such as chamomile and rose are of value in all inflammatory conditions of the skin. Essential oils are valuable as antiseptics. Bergamot, juniper, and lavender are helpful for oily hair or dandruff and our grandmothers were very well aware of these properties.

EVERGREEN BRANCHES can often be kept from breaking after a heavy snowfall if given a gentle shaking.

EYES HAVE IT I always advise my gardening friends to wear dark glasses when working in the hot sun: they not only shield the eyes from the strong rays but also help to prevent wrinkles. For tired eyes make a compress of grated raw potato, put the pulp between two layers of gauze or fine cotton. Place the potato pads over your eyes; lie down and relax for fifteen minutes to a half hour, and allow the compress to do its work. Another remedy is tea bags. Drink your tea and then lie down with a cold tea bag placed over each eye. Particularly good if you've had an emotional upset.

Fig, grape, and quince, each in his time doth come . . .
BEN JONSON

FACIAL MASKS Those who work out-doors, even in the most favorable conditions, receive a certain amount of exposure from sun and wind and—this goes for the boys as well as the girls—need to take care of their skin.

A good face mask once a week or so is an excellent way of sealing moisture in your skin, drawing out impurities and tightening pores. The tightening power of masks that dry on your skin helps draw the blood to the surface—an excellent aid to circulation, causing a flushing, restoring process. This is an important function, particularly as you get older and may be less active. Of course you can buy all kinds of commercial masks, but why not make your own from ingredients right in your garden or refrigerator? Here are some suggestions you can use alone or in combination—I've found equal portions of each ingredient work fine:

For dry skin: egg yolks, mashed bananas, peaches, avocados, olive oil, yogurt, powdered milk, cucumbers, sour cream, honey, brewer's yeast, lemon, grated carrots, cornstarch.

For oily skin: papaya, strawberries, tomatoes, lemon juice, oatmeal, cornmeal, brewer's yeast, cucumber, apple juice, whipped egg white and cornmeal or oatmeal, thyme.

For normal skin: chamomile, rose hips, strawberries, bananas, egg yolk, yogurt, mayonnaise.

Garden and kitchen cosmetics are great fun. Make up your own recipes. Leave the concoction on your face while you lie down and relax with your feet up for twenty to thirty minutes or so. Rinse off with warm water. You'll be very pleased with the difference in texture and the new glow of your skin.

FACTS OF LIGHT Light is radiant energy. Visible "white" sunlight is really a blend of red, orange, yellow, green, blue, and violet rays—all the rainbow hues. The blue and violet rays promote foliage growth. Plants grown with blue light alone are compact and have lush, dark green leaves, but very few flowers. Research has not yet revealed any major effects of yellow or green rays on plant growth. A photoreaction of red and far-red light triggers the elongation and expansion of various plant parts and, notably, flowering.

Diana Mandoli, a Stanford University plant biologist, has discovered that some plants transmit light similarly to the way the phone company transmits telephone calls. She placed tissues of oat, mung bean, and corn in a dark room, focused a laser beam on one end of a tissue segment and measured light at the opposite end. Acting as optical fibers, the tissues sent light one inch or more along the plant stem, even around curves. Mandoli found that this ability of the plants to transmit light may explain what enables them to sense in which direction to grow in order to face the sun.

Her research is also believed to explain why a seedling can respond to light, even though most of the plant is underground, a process that has long been a puzzle to plant scientists.

FALL GARDENING What you do in the fall largely determines what happens in the spring. This is a good time for "sheet composting." Plow in compost, manure, leaves, grass clippings and let it all decompose over winter. Fall plowing also kills many insects. Vines and stalks should either be composted or burned, especially cucumber, bean, and tomato vines, which help insects and diseases to overwinter. Cornstalks help the corn borer. In the flower garden remove all tops of dahlias, iris, peonies, or any debris that might harbor borers. Spread rotted manure, peat moss, or straw (I use alfalfa hay) around roses and other perennials. Mulch evergreens with peat moss.

No matter how hot and dry it is I always plan to plant my turnip seeds the last of August. They seem to pick up a little moisture anyway and are ready to sprout and grow with the first fall rains. In early September I start planting tender-greens, mustard, pakchoy, and other greens that will grow crisp and tender in the cooler days of early fall.

Not every variety of fall vegetable should be planted in August, but in the South several of the most popular—new potatoes and tomatoes—certainly should. This is also the time to start green beans and onion seeds as well as your ornamental pansy and viola seeds.

You can, of course, buy seedlings from your neighborhood nursery, but they may not have the variety you want. Here's a tip worth having; in the spring when you buy your seeds, plan also for your fall garden and buy the seed varieties you want at that time and simply hold them until they are wanted. It's so easy to start your seedlings in the filtered shade and have them ready to transplant when cooler days arrive. I always do this with broccoli, Chinese celery cabbage, brussels sprouts, cabbage, onions, and other veggies my family likes.

Sometime in late November or early December you will get a killing frost. That's the time to harvest your green tomatoes. Hang the plants in a frost-proof place and let them ripen, or wrap the individual tomatoes in newspapers and place in a cardboard box. Put the box in a well-ventilated dark place. Check every few weeks; they will slowly ripen. Or pick the small green ones and make green tomato chow-chow or relish.

FARMERS' FANCY The farmers in Lincolnshire, England, once practiced an unusual custom for determining planting time. They removed their trousers and sat on the earth; if they found it warm and comfortable, they reasoned, plants would also do so.

FATSIA (*Fatsia japonica*) This big, bold, and beautiful plant with the funny name grows best in the lower and middle South but can be grown as a container plant in colder climates if brought indoors to overwinter in a brightly lit room. The deeply lobed foliage of Japanese fatsia can be used to accent an entrance, grace an atrium, or form a rich, dark-green border in front of a wall. The plant is equally handsome in a woodland beneath a high canopy of trees or in a contemporary setting. Give it full to partial shade and rich, well-drained soil. It will grow 6 to 8 feet tall but, once established, growth slows.

FEET Out of sight, out of mind . . . until they hurt! Adding a cup of salt to a simulated "sea water" footbath is refreshing. Or peel a potato and cut it in half. Rub the potato all over your feet. Try to use a circular, round-and-round motion as you massage. Let the juice dry and leave on overnight, rinsing off in the morning. This is a good treatment for swollen feet. Curative juices in garlic work wonders on corns.

FENDING OFF FLAMES   Those who live in the hot, arid regions of the American Southwest, where dry brush covers much of the landscape, must always face the threat of fire, especially during the hot summer months. But landscape design can offer a protective barrier. Four key guidelines are the secret: 1. Clear your garden and surroundings of highly combustible dead brush; 2. Use water-retaining succulents and low-matted species that don't burn well; 3. Avoid plants such as chamise (*Adenostoma fasiculatum*) and rosemary (*Rosmarinus officinalis*), with flammable oils, and such trees as eucalyptus; 4. Use nonflammable groundcovers, including raked earth, slate, and pebbles.

Native plants such as dwarf coyote brush (*Baccharis pilularis*), salt bush (*Atriplex* spp.), and Saint Catherine's lace (*Eriogonum giganteum*), can form the background of your garden. Naturally well-groomed and of relatively easy care in a hot, dry climate, they don't accumulate too much deadwood or debris. Also most are low-growing plants so there is little foliage to burn. Isolate more combustible species with open spaces between them, separating them with gravel or bare earth, to prevent a brush fire from traveling rapidly from plant to plant through the garden. Create your greenbelt with a limited number of species to give your garden a unified look.

Consider using fire-retardant plants. If you live in a high-risk area, sometimes just a few minutes' delay can make the difference, giving you time to take safety measures. But we must remember that no plant will completely stop a fire from advancing. The most we can hope for is plants that will resist burning, thereby slowing the fire's progress. Remember, too, that on a windy day sparks will be carried and thus breach even protective fire-retardant plantings.

From Sunset's *New Western Garden Book* come these suggestions for trees and shrubs that resist burning better than most:
Trees and Shrubs: Callistemon, *ceratonia siliqua*, *Heteromeles arbutifolia*, myporum, *Nerium oleander* (dwarf kinds), *Prunus lyonii*, *Rhamnus alaternus*, rhus (evergreen types), *Rosmarinus officinalis* 'Prostratus,' *Schinus terebinthifolius*, *Teucrim chamaedrys*.
Perennials and Vines: Achillea, agave, aloe, artemisia (low-growing varieties), atriplex (some), campsis, *Convolvulus cneorum*, gazania, ice plants, *Limonium perezii*, *Portulacaria afra*, *Santolina virens*, *Satureja montana*, *Senecio cineraria*, *Solanum jasminoides*, and yucca (trunkless varieties).

FERNS   Here are some timely tips from thrifty Louise. Are your ferns suffering from "tired blood"? Chop up two raw oysters and use as fertilizer. Or cottonseed meal can be used. This will keep them garden-green and forest-fresh. To revive "sick" ferns, water them with ½ pint salt, added to 6 pints of lukewarm water. If infested with worms, try sticking matches into the soil, sulphur end down. Four for a medium-size pot, six for a large one.

The fronds of leaf-losing ferns should not be removed until spring, as they provide protection for the young fronds. These young fronds, or fiddle-heads, very attractive in spring, are steadily gaining in popularity as a gourmet food item, but we are warned not to eat too many, and to be careful as to variety.

Quite a number of ferns, according to Nelson Coon, give off, in varying degrees, delightful odors when they are dried or brushed when walking through them. Gertrude Jekyll, the famous English writer, said: "The scent of bracken is 'like the smell of sea as you come near it after a long absence.' " Maidenhair fern, Louise Beebe Wilder tells us, has a delicate haylike scent when dried. *Aspidium fragrans* has a fragrance that has been likened to that of strawberries, raspberries, and primroses. The lovely bladder fern, *Cystopteris bulbifera*, found on dripping cliffs in limestone regions, is exceedingly fragrant. There are many others.

FERNS IN SUMMER When it's time to take your ferns and other hanging baskets outside for the summer, try hanging them from the limbs of a large tree. Not only will they look just beautiful, they'll thrive on the shade and gentle breezes the tree provides. And, since they'll catch rainwater, they'll also need less watering.

FIGS (*Ficus*) Figs are more alkaline and contain more mineral matter than most fruits, and have been recommended as everything from an anemia cure to a laxative. They are especially delicious cut in two and soaked in orange liqueur an hour or two before being served with whipped cream. For years I have made a fig marmalade of chopped figs laced with softened lemon and orange peels that is out of this world. Fresh figs with honey make a superb dessert.

Generally grown in bush form, figs are tender plants. Even so, I have wintered over my "everbearer" for many years by giving winter protection to its low-growing branches. These usually start bearing in July. New growth bears later into the fall, giving almost continuous fruit until frost. Figs contain vitamins A, B, and C as well as calcium, iron, and phosphorus.

FIRE ANTS (*Solenopsis invicta*) When considering the fire ant I am reminded of a story I once heard about a kindly woman who had a word of praise for everyone. One day a friend said to her, "Mary, I believe you could find something good to say about the Devil himself!" "Well," said Mary, after due reflection, "He certainly keeps busy." And that's about the best thing you can say about fire ants!

According to Richard Conniff, writing in the 1991 edition of *The Old Farmer's Almanac*, fire ants were first noticed by a U.S.D.A. researcher, William F. Buren, who stopped to examine a large ant nest along U.S. Route 98 near Daphne, Alabama. This was just the beginning: "Over the next four decades they were to spread from their port of entry, Mobile, Alabama, across 260 million acres to eleven southern states and put themselves in a position to sting (usually more than once) an estimated three to five million outraged Americans a year."

Being stung is no joke. Symptoms include burning and itching, followed by development of a white sore or pustule that may leave a permanent scar. Persons reacting severely to fire ant stings should see a physician immediately, and those who are hypersensitive should see an allergist for treatment if fire ant contact is a possibility.

So what, if anything, can be done about fire ants? The following information is excerpted from Bulletin B-1536, Texas Agricultural Service, written by Bastiaan M. Drees and S. Bradleigh Vinson, Extension Entomologist and professor, Department of Entomology, the Texas A & M University System.

What should you do if you suspect fire ants on your property? Advice is to collect a sample for identification by pushing a small vial or jar into the mound for ten to fifteen minutes, then removing with alcohol added if needed, and capped. Care should be taken to avoid being stung. Then contact your county extension agent for information on submitting specimens.

Each mound was thought to contain a single queen. Recently, however, populations of red imported fire ants have been found that contain many reproductive queen ants. These are called "multiple queen" colonies. The imported fire ant spreads naturally through mating flights; however, the queens

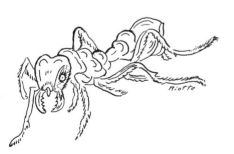

also spread by crawling, drifting downstream on or in logs, or traveling aboard cars, trucks, or trains. Shipments of nursery stock or soil from an infested area may relocate an entire colony or nest. Imported fire ants build mounds in almost any type of soil but prefer open, sunny areas such as pastures, parks, lawns, meadows, and cultivated fields. Mounds are less well developed in very sandy soils.

Red imported fire ants are a pest of man, animals, and several agricultural crops. Currently there is no single, universal solution to the fire ant problem. However there are a number of options available.

In areas where fire ants are not causing a problem it may be best not to attempt any control measures. Often attempts at control simply spread the ants. Maintaining several large, stable colonies in locations that do not interfere with the activities of man may be an ecologically sound method of stabilizing the fire ant population in certain areas. Established ants defend territories, preventing the establishment of new colonies in their territory.

The suppression of fire ants by several nonchemical control techniques may be appropriate in certain situations. A mound can be dug up or moved and dispersed. Take care to prevent ants from attacking by crawling up the handle of a shovel or out of a bucket. Talcum powder, liberally dusted on handles and the inside of a bucket, will deter fire ant movement across the dusted surfaces.

Boiling water is reportedly a fairly effective treatment for individual fire ant mounds. Approximately 3 gallons of hot water poured on each mound will eliminate about 60 percent of the mounds treated. Surviving mounds will need to be treated again. This method may work well in certain situations, but take care not to pour hot water on desired plants. Exercise care in handling large volumes of hot water to prevent serious burns.

There are a number of organisms that kill newly mated fire ant queens. These include dragonflies, other ants, birds, lizards, spiders, and toads. Animals that eat ants, such as armadillos, may disturb the mound and eat some workers but are not really useful in control. Some parasites are known to attack ants.

A vinegar/diatomaceous earth solution is a possible fire ant control on individual mounds. For larger areas try Logic, Affirm, or Pro-Drone. Once ingested the queen stops laying eggs and the colony eventually starves to death. Maximum results take twelve to sixteen weeks, but starving a mound is an environmentally sound method, according to Steven George, Ph.D.

Remember that fire ants are key predators of some pests such as the boll weevil in cotton, and thus may be considered beneficial insects in some field crops—so they are not all bad. Conversely, fire ants and other ant species will protect and disperse aphids because aphids produce a sugary substance called "honeydew" on which the ants feed.

FIRE BLIGHT This bacterial disease attacks apples and pears but may also be a problem on related ornamentals such as photinia, cotoneaster, firethorn (pyracantha), flowering quince, hawthorn, loquat, and roses. Fire blight starts in spring, with the bacterium carried by bees from infected specimens to the flowers of other plants. The growing tip of an infected branch will bend downward, the leaves turning black as if burned. As it continues downward it may kill the plant.

The best method of preventing this disease is to plant resistant selections such as Red Delicious apples, Winesap, Golden Delicious, Stayman, and Yates. Resistant pears include Orient, Magness, Kieffer, Ayers, and Moonglow. To prevent an infection spray susceptible plants with streptomycin (Agri-Strep) during flowering, being sure to read the label and follow directions. If plants are already infected, pruning out infected portions will help to keep the blight from spreading. Sterilize your pruning tool between each cut by dipping in a solution of household bleach (Clorox) mixed at a ratio of 1 part bleach to 9 parts water.

FIREFLIES (*Lampyridae*) Fireflies are not just of material benefit to man, but of spiritual benefit as well, according to Dr. Roy Parker, Texas Agricultural Extension Service entomologist in Corpus Christi, Texas. "Fireflies remind many adult urbanites of their childhoods in more rural areas," he says. I believe this is true, for I well remember what fun it was to chase them on midsummer evenings.

Fireflies on a summer night,
Add beauty with their flashing light,
They take us back to childhood's scene -
But what does all that flashing mean?
Their light, at night, means love's delight!
—Louise Riotte

It's the flashing that makes the fireflies unique in the insect world. They are the only luminescent insects that can actually turn their lights on and off—all others glow continuously. In the U.S. and Canada 125 species have been recorded. But just what is all that flashing on and off meant for?

Love lights! When these lights are being sent out the females are using codes each species recognizes. And she can produce an almost infinite number of codes by frequency variations and duration of flashes and also the intervals between.

Again that innocent-looking little firefly proves that, like the spider, "the female is more deadly than the male," for some female fireflies prey on the males of other species. The predatory female deliberately mimics the love code of another type of firefly and when the hapless male comes looking for a mate he ends up as dinner.

How does the firefly do its flashing? Five chemicals—adenosine, triphosphate, luciferin, oxygen, magnesium, and luciferase—are bound up in the firefly's abdomen by a chemical controller. When nerve stimulations release another chemical, inorganic pyrophosphate, the bond breaks and the reaction produces the light which usually appears on the sides of the firefly's abdomen.

Is the delightful firefly friend or foe? Friend: in the larval stage the firefly can be considered of material benefit to man. Adult fireflies eat very little according to Dr. Parker, but the growing juveniles eat animals that feed on the leaves. Their favorite foods are the small snails they share living quarters with in decaying wood and soil. The larvae attack them by injecting them with a predigestive enzyme. After the snails die, the larvae dine at leisure. The most common type of firefly in the southern and southwestern states is *Thotinus pyralys*. People in tropical countries sometimes put fireflies in a bottle and use them for lanterns.

FIRE STARTERS Save pine cones and dip them in leftover kitchen grease and drippings. Let the cones harden and store where mice can't get at them. They'll make great fire starters for your wood stove—but go cautiously for they really burn! You'll be glad to have these when winter winds begin to blow.

FISHING SCENTS Many news articles have centered on how the olfactory system of bass and other fish species actually works, but that fish do have a keen sense of smell there is no doubt. While it is reputed that fish do not like strong aromas, many fisherpersons believe that bait rubbed with oil of anise will attract the fish. Others swear by lovage, or smallage. Howard Sparger, a former game ranger, states, "When you think seriously about what a fishing scent should do for you as an angler, keep three important things in mind:

"First and foremost, the scent we spray on our baits, live or artificial, should act as an attractant. It should trigger the quarry to at least move a few inches, if not more, to get a better whiff of what is oozing that great odor.

"Second, the ideal fish scent should also taste great (anise is used to flavor all sorts of cakes, cookies, and baked goods). When the bass or other game fish you're after picks up the lure sprayed with magic elixir, that fish should want to mouth it at least one-tenth of a second longer than it normally would, and hopefully for a lot longer than that.

"Third, the ideal fish scent should also mask a number of scents—human odor, gasoline, grease, and so forth. Scientists have proven that fish can be repelled by these and other scents repulsive to them."

Plant anise where it is to remain. It does not transplant well because the delicate root is liable to break and the plant does not readily recover. It is best grown in fairly dry, light, sandy, well drained, moderately rich soil in a warm, sunny spot. Oddly it is also an attractant for mice as well as for fish and issued as bait.

Of lovage, or smallage, Rossetta Clarkson says, "Our grandmothers called it 'smellage.' " This is a handsome, tropical background plant, growing to 7 feet, with very aromatic leaves. Clarkson says the leaves, fresh or dried, are similar in odor and taste to celery and may be used in place of it. The oil is also used in perfumery.

FLAME BOTTLE TREE (*Brachychiton acerifolius*) This is a tropical tree suited to sections of the United States such as Florida where exotics may be grown. The flame bottle tree grows to a height of about 40 feet, with the lower part of the trunk usually swollen to form a bottle shape. The glossy green leaves may be as much as 10 inches wide. In July and August, the scarlet-red flowers appear. Dramatically, just before the blooming period, the leaves drop and the branches turn red.

FLORATAM GRASS In areas where the southern-lawn chinch bug is a big headache, floratam, a variety of St. Augustine, may be the answer. This vigorous, broad-leaved, deeper-green variety, developed jointly by the Texas and Florida agricultural experiment stations is not only chinch-bug-resistant but also resistant to St. Augustine Decline (SAD). SAD is a mosaic virus disease. Floratam, like other St. Augustine grasses, is versatile and more salt-tolerant than other warm-season grasses. Thriving well in full sun or moderate shade, its low-maintenance requirements compare well with most other turf grasses. Unfortunately—

you can't have everything—like common St. Augustine, floratam is not resistant to brown patch or rust. The protectant Terrachlor is recommended to reduce these two diseases.

FLORENCE FENNEL (*Foeniculum vulgare*) This is probably the most bizarre-looking plant you've seen in the garden since you discovered kohlrabi. And—hold onto your hat—this vegetable/herb tastes like licorice! Florence fennel, like kohlrabi, also is grown for its swollen base, which is enjoyed as a vegetable. Other parts of the plant may be used as well, the foliage adding flavor to salads and dressings and often used to season fish or soup. You can make a tea with the fresh leaves, or dry them for year-round use. Fennel is one of the umbel plants, similar to dill, and you should harvest the seeds when they are a light brown. Use them for spicing cookies, sweet breads, or candy. Stored in the refrigerator you can plant them the following spring.

Florence fennel is a hardy perennial in all but the coldest regions of the South, but it is most commonly grown as an annual. As with most herbs, it prefers slightly alkaline soil. Sow outdoors when danger of frost is past. Mound soil around the bulbous portion to blanch it, harvesting when it reaches 2½ to 3 inches in diameter.

Herb fennel has a centuries old reputation as a slendering agent. *The Good Housewife's Jewell* (1585) praises it "For to make one slender." Herbalist William Coles (1650) stated in *Nature's Paradise*: "Both the seeds, leaves and root of our Garden Fennel are much used in drinks and broths for those that are grown fat." And, quite probably, the ancient Greeks were also aware of the properties of this herb, for they called it *marathon*, derived from *maraino*, to grow thin. (See also "Umbel Ones.")

Reducing Aid: Simmer for 5 minutes in 2 pints boiling water ½ teaspoonful each of licorice and sweet flag roots, kelp, sassafras bark, and 1 teaspoon of fennel seed and chickweed. Cover 15 minutes and strain. Take about ⅔ cupful (warm) morning, afternoon, and evening. It is also an important ingredient in eye lotions: Steep ⅛ teaspoon each of fennel, chamomile, and/or eyebright, in a cupful of hot boiled water and cover until cold. Stir, strain and filter carefully through absorbent cotton. Wash eye with eye cup every 2 to 3 hours or as needed.

FLOUR OF SULFUR This is the crude or dusting type and it is useful as a coating for seed potatoes after they have been cut for planting. Just put them in a paper bag and shake them up as you would when coating chicken with flour. The sulfur helps to prevent rotting and also deters potato beetles and other chewing insects as the plants grow. You may also use sulfur in transplanting holes for tomatoes, peppers, and eggplants, mixing it with the soil. The theory is that the sulfur goes from the roots up into the top growth and makes the plant unappetizing to insects, but it does not impart any flavor to the fruit. A light sprinkling of sulfur around plants also helps retard cutworms. I also find dusting with sulphur helpful when humid weather causes mildew on my English peas.

> Any man that walks the mead
> In bud, or blade, or bloom, may find
> A meaning suited to his mind.
> —Alfred Lord Tennyson

FLOWER MESSAGES Back in the Victorian age people capitalized on the ability of flowers to communicate a message by sending tussie-mussies, carefully chosen flowers and herbs. It was considered a great way of communicating when they were at a loss for words. Of course, today, if you send a friend a bouquet of parsley—and they don't know how to play the game—you may be in deep trouble!

Even so, this is a lovely custom and a tradition that deserves to be kept alive because it can be a lot of fun. One of the best and most popular books was by Kate Greenaway called *Language of Flowers*, which can still be found in bookstores today. I am fortunate in possessing another, *Messages of Flowers*, by George H. O'Neill, published in 1917. George, too, had a lot to say and even included messages of vegetables.

A tussie-mussie is not a big deal; it is meant to be small enough to be held comfortably in your hand. Surround the flowers and herbs with small fragrant leaves or ferns and tie securely with a pretty ribbon bow.

Here are a few suggestions:

Abutilon—Meditation, truce

Acacia—Affection, friendship

Acacia, Yellow—Secret love

Azalea—Temperance

Bachelor's Button—Celibacy, obstinacy

Balloon Vine (Love-in-a-puff)—No trace

Balm of Gilead—Relief

Basil—Hatred

Basil, Sweet—Good wishes

Beech Tree—Prosperity

Candytuft—Indifference

Celosia—Lovely, exquisite taste

Chrysanthemum—Cheerfulness

Clover, Four-leaves—Be mine

Daisy—Innocence

Datura—Evil

Edelweiss—Purity, faithfulness

Elm—Dignity, patriotism

Endive—Frugality

Fern—Fascination, sincerity

Fleur-de-Lis—Eloquence

Forget-me-not—Think of me

Four-o'Clock—Promptness

Geraniums, Scarlet—Kindness

Gladiolus—Telephone

Goldenrod—Precaution

Hazel—Reconciliation

Herbs—A cure

Holly Wreath—A Merry Christmas

Honeysuckle—Generosity

Immortelle—Remembrance of beauty

Jacob's Ladder—Elevation, return

Jasmine—Happiness

Jonquil—Returnable affection

Kudzu Vine—Elopement

Lady's Slipper—Gayety

Lilies—Purity

Magnolia—Nature lover

Marigold—Grief

Narcissus—Egotism

Nasturtium—Patriotism

Obedient Plant—Docility

Olive Branch—Peace

Orange Blossom—Bridal

Palm—Victory

Pansy—Thoughts

Parsley—Festivity

Peppermint—Warmth of feeling

Peppers, Sweet—Banter

Plum Blossom—Keep your promise

Poppy—Dreams

Quaking-grass—Agitation

Rhododendron—Alertness

Roses:
> American Beauty—Adoration, intended visit, may I call?
> Austrian—Flattery
> Bridal—Happy love
> Burgundy—Unconscious
> Cabbage—Ambassador of love
> China—Beauty always new
> Musk—Capricious
> Moss—Merit
> Pink—Arrange meeting
> Scarlet—An angry "NO!"
> Thornless—No danger
> Yellow—Jealousy

Rosemary—Remembrance

Rubber Plant—Domesticity

Sage—Domestic excellency

Snapdragon—Presumption, no

Snowdrop—Atonement

Spearmint—Sentimentality

Thistle—Austerity

Tiger Lily—Anger

Tulips—Apology

Umbrella Plant—Have covered everything

Valerian—Don't be nervous

Violet—Modesty

Wallflower—Fidelity

Xerantheum—Rudeness

Yarrow—Assistance

FLOWERS FOR NATURALIZING   Perennials that spread without care and work well are aster, lily of the valley, lossestrife, bee balm, coneflower, and false Solomon's seal. Narcissus, crocus, ornithogalum, muscari, puschkinia, and chionodoxa are bulbs recommended for naturalizing. You can try for a random effect by scattering marbles on the prepared soil and planting wherever the marbles fall!

ARE YOU IN A FOG?   For many coastal residents and those who live in certain inland valleys, fog is a fact of life. Even here in hot, dry Oklahoma we have "pea soupers" at certain seasons in the spring. Fog can be a friend, helping to keep temperatures mild year-round. Cool-weather vegetables dote on fog and you can have a great garden if you know what to plant. For starters three vegetables that thrive in fog are artichokes, garlic, and fava beans—all very easy to grow. Others include broccoli, cauliflower, brussels sprouts, chard, cabbage, chives, potatoes, peas, lettuce, endive, Chinese cabbage, kale, mustard, spinach, onions, and leeks. Radishes are so easy to grow that you should make continuous plantings. Fava beans, sometimes called broad beans or long beans, are an excellent source of protein. Many fog-zone gardeners not only grow them as a good winter, spring, or early summer crop, but also to return nitrogen to the soil. Fog also helps to extend the gardening season. In some regions gardeners can expect to get corn in the late fall, tomatoes in the middle of winter, spinach and head lettuce in midsummer, and pumpkins as late as December.

FOLIAGE PERKER-UPPER Iron sulfate is beneficial where iron in the soil is low, chiefly useful in greening foliage. It has no effect on flower color.

> And here's the happy bounding flea -
> You cannot tell the he from she,
> The sexes look alike, you see;
> But she can tell, and so can he.
>> "The Flea"
>> —Roland Young (1887–1953)

FORCING FLEAS TO FLEE! The spring of 1991 was unusually hot and humid and the muggy weather apparently triggered an explosion in the flea population the like of which we had not seen for several years. Along with many others who kept house pets I soon found I had a flea problem. Not only was Bootsie, my Siamese, scratching frantically, but my carpets were hopping with fleas as well. I panicked and spent a young fortune on sprays and powders, all to no avail. Cube powder, containing Rotenone, a derivative of derris, which I had used effectively in the past, no longer corrected the problem. Then my daughter-in-law came to my rescue and saved both my sanity and my pocketbook. She told me about a family owning two small house dogs who had a terrible flea problem and said that they had cleansed the house of fleas by sprinkling *salt* all over the house—just plain old common table salt.

I determined to try this; of course, by then I would have tried anything. First, we thoroughly vacuumed the carpet, then we sprinkled salt liberally all over and left it down for several days, again vacuuming thoroughly, and spreading a second time to kill any hatch-out that might be remaining. It worked! Why? I am not sure but think, since salt is not a poison, that it may work on the same principle as diatomaceous earth by cutting their bodies.

I approached the problem of fleas on the cat two ways. I bought a steel flea comb (a British product), and started a program of daily grooming. The closely set teeth (22 per inch) extracts fleas and flea eggs which may then be killed by dipping the comb into a flea solution. Used gently but thoroughly the cat really seems to enjoy the grooming. (*Gardens Alive* has several types of flea combs).

FOUR-O'CLOCK (*Mirabilis Jalapa*) Marvel-of-Peru. Native of tropical and North America, the name *mirabilis* means wonderful and refers to the color of the flowers which open in late afternoon—hence its common name—four-o'clock. According to the variety flowers may be red, yellow, white, pink, or violet. Give them a sunny position and light, well-drained soil.

Indians used the root of the plant medicinally. When a sore reached the appropriate state, the scab was peeled off and the powdered root of the four-o'clock blown over it. Every tribe has its special name for this, but government field nurses referred to it simply as *impetigo plant*.

FRAGRANT GARDENS FOR THE BLIND There is more good gardening news for caretakers whose charges may have impaired sight. Many easily grown garden flowers are both fragrant and edible, which is a bit like "having your cake and eating it too."

Who doesn't love the scent of **violets**? According to Euell Gibbons the blossoms are three times as rich in vitamin C, weight for weight, as oranges. And the leaves are an excellent source of vitamin A. Gibbons speaks joyfully of violet syrup, violet greens, violet jam, violet jelly, violet ointment, violet sherbet, and candied violets. **Pansies** have a warm sweet scent, sometimes sharp.

Scented-leaved geraniums are a little-known treasure. Rose-geranium is justly famous as an ingredient of apple jelly, but it also makes a delicious custard. That's just the "tip of the iceberg" so to speak. Louise Beebe Wilder, in *The Fragrant Garden*, tells us of geraniums whose odor is reminiscent of lemon, nutmeg, filbert, cinnamon, almond, orange, apple, anise, pine, musk, violet, lavender, balm, peppermint, and oak. You might not want it, but there is also one that smells of fish!

Roses, of course, are just about everybody's favorite flower, but if you want the most fragrant, the antique varieties are quite likely to be your selection. Let 'American Beauty,' 'La France,' 'Mermaid,' 'Musk Rose,' or 'Reine des Violettes' provide enchanting fragrance. Tillotson's Roses (Brown's Valley Road, Watsonville, California 95076) has a wide selection.

Daylilies are another good choice, like the sweet-scented and free blooming 'Catherine Woodbury.' And some people love the sharp scent of **marigolds**; others can't stand 'em! But marigold petals are highly edible in such recipes as marigold cheese balls, chicken pie, chowder, potato puffs, rice, rice pudding, scalloped oysters, and Marigold Beef Casserole, according to Francesca Tillona and Cynthia Strowbridge (*A Feast of Flowers*).

Carnations, especially the Clove strain, have an unforgettable fragrance, and they come as both annuals and perennials. **Nasturtiums**, according to Wilder, have a "smokey-sweetness." She explained that "the name comes from an old Latin word, used by Pliny, and derived by him from *narsus*, the nose, and *tortus*, twisted, in reference to the supposed contortions of the nose caused by the hot pungent odor and taste of these flowers." Many find the leaves delicious in salads and sandwiches. And the blossoms are delightful stuffed with tuna salad and served surrounded by violets and violet leaves.

Spicy **chrysanthemums** are beloved of the Chinese, who grow especially edible varieties. The Japanese love them as well and serve them as "Chrysanthemums Nipponese," petals simmered in salted water until just tender, drained and sprinkled with orange-flower water and soy sauce, and served on steamed rice.

Lavendula vera is the true English **lavender**. The finely scented *L. Stoechas* is called French lavender. It was once strewn on the floors of churches and dwellings on feast days. It is delicious made into lavender-mint jelly.

Which brings us to the mints. "Pennyroyal," says Wilder, "is one of the few herbs that floods the surrounding air with its searching aroma without encouragement."

Catnip (*Nepeta cataria*) is my own favorite. Wilder said her favorite is the variegated apple-mint. Orange-mint (*Mentha citrata*) she says is good but not easily come by. And of course there are the well-known peppermint and spearmint (*M. piperita* and *M. viridis*). These julep-mints were beloved in the old South served in the hot, breathless days of summer.

I have room to mention but a few of the delightful possibilities of flowers and herbs to tease our noses and our palates. Just don't get carried away, for some flowers are poisonous and should never be eaten. Be sure and be safe.

FRAGRANT INDOOR PLANTS I am firmly of the opinion that more homeowners would use fragrant container plants if they knew which plants to choose. I happen to love **gardenias**. Years ago a young boy who took me to the prom gave me a gardenia. I pressed the corsage down under a heavy book and I still have it, although a week after the dance he took off with another girl! (Looking back I realize I should have weighted the boy with the book, but I wasn't as sharp then as I am now.) Don't let your gardenia plant slip away from you; give it early morning sun, then diffuse light, and supply lots of humidity. Keep it on pebbles and mist often with water. It likes a temperature of 65 to 70 degrees.

The **sweet olive**, another favorite, is one helluva fine trooper; it just goes and goes, flowering practically continuously. The little white flowers, however, don't amount to much, but the punchline is their fragrance filling a whole room. An evergreen native to the Orient, it has shiny green leaves and the flowers appear in clusters in the leaf axils. It grows from 12 inches to the size of a small shrub. Give it sun, but in summer's heat you may find it does best in filtered light. Keep it on a saucer filled with pebbles and water and mist often.

Night-blooming jessamine is the type that pours out the fragrance. It has bright green leaves and a midwinter flowering period, though some bloom off and on all year. Plants seldom grow over 2 feet tall, making it a compact plant for the house. Give it lots of sun, but filtered sunshine is best in summer heat. Humidity is important; keep the soil evenly moist and keep spraying. This also helps to ward off red spider and mealy bugs. If plants have aphids or mealy bugs, apply plain rubbing alcohol directly on the insects with a cotton-tipped swab.

Have you heard about **hoyas**? Wonderfully fragrant, the flowers have a shiny, waxy look that gives them the name wax plant. The very lovely flowers are white with pink or red stainings on them. This is another little tough guy—just keep it in partial sun and give it average house temperatures and humidity. Don't drown it, for too much water can kill it. The neat trick is to give it lots of water at one time, let it drip out of the draining holes and then leave it alone. Don't water again until the top inch or so has dried out. But, of course, don't let it wither away. It needs the semidry period to develop its root system.

"FRESH" FRUIT FOR WINTER When grapes have ripened put them in a freezing container. Make a purée of apricots, peaches, or apples and pour over stemmed grapes, filling all air spaces with the paste. Grapes will stay their natural color and give you a delicious dessert in winter when fresh fruit is scarce.

FREEZING VEGETABLES After blanching I save the cooking water. After placing the vegetables, peas, carrots, etc. in a leakproof container I pour the water over them leaving ½ inch at the top for expansion. Frozen like this they do not dry out and have a much better flavor. When I plan to use a carton I place it in the refrigerator and let it thaw out a little overnight.

By all means freeze your surplus corn, which often tends to mature all at one time. Some prefer to freeze without blanching, simply husking and wrapping individually in waxed or freezer paper; others prefer to blanch for a few minutes. Whichever

method you prefer it is the thawing that is important. Corn, so far as I am able to determine, is the one vegetable that should be thawed before cooking.

To freeze onions, spread sliced on cookie sheets until they freeze, then pack them into plastic bags. This method keeps them loose and you can take them out as needed. This method works well also for brussels sprouts or other small vegetables.

FROST AND THE BUD MOTH
Weather conditions sometimes play a large part in controlling certain insect pests. Frost, for example, was found to be the chief factor with the bud moth, a pest of apple orchards. Customarily, growers in the Province of Quebec had sprayed against this insect twice during the growing season. But when it was discovered that bud moth larvae perish whenever temperatures go down to -21°F, even if only for a single winter evening, their spraying against this insect was eliminated during the following season.

FROST DAMAGE Of course you should listen to your weather report, but sometimes such reports are quite general and due to certain microclimate conditions may not apply well to your particular garden spot. It pays to develop your sixth sense about the weather—a late frost can do a lot of damage. Here are some signs to look for:

- If the sky is clear and the air is calm and still with no breeze blowing as dusk falls . . . watch out for frost.
- When the thermometer dips to 40°F by early evening, there's a good possibility that it will drop to the freezing point by the early morning hours.
- No one knows why, but frost is often likely during the last week before a full moon.

So with a late frost imminent, what can you do? Covering as much as possible is usually the answer, but many gardeners are now finding that the use of a seaweed spray on their vegetables is often effective. According to E. Booth of the Institute of Seaweed Research, writing in *The Grower* (November

27, 1965), experiments indicate that it is sometimes impossible for plants to synthesize the necessary components of growth when the temperature is too low. Kelp is not only a rich source of trace minerals, it also contains alginic acid and other substances, known to chelate metals, thus making some of the trace elements more readily available to the plant. Thus the seaweed helps the plant to compensate for the inhibiting effect of low temperatures by supplying in ready-to-use form those vital elements of growth that the plant would otherwise be unable to make for itself.

Eskimos, in their far-north, short-season gardens have been doing just that for years. Granular kelp may be applied to the soil, but the foliar spray is more rapidly absorbed. To apply kelp solution, mix one tablespoon of the bottled concentrate with one gallon of water and spray it on the foliage with a small hand sprayer. Frequent light applications are more effective than occasional heavy treatments.

FROST-NIPPED PLANTS   These can sometimes be saved by sprinkling well with water in which common salt has been dissolved—a tablespoon or two to the gallon. This treatment must be given before the plant has been exposed to the sun or thawed.

FRUCTOSE   People who want to do without sugar can. Vegetables and fruit contain enough sugar to satisfy both our sweet tooth and our energy requirements. Called fructose, this fruit sugar is also a bit easier on our teeth than sucrose (table sugar) and is a natural product of food that offers many other nutrients.

Fructose does not give the "quick hit" of table sugar, which often stirs our bodies into a "flight or fight" reaction, then drops us into a post-sugar depression. Rather, fructose provides slow and steady energy, with enough in reserve to meet a sudden demand.

Honey is basically a blend of fructose and glucose. When you eat white sugar, your body breaks down the sucrose into fructose and glucose, the two main ingredients of

honey. Yet honey is a caloric bargain; because it is sweeter than sugar, you need less to get the same sweet effect.

Maple syrup, though expensive, is another source of sweet power. When shopping for this be sure to check the label. Blackstrap molasses, a third sweetener, is your best bet nutritionally. It is high in calcium, iron, potassium, and provides some B vitamins, phosphorus, and sodium.

A FRUIT BOUNTY   Bending the branches of your fruit trees downward induces earlier bearing. Green apples will color up if placed on straw under a tree. Grafting will convert an undesirable tree into one with top quality fruit. Plant young trees (so much less expensive, too!). A one-year old tree for transplanting will usually bear quicker than a five-year-old tree. Early fruit drop ("June drop") is nothing serious. It's nature's way of helping you have larger and better fruit. If your space is limited, grow espaliered trees, which are trained flat against a wall or terrace. Trees carefully located often are warmed by the sunlight reflected from a wall and bear earlier than trees in orchards or other locations about your property.

FUCHSIA (*Fuchsia*)   There are about 100 species in the genus *Fuchsia* and it is not generally realized that a number of them offer edible berries. Some were undoubtedly

Fuchsia exoniensis

known to the Incas and Aztecs and possibly cultivated by them. One species was, in fact, discovered growing in the ruins of an Inca city in the Andes. Another species, native to New Zealand, provided edible berries for the Maori. However, the fruit-bearing species, such as the Peruvian *Fuchsia corymbiflora*, does not compare with the really lovely fuchsia known to most people; these beauties are hybrids and are the result of patient breeding over the past 100 years. The berries of *corymbiflora* are said to taste like ripe figs.

Fuchsia exorticata from New Zealand is a most hardy species. It is also remarkably different from other fuchsia species and its flowers are produced on its trunk right down to the ground, as well as on the branches. The flowers, 1 inch long, have a yellow calyx and sepals of violet-green. The pollen of the flowers is bright blue, giving the tree a purple-blue sheen when in bloom. Maori girls once used this blue pollen as a face powder to beautify themselves. The berries from *F. exorticata* are purple-black and sub-acid.

FUGITIVES FROM A FAIRY TALE

Large gourds (*Lagenaria leucantha*) have been making headlines for years. They come in various shapes and sizes and have fragrant, showy white flowers. Perhaps none of them is more spectacular than the Hercules Club (Park Seed), which has club-shaped fruits, sometimes 6 feet long! Cave Man's Club has bat-shaped fruits that may attain 3 feet. The turbanlike Aladdin is bright red-orange with yellow and green stripes and is very popular as a Thanksgiving decoration, as is also Turk's Turban, a giant ornamental. Dolphin, or Maranka, is dolphin-shaped with deep ridges. Then there is the Snake Gourd (*Trichosanthes cucumerina anguina*), which is so like a real snake that it can serve you in your garden as a scarecrow for the birds. Get acquainted with these fascinating annuals and you'll want some of them every year.

FUN WITH ASTROLOGY
As mentioned in my books *Planetary Planting* and *Astrological Gardening*, many people like to plant by the astrological "signs," believing

that to do so enhances their chances of gardening success. This practice is centuries old and has endured throughout the ages. Moreover, each sign, if used correctly, has something going for it that can be of benefit. I have summed this up in my little "fun poem":

The Gardener's Almanac
Learn to watch each new-born day,
Check to see what "the Signs" say.
Water in Pisces, very wet. Plant vines
In Virgo as your best bet . . .
Is the weather hot and dry?
Capricorn planting is good to try,
Taurus planted trees will be,
Short and sturdy and fine to see.
If you want flowers, Libra's for you.
For veggies, Cancer's a great sign too.
Leo's the sign for killing weeds,
Scorpio plants fill the garden's needs.
Gemini's good for eradication,
Sagittarius' day is for cultivation,
Aries is your harvest sign,
Aquarius keeps bugs and slugs in line.
From moon-moist night, to sun-warmed day,
The stars themselves come out to play.
And planets that slowly roll and turn,
Become a gardener's great concern.

It has long been considered that plants bearing above ground should be planted in the first and second quarter of the moon, and plants, such as roots, bearing their fruit below ground should be planted in the third and fourth quarters. However, according to the astrological practices advocated by Rudolf Steiner, the "day sign" takes precedence, that is, if the calendar shows third quarter and Cancer, it is still a good planting sign. This also holds for other gardening practices such as weeding, cultivation, and harvesting. Of course no astro/organic gardener believes that "planting by the signs" will effect a miracle. Other good organic gardening practices are followed by sensible gardeners such as composting and adding organic fertilizer to the soil. As I have repeatedly said: "Organic gardening teaches us *how* to plant, astrological gardening tells us *when*."

FUN WITH FLOWERS   Carnations are surprisingly sweet. To use the petals in desserts, cut them away from the bitter white base of the flower. Add dried petals to cake batter or sprinkle fresh minced petals over a bowl of berries.

Gardenias have tender sweet petals that make delightful dessert fritters. Make a batter by mixing one egg yolk with ⅔ cup of cold water, ¾ cup flour and a dash of brandy. Remove petals from gardenia, dip into batter and deep-fry until golden brown. Sprinkle fritters with powdered sugar and serve with ice cream.

Pansies look dramatic frozen into ice cubes for drinks or ice rings for punch. To make a memorable jello salad, try putting pansies face down in the mold before adding the gelatin.

Violets can, of course, be candied by dipping into egg white and then into finely granulated sugar, and set to dry. They are pretty for decorating cakes and other pastries. If you want the flowers to last for more than two days dip them into gum arabic instead of egg whites. Violets, whose flowers and leaves are both edible (and high in vitamin C), also make a dainty addition to an early spring salad.

Gardens were before gardeners,
and but some hours after the earth.

SIR THOMAS BROWNE

GARBAGE, like beauty, is often in the eye of the beholder. Waste not, want not. Regard carrot tops, squeezed-out orange and grapefruit halves, moldy and inedible leftovers, eggshells, potato parings, and apple cores as manna for the garden compost heap. The heap, which you may prefer to box, really epitomizes the whole ecological process, recycling waste into the total scheme, turning unlovely garbage into lovely and useful humus. Garbage power is too good to waste.

GARDEN HOSE makes a handy tape measure for outdoor use! Usually 50 feet long, it can be divided into smaller increments by using waterproof tape in different colors. Fold the hose by placing both ends together, and mark the center (about 25 feet) with one color of tape. Put the center and both ends together (about 12½ feet from each end) with another color. Now you've just made a weather-proof, durable marker that still serves its original purpose.

GARDEN HUCKLEBERRIES (*Solanum melanocerasum*) The first thing to know about garden huckleberries is that they are neither blueberries nor huckleberries. They are an edible member of the nightshade family, close cousins to the Irish potato and the eggplant. Yet by some alchemy, when cooked, they taste just like blueberries!

Care for the plants as you would tomato and pepper plants. They also die after frost. Garden huckleberries, while needing plenty of water, will grow in almost any soil, even that wasted place back of the garage where nothing else will live. Just give them plenty of room, perhaps even a bit more than the seed packet directs. They start to bloom early, continuing throughout summer into fall, right up to frost. You may have ripe berries, various sizes of green berries, and blossoms all together. However, just because some of the berries are shiny black doesn't necessarily mean they are ripe. It's best to leave them on the plant until a light frost or two mellows them, for they will probably still be bitter. The berries do not wither, remaining firm on the vine. Watch the weather and pull before a hard frost, however.

To cook, bring a large pot of water to a rolling boil. Add berries, and bring back to a boil, then add one teaspoon of baking soda. Boil one minute longer and quickly drain. It may be a bit of a surprise to see the water turning bright green, even though the berries are purple. Allow about 4 cups to a pie, using any good blueberry pie recipe. Tapioca makes a good thickener and the juice of half a lemon adds flavor.

I want to emphasize again the distinction between huckleberries and garden huckleberries, for many people assume they are the same thing. Often garden huckleberries are thrown away as being bitter because no one knew that cooking is the secret to eating them.

GARDEN RESULTS ARE OFTEN GEO-GRAPHICAL   *Don't* worry if the ad said your plant would grow 18 feet high and yield 200 pounds of fruit and your plant grew only 4 feet high and yielded 10 pounds of fruit. *Do* worry if your next-door neighbor planted the same thing in the same amount at the same time and had twice as much as fruit as you did.

GARLIC AND PETS   A clove or two crushed daily into your dog's food can:
- Reduce the population of intestinal worms, if fed along with a good nutritious diet.
- Stimulate better digestion and relieve the distress dogs sometimes suffer from overindulgence or eating improper food.
- Relieve a tendency toward constipation—often we don't realize that a dog suffers from this, particularly one that doesn't get enough exercise.
- Help some cases of bronchitis and tracheitis with coughing spells.
- Act as a natural pain reliever in dogs with painful hips.
- Help repel fleas. (I say "help," but if he's a walking city of these little nasties, you'll need more than garlic!)

GERANIUM LIFE IN WINTER   Don't let frost kill your geranium plants. There are several ways to carry geraniums through the winter months. Those methods are bare root, potting the entire plant, or propagation through cuttings.

Bare root requires removing plants from the garden before the first frost in the au-

tumn. Tie the plants in bundles and store them in a cellar or cool, moist area with temperatures of 45°F or less and humidity of 80 percent or higher.

In potting the entire plant, remove some of the root system. Cut back to six inches in height and place in a pot just large enough to hold the root system. Keep in a sunny window and water and fertilize as needed.

Cuttings of 3- or 4-inch terminal sections of stems may be rooted in perlite, peat moss, or sand. Water as needed and when well rooted, transplant to 4-inch pots and place in a sunny window.

GERMAN "LADY FINGER" POTA-TOES   These little yellow-fleshed potatoes were brought to the United States by early German settlers. Dainty little nuggets only one inch in diameter and a few inches long, they have a wonderful flavor and quality that is simply unique. They are far superior to any other potato when used in potato salad—and delicious fried as well. May be served boiled or baked. (Gurney's)

GETTING STUNG   Unless you are seriously allergic, in which case you should see your doctor, home remedies often help alleviate the pain of insect stings. Bee stings should be removed before treatment, using a small pair of forceps, a sterilized needle, the blade of a pen knife, or a clean fingernail. Ammonia is helpful against bees and horse flies. Dab it on or make a poultice: dampen a cloth with a strong solution of bicarbonate of soda. Vinegar or lemon juice is useful against wasp stings. You also may try rubbing with a slice of raw potato, particularly useful if you happen to be working in your garden. Another oldtime remedy is to simply rub the sting with damp earth.

GIANT ONION (*Allium giganteum*)   is really impressive, growing as high as 5 feet in early summer and bearing large violet flower heads. There are many delightful *Alliums* which may be planted among your flowers which will serve the same protective purpose as ordinary table onions. They are excellent for borders or at the back of flower beds if you use the taller ones.

Among the best are neapolitanum (white); azureum (blue); flavum (yellow); aflatunese and rosenbachianum (purple lilac); and albopilosum (violet). Shorter kinds for rock gardens and foreground planting are kartaviense (silvery lilac); moly (yellow); reseum grandiflorum (rose); stellatum (pink), and schoenoprasum (rosy purple). All grow best in a light, well-drained loam and most prefer sun. Divide and transplant when crowded: either fall or early spring. Most are very easy to grow.

GINGER (*Zingiberaceae officinale*) Fresh ginger is a snap to grow and you can do it in a flowerpot. A tropical plant, ginger does not grow in northern gardens but it can be grown quite successfully indoors. The root, a gnarled, dry-looking tuber, is light brown outside and pale yellow inside. It's the tuber you both plant and eat. You will often find them in the vegetable section of your supermarket. Try to choose a plump, shiny-skinned, healthy specimen, avoiding any that are shriveled or wrinkled.

Plant the root in a 6-inch container using a mixture of potting soil, sand, and humus. Bury it just beneath the surface, then give it a thorough soaking with warm water to settle and place in a south or west window. Its rate of growth is largely dependent on humidity and light and is more rapid in spring and summer, but some plants will do surprisingly well when planted in late fall.

Shoots eventually push their way through the soil and, if you're lucky, a sterile white flower will bloom at the end of each spike. Harvesting is also a snap. When the root fills the container, unpot the plant, cut off a two-to-three-inch piece to start a second crop. To store the root, keep it in a dry place or cut in thin slices and put in your freezer. Use the root with caution if you're not used to cooking with ginger. It's hot, spicy flavor is more powerful than commercially ground

ginger, but used correctly, it's absolutely marvelous for fresh gingerbread and pumpkin pie.

Ginger also is used to make ginger tea, a home remedy for stomache ache. Candied ginger is popular for putting in fruit cakes and then there are the drinks ginger ale and ginger beer. Oil of ginger is used as a medicine, internally for the stomach, and externally for pains like toothaches.

Wild ginger (*Asarum canadense*), common in American woodlands, is in the family *Aristolochiaceae*, a plant of the birthwort family, and is not related to true ginger. It grows in the shady woodlands of the northern United States. Like true ginger, its root is a stimulant, and it also is used as a spice.

GLAD TIDINGS Do you have trouble keeping your gladiolus standing upright? Here's a trick that will keep them in line. First, use your tulip setter to make the planting hole, then put the glad corm in the bottom (using kitchen tongs is helpful) and set in a soup can with both ends removed. Add just enough soil to cover the corm and fill in as it grows. This method also makes for easy watering if needful and the plants grow sturdy, strong, straight, and beautiful.

GLOXINIA (*Sinningia speciosa*) This is a lovely plant with its richly colored velvety leaves and large bell-shaped flowers. Gloxinia can be grown from seed as a houseplant. Sow seeds at 65°F to 75°F at any time of the year using milled sphagnum moss. Spring- and summer-sown plants bloom in five to six months; autumn and winter seven to eight months. Young plants grow best in no less than 70°F. Gloxinias love summer heat, humidity, and 16 hours of daylight. Shield from direct sunlight and wind at all times.

When bloom ceases, tend plant for three additional weeks and you will find a bulb has formed in the pot. Cut leaves off at bulb and keep it in pot in a dark place at 50°F to 60°F for six to eight weeks. Do not water. Then remove bulb carefully, use a 5- to 6-inch pot and plant in fresh, coarse sphagnum moss, covering top of bulb with ¼ inch of moss. Plant will soon bloom again.

GOBERNADORA (*Larrea mexicana, Corillea tridentala*)   This valuable antiseptic plant is native to the arid regions of the Coahuila Province of Mexico. It is known to contain tannin, silica, carbonic, anhidrade, phosphoric acid, chloride, potash, lime, magnesia, iron, and soda. It is a small low-growing shrub with very downy leaves (nature's way of conserving moisture), covered with a sort of resin, and has yellow flowers and very knotty stems. The flowers are eaten for their wholesome properties, and the leaves are aphrodisiac. The whole plant is strongly scented and the flowers are eaten as capers. Gobernadora is used to make soap and varnishes.

GOPHERS GONE   If you have a problem with gophers digging in your lawn or garden try this to discourage them: put two or three bulbs of garlic, several chili peppers and some water in your blender and blend well. Pour this down some of the gopher holes and rinse it down with a strong stream of water from the hose. It is seldom necessary to repeat the treatment.

GRAPES, AMERICAN BUNCH (*Vitis aestivalis*)   These varieties were derived primarily from wild grape species native to North America. Most have some mixture of European varieties in their ancestry. You, as a home gardener, should know about them, for they are one of the most popular and extensively grown fruits in home plantings. They are easy to grow (just what the fun-loving gardener needs!), bear early and regularly, and are small but long-lived plants. Insects and diseases are usually easily controlled.

The grapes are grown for fresh fruit and for wine, juice, jams, jellies, and frozen products. Many of us know them by the name "Concord," and they are grown over a far wider area than other types of grapes.

Growing American bunch grapes is limited or entirely unsatisfactory only in arid sections without irrigation, locations with very short growing seasons, locations with extremely severe winter temperatures, areas with high temperatures and extremely high humidity. The grapes are susceptible to several diseases which thrive under hot, humid conditions.

Grapes will grow, and grow well, in many different soils. The fertile, deep, and well-drained loams are best, but soils that contain sand, gravel, shale, slate, or clay can also be used. Avoid extremely wet or extremely dry soils. Good drainage, which also includes good air circulation, is essential.

Varieties derived mainly from *V. riparia*, the frost grape, are adapted to Northern areas. The fruit tends to be small but ripens early, and the vines are extremely cold hardy. Varieties derived mainly from *V. labrusca*, the fox grape, include many of the varieties best adapted to the North and Midwest. The fruit is large and usually has some of the "foxy" flavor characteristic of Concord. Most varieties adapted to the South are derived from the species *V. rupestris*, *V. champini*, *V. lincecumii*, and *V. bourguiniana*. The fruit is medium size and ripens late. The vines may sometimes lack winter hardiness.

Grapes are natural "swingers"!

"GRAY WATER"   If, during a drought, you may no longer use fresh water to irrigate outdoor plantings, you can safely use "gray water" (household bath or laundry water, even dish water) if you're reasonably careful. Avoid, for example, the use of wash water containing chlorine bleach or high levels of boron (found in many laundry detergents) and sodium (salt); if such water must be used, dilute it first with water from the rinse cycle or other source, such as collected rainwater.

Be sure the plants you water really *need* it. Lawns, for example, though they turn brown, survive for long periods without supplemental moisture. The woody plants in your landscape, such as azaleas, are probably the plants which need water the most.

GREENHOUSE WISDOM Sooner or later every gardener has a yearning for a greenhouse, so give in—a small greenhouse is within the reach of nearly all gardeners. Windowboxes add cheer and gaiety to a home so build yourself a small box and grow your own plants in it—the exact varieties you want. A larger greenhouse will enable you not only to grow your own plants but often you can raise enough to sell to your neighbors, or trade for something they have but you don't. During the hot summer days, apply a shading compound to your glass roof to keep the sun out. Most garden supply houses handle shading compounds. A low night temperature (45°F to 50°F) is ideal for most plants. During the day a temperature of 65°F to 80°F will keep them comfortable. Good ventilation is important in a greenhouse or coldframe, so plan for this. Liquid feeding is simple, effective, and a timesaver for those who own a small greenhouse. Don't be afraid to change greenhouse bench soil, or to use new soil in porch or windowboxes. Disease organisms tend to build up on used soils, unless you sterilize them.

Pay a visit to a successful commercial greenhouse operator and learn some of his tricks; his experience can help you get more mileage from your greenhouse efforts. Often you can learn a lot as well by reading the literature offered by commercial suppliers of greenhouses, seeds and related topics—a wealth of information free for the asking. Ask your librarian to help you select some good books on greenhouse growing.

GREEN MANURE Both winter rye and perennial rye grass make excellent green-manure crops. Both can be sown anytime from midsummer until frost, and are perfectly hardy through the winter. Rye germinates somewhat faster and makes a more rapid early growth. It is coarser and more difficult to dig under in the spring if the job is not done early. Rye produces more bulk in a shorter time than rye grass, but both are satisfactory.

GROUND CHERRY (*Physalis pruinosa*) Ground cherries, also known as husk tomatoes, make a highly decorative garden addition with their delicate parchment lanterns, each of which contains one golden fruit. Plant after danger of frost is past, spacing 12 to 18 inches apart. Plants may be staked or allowed to roam. When harvesting, gently shake the plant and you can easily pick up the ripe fruit. Kept clean by their parchment coats, a gentle pinch at the stem end causes the golden cherry-sized fruit to pop out. Delicious eaten raw or in salads, they freeze well and may also be used for pies and preserves.

GROWTH HORMONE When setting new cuttings to root (to get new plants), place a few grains of wheat near the base of each slip (sometimes called "clone"). The originator of this idea maintains that the wheat, as it germinates, gives off a hormone that promotes new root growth.

GUAYULE (*Parthenium argentatum*), a shrub native to the Southwest desert, is a plant with commercial possibilities. It is a source of natural rubber that can be used in the manufacture of numerous products. It also produces wax, cork, and fiber. Guayule rubber is distributed throughout the entire plant in the individual cells rather than in latex tubes or vessels. It is used as an emergency rubber plant. The rubber produced is highly resinous and must be deresinated to extend its general usefulness. The leaves are useful as fertilizer, as top-dressing, or for composting material. The seeds have a protein content of 11 to 14 percent and are useful as animal feed.

The soil welcomes the seed and guayule is locally abundant in calcareous deserts in the southwestern United States and the adjacent central plateau of Mexico. It is cultivated in the Salinas Valley in California, Arizona, New Mexico, and Texas. It also has been introduced and cultivated in Australia, Turkey, Russia, Italy, Spain, and Argentina.

Guayule is a shrub or perennial herb, living thirty to forty years. In its native habitat it is restricted to limestone soils in regions having rainfall of 25 to 37 cm per year, with most of the effective rain falling in the summer. But plants will grow better with higher rainfall and in more fertile soil. However, the rubber content will be lower unless the plant is given moisture for a few months to grow and then allowed to become dry. Guayule must have a growth period and a dormancy period during which the rubber is produced. Guayule cannot tolerate waterlogging even when caused by irrigation practices.

GYNOECIOUS CUCUMBERS ANYONE? Gynoecious cucumber varieties produce all female flowers and usually are very productive. A standard variety must also be planted to pollinate the gynoecious plants and assure a good crop. You can't tell the seeds of the pollinator from the others. Burpee Hybrid II, Early Pride hybrid, Burpeana Hybrid II, and Streamliner Hybrid are all examples. There is a good mixture of seeds in each packet, so you just plant any six or more seeds to make sure you are growing plants of both varieties. It's lots of fun to grow these cucumbers, especially if you like salads and pickles.

Here at my feet what wonders pass,
What endless, active life is here!
What blowing daisies, fragrant grass!
An ant-stirred forest, fresh and clear.
MATTHEW ARNOLD

HANGING BASKET HELP   This moist midair cushion will fend the fiercest blast: for insulation and extra moisture put the plant in a clay pot two inches smaller, center it in the basket, then fill the space between with vermiculite kept moist. This way soil in the pot does not dry quickly, and plants do not wilt in hot wind.

HAY   How often have you heard the expression "big as a barn door"? And have you ever wondered why they were so big? Actually, the doors had to be large so a loaded hay wagon could drive into the barn. The man-sized door, cut into the big door, is called "the eye of the needle," and is useful for admitting both humans and barn cats. (Cats are an essential part of farming operations, for mice like to hole up in barns.)

Most of us are so busy trying to produce succulent vegetables and tasty fruits that we seldom give a thought to hay. What bread is to man, so hay is to the animals we have domesticated. And hay is not merely food, it is also medicine.

What is hay? For one thing it is not a herb. It is composed of dried grasses and wildflowers. It is often highly aromatic, the scents at cutting time alone give belief to its mystical powers, a comforting fragrance for the animals for whom it is gathered and stored. As food the cereal grains and grasses are important to us also. Barley, buckwheat, oats, rice, wheat, and corn figure more often in our diets than we may realize. Alfalfa products are medicinal both for humans and animals.

Hay to be at its best should never be kiln-dried. It should be stored in mounds, shaped like old-time bee skeps, and daily turned and tossed until fully and naturally weathered and dried. This is *true* hay, with juice and body, and the vitality only carefully seasoned hay possesses!

Hay, as a nutritious, mineral-rich, and medicinal fodder, maintains animals during times when inclement weather makes grazing impossible (as when land is under snow or frost). It also lines animals' stomachs with bulk food to prevent "blow" or colic when animals are to feed on pastures that are dew-wet or very lush. Hay's healing properties are also released when it is steamed, but care should be taken not to spoil it by letting it get overly hot. The addition of honey is also helpful.

Another medicinal hay which is not a grass but an herb is nettle hay. This old-fashioned but effective sheep tonic, also valuable for other animals, is made from two parts cooked hay and one part nettle greens. Cover mixture with water, heat gently but do not allow to boil. After ten minutes on the heat, let it stand to brew. When tepid, strain, sweeten with two tablespoons honey or molasses, and use in the drinking troughs.

HEELING IN   This is the temporary planting of trees or plants, close together, in a trench or hole, with at least the roots covered and properly watered. It serves to tide plants over an interval between their arrival and permanent planting. If so kept over winter, they should be set in a little deeper and covered, overall, with a thick layer of straw, leaves, or other mulch.

HERBAL BEAUTY   David Conway, writing in *The Magic of Herbs*, tells us that common burdock (*Arctium minus*), made into an infusion and used externally, provides a soothing skin and scalp lotion.

Burnet (*Sanguisorba officinalis*), used as an infusion, promotes the healing of wounds and will cure most skin ailments.

Chamomile (*Anthemis nobilis*), prepared as an infusion, is useful as a facewash, for clearing the complexion, and, as a rinse, for lightening fair hair and adding highlights. (Sage is a fine rinse for brunettes.)

Chickweed (*Stellaria media*), infused, refines the texture of the skin when it is applied as a face lotion.

Cleavers (*Galium aparine*) is a good tonic for the scalp, helping to clear dandruff, and may be used as a skin lotion.

Garlic (*Allium sativum*), which seems to be good for just about everything, will also rid the skin of parasites. Taken internally it promotes skin beauty, and it's easy to grow.

Heartsease (*Viola tricolor*), used as a lotion, heals sores and other skin ailments. There are many other herbs helpful to skin, but what about eyes?

Comfrey (*Eupatorium perfoliatum*) combined with boneset is helpful to eye injuries. You may use an infusion of the leaves or a decoction from the bruised root.

Loosestrife (*Lythrum salicaria*). According to Culpepper, this herb was one of the best for the sight, and it is still used, often in the company of eyebright (*Euphrasia officinalis*), as an eye lotion. Use half an once of herb to half a pint of boiling, slightly salty water. Steep thirty minutes, strain and use.

Other useful eye herbs are lady's mantle (*Alchemilla vulgaris*), lovage (*Ligustrum scoticum*), summer savory (*Satureja hortensis*), and mugwort (*Artemisia vulgaris*). Pimpernell (*Amagallis arvensis*) was a favorite eye herb of the ancient Greeks, who used it in the treatment of many eye diseases. It has cosmetic properties as a skin lotion, the infusion regulating pigmentation, and is helpful in the removal of freckles and other minor blemishes. It also has a reputation as a hair restorer.

Try a slice of potato on tired eyes. This is particularly soothing after facing or working with a bright light.

Maidenhair fern (*Adiantum capillus-veneris*), infused, may be used as a scalp lotion to improve the hair and stop premature baldness. The leaves, eaten raw, are said to have a therapeutic effect on the heart and lungs.

Rosemary (*Rosmarinus officinalis*) has a well-deserved reputation as a fine skin tonic for the scalp and a lotion for the complexion, adding lustre to the hair. It is a common ingredient even today of many commercial shampoos.

Elder (*Sambucus nigra*): a balm of elder flowers is said to keep crow's feet at bay, and the berries are soothing to burns and scalds.

Tansy (*Tanacetum vulgare*), used medicinally, is said to improve the circulation and is invaluable in treating varicose veins. It may be applied externally to varicose veins as well and to bruises, styes, and minor swellings.

Seakale (*Crambe maritima*), a mineral-rich herb, is used to fight an assortment of ills, including dental decay, general debility, and rheumatism. Raw in salads it is laxative, so use discretion. Used as a mouthwash it strengthens gums, heals ulcers, and fights against oral infection.

Strawberry (*Fragaria vesca*) is rich in minerals and antiseptic. The juice is used in treating serious skin ailments such as eczema and pruritis. An infusion of the leaves is helpful in curing styes. Even discolored teeth encrusted with tartar may be cleaned with strawberry juice.

The "standard infusion" herein referred to: Pour a pint of water over an ounce of dried herb leaves, or three handfuls of fresh, and leave the mixture for three or four hours. Cut large leaves and finely chop tough herbs before using. Strain. Infusions will usually keep for three of four days (refrigerate in hot weather). They should be poured into bottles and stored in a cool, dark place. Do not cork tightly but place a piece of muslin or perforated greaseproof paper over their tops. Decoctions are made from the hard parts of the herb, stems, roots, bark, and seeds, and they must be boiled for some time to extract their full value.

HERBAL FREEZE Here's a fun way to preserve fresh herbs. Blend them with a little water and freeze in ice-cube trays. Transfer frozen cubes to plastic bags or freezer containers. Drop cubes into soups, spaghetti sauce, stews for color and flavor of fresh herbs. And they look beautiful, too, in iced drinks like lemonade, tea, or mint julep.

HERBAL GIFTS The calming effects of several fragrant herbs have long been used in association with headaches. Lemon verbena, steeped in alcohol, has long been a favorite for mopping the troubled brow. Another custom of years gone by is the small "peace pillows." Small pillows of dried balsam, pine, and chamomile were made to be placed

under the larger bed pillow and their aroma was said to be very relaxing and an aid to sleep. Even today, a small yellow flower native to Switzerland called life-everlasting (*Anaphalis margaritaceae*) is greatly in demand for use in peace pillows. This flower supposedly releases an "ozone" that is most welcome to the sleepless. A peace pillow would be a delightful gift for an invalid, a sick friend, or those who live in a nursing home.

> When chamber is swept
> And Wormwood is thrown,
> No flea for his life—
> Dare abide to be known!
> Old Elizabethan saying

HERBAL REPELLENTS Wormwood has been used since earliest times by wool manufacturers to protect their cloth from clothes moths. And a water spray of wormwood is said to keep beetles and weevils out of granaries. Wormwood is also an ingredient of a popular liniment used to rub on bruises and sore muscles. Both mice and rats are repelled by wormwood, lavender, corn chamomile, fresh or dried leaves of mints or their oils, pitch pine, and camphor.

Cats dislike the odor of rue and it is helpful rubbed on furniture to keep them from clawing upholstery. Oldtimers plant catnip near barns to repel rats. Plain water is somewhat effective against red spider. One Early American gardener used tobacco tea, reporting good results. Sulphur and garlic were effective against moles according to Albertus Magnus. Pliny declared thyme, when burnt, would put to flight all venemous creatures.

HERBAL SUNSCREEN An herbal sunscreen? Recently my friend Howard Garrett, who hosts his radio program "The Natural Way" over station WBAP, Dallas, Texas, asked me if I knew of an herbal sunscreen. At the moment I could not give an answer. However, always intrigued by a challenging question, I was soon off and running, excited by a new idea for research.

I did find an answer. And the following Sunday, when he interviewed me, I was just bubbling over with my newly acquired knowledge.

Flower Essence Services (see "Sources") whose motto is "Body-mind wellness through Nature's living archetypes," lists among their products Saint John's Wort Flower Oil. "Saint John's Wort is a plant long-esteemed in herbal tradition for protection at times of too much vulnerability and openness. . . . *[The oil] makes an excellent sunscreen*, shielding from an overly intense light and is helpful also in sleep disturbances. Many people like to apply the oil directly to the body or disperse it in a warm bath."

Flower Essence Services lists many other helpful herbal oils and sachets such as mugwort flower oil, a sister remedy to St. John's Wort, helpful applied to sore muscles and bruises and dandelion massage oil, helpful for releasing strain and constriction of the body. Prepared in a base of peanut and olive oils, it is blended with rosemary essential oil and castor oil for extra warmth and penetration.

HERBAL TEAS   The delightful English custom of "taking tea" became popularized when black tea became available as a luxury import. But "tisanes," as they are known in France, have been popular for much longer as enjoyable beverages. They are calorie- and caffeine-free, health giving, and refreshing to both the body and the spirit. The Shepherd Seed Company offers four pleasurable possibilities for herbs that can be grown in the garden: lemon balm, a sweetly cordial lemon flavor with citrus aroma; cinnamon basil, an exotic flowering basil making a rich spicy tea; chamomile (beloved of our grandmothers for curing a headache), very restorative with an apple/pineapple scent; and anise hyssop, with lovely lavender flowers and green leaves for naturally sweet anise-scented tea.

"Many herb gardeners," says Renee Shepherd, "don't worry about measuring exactly. They simply take the teapot out into the garden and fill it loosely with an im-promptu blend of their favorite herbal leaves and flowers. Try mixing tea herbs in different combinations and strengths to suit your pleasure." Here in the Southwest iced teas are very popular in the summer months—we tea lovers like to set a big glass jar of freshly made herbal tea in the sun to steep. "Sun tea" makes a fine base to keep on hand to drink iced on hot summer days.

To make herbal tea bring cool water to an audible rolling boil. Rinse out a glass or china teapot with hot water to warm it. Add herb leaves and flowers using about 2 tablespoons fresh herb or 1 tablespoon dried herb per cup, plus an extra 2 tablespoons fresh or 1 dry "for the pot." Pour boiling water over the herbs and brew or steep for about 3 to 5 minutes, tasting occasionally until it is to your liking. Strain out leaves as you pour each cupful. For iced tea follow the same directions but make the tea stronger, 3 tablespoons fresh or 2 dried.

To dry herbs pick as soon as the dew has dried and hang small bundles of leafy branches out of the sun in a shaded place where the air will circulate freely. When leaves are crackling dry, strip from the branches, crumble, and store in glass jars. Be sure to keep out of direct sunlight.

HERB GARDEN GUIDE   Dill, marjoram, mint, basil, rosemary, chives, sage, summer and winter savory, tarragon, and thyme are popular for cooking; lavender, lemon balm, lemon verbena, and scented geraniums for their fragrances. They are easy to grow from seed but you may be more successful starting with small plants. Most herbs require full sun and average, well-drained soil. In nutrition-rich soil, herbs produce a lot of foliage, but their flavor and fragrance is less potent.

Prepare your soil bed by working in well-rotted manure or compost. Spread about 3 inches over the garden and turn under, digging down about 10 inches into soil. One or two plants of each perennial herb is generally enough. Perennial plants tend to spread over the years, so space them accordingly.

For basil, parsley, or herbs you especially like, you may want to reserve larger sections. Care of established plants is minimal and consists mostly of keeping down weeds or an occasional watering.

Unless you are growing a herb for its flowers, such as lavender, pinch off flower buds as flowering diminishes flavor and fragrance potency and causes plants to become spindly with tiny tough leaves. During summer, harvest leaves as needed. Pruning encourages bushy growth. Plants will often overwinter successfully if covered in late fall with evergreen boughs.

HERB JAR Here's an easy way to make your own strawberry jar herb garden. All you need is a set of nested clay pots, pebbles, and soil. Cover the bottom of the largest pot with pebbles. Then place the next size pot inside, filling around the edges with soil. Continue this procedure for the remaining pots, making sure there's enough soil around each pot to hold plants. Succulents, as well as small herbs, will do especially well in your homemade strawberry jar.

HERBS IN OIL For thousands of years the only way people could hold herbs for future use has been to dry them. Preserving in oil is an alternative and gives more lasting flavor. For success you must follow these rules but the results are well worth the care. Begin with proper harvesting:
1. Harvest can begin any time after there is sufficient growth so plants can withstand cutting. Do not cut too closely on any one plant.
2. Midmorning is the best time, after moisture has burned off, but before the sun causes wilting.
3. Do not wash cut herbs unless absolutely necessary. Then, shake off moisture and air dry. Washing may be avoided by giving the plant a good rinse the evening before cutting.
4. Don't cut more than you can handle.
5. Scissors are better than pinching off. If there are blossoms on the herbs, it is all right to use these also.

Any vegetable oil you prefer (except olive oil) can be used for blending. The ratio is about ½ cup of good quality cooking oil to about 2 hard-packed cups of fresh herbs. Oil should be added gradually, using only as much as is necessary to achieve a texture similar to that of heavy cream. Mix well in a blender or food processor, then seal the herbal concentrate in airtight containers and store in freezer or refrigerator. To prevent mold always be sure to return your herbal oils to freezer or refrigerator quickly after each use.

The best herbs for preserving in oil are dill, tarragon, oregano, sage, mints, marjoram, and lemon thyme. For smaller herbs you may add fresh parsley for bulk. Combinations of herbs also work well. Try a blend of thyme, marjoram, and savory for basting poultry—especially delightful when parsley and chives are also added. Basil, rosemary, and oregano are great for pasta dishes and also may be used for chicken. When combining herbs do not use more than one or two very strong-flavored specimens. Be sure to label your jars, listing the ingredients used.

Using your herbal oils:

- About one teaspoon per pound may be added to meats or vegetables.
- Use as part of total oil measurement in salad dressing.
- Use as part of total oil measurement for sautéeing meats or fresh vegetables.
- Herbal oils are delightful stirred into sour cream or cream cheese, then add salt and garlic if desired for a great dip with chips or raw vegetables.

Orange-mint or apple-mint oil is delicious with carrots cooked with a little butter and honey. Either one is wonderful with English peas or in fruit-salad dressing. Or try in vanilla custard over fruit.

HIGH-ALTITUDE GARDENING This can be a pain in the neck, but many crops actually taste better when grown a mile high! So, if you live "way up there," plan well. Grow tomatoes in a protected place; a wall that provides reflected heat and light helps.

Use a determinant (bush type) early yielder and get a head start indoors. You might try Gurney's Cold Set, Fantastic, or Early Girl. For lettuce, the loose head varieties like Buttercrunch and Valamaine do best. Peas such as Early Alaska and Early All Sweet which mature quickly and also bush types of green beans are good possibilities. Broccoli, brussels sprouts, and cauliflower will mature if started in the house and transplanted early. You can even grow corn such as Early Sunglow and the marvelous-flavored Kandy Korn for a later crop. Cucumbers need warm sunshine but Nantes carrots will grow well if planted early. Also experiment with different varieties of short-season crops and you can have just as good a garden as any lowlander. One more tip: plan well for irrigation as rainfall may be scanty during the summer months in some high-altitude areas.

HIGH-ALTITUDE WATERING   When my garden crops grow waist- or knee-high is just about the time summer starts and natural rainfall quits. To get enough altitude to do a thorough job of watering over a large area I take my kitchen stepladder to the garden and put my sprinkler on top of it, covering the top of the stepladder with a piece of plastic to preserve it from the wetting.

HONEYBEES AND HAYFEVER   There is a theory that hayfever sufferers who eat honey produced within a few miles of their homes will find that it alleviates their misery. The pollen of the flowers and weeds, which the honeybee makes into honeycomb, is believed to provide a natural antitoxia.

HONEYBEES AND INSECTICIDES   Insecticides that are hazardous to bees include carbaryl (Sevin), diazinon, malathion, and ethion. Those that are not harmful include kelthane and sulfur. Insecticides should not be used whenever possible. Sprays and granules should be applied rather than dusts in areas where bees are foraging.

HONEYSUCKLE (*Lonicera* spp.)   These vigorous climbers are widely renowned for

Lonicera caprifolium

the fragrance of their blossoms and *L. fragantissima* is one of the sweetest of them all. Sometimes called the winter honeysuckle, its creamy-white, lemon-scented blossoms appear in late March or early April, lasting three to four weeks. They are followed by small red fruits, extending its attractiveness. The everblooming *L. Heckrottii* has bright carmine buds that open to reveal yellow inside, giving a lovely two-tone effect to its fragrant clusters. Dropmore scarlet is an extremely hardy, everblooming honeysuckle developed in Manitoba, Canada. The long-tubed, brilliant scarlet flowers cover the vine. *L. Henryi* is a dependable evergreen viner that holds its dark green leaves well through the winter in the colder parts of the country. *L. japonica* 'Halliana,' often called Hall's honeysuckle, is an old favorite growing well and rapidly in sun or shade.

There is even a honeysuckle that makes an excellent groundcover. *L. pileata*, royal carpet honeysuckle, is truly an aristocrat with dark, shiny evergreen leaves. (Wayside Gardens)

HOPS (*Humulus*) I often wonder why this vine is not more often planted. Both annual and perennial hops thrive in ordinary garden soil, but grow more vigorously in a deep soil enriched with manure. Hop plants grow very quickly. Arches, pillars, porches, verandas, arbors, and horizontal wires supporting perpendicular strings provide a means of support for the plants, which make excellent screens. The hops used in brewing are cultivated varieties. The variety aureus has golden-yellow leaves and is an ornamental-leaved climber.

HORSERADISH, HOME GROWN AND HOT This member of the mustard family is often found wild, growing along streams, in meadows, and in other moist locations. It makes a really tasty condiment for meat and fish courses and is one of our most valuable concentrated foods, being an excellent solvent of excessive mucus in the system, especially in the nasal and sinus cavities. It is recommended for colds, coughs, and asthma. This wonderful vegetable stimulates appetite as it aids in the secretion of digestive juices. The best preparation of horseradish is to grate it very finely and combine with equal amounts of lemon juice, taking one-quarter teaspoon four times daily. There's no match for the fiery flavor of fresh ground horseradish roots.

To grow roots of horseradish really well you will need plenty of moisture, a deep, fertile loam soil, deep cultivation, and careful weeding. In planting, the roots are placed with the upper end of the cutting 2 to 5 inches below the soil surface, packing the soil firmly to ensure good contact and resultant prompt growth. For long, straight roots you must maintain a deep, mellow soil. Gardeners usually dig just a few roots at a time, allowing the remainder to lay in the soil, since the root is hardy.

HOSE-COVERED CHERRIES This idea is really *not* for the birds. Birds are notoriously fond of cherries and often eat most of them, spoiling the rest. Tom Alston of Bicknacre in Essex, England, found a novel way to protect his cherries by cutting the legs off his wife's old pantyhose. He then draws them carefully over the fruit on his cherry tree before it ripens. By this method the owner of the tree also gets his share.

HOTHOUSES FOR FREE Save clear plastic grocery and dry cleaner bags to make inexpensive temporary hothouses. Place started seed pots or cartons inside bags to retain moisture. Aluminum foil reflectors may be made by stapling foil to cardboard of appropriate size for plants set in a window; foil reflects sunlight back on plants causing stems to grow straight instead of leaning. Or cut front from a cardboard box and line back and sides with foil, placing plants inside box.

HOT PEPPERS DE-HEATED *Capsaicin*, present in great quantities in hot peppers, causes the hotness. It is found in tiny, blisterlike sacs between the lining and the inner wall of the pepper. Can anything take it out? Not entirely, but it can be decreased in those you grow in your own garden.

Roll a fresh chile pepper on the table as if you were rolling dough. This is to dislodge the seeds and break the capsaicin sacs. Then take a sharp knife, cut the pepper from near the stem end down to the bottom. Cut only the wall; don't cut pepper into pieces. Repeat cut in two other places. This gives you a pepper in three sections, held together by the stem end. Hold by the stem and dip the pepper into a glass of water. After a minute or so the pepper should be ready to eat, the water washing out the seeds and much of the capsaicin. If it is still too hot for your taste, repeat dipping.

HOT SPOTS   Have you a garden hot spot? The one location that never seems to look anything but awful. What you need are annual flowers that will thrive in hot, dry locations, something that will provide unceasing bloom in a most inhospitable environment. Try verbena and vinca. Suggestions are 'Sangria' verbena, an All-American award winner that comes in a rich red wine color unique to the verbena family, and 'Little Rosie' vinca, which produces deep violet-red flowers, however hot or dry the summer.

HOUSEPLANTS,   after summering outdoors, need a gradual introduction to indoor conditions. A few weeks before frost is expected bring them in at night and take them back out as long as the days are warm. Prune back any straggly growth, rinse thoroughly in tub or shower, and watch them carefully for signs of insect problems.

HOUSEPLANTS AND POLLUTION
Did you know that houseplants can help fight indoor air pollution? Some of the best at fighting are spider plant, golden pothos, peace lily, and Chinese evergreen.

HOUSEPLANT "COMPOST"   So you are an apartment dweller with neither garden nor outside space in which to make compost! Try these organic foods for soil and plants, most of which you've probably been throwing away:

Cigar and cigarette ash, in small quantities, are good additives to houseplant soil, containing potassium, which enables leaves to remain green.

Coffee grounds, used and well washed, are good for plants that need an acid soil. Dry them in a low oven and mix in with the rest of the soil.

Peanut shells, both the outer husk and the inside skin, mixed in with the potting soil help aeration and are beneficial as they decompose.

Eggshells can be crunched up and mixed with the soil, or you can make a liquid fertilizer of them. Fill a glass jar halfway with shells and then add enough water to fill the jar. Cover and let stand three weeks in a dark place and then use the liquid to water your houseplants.

Tea bags—houseplants love tea too! Save used tea bags, dry them, and then pour hot water over them. Cool water and use to water houseplants. Miniature roses, in particular, just love this treatment.

Beer is another natural nutrient. Collect the stale beer left over in glasses or cans, add water, and douse your plants and they can have their own beerfest. Beer, diluted, can be used as a leaf-wash and conditioner; try a half and half mix and use it on fully matured leaves but not on new growth. Do not wash fuzzy or downy leaves, these should be gently brushed with a fine brush.

Milk is also a leaf cleanser that puts a shine on solid-surface foliage.

If you live in a hard-water area, catch *rainwater* or use melted snow on your houseplants, they'll love you for it.

Carrot tops, potato peelings, outer leaves of cabbage, lettuce, citrus rinds are all compostable. Layer them with some purchased garden soil, if you have none, in a plastic can, turn them occasionally and you have compost for plants.

Cigarette smoke will do in the bugs in an infected terrarium or bottle garden. Just blow the smoke down the spout, replace the cork or cover the opening with foil, and the nicotine, trapped inside, will do in the bugs.

Music?   I don't really know, but it's a nice idea. Some say high-frequency sounds persuade plants to open their pores wider and keep them open longer, thus providing stimulation. This could be fun to try if you have a budding pianist or violin player in the house.

HUMUS Whole books have been written about humus, what it is, and how to make it. Essentially humus is organic matter in a more advanced stage of decomposition than compost in its early stages. In a compost heap some of the organic matter has turned to humus, but generally the remaining portion will complete the decomposition process after it has been placed in the soil, often aided by earthworms. The most noticeable difference between humus and organic matter is that the latter is rough-looking material, such as coarse plant matter, while in the humus form we find something that has turned into a more uniform-looking substance. Humus is very beneficial for almost all plants, having good moisture-holding capacity and various nutrients and minerals, depending on the sources from which it has been made.

Appetite furnishes the best sauce
—Typee Indian Wisdom

HUSH PUPPIES are a Southern legend with many versions of how they got their name. Back in the old days just about every farmer and rancher kept a pack of dogs. They were used for many purposes but most everyone was especially prideful about their hunters, with many stories to tell and friendly competition about who had the best. But hunting wasn't the only recreation—fishing down by the crick was a pastime frequently indulged in as well, and naturally the dogs went along.

Now there just ain't anythin' better than fresh-caught fish, cleaned and plopped into a deep vat of fat bubbling over a fire on the bank of a stream. A warm spring day and the aroma of the frying fish wafting on the air gave everybody a great appetite—and that included the dogs. A hungry hound jest natcherally sets up a-howling—how can you blame him when your own mouth is a-waterin'?

Well, the story is that the dogs, attracted by that great smell would gather around and to quiet them the cook would throw them bits of fried dough of another southern dish—cornmeal mush—with the command, "Hush puppies!"

Of course you can make hush puppies and fry them in some purified oil but to be really authentic they should be fried in the same oil as the fresh-caught fish—you just can't beat the original way of doing things. Try it sometime and give yourself a treat using this really great hush puppy recipe:

Texhoma Hush Puppies

2 cups cornmeal (once called "Indian meal")
2 tablespoons flour
1 teaspoon baking powder
1 teaspoon salt
1 large egg, beaten
1 cup buttermilk
4 tablespoons minced red onions
1 tablespoon finely chopped jalapeno pepper

Blend together dry ingredients. Add egg, buttermilk, onion, and pepper. Mix well. Drop by tablespoons in deep fat (preferably in which fish has been fried), heated to 375°F. Fry until golden brown, remove and drain on paper towels. Serve piping hot.

I know a little garden close,
Set thick with lily and red rose,
Where I would wander if I might,
From dewy morn to dewy night.
WILLIAM MORRIS

ICE CUBE TIP Potted plants that sometimes form thick root masses (such as asparagus fern), or whose roots store water (like amaryllis), may not absorb enough water because it drains through the pot. Instead of watering such plants, pile some ice cubes in the pots. As the cubes melt, the roots will absorb the moisture. Ice will not harm the plants as long as you keep it away from the stems.

ICELAND MOSS (*Cetraria islandica*) A water spray of Iceland moss, a lichen, has been used to destroy eggs of leaf-eating caterpillars on trees. A pound is boiled for an hour in five gallons of water, more water being added as needed to maintain a constant volume.

IMPATIENS (*Impatiens*) By now most of us know that the native jewelweed (*Impatiens capensis*) is useful to treat poison ivy. However, for those who live where jewelweed is not native, an even more powerful remedy may be found in the ornamental impatiens hybrid Futura (Park Seed), which may be grown as a pot plant. Futura, which comes in a galaxy of colors, produces blossoms 1½ to 2 inches across on 8- to 10-inch plants. It is compact growing and free flowering. Great for hanging baskets, it will grow well even in heavy shade, thriving under the same conditions as tuberous begonias. Easy to progagate by cuttings, they will also grow from seed.

To use, take a one inch or smaller leaf, crush to produce enough juice to treat the affected area. Relief from itching is usually immediate and blistering generally dries up within 48 hours.

INCREDIBLE SOYBEAN Soybeans are one of the principle sources of lecithin, the almost magical substance that is known to have an emulsifying action on fats, which helps keep the arteries free of cholesterol deposits.

Soybeans are easy to grow, sprout quickly and grow lush just like other beans, but they do take a long season to mature and dry on the vine. Fiskeby V is earlier and well suited to Northern gardens. Like limas they are bushier than other beans.

To shell soybeans, dip pods in boiling water for a few minutes and they'll give up their beans easily. Dried on the vines you can thresh and winnow them like other dry beans and store them in airtight containers. Return vines to the compost heap.

In addition to cooking, soybeans can also be toasted and eaten like peanuts, or used for bean sprouts. For this, Burpee recommends their bush soybean, Prize. Soybeans may also be frozen or canned.

INDIAN COOKERY Several years ago while attending the annual Festival of the Plains Indians at Anadarko, Oklahoma, we were privileged to partake of the evening meal with an Indian family camping in "Tent City"—an area set aside by the city of Anadarko to accommodate its many Indian visitors, usually 500 or more.

For me the high point of the meal was "fry bread," which I found delicious. It's something like an unsweetened doughnut with a crispy brown crust and a breadlike texture inside. Mrs. Campbell, our hostess, explained how it was made, showing me how to pinch off a golf-ball-sized bit from the large roll of dough, dexterously pat it with her fingers, cut a slit in the center, and place it in the skillet. The grease was a combination of pork lard and beef tallow, and the wood used was blackjack, which makes a very hot fire. Here is the recipe for the Chickasaw version:

Chickasaw Fry Bread

2 cups flour
1 teaspoon salt
3 teaspoons baking powder
1 cup milk or water

Combine flour, salt, and baking powder. Add liquid and stir all together to make a stiff dough. Turn out on a floured board and pat down to ½-inch thickness with floured hands. Cut into strips or squares and slit middle of each. Fry in deep, hot fat until brown on both sides, like a doughnut. This bread is served with a main dish or eaten with syrup as a dessert.

This main dish was another Indian favorite.

Wild Onions and Scrambled Eggs

1 cup green onions, using both stems and
  tops, chopped
12 eggs
1 teaspoon salt
½ cup bacon drippings (I use canola oil)

Dig wild onions in spring. Clean onions, wash thoroughly, and cut into lengths of 1 to 1½ inches. Place in small amount of water and boil from 3 to 5 minutes. Drain. Place in preheated skillet with bacon drippings, add the well-beaten, salted eggs, and cook until eggs are done. Serve hot. The flavor of wild onions is milder than the garden variety and the flavor is distinctly their own. Look for them on the damp prairie and along small streams in early spring.

The many wild greens and other plants the Indians utilized are still right out there waiting for us but now we must be careful not to pick any that have been sprayed. Be especially careful of roadside plants.

Other wild greens that may be prepared are "Poke salit" (salad)—pick only young, tender shoots (stalks and leaves)—sour dock, dandelion (including flower buds), wild lettuce, tops of wild beets, lamb's-quarter, and wild mustard.

Pashofa

Pashofa, which is both the name of the food served and the social gathering, is usually cooked in a huge iron kettle for it is a great Indian favorite.

1 pound cracked corn (pearl hominy)
1 pound fresh lean pork (preferably meaty
  back bone)
2 quarts water (add more as needed)

Wash and clean corn. Bring water to boil and add corn. Cook slowly, stirring often. When corn is about half done add fresh pork. Cook until meat and corn are tender and soft. Mixture should be thick and soupy. Cooking time about 4 hours (plenty of time for socializing). Add no salt while cooking: it is customary for each individual to salt to his own taste when *Pashofa* is served.

Banaha

My friend, Mrs. Neoma Rainwater, gave me this recipe for "shuck bread":

2 cups cornmeal
1 teaspoon soda
1½cups hot water
1 teaspoon salt
Cleaned corn shucks should be boiled
   about 10 minutes before using

Mix dry ingredients; add water until mixture is stiff enough to handle easily. Form small oblong balls about the size of a tennis ball, and wrap in corn shucks. Tie in middle with corn shuck string. Drop covered balls into a deep pot of boiling water. Cover and cook 40 minutes. Serve.

A variation is to add ½ cup cooked black-eyed peas or red beans to recipe.

The Indians also love desserts and they make the most of wild strawberries and gooseberries, and no feast is complete without possum grape dumplings. Fried huckleberries and hickory nut pie, pumpkin pie, or baked persimmons are also served. Beverages may be sassafras tea (*iti kafi*), possum grape drink, coffee (boiled parched corn), sage tea (*ti kostini*), or boiled cedar bark.

When I have traveled outside of Oklahoma, however, the recipe I have been asked about most often is "Corn Cob Jelly." Here is the recipe from *Indian Cookin*, published by Norwega Press, 1973:

"Boil 12 bright red corn cobs in 3 pints water for 30 minutes. Remove from heat and strain. If needed, add enough water to make 3 cups liquid. Add one package fruit pectin and bring to boil. Add 3 cups sugar and boil 2 to 3 minutes until jelly stage. Tastes like apple jelly and is a glowing red color."

INDIAN CORN   Improved varieties, Calico or Rainbow corn (Park Seed). Also multi-color hybrids, with red, white, blue, and gold kernels, some cobs almost entirely black or deep red. The novel, decorative ears are superb for decoration. This corn looks pretty enough to eat, and it is . . . after all, the Indians have been eating it for a long time. Try roasting the ears, grinding the corn into meal and making corn bread. You will be in for a treat, the flavor is so great that it makes yellow meal seem ordinary. Red Strawberry Popcorn is another unusual corn. The tiny, 1½-inch strawberry-shaped ears are crowded with small deep crimson kernels. Attractive as a decoration and a good popping corn as well.

INDIANS AND THE "THREE SISTERS"   The natives of South American tropical forests plant corn and beans and squash in the same plot. The corn provides a pole for the beans to climb on. The beans fix nitrogen for the corn. The squash provides a groundcover which crowds out some of the weeds and keeps the soil from eroding.

Here in our own country, it has been traditional with the Cherokees since time immemorial to plant beans, corn, and squash together, because of a legend that they were the Three Sisters. The Indians knew a great deal about nutritional values, that is, they recognized results, without, perhaps, realizing the "why." We know today that the protein of these three vegetables, though individually incomplete, is equivalent to beef when eaten together. This is a fact well worth knowing in these times of high meat prices.

INSECT ATTRACTANTS   Certain female insects give off secretions so highly attractive to the male that these substances have been called the most fantastically potent biologically active materials ever discovered. Though odorless to humans, they attract male insects to the female from great distances, even miles away. *Pheromones* are subliminal scent signals that nearly all animals exude to elicit sexual response and were the subject of many experiments by Fabre, the celebrated French naturalist. They are often effective in incredibly small concentrations; one caged virgin female of the pine sawfly attracted over 11,000 males! Some of these lures have been chemically identified and even synthesized. As a control for undesirable insects, sex attractants may prove to be one of our most desirable tools and have already been proven useful against the gypsy moth. Male moths have been lured to the substance from more than two miles downwind. The extract can be stabilized by hydrogenation and will keep its potency for ten years or more.

INSECTS CAN'T SLIP BY Some insects damaging to fruit trees crawl from the soil to the branches to lay their eggs. They can be stopped by wrapping the trunk with six to eight inches of tape or grease-resistant paper and applying vaseline or other grease to the tape. Don't put vaseline directly on the tree as it may cause damage.

INSOMNIA Most gardeners sleep well, but just in case you don't, try a spoonful or two of honey as a before-bed snack. A chemical balance is needed within the body to allow it to achieve its required state, whether that state be wakefulness or sleep. Honey helps gear your body to the required action; milk helps prolong the effect. Other soothers which help overcome sleeplessness by helping the body to balance and regulate itself are lecithin and kelp. A pillow filled with hops is also helpful in inducing sound, restful sleep.

INSULATE WITH FOUNDATION PLANTINGS The term "foundation planting" often brings to mind a stiff and formal parade of green foliage, standing at attention across the front of a house, sheared to perfection, not a leaf out of place. That concept may have been valid ten or twenty years ago, but today's relaxed atmosphere responds better to loose, unsheared shrubs, planted in informal groups around your home. They look more natural, they need less maintenance, and they serve the same purposes as their earlier relatives.

Plantings along the foundation of your home not only look beautiful, but will add extra insulation against chilling winds in winter and help reduce solar radiation, both direct and reflected, at windows during the summer.

Proper landscaping will reduce air leakage in all seasons through cracks and joints around windows and doors, at roof eaves, building corners, and at the foundation line by lowering the wind velocity. Dense shrubs, such as arborvitae, hemlock, or spruce, when planted close to your house, will affect its outside surface temperature by blocking the wind, creating shade and providing an insulating dead air space between the shrub and the house. Experiments by the Lake State Forest Experimental Station in Nebraska have shown that with good protection by dense shrubbery on three sides of the house, fuel savings could run as high as thirty percent.

The American Association of Nurserymen suggests homeowners remember these few tips when planning their foundation planting. Select plants that enhance the facade of your home, rather than overwhelm it. It is important to keep in mind the *mature* height and habit of the plants you choose for this purpose, and leave enough room for them to grow naturally.

There is a wide choice of low and slow-growing plants for placement under windows, e.g., boxwood, Japanese holly, dwarf varieties of hemlock, spruce, rhododendron, euonymus. If your windows are very low to the ground, consider using a groundcover. Avoid framing windows with tall shrubs since this effect will make your home look smaller.

The corners of your house often have higher winds than along the sides, so place groups of plants there, and extend them around the house to give a feeling of unity to your plan. This technique will make your house look wider as well.

Whether you prefer the clipped precision of a boxwood, or the free-form of an unsheared laurel, the importance of foundation plantings can be counted in energy savings as well as beauty. It's another expression of "Green Survival."

IRIS (*Iris*), **THE BEARDED LADY**   I am an iris fancier—my ten-foot-wide beds extend for over 300 feet on a sloping terrace on the west side of my property. In spring they are a rainbow riot of color, interplanted with daffodils and grape hyacinth to extend the blooming season. This is a perfect site, with full sun and excellent drainage, in both of which iris revel. Plants in poorly drained soil are highly susceptible to crown and root rot.

To prepare your bed, work the soil 12 to 18 inches deep and add a complete fertilizer. When planting the rhizomes, first build a cone-shaped mound of soil in the bottom of a hole so that the top of the cone is about even with the soil surface. Set the rhizome on top of the cone and allow the roots to spread downward. Then fill in with soil and water to settle the soil around the roots. Space transplants 12 to 18 inches apart.

Growth occurs in the leaf end of the rhizome, so place the leaves in the direction of desired growth. Also trim back foliage to one-third of original height. If root rot occurs, cut off diseased portion, and dip rhizome in a water-Clorox solution (one quart water, ¼ cup of Clorox). In summer, during extremely hot weather, do not water iris; they can stand the heat but watering may cause them to bake and rot.

IRISH MOSS   Have you ever wondered why those Irish colleens have such pretty complexions? The ones with creamy skins and violet eyes? If they make you jealous, remember Irish seaweed, sometimes called carrageenan, is a powerhouse of vitamins and minerals offering one special and unique benefit:

The rich alkaline source in Irish moss makes it a very soothing food that is said to help restore the delicate acid-alkaline balance that enters into the rhythmic flow of thyroxine from the thyroid gland. The thyroid is the two-part endocrine gland that looks like a butterfly and rests against the front of the windpipe and helps to regulate our health and personality. As an added benefit Irish moss is very low in calories and high in calcium and phosphorus, which help to build strong bone structure, firm up the nerves and skin-hair cellular network, assist in metabolism and boost the health of the body.

In Germany, a mucilage from *Chondus crispus*, a variety of Irish moss, has been used to control insects in orchards and vineyards. A pound is boiled in five gallons of water for an hour. When thickened, the mixture is sprayed on infected plants. As the spray dries, pieces flake off, taking with them eggs and larvae of injurious insects.

Most of us want to live, not only a long time, but in full possession of our health and faculties. So look to the natural food products such as the various seaweeds, kelp, and Irish moss, as excellent sources of iodine-rich food.

IRRIGATION IDEAS   Instead of using solid stakes for vegetables or shrubs, use 2-inch galvanized or plastic pipes. They can double as a watering system. Simply drill a few holes along the section of pipe that will be embedded in the ground. Place it and fill with water. The entire root zone of the plant will be filled with water without the foliage being touched. Fertilize plants with this system by packing the pipe with fertilizer or compost and then watering.

You can also use pipes with holes to supply air and water to compost piles. Place the pipes upright in the compost, water weekly, and they will supply all the moisture needed, hastening decomposition. When water is not in the pipes air will flow through them and into the compost.

IS SLEEPING WITH HOUSEPLANTS HAZARDOUS?   Every now and then one of my readers asks me this question. According to leading horticulturists the answer is "No," the amount of oxygen that plants take is too small to matter, and this occurs during photosynthesis in the daytime. At night, in the dark, this process is not taking place.

Only in more recent times have human beings evolved into an interior people who are inherently unhappy without plants in their presence. Ancient peoples slept under the trees. Now, it seems only natural to bring the outdoors inside. So, sleep with plants if you like—their beauty will add a sense of calm that is all the more appreciated in a bedroom.

IT'S IN THE CAN   When crocus and daffodils bloom in the spring, it's easy to spot blank spaces where you need more bulbs. But since they cannot be planted until late fall, you'll need to mark these places so they won't interfere with summer gardening. Use flat cans from tuna or cat food. Just set the can face down where you'll place the bulb and step on the can, sinking it flush with the surface so it can be hidden by the annuals in the flowerbed. In the fall the cans are easy to spot and can be flipped out with the point of a trowel. Presto! You've got a round, bulb-size hole already started. A handy garden tip for any situation where planting is delayed.

IVIES IN YOUR LIFE   Boston ivy and other deciduous types can make your home cooler in summer and warmer in winter.

That's because they will shade a wall in summer and then lose their leaves in winter, allowing the sun to hit the wall. If your wall is brick, stone, or concrete block the ivy may be allowed to climb on the wall itself, but if your wall is wood it is best to place the ivy on a trellis about two inches away from the wall so the moisture from the ivy will not rot the wood.

English ivy (*Hedera helix*) makes an excellent groundcover for a steep bank and will even do well with a northeast exposure. You can root cuttings in a propagating frame. Prepare the soil well with leafmold and rotted or dehydrated manure. Plant rooted cuttings 6 to 8 inches apart in early spring and keep watered until established.

Baltic ivy (*Hedera helix* 'Baltica') is the hardiest evergreen variety of ivy. Its leaves are slightly smaller than those of the typical English ivy, and the white veins are often more prominent.

Ground-ivy (*Nepeta hederacea*) is an interesting and practical groundcover, but take care if it is grown where flowers (perennials and annuals) grow, for it may smother them if the plants are small.

The joys of earth and air are thine entire,
That with thy feet and wings dost hop and fly.
"The Grasshopper"
RICHARD LOVELACE

JALAPEÑO (*Capiscum annuum*) Little boys are often changelings. Angelic until they are about five years old, they suddenly turn into "little monsters" right before your eyes as little boy mischief begins to take over. My own little monster and the son of my best friend across the street were partners in crime. Just a month apart in age, they were constantly up to no good and driving both of us mothers to distraction. Like the time they fed jalapeño peppers to the kid next door who was a couple of years younger, considerably more naive, and the neighborhood pest. The result was a holy war, his mother was outraged, and Bessie and I went around on our knees for about six weeks afterward in a constant state of abject apology.

I have always grown jalapeño peppers—robustly flavored, thick-walled, dark green that turns a brilliant red when mature. My all-time favorites, I use them in everything—pimento cheese, soups, salads, even chopped fine in corn muffins. But most of all I favor them for:

Jalapeño Jelly

7 sweet green peppers
1 jalapeno pepper (I use 2 or more)
1½ cups vinegar
1½ cups apple juice
½ teaspoon salt
5 cups sugar
1 package powdered pectin
Green food coloring (optional)

Wash peppers, remove stems and seeds, and cut into ½-inch squares. Purée half of peppers and ¾ cup vinegar in blender or food processor. Purée remaining peppers and vinegar. Pour into a large bowl and add apple juice. Cover and refrigerate overnight.

Strain puréed mixture through several thicknesses of damp cheesecloth. Measure 4 cups juice into a large saucepot. If needed, add water to make 4 cups. Stir salt and pectin into juice. Bring to a rolling boil over high heat, stirring constantly. Remove from heat. Skim foam if needed. Add a few drops of green food coloring. Pour hot into hot, sterilized jars, leaving ¼-inch head space. Adjust caps. Process 5 minutes in boiling water bath. Yields about 6 pints. (Recipe from the *Ball Blue Book*)

To my thinking, peppers are the prettiest plants in the garden, especially when they are loaded with dozens of red, green, orange, yellow, and even purple peppers. The warm Southwestern soil welcomes the seed and they are easy to grow—but take care not to give them too much fertilizer, for you will have more leaves than peppers. Bad weather can plague peppers and sometimes blossoms will fall off in a cold spell—they like it HOT! Pack the row with plants: peppers can grow close together and yield a big harvest. A few matches, mixed in the soil beneath the plants, will add sulfur and help the plants to grow, for they like a slightly acid soil. Spray plants with 1 teaspoon Epsom salts mixed with a pint of warm water when they start to blossom to add magnesium.

Jalapeño is the really hot pepper variety you should use to make pepper spray for insect control. To make pepper spray take 3 large onions, 1 whole garlic clove, 2 tablespoons of hot red pepper, 1 quart water, 1 tablespoon soap. Whiz together first four ingredients in blender, stir in soap. May be used in standard sprayer.

IN A JAM Not having room to grow everything, I've gone to jell with wild berries and gotten into a jam with wild plums for more years that I'd care to count. Wild fruits grow just about everywhere. In my area we have wild dewberries, blackberries, tiny, indescribably delicious wild possum grapes, elderberries, wild plums, and those social climbers, the mustang grapes, that hang on to the coattails of sturdier trees and bushes. When picking these be sure to wear gloves, as the grapes are acidic and will do in even dishwater-hardened hands.

You can adjust your "take" to the instructions that come with "store-bought" pectin, which I find easy and usually foolproof. The Ball and Kerr companies put out inexpensive books on canning with excellent recipes,

and your County Agent Extension Department has recipes on jam and jelly making. Or you can use this recipe for a starter:

Dewberry Jam

2 lemons, coarsely ground or chopped
½ cups water
6 cups dewberries
7 cups sugar

Combine lemons and water and cook for 20 minutes. Add berries and sugar and cook 20 minutes longer or until the mixture has thickened (reached jellying point—as the boiling mass reaches this it will drop from the side of the spoon in two drops, running together and sliding off in a flake or sheet from the side of the spoon). If your hands get stained in the process of your wild fling you can get them clean with a little bleach.

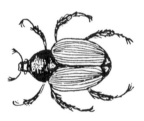

JAPANESE BEETLES Besides Milky Spore Disease there are biological controls. Spiders are their sworn enemies, especially the big black-and-yellow garden spiders that appear about August every year. They will spin their webs about eighteen inches apart over a field and voraciously devour every beetle they catch, wrapping and binding them up very quickly in just a few minutes. Wild primroses have been used as a trap crop; the beetles seem to prefer them to other plants. Another favorite plant is white geranium. There is some evidence that planting angel's trumpets in a garden will repel them.

JAPANESE-BEETLE-FREE FLOWERS
Probably no flowers are entirely free but phlox and the Heavenly Blue morning glory are bothered less than many other flowers.

Roses, marigolds, and zinnias are a favored plant food; delphiniums are seldom bothered but they are not easy to grow. Blue eupatorium will contrast well with phlox and give good color until frost. It has few insects; if it blights, you can always remove a plant and have plenty left. To replace marigolds, try 'Orange Flare' cosmos. It has almost no pests and diseases and grows with no effort at all (just what the fun-loving gardener wants!). Scatter the seeds in any odd corner; rake them in lightly. With no more attention they bloom from early July to November.

Most vegetables are little affected by Japanese beetles. However, the beetles are extremely fond of soybeans and sometimes appear on snap and lima beans; they injure the silk of corn; they are numerous on, but seldom injurious to, asparagus foliage; but they often play havoc on rhubarb leaves.

JAPANESE BLACK PINE   This beautiful pine grows somewhat irregularly and is an excellent choice if you have a garden near a windy seashore, as it is very resistant to wind and salt spray. I have also found it to be an excellent choice for dry, windy Oklahoma.

JICAMA   The jicama is well known and often sold at roadside stands in Mexico, but is only recently catching on here. This intriguing plant grows from a small beanlike seed to a tall vine with attractive blue flowers. These should not be allowed to remain: pick them off promptly to encourage growth of the large edible root. Depending on climate and soil factors this root may vary from about the size of a baseball to that of a fairly large cantaloupe. The skin is light brown, sort of coffee-and-cream color, with a white, fine-textured interior whose crunchy goodness brings to mind the water chestnut. The plant requires a long, frost-free growing season and I have grown them successfully in southern Oklahoma. Farther north it may be grown in a greenhouse, or started indoors and set out when weather warms up. Jicama seeds are toxic, so take care to keep them away from small children or animals. Seeds

may be obtained from Horticultural Enterprises or Gurney's.

JOJOBA   (*Simmondsia Chinensis*)   Jojoba, pronounced "ho-ho-ba," grows wild in abundance in Cave Creek, Arizona, but in other areas of the state is being carefully cultivated in controlled quantities. Jojoba is native to areas of northern Mexico, lower California, the islands off the coast of California, New Mexico, and Arizona. It inhabits the mountains bordering the Salton Sea basin in the Colorado Desert in California and the southern portion of San Diego County. The plant will grow in frost-free, arid, subtropical, and tropical zones. However, seedlings are sensitive to light frosts just below freezing.

According to Dr. J.A. Duke, writing in *Handbook of Nuts*, oil of jojoba is light-yellow, unsaturated, of unusual stability, remarkably pure, and need not be refined for use as a transformer oil or as a lubricant for high-speed machinery or machines operating at high temperatures. The oil does not become rancid. The residual meal makes an acceptable livestock food. It is an important browsing plant in California and Arizona, the foliage and young twigs being relished by cattle, goats, and deer—hence such names as "goatnut."

Jojoba

Jojoba has a long history as folk medicine. Indians of Baja California highly prized the fruit for food and the oil as a medicine for cancer and kidney disorders. Indians in Mexico use the oil as a hair restorer. Reported to be emetic, jojoba is a folk remedy for cancer, colds, obesity, parturition, poison ivy, sores, sore throat, warts, and wounds. Seri Indians applied jojoba to head sores and aching eyes. They even drank jojoba-ade for colds and to facilitate parturition. In recent years jojoba products have appeared on the market for hair and skin use.

JUNE BEETLES Grubworms are the larvae of June beetles. You will recognize them as soft-bodied white worms with brown heads, their curved bodies being ½ to 1 inch long. They resemble Japanese beetle grubs but are a little larger. They damage lawns in the same way and are much more injurious to root vegetables than are the grubs of Japanese beetles. There is a three-year cycle, the grubs staying in the ground two years and the large brown beetles flying the third year and eating tree foliage. Injury from the worms is greatest the year after beetle flight.

Prevent trouble, if possible, by not planting garden crops on sod land or land grown up to weeds and grass the preceding year. If such land must be used, plow in the fall, or spade. Legume crops will suffer less than corn or potatoes.

JUNIPER BERRY (*Juniperus communis*) Usually found in dry woods of the United States, Europe, Asia, and Northern Africa. The parts used are in the berries or fruits, which are smooth and shiny, ranging from one-quarter inch to one-half inch in diameter and are purplish-black to dusky red purple. The berries are prepared as an infusion by first soaking several tablespoons of the berries, then adding them to a pint of boiling water for one-half hour or more. After cooling the drink is divided into four portions and taken morning, noon, afternoon, and evening.

The drink acts as a stimulant on the body functions. As an aphrodisiac the herb increases or tends to increase sexual passion or power, stimulating the sexual appetite.

Skin itches, scabs, and even leprosy are reported to be aided by this herb. Bathing the skin with the juniper solution has given reportedly beneficial results. Good results have also been reported for aiding conditions of sciatica, as well as general strengthening of limbs of the body. The brain is also helped: memory is aided and the optic nerve is strengthened. The herb is also said to be valuable in treating diseases of the prostate gland, one of the symptoms of the disease of this gland being an excessive discharge of fluid.

The oil of the juniper berries is used to flavor gin; it also gives this drink its diuretic power (ability to increase activity of the kidneys) that is generally associated with drinking gin.

Juniper berries are widely used when preparing game to remove the strong, gamy taste that is objectional to many diners. Before roasting game, it is best to parboil the game in a good beef stock in which lemon, bay leaves, and juniper berries have been added. The berries also add a pleasing flavor to meat and game stews. Four to six berries are usually considered sufficient.

The kiss of the sun for pardon
The song of the birds for mirth
One is nearer God's Heart in a garden
Than anywhere else on earth.

DOROTHY FRANCES GURNEY

KALE Kales are primitive types of the colewort family, with large, loose leaves growing
up the sides of the stalk. The leaves on kales
are curly, while the leaves on collards are
smooth. Scotch kale has extremely crumpled
and curly gray-green leaves. The leaves of Siberian, or blue, kale are less curly and have a
bluish cast. Flowering kales are decorative
forms that have variegated leaves in cream,
red, rose, lavender, or silver. Actually having
no conspicuous flowers, they get their names
from their beautifully colored leaves, which
give them the appearance of a giant rose.
Grow kale in the fall garden; it is very hardy
and often grows well all winter, even under
snow. Kale has a good content of vitamin C,
calcium, and phosphorus, as well as traces of
iron, riboflavin, and niacin.

KAVA-KAVA (*Piper methysticum*) The
root of this plant, found in the South Sea Islands, is used as a general tonic and relaxant.
It is also considered to be a potential longevity preparation. A resin extracted from this
plant named *kawain* has recently been found
to clear up pigmented age deposits which
clutter up aged cells and tissues.

KEEP POTTED PLANTS SMILING
Problems with potted plants generally fall
into just five areas, all of which are easily
remedied if you are aware of the plant's
needs.

1. Overwatering. This is a very common
problem. Generally speaking, water only
when the soil is dry to the touch.
2. Underwatering. Apparent by signs of
wilting.
3. Salt accumulation. Overfertilization,
lack of drainage, or minerals in the water
can cause this. Frequent but very weak dosages of fertilizer are preferable to infrequent,
heavy doses. Be sure hole in pot is not
plugged up, interfering with drainage. Don't
let pot sit in water in the saucer. One quarter teaspoon of Epsom salts to each gallon of
tap water will help counteract minerals in
city water.
4. Insufficient light. Weak, spindly growth is
a symptom. So is a light green or yellowish
color. Move the plant to an area of stronger
light (but do not place it in direct sunlight
for a few days), or try a wide-spectrum fluo-
rescent light.

5. Low humidity. Occasional misting of the foliage with a hand sprayer helps most plants growing in the dry atmosphere of the house. The exception to this rule is any plants with fuzzy-surface leaves.

KEEP YOUNGSTERS AND PETS away from dieffenbachia, caladium, philodendron, and monstera. These common houseplants contain crystals of calcium oxalate which, when taken into the body, can cause lips and tongue to swell and make breathing difficult. The juice of these plants can also cause skin irritations. If you have an indoor cat place these plants out of its reach. Cats like to nibble on plants. Kitty will bless you if you give him some grass occasionally or grow some pots of oats and catnip.

KEEPING YOUR COOL Incredible as it seems, there was a time not so long ago when we didn't have air conditioning—or even electric fans before that. And today, because of the high price of electricity, many people who have air conditioners don't use them. Through careful planning it is possible to put your landscaping to work to make your home cooler in summer and, yes, warmer in winter. You can save $$s.

Most gardeners tending lawns, trees, and shrubs don't realize it, but they are putting their plants to work, purifying the air and replacing oxygen back into it, making breathing much easier. Do you realize that an acre of grass in front of your home gives off 2,400 gallons of precious water every hot summer day? And that same grass has a cooling effect equal to a 140,000-pound air conditioner—a 70-ton machine! A deciduous tree near your home can produce a cooling effect equal to ten room-size air conditioners running twenty hours a day. An apple tree in your lawn not only produces all the apples you can use, but also produces enough oxygen to supply four people for one year. And, in winter, when leaves drop, the tree lets the sunshine in to warm your home and help save on fuel bills.

Furthermore, the trees, flowers, grass, and, yes, even vegetables in your backyard act as natural "garbage" collectors, blotting up dust and noises as well. As a matter of fact plants are the best "dust mops" of all, catching much of the falling particles found in 12 million tons of pollutants (dust, grit, and cinders, according to George "Doc" Abraham) released into the atmosphere above the United States each year. It's the hairy surfaces of plant leaves on trees, bushes, grass, vines and other plants that catch the particles from the air. Then, when rainfall occurs, the pollutants are washed into the soil, where they are no longer a danger to our breathing apparatus. Yes, we can even improve our world through gardening, and save money as well.

But don't stop there! Close your draperies to keep out the heat of the sun. Open windows at both ends of your home to create an air flow. Also, open both the lowest and highest windows so that the hot air will be drawn out the top windows. Stay cool with a shower or bath. Soak your feet in a pan of cool water. Use a cool washcloth on your forehead or neck. Cook outdoors on a grill to keep heat out of your kitchen. Wear loose-fitting cotton garments and avoid synthetic fabrics. Slow down!

KENAF (*Hibiscus cannabinus*) A young friend of mine, a schoolgirl, with the aid of her family, has been conducting a successful experiment in growing kenaf in southern

Kenaf

Oklahoma. Her enthusiasm has been so contagious that I wanted to learn more about this plant so I wrote to the U.S.D.A. Agricultural Station at Beltsville, Maryland. Dr. James A. Duke, Economic Botanist, has been kind enough to give me some answers. According to Dr. Duke:

Kenaf is cultivated for its bast fibers which resemble and substitute for jute fibers. The fiber strands, from four to nine feet long, are used for rope, cordage, canvas, sacking, carpet backing, and fishing nets. It is cultivated secondarily for the seeds, which contain about 20 percent oil and are used for salad, cooking, and lubricant oils. Oil is also used in the manufacture of soap, linoleum, paints and varnishes, and for illumination.

Kenaf, a woody to herbaceous annual, is fast-growing. It has prickly stems and yellow flowers with purple centers. The deep-penetrating taproot has deep-seated laterals, making it a good crop for warmer climate. It is less exacting in its requirements than jute and is adaptable to a variety of soils, best being a deep, friable, well-drained, sandy loam with humus. Propagation is by seed, which is broadcast or planted with a grain drill in rows. Highest-quality fiber is obtained when plants are harvested during the flowering period, usually in August north of the equator.

As folk medicine kenaf is reported to be anodyne, aperitif, aphrodisiac, fattening, purgative, and stomachic. It is a folk remedy for bilious conditions, bruises, fever, and puerperium (Duke and Wain, 1981). Powdered leaves are applied to Guinea worms in Africa. Africans use peelings from the stems for anemia, fatigue, lassitude, etc. In Gambia, the leaf infusion is used for coughs. Seeds are applied externally to aches and bruises. Medicinally, juice of the flowers with sugar and black pepper is used in biliousness with acidity. The seeds are considered to be an aphrodisiac and fattening.

KENILWORTH IVY (*Cymbalaria muralis*) This dainty little vine, with its violet flowers and leaves tinted with red beneath, will grow well in a sunny window if the atmosphere is not too dry. It needs only standard potting soil and will often seed itself in the soil about the base of other pot plants. In summer it grows riotously in a wall or rock garden out-of-doors.

KIWI FRUIT (*Actinidia chinensis*) This attractive climbing shrub has bright red young foliage and mature leaves that are glossy dark green above and whitish beneath. Cream white flowers in April are followed by oval hairy fruits with an almost indescribably delicious flavor, somewhat suggestive of a tangy banana and strawberry combination. Fruits mature in October and November, a frost-free growing season of 235 days being required. They are an interesting and decorative ornamental plant for greenhouses or container culture.

Both male and female plants are needed to set fruit. Kiwi grows very rapidly but produces no blooms until four or five years old; usually, no fruit appears for five to nine years. Best to start with two-year-old plants, but they can be grown from vines. Fertilize in spring with compost, applying at the rate of one cup per plant. Provide a support (this is really a climbing shrub) such as a trellis or wire fence. Unless pruned quite heavily, kiwi will become a tangled mass. Prune after the leaves drop, removing the weaker canes to encourage the stronger canes to be more productive. (Wayside Gardens)

KOHLRABI (*Brassica oleracea caulorapa,* var. *gougyloides*) Kohlrabi is the flying saucer of the cabbage world, a strange-looking vegetable resembling a sputnik. It looks like the root of a turnip growing out of the ground, but it can be grown in places where the summers are hot and dry and where turnips, therefore, are likely to fail. It can stand drought and heat without losing flavor but it should be used when young. Start the durable plants with seed—insect- and disease-free—it is well worth growing. Excellent in stir-fry dishes, and don't forget to include raw slices in all your summer party dips. Grows well with beets.

Leaves of a rose not yet unfolded—
A lovely being not quite molded,
Waiting for the sun-kissed morn
To be in fullest beauty born.

LOUISE RIOTTE

LAMB'S-QUARTERS (*Chenopodium album*) May sometimes act as a wild host for leaf miners which work inside beet leaves, turning the tissues brown. No spray will prevent these maggots. Pick off the infested leaves and destroy the lamb's-quarters. Incidentally, lamb's-quarters when young is a perfectly delicious vegetable, preferred by many to spinach, so a good way to destroy it is to cook it for dinner!

LACEWINGS (*Neuroptera*) Never lay a hand on a lacewing! These beneficial insects deserve every consideration and are one of the gardener's best allies. Along with that fantastic consumer of aphids, the ladybug, the lacewings go right after this little pest and many others as well.

LAWNS Shall you seed, sod, plug, or sprig? When shopping for seeds you'll find blends and mixtures as well as seeds of a single type. Blends are several selections of a single type of grass; mixtures combine several different kinds of grass. Both have the advantage of combining disease resistance, drought resis-

tance, shade tolerance, and other desirable qualities of their component lawn grasses for a single lawn. Be sure to read the tags and buy seeds that are at least 90 percent pure, with a germination percentage of not less than 85 percent. The testing data should not be over one year old. A good mixture is Kentucky Bluegrass, Fescue, Meadow Grass, Bent, and Redtop.

A sprig is a single stolon of grass with 3 to 5 nodes (joints) and no soil attached. Plant in furrows 1 to 2 inches deep, spacing 4 to 6 inches apart, in rows 10 to 18 inches apart. Sprinkle daily around noon to keep the soil moist. Each week, cover sprigged area with a ¼- to ½-inch layer of soil or compost to tack down new growth. Use this method for Zoysia, Bent grasses, Bermuda, St. Augustine, or centipede.

Plugs are 2-inch pieces of sod, and have a better chance of survival than sprigs. Recommended spacing is 6 to 8 inches apart. If you can't get plugs you might be able to buy sod and cut your own with a knife or hatchet. Plugging gives good results with Zoysia, centipede, Bermuda, and Bent grasses.

Sodding not only results in an immediate lawn, but also minimizes weed growth and erosion. Any grass can be sodded; but centipede, Zoysia, and hybrid Bermuda are the most common. Keep sod moist if you must hold it a day or so and preferably lay it in either early morning or later afternoon. Pack it in tightly. If possible roll the area with a water-filled roller to ensure good contact with the soil. Lightly water each day between noon and 2 p.m. Do not fertilize for a month and keep traffic off the sod. When growth starts, mow just as you would an established lawn.

LEAD IN YOUR VEGETABLES If your garden is an unprotected plot near a busy road, your harvest could be tainted with a mineral you don't need: lead.

Tests at Cornell University show that the best way to keep down the uptake of lead in plants is to mix organic materials at a rate of 25 percent by volume into the soil. Keeping the soil's pH balance between 6.5 and 7.0 is also important as this is mildly acidic, according to Dr. Nina L. Bassuk, who conducted the test. If the lot is shielded by a hedge fence and is located several hundred feet from a roadway, lead contamination will be greatly minimized. If you are unsure, your county's agricultural service can make a test for lead or pH balance.

LEAF MOLD I regard it as sheer madness to pack leaves into plastic bags to be carted away and burned. Leaves should be reincorporated into the earth, preferably after being shredded and composted. But, while leaf mold is wonderful organic fertilizer, remember that leaves used alone as a mulch tend to pack and may keep water away from plants. Shredded and mixed with grass clippings they make a good mulch, decomposing more rapidly and giving the mulched plants the benefits of their many nutrients.

LECITHIN A product of the soybean, it is not only an able cholesterol fighter breaking up fatty oils in our foods, it is also now believed to be a great memory improver.

Manufacturers used to make their lecithin products out of eggs, which are a rich source, but when eggs became too expensive they discovered that soybeans also contained lots of lecithin. Lecithin is defined as a phospholipid—a colorless, waxy solid widely distributed in the human body. It is especially abundant in brain and nerve cells, suggesting that people who get enough lecithin are likely to be well off, nutritionally speaking, in these departments.

You can add lecithin in powdered or granular form to almost any food where it is appropriate. When you're baking bread, add a tablespoon or two of lecithin to the dough when you add the wheat germ, bran, or whatever other nutritional goodies you use. Or put it in homemade muffins, biscuits, or crackers. Add it to breakfast food, along with wheat germ and bran. Add it to scrambled eggs, gravies, and blender drinks—remember, it is a food and completely harmless. And did you know that Pam, the spray you use to keep foods from sticking, is pure lecithin?

LEEKS (*Allium porrum*) Few vegetables have been honored like the leek, which has been adopted by the Welsh as their national emblem. And the emperor Nero believed that leeks were good for his singing voice. The Romanies believe that they are good for their hair. Most of us simply believe they are good to eat. Leeks, which are members of the onion family, are easy to grow. You can grow them from seed but I simply buy several bunches of leeks (which are usually sold with roots still attached) in the supermarket and plant them. In time the bulbs split, much like garlic, and I have loads of new plants and increase my stock from year to year. Leeks are not as greedy as onions but will grow bigger and better on a diet of compost or well-rotted manure.

LEGUMES Early planted beans often rot when the ground is too cold. To prevent this choose beans that have been treated with Captan. With treated seed you can plant an earlier crop in northern states. You can also increase your bean crop by dusting the seeds with a nitrogen inoculant powder to aid the plants in capturing nitrogen with bacteria in the roots. And, last, be sure to return your spent bean plants and pods to the garden by way of the compost heap to increase your soil's fertility by again adding the nitrogen stored in the plants.

LEMON AID   Instead of sprinkling granulated sugar over cut fruit, sprinkle an equal amount of presweetened, dry lemonade mix over the fruit. It's different, has a terrific taste, and also keeps the fruits from turning dark.

LEMON-SCENTED   Wouldn't it be nice if we could see scents and smell colors? Of course we can't, but when it comes to lemon-scented plants we can almost taste them! Some we actually can, like lemon basil (*Ocimum Basilicum*), which has a concentrated clear lemon fragrance we can enjoy wherever we want a summery "bouquet-of-lemons" taste combined with the aromatic scent of basil. (Shepherd's)

- Lemon balm (*Melissa officinalis*), beloved of bees and no wonder, for it has a pronounced lemon fragrance and a soft flavor when the leaves are brewed. This tea is said to "renew youth and strengthen the brain." Couldn't we all use some of that?
- Lemon catnip (*Nepeta cataria citriodora*) is identical to regular catnip but with an appealing lemon fragrance. (Park's)
- Lemon thyme (*Thymus Serpylium*), makes a great addition to any garden as a border plant. Common lemon thyme (*T. Serpylium citriodorus*) is bushy and vigorous with a cloud of pink blossoms in June and attractive dark green leaves. Other varieties of lemon thyme, silver lemon (*T.S. argenteus*) and golden lemon (*T.S. aureus*), display leaves bordered in white and yellow and are striking in mixed borders.
- Lemon verbena (*Aloysia triphylla*) is a delicate plant possessing the strongest lemon scent in nature. Native to South America, it may not survive winter, but in a fine summer it will grow from 3 to 6 feet tall if given full sun and a friable, well-drained soil. A shy bloomer, lemon verbena produces its flowers in panicles of palest lavender in mid-August. It will grow well in a pot if given a light dressing of fertilizer.
- Those scent-mimics, geraniums, also have a lemon-scented family member: *Pelargonium crispum* 'Prince Rupert' is a tall-growing variety, but pinching back will cause it to fill out nicely. The crinkled leaves have an impressive lemon fragrance.
- Lemon Mint (*Monarda citriodora*) has lemon-scented leaves and flowers that attract bees. Indians used the oil to treat wounds.
- Moonflower (*Calonyction*)—Burpee's Giant White unfurls itself at twilight, emitting a strong lemon fragrance on the evening air that attracts the big hawkmoths.
- The Southern Magnolia (*Magnolia grandiflora*), native from North Carolina to Texas, is not only dramatically beautiful but has a lemon-scented fragrance as well.

LENTILS (*Lens esculenta*)   Lentils seem to be the stepchildren of the pea family, growing on a straggling 12- to 18-inch vine and producing inconspicuous whitish to lavender pealike flowers, that are a good source of honey. The blossoms are followed by flat pods containing two seeds each, in three varieties: small flat brown, small yellow, or larger pea-shaped. Lentils have been a staple food in Mediterranean countries since antiquity. They are used for soup, as beans, or, with the larger pea shape grown in Provence, as fodder. Seed is sown in early spring, preferably in sandy soil, the rows 18 to 30 inches apart. Seed keeps best when left in the pod.

They are a very nourishing food and a good body builder. They are very rich in vital minerals and are recommended in cases of low blood pressure, anemia, and emaciation. Lentil soup is good for cases of ulcerated stomachs and ulcerated digestive tracts.

Lentil Loaf
Take 2½ cups cooked lentils and combine with 1 cup cooked millet; 1 beaten egg; 2 slices chopped, broiled bacon; 2 grated onions; 1 clove garlic, minced; ½ teaspoon salt; ¼ cup parsley; 1 teaspoon chopped chives; ¼ teaspoon thyme; and a pinch of nutmeg. Blend ingredients together with enough stock to moisten, place into oiled (or Pam-sprayed) loaf pan and bake at 375°F for 40 to 45 minutes. Serve with your favorite sauce.

Lentil forest: A sprinkling of lentils on a flat dish or a paper towel is all you need. Keep damp and the lentils will sprout into a green carpet in a few days.

LETTUCE (*Lactuca sativa*)   Lettuce comes in infinite variety and, so far as my experience goes, all varieties are easily transplantable, a fact not generally known. Lettuce seed needs a cool temperature (about 70°F) to germinate well, and won't come up in hot weather. Planting early, heat-resistant varieties is the way for Southern gardeners to go if they want lettuce during the warmer months. Giving seed the cold treatment in the refrigerator will also help to ensure germination during warmer weather. Mix seed with moist peat moss and perlite, keep in refrigerator five days, then plant in the garden. Among the best bets for home gardens are hybrids bred for heat tolerance and slow bolting (seeding). Buttercrunch, my own favorite, is an outstanding All-America winner. Or try Burpee's Dark Green Oak Leaf, another heat-resistant salad type which stays sweet and succulent even during summer heat. The dwarf variety, Tom Thumb, is great for growing under lights or in a sunny window for winter salads. It produces compact, well-folded heads, medium green on the outside and creamy white inside.

There is a substantial amount of vitamin E found in lettuce, especially in the Romaine variety, which contains more vitamins and minerals than head (iceberg) lettuce. The high percentage of iron in lettuce makes this food desirable for anemic conditions.

LETTUCE, SWEET LETTUCE, DON'T BOLT!   If you've tried to grow head lettuce year after year, only to have it bolt when the weather turns hot, try this. Broadcast 85-day iceberg head lettuce seed into an area of well-prepared soil (lettuce, like most leaf vegetables, can stand some shade or filtered sunlight). In about 30 days you will have firm lettuce leaves—don't worry about the lettuce forming heads, just use the large crisp leaves instead. Once some leaves are ready pull a week's supply from an area of about a foot square. Then work up the soil again and broadcast more seed. Keep this floating crop game going and you can have lettuce for sandwiches and salad from May through October!

LIBATION LIGHTS UP LANGUISHING PLANTS   Try feeding vinegar water to azaleas and other plants needing soil acidification. It works. Use 2 tablespoons per gallon of water and soak the entire root area; repeat every three or four months, or as leaf color begins to fade. Also perks up camellias, heather, laurel, pieris, rhododendrons, as well as helping hydrangeas produce blue flowers.

LICORICE (*Glycyrrhiza glabra*)   From this herb we get a valuable flavoring material that comes from its long, sweet roots. Licorice is a hardy perennial of the pea family. Licorice in medicine disguises the flavor of disagreeable drugs and it is contained in some cough medicines. It is also used to flavor tobaccos, cigars, and cigarettes, as well as soft drinks, candy, and chewing gum. In Oriental medicine licorice is also believed to have healing and tranquilizing properties owing to the triterpenoidal glycosides within its roots. In the West licorice has been used in the treatment of gastric ulcer.

LIGHTNING Lightning, according to Merrill S. Timmins, Jr., Agricultural Engineering Research Division, Agricultural Research Service, is one of the most destructive forces of nature, and it's a particularly dangerous and costly peril for the farm. Lightning is a major cause of farm fires. Barns, loafing sheds, and other livestock buildings are particularly vulnerable. Lightning bolts cause more than 80 percent of all livestock loss due to accidents. (For more complete and detailed information you may wish to get Farmers Bulletin No. 2136, U.S. Department of Agriculture, Supt. of Documents, U.S. Government Printing Office, Washington, D.C.)

But primarily what we are concerned with is protection for trees that may be ruined or severely damaged by lightning. If sufficiently damaged they may even fall on a building.

Trees that most need protection include those within ten feet of any building, those under which livestock usually shelter, and those that are valuable in themselves. Where there is a small grove of trees, only a few of the tallest need to be protected. To protect a tree, install air terminals at the top of the trunk (or main branch) and at the end of the main branches. Install the terminals as far out on the branches as it is possible to securely fasten them. Run the main conductor from the trunk terminal down to ground. Connect other terminals to the main conductor with branch conductors. Course the conductors along the trunk and branches. Trees with trunks more than three feet in diameter should have two down conductors.

To make ground connections, bury the conductor in a trench extending away from the tree at least twelve feet or to the extremity of the overhanging branches. The trench should be shallow near the tree to prevent damage to the roots. Ten-foot ground rods may be driven beyond the root spread.

To protect the exposed part of the conductor from damage by livestock, cover it with a suitable casing.

How often have you heard, "Don't seek shelter under a tree in an electrical storm?" *Now* you know why. . . .

LIGHTNING GARDENING A thunder-and-lightning storm has an extremely fertile effect on your garden and lawn. Immediately after one of these supercharged storms your plants seem to literally turn green instantly. As a matter of actual fact they do, as a result of the electrically charged oxygen, which is turned into 78 percent nitrogen.

Many believe this condition can be created in their gardens by practicing a special type of gardening called electroculture. This is done by making use of metal objects like copper wire, metal trellises, and tin cans to attract the static electricity in the vicinity of the vegetable garden. The atmosphere becomes charged in the form of gentle and free-growing elements which increase size, health, and yield of the garden.

One method is to stretch a piece of copper wire over the top of the vegetables, fastening it to wooden stakes at each end of the row. Wire should be high enough so it does not touch tree plants. Another way is to place tin cans every 12 to 18 inches apart in your row with tops and bottoms removed. Bury the first few inches in the ground so cans will not blow or fall over.

Grow melons and other vine crops such as peas and beans on metal fences. Copper is believed to give the best results.

LIMONOIDS TO THE RESCUE Research at the University of California at Berkeley by Isao Kubo and James A. Klocke has found that a group of bitter-tasting chemicals found in the rinds, juice, and seeds of citrus, called limonoids, will discourage several types of caterpillars from feeding. You can try this deterrent in your own garden by grinding up citrus rinds and seeds left over from breakfast. Soak overnight in warm water, strain, and spray on your plants. Research has shown this spray to be effective on corn earworm, fall armyworm, tobacco budworm, and pink bollworm, but you might find it effective on other pests as well.

LIVING CHRISTMAS TREES A living tree costs little more than a cut tree and you can plant it in your yard for a permanent memory of the Christmas past. Possibilities include the Aleppo pine, Japanese black pine, Deodar cedar, Douglas fir, Scotch pine, white spruce, or even the Norfolk Island pine, which makes a lovely house plant. Leave your living Christmas tree outdoors in the sunshine as long as possible; ten days to two weeks is the recommended maximum length of indoor time. The day before you bring it inside, water it thoroughly by saturating the soil and spraying the foliage. Place it under the strongest light available, under a skylight or near a sunny window, and away from heating drafts. Set container on a plant stand or piece of plastic to protect the floor or table surface.

If you plan to use electric Christmas lights, select strings of small lights rather than the large, hot lights. A floodlight can illuminate the tree quite effectively without burning the foliage. Decorate the tree with small ornaments, avoiding anything heavy that might weigh down the branches and spoil the tree's symmetrical shape. Water soil just enough to keep it moist.

When you take the tree outside after Christmas, place it in a shady spot rather than in the sun until it recovers from being indoors. Thoroughly water the soil and the foliage. Misting the foliage is a good idea. When planting your tree prepare a hole deeper and wider than the container. Enrich the existing soil with humus and fill the hole with water. Plant the tree, fill in the hole and again water thoroughly, spreading mulch over the surface of the soil. Continue to water at least once a week, particularly during dry spells. A large tree should be guyed for protection against the wind.

A small tree can be repotted into a larger container and left on a patio or balcony until next Christmas. It should be watered thoroughly at least once a week and more often during the summer months, as container plants always need more moisture than those in the ground.

LIVING STONES (*Lithops*)   Perfect houseplants for those who must often be away from home. These attractive and unusual succulents from Africa are stemless and form clumps of paired leaves, often with transparent windows to focus light. The markings mimic the pebbles of the desert floor. In nature they lie half-buried in the sand, resembling rocks and minerals. These tiny, interesting plants have a silvery or bluish tinge and at maturity may reward you with a few white or yellow daisylike flowers. Especially suited to dish gardens, they are best grown on hot, sunny window sills. They thrive on dry air and heat from radiators or vents. Always be sure they have good drainage. Water very sparingly and wait until the soil feels very dry before watering again. Will grow out of doors in rock gardens in frost-free areas.

LIZARDS   If lizards are abundant in your area, catch a few and set them loose in your garden. A noose-type knot on the end of a rigid fishing pole serves as a good trap. Their diet is primarily insects and good species to adopt include fence lizards, six-lined lizards, blue-tailed skinks, and horned toads (really a species of lizard). They will eat lots of beetles, grubs, caterpillars, and fire ants— helping on the ground floor as birds do in the air.

LOGANBERRY (*Rubus loganobaccus*) These berries resemble blackberries, except they're red instead of black. A trailing variety, it is not hardy in the Northeast but can be grown with winter protection in places where temperatures do not drop below zero. It is self-fertile and does not require pollenization. Use fresh, cooked, dried, or for juice. (Gurney's)

LOLLIPOP PLANT (*Pachystachys lutea*), or yellow shrimp plant. To keep your "lollipops" coming on, keep it short. Prune each spring by clipping back into a neat shape. If it's very straggly cut back the stems to about 2 inches long, and let the plant start all over. Propagate every other year. When cutting back, insert cuttings in a mixture of moist sharp sand and sphagnum peat moss, covering the container with a clear plastic bag to maintain humidity. Place in moderate light in a temperature of 65°F to 79°F and you should see root development in about two weeks.

LOSS OF THE GENETIC DIVERSITY of some of the world's crops has accelerated in recent decades with some crops becoming increasingly susceptible to diseases, pests, and environmental stress. A global network of gene banks has therefore been established to provide plant breeders with the genetic resources necessary for developing more resistant crops that will enable farmers to maintain high yields. Most of the gene banks now store the germplasm of only the major crops such as cereals, potatoes, and grain legumes. Cultivated varieties of these crops are conserved as well as wild species that might otherwise become extinct. Tropical crops such as bananas and coconuts also need to be conserved as well as germplasm of other important plants such as plantation crops, medicinal herbs, and fruit and timber trees.

LUFFA (*Luffa cylindrica*) You can eat your vegetable and have it, too, if you grow luffa. Luffa, sometimes called the flesh-brush gourd, is a subtropical annual climber of the cucurbit family, somewhat resembling zucchinis. However, they are not only edible, you can also wash with them! Luffa sponges are highly recommended for their slightly abrasive action which stirs up the circulation.

Luffas, though they may grow as large as 15 inches in fertile soil, are best eaten before reaching 8 inches. After that let them mature, cure them and you will have sponges useful for many purposes. Since luffas like to vine, the flat black seeds are best planted near a fence. Let them climb and ramble about, showing off their handsome lemon-yellow blossoms which cluster at each node.

By fall luffas turn olive green, a sign of maturity. Cut them from the vine, leaving a few inches of stem so you can tie a cord on them. Hang in an airy, dry place for several weeks. Peel off skin as it becomes cracked and shrunken and you will have a network of strong yellow fibers—your sponge. Save and dry some of the seeds for next year's garden. Lay sponges where they can dry completely and you will have useful sponges for your sink, washing the car, your hands, body, or whatever. Both Egypt and Japan export luffas for use in industrial filters.

LUNA MOTH Rarely occurring in large numbers, this beautiful green moth is helpful as a pollinator to night-blooming flowers. Its caterpillar stage, like that of butterflies, may be harmful to plants. Most harmful moths include the tussock moth, tent caterpillars, gypsy moth, and brown-tail moth in their caterpillar stage. Also harmful in this stage are the army worm, corn borer, corn-ear worm, cutworms, codling moth, peach moth, and the pink bollworm, which attacks cotton.

Merrily, merrily shall I live now
Under the blossum that hangs on the bough.
WILLIAM SHAKESPEARE

MAGNOLIA (*Magnoliaceae*) is the name of a group of trees and shrubs that grow in North America and Asia. Eight of the thirty-five kinds grow wild in the eastern United States. Southern magnolia is especially popular because of the beauty and fragrance of its large creamy white flowers. The leaves of the umbrella tree and the big-leaf magnolia tend to stretch out from the ends of the branches like the ribs of an open umbrella. Big-leaf magnolia has the largest flowers of any native tree in the United States. They measure about 10 inches across the 6 creamy white petals. It also has the biggest undivided leaves, with blades 15 to 30 inches long and up to 10 inches wide.

Magnolia lumber is used mainly for furniture. The bark is said to cure the tobacco habit if chewed. It is used in medicine for rheumatism with stiffness and soreness, especially when the heart is affected and there is oppression in the lungs. It is given in fevers, catarrh, malaria, gout, and chronic rheumatism. It arrests the paroxysms in fever and has a stimulating and tonic effect. The tulip tree is also used for the same purpose, the bark being given in intermittent fever and chronic rheumatism.

MAIDENHAIR FERN (*Adiantum pedatum*) Native from Canada to Georgia and west to Oklahoma and coastal Louisiana, it grows 1 to 2 feet tall, spreading its fronds in a fan pattern held parallel to the ground. Southern maidenhair (A. *capillus-veneris*) reaches a height of 6 to 20 inches, and its elongated fronds of wispy leaflets are identical in shape to the foliage of the maidenhair tree (*Ginkgo bilboa*). This type grows from Virginia to Florida. Maidenhair ferns, in their natural habitat, like shelter from drying winds and full sun. To grow them in a landscape situation you'll need to duplicate these conditions, like tucking them into rocky crevices next to a pond, fountain, or trickling stream. Once you've satisfied their basic needs for light, filtered shade, and rich, well-drained soil, their care is simple. Prepare the planting site by working in generous amounts of rotted compost, decayed manure, or sphagnum peat moss, adding a little at a time. Be sure to keep the soil moist. In time, you will need to divide. Do this by digging up the bed and cutting plants apart with a sharp spade, replanting divisions from one to two feet apart.

MAKE YOUR OWN BROOMS Grow broomcorn just as you would other corn. Cut the heads at about three months, or when they begin to fill out and the seeds and sweeps are still green. Fully mature broomcorn will have red heads that make an attractive broom, but the fibers are not as strong as green ones. Cut stalks about 3 feet from the tip. Hang heads or lay flat to cure. Dry carefully as broomcorn mildews easily.

MALABAR SPINACH (*Basella alba*) is a climber. It is excellent cooked or raw in salads. Large, bright glossy green leaves grow abundantly throughout the season on long viney stems. Quick-growing, it takes little space if trained on a fence and will thrive in hot weather when ordinary spinach goes to seed.

MANICURE MAGIC If you like to garden without gloves, scrape your nails over a bar of soap before digging and weeding. This saves a lot of cleanup time and keeps earth from under your nails.

MANURE, DOG Dog manure, like that of the cat, is, owing to the diets of these animals, especially rich in phosphoric acid. This may be as much as 10 percent with a nitrogen content of about 2 percent. Dogs allowed to eat bones will have manure higher in phosphorus and calcium than when they are fed only canned foods. While dog manure has value and may be composted and used advantageously for lawns, flower beds, or orchards, I do not think it is advisable to use such compost on vegetable gardens. This is because the excrement of dogs can contain a dangerous parasite, a worm known as toxocara. This worm can live in the dog's intestine for as long as ten years and is very difficult to eradicate. For this reason it is also best to keep your dog out of the vegetable garden as well.

MAPLE SUGAR TREATS Try taking maple syrup that hasn't *quite* boiled down to the syrup stage and pour the liquid into popsicle holders to freeze. Best goodies ever!

MAPLE SYRUP IN THE WEST It has been reported that maple syrup can be successfully produced by tapping the big-tooth maple (*Acer grandidentatum*) trees that grow abundantly in higher elevation canyons in the western states. Another western tree from which the sap may be boiled into sugar is the box elder (*A. negundo*). The trees do not grow as large as those in New England but do produce real syrup.

Tapping is begun in mid-January when daytime temperatures in the canyons pass the freezing mark. The season ends in late March when the days become too warm and too wet for sugar production. The sap is collected and boiled in the traditional way.

MAPPING FOR GARDEN TREASURE Many have not only limited soil area but also limited sunshine, so make a sun map. Begin by drawing in your yard and all the gardening areas. Mark those that receive the most sun, those that get only noonday sun, and those that receive late afternoon sun. You can then regulate what you plant, according to the requirements of certain plants. Don't, for instance, plant something that will tolerate partial shade in the sunniest part of the yard. Blooming plants such as tomatoes, eggplant, and peppers generally need more sun than leafy or root plants which may grow quite well in partial shade.

MARKERS You can make charming, permanent, and unobtrusive plant markers for identifying individual plants. Stone markers have the advantage of lying flat on the ground, so they don't compete with your plants for attention—and they also add a natural look. Their surfaces should be rather smooth, so painting the plants' names on them will be easy. It is best to use only one type of stone. All you'll need is a small paintbrush and some white acrylic paint. Weathering might cause the paint to flake off in time, but repainting the stones is easy. Especially nice for irises, which tend to all look alike when not in bloom.

MARSH MALLOW (*Althaea officianalis*) Did you know that here in America the root of the marsh mallow really was once used to make marshmallows, which are now made with cheaper gelatin? The Romans were said to stew oysters with mallows for a tasty love dish—maybe that's how cooking marshmallows got started. Originally, according to Euell Gibbons, marshmallows were considered more a medicine than a sweetmeat. They were chiefly used as a very pleasant method of treating a cough, sore throat, or bronchitis. The edible roots were mentioned in the Book of Job in the Old Testament, making this one of the first wild food plants to be written about. And those discriminating connoisseurs, the Chinese, still use mallows in some of their fine dishes.

Mallows are magnificent flowers, growing in stately ranks among the tall sedges and "cat-tails" of the marshes, making the most insensitive traveler exclaim at their amazing loveliness.

MELONS   Melons need warm soil to grow well. Researchers at Virginia Tech found that melons directly seeded into black plastic yielded earlier and twice as heavily as those planted in bare sod. They also grew faster and began running sooner. Black plastic absorbs heat from the sun, holds it in at night, keeps down weeds, and retains soil moisture.

MEXICAN BEAN BEETLES   A nonstinging predatory wasp, *Pediobus foveolatus*, has been found very effective against Mexican bean beetles. They lay their eggs in the beetle larvae and the young wasps kill the larvae by eating their way out. The wasp is not native and cannot live through the winter in most areas, so must be released each season. Gardens Alive (see "Sources") also recommends spined soldier bugs to control Mexican bean beetles.

Ladybugs often take over and take care of this problem. Planting marigolds with beans is helpful. A parasitic fungus, *Beauveria globulifera*, affects Mexican bean beetles, which are susceptible in all stages of development, including the egg. A spray made with Octagon soap will also alleviate the condition.

MICE   Mice sometimes completely girdle young fruit trees. Painting with standard tree wound paints is helpful. Or you might try, as one gardener recommends, covering the wounds with white corn syrup and then wrapping with aluminum foil. If you live in an especially warm climate, as I do, with blazing summer temperatures often going over 100°F, it is also very helpful to use tree wrap. This will protect new trees for one year from sun and gnawing animals. (Not always obtainable in your local area; look in your seed and nursery catalogs—Gurney's has it.)

MIDGET VEGETABLES   Even though you may have only a tiny backyard or city terrace your garden can produce a rewarding crop of fresh vegetables if you select varieties with care. Most practical in limited space are small growing hybrids bred for maximum production on midget plants. Possible suggestions are such space-savers as Cucumber Bush Whopper, with short vines and no runners, Cabbage Darkri, which makes firm heads 6 to 8 inches in just 47 days, and Eggplant Morden Midget. Also: Squash Park's Sun Drops hybrid, with space-saving bushy plants, Sweet Corn, Golden Midget, which makes 4-inch butter-yellow ears on 30-inch plants, and Lettuce Tom Thumb, a miniature butterhead type. For garnishing there is a Parsley Paramount and for dessert you can grow Watermelon Bushbaby, with round-oval 8-pound fruit.

MILK CARTON PLANT PROTEC-TORS   In southern Oklahoma you can have 80°F temperatures one day and freezing temperatures the next, so when I set out tomato, eggplant, and pepper seedlings in the spring I must prepare for weather extremes. I cut three sides off the bottom of my milk cartons, leaving a flap that can be covered with soil to hold the carton in place. I then cut the top on three sides so it can be folded back or closed depending on weather conditions. These cartons also protect my plants from the extremely high, drying winds we often experience in the spring. Sometimes when I set out eggplant I tape a piece of clear plastic over the top to protect it from the tiny insects that can so often completely devastate the leaves.

Coffee cans with the bottoms cut out also make great plant protectors. Save the plastic lids for covering if cold weather threatens.

MILKWEED (*Asclepias* spp.)   Sometimes called silkweed or butterfly weed, this plant is well suited for the wild garden. Orange milkweed (*A. tuberosa*) and some others are fine flower border plants. It is deeply tuberous rooted but can be transplanted with a ball of earth dug with it in order not to break the tubers. Can be grown from seeds sown in fall or spring, preferably the latter.

A report from the Office of Technology Assessment states that milkweed contains a potential source of natural insect attractants, repellents, and toxicants which may prove to be of great future value. It is, of course, a favorite host plant for butterflies.

The Shoshones, a Native American tribe, learned the knack of collecting milkweed milk, pressing and molding it in the hand until it was firm enough to chew. The Indians have also used the plant medicinally for centuries, as well as using it for food, including the leaves and pods. Blossoms and buds become both flavoring and thickening for meat soups. The most graceful gastronomical gesture, however, is their habit of sweetening their wild strawberries by shaking on them the early dew from the milkweed blossoms.

Fremont found the Indians of the Platte River cooking the young milkweed pods with buffalo meat. Even today in Taos, if one is invited to an Indian home, one may dine on meat dishes to which have been added young milkweed leaves or pods cooked as we cook green beans.

MINTS (*Mentha* spp.)   Mints are promiscuous. Notorious cross-pollinators, they should not be permitted to bloom. The resulting mint growth often has a muddy or muddled fragrance, not sharp and clean as you want it to be. Mints should be propagated from plants or stolons in order to be true. Stolons are small roots growing near the surface with wild abandon, as though mint was seeking Proserpina or Pluto.

MONOCULTURES   Monoculture is defined as the growing of one crop in an area to the exclusion of all others. This should be avoided, for growing a diversity of plants will bring about a diversity of pests and consequently a variety of benefits. On a large scale this means strip-farming, using two or more crops; in the home garden, rows and patches should be broken up. Strips of corn or small grains in a large planting could be broken up with strips of meadow. Strip-cropping alfalfa and cotton tends to increase the effectiveness of natural enemies. In the garden interplanting lettuce and cantaloupes will reduce leaf miner damage.

MOLES   Foil the critters by soaking seeds of corn, beans, etc. in a solution made by boiling a few pods of hot pepper for about five minutes. Dilute this mixture with just enough water to soak the seeds in for an hour or so. Just be sure to wear rubber gloves when planting.

Protective plantings also help to keep away moles. Spurge (also known as the mole plant) will discourage moles. Seeds are commercially available and the plant is decorative and self-sowing. Castor beans are

also effective but care should be taken if there are children about as the attractive seeds are poisonous. Dog droppings placed in their tunnels are said to repel them. Vibration vexes moles, and pinwheels may drive them away if stuck in several places. Empty bottles placed in their tunnels have also been used by some gardeners with good effect. Scilla is another plant they are reported to dislike.

MONKEY GRASS (*Liriope*)   Mostly we are so concerned with the flower picture that we forget the frame! This evergreen wonder plant grows well in sun or deep shade. Park's *Muscari exilflora* has blue flowers resembling grape hyacinths which appear in late summer or fall, followed by polished black berries. Use as a border, grouped in the landscape, or as a groundcover. To maintain health and aesthetic appeal, cut back old foliage in early spring before growth starts. Chopped foliage may be used for seasoning.

MONSTERA DELICIOSA   The genus *Monstera* consists of about thirty species of evergreen climbers coming mainly from South America. Among the species only one, *Monstera deliciosa* (sometimes called *Philodendron pertusum*), offers an unusual fruit. This ornamental climber has large, curiously perforated, dark green leathery leaves. The fruit, which is seldom borne outside the tropics, turns from green to yellow when fully mature and the scales that cover the surface gradually fall off. The fruit can be cut from the stem and placed in a glass of water. It ripens from the base upwards gradually and not all at the same time, so that a portion may be eaten at a time as it ripens, provided it can be stored properly, preferably in a refrigerator. The soft pulp of the fruit has a pineapple-banana odor and a sweet pleasant taste.

MOONS, SEEDS, AND WATER   Dr. Jane Joy Panzer, a biologist at Tulane University, after three years of research, concluded that seeds have "some kind of biological control." As reported in *Organic Gardening*, her experiments showed that seeds take in water and germinate on a well-established monthly lunar cycle. "Water intake charts on the seeds peaked at every quarter moon, and were especially marked on the full moon," according to Dr. Panzer's observation. "In fact, seeds took in twice as much water on the full moon as at other times in the monthly cycle." Water intake is closely related to germination. Her studies also revealed a seasonal variation among different kinds of seed. Corn was found to be "livelier," taking in more water and germinating faster in May and June. "Nobody knows the seeds control their behavior because nobody ever assumed that they had any control," Dr. Panzer stated, "The assumption has been that seeds germinate and take in water in a passive automatic way." Further evidence that seeds react to environmental changes such as lunar pull, the earth's electromagnetic field, and other factors came during hurricane season in New Orleans. As Hurricane Carmen raged far out at sea, Dr. Panzer's seeds began to show a decidedly "nervous" reaction. Weeks before the storm approached land, she noticed the seeds were behaving strangely. The rhythm of the water intake charts broke. The curve changed, and the peak lessened, as water intake activity dwindled with the approach of the storm. "We don't know what triggered this reaction specifically, but several weeks after the storm passed, the seeds resumed their normal water intake rhythm." Dr. Panzer also found some evidence to suggest that seeds interact with each other, possibly because they have their own electromagnetic fields.

MORMON TEA (*Ephedra nevadensis*) This herb was widely used by early settlers for medicinal purposes and may still be purchased from dealers in herbs. The active principle is ephedrine, which is a powerful decongestant. It is a stimulant and may cause a moderate rise in blood pressure, increasing the heart rate and cardiac output. The bronchi are relaxed and dilated. It is used by the Chinese to treat coughs, colds, headaches, and fever—they call it *Ma Huang*.

Ephedrine has sometimes been compared in its effects to adrenaline, but unlike adrenaline it may be taken by mouth. It is especially valuable in relieving the choking spasms in asthma and has also been used to relieve hay fever.

Mormon tea is fairly widespread throughout the American Southwest. It likes a shady habitat. The herb has both male and female flowers and the fruit consists of two pistillike capsules containing a juicy cone-shaped seed in each capsule.

MOSQUITOS (*Culex pipiens*) Few things can make a gardener more miserable. Only the female mosquito bites—but how she bites! Generally, dark clothing, the carbon dioxide we exhale, and the warm, moist currents of air always circulating just above our skin attract the hungry female. Perfume, perspiration, and other body chemicals make the trail even stronger, leading her right to you. To avoid her attentions wear long pants and long-sleeved shirts of light colors, such as white, light green, or yellow. Avoid perfumes or highly scented deodorants and soaps. Finally, the best insurance is a strong repellent. The repellent works by clogging the pores of a mosquito's receptors. You may use a gel, oil, stick, or spray. Researchers believe the most effective repellents usually contain deet—diethyltoluamide—and they also suggest diluting with alcohol to make them less greasy and easier to use.

MOSS In certain seasons and under certain weather conditions, moss often grows in a shady patio or between paving stones or bricks, resulting in a slippery condition that may prove hazardous. One of the best ways to control this moss is with a good cleaning material. Mix 2 gallons warm water, 1 cup TSP (trisodium phosphate, obtainable at most hardware stores), 1 cup powdered detergent, and 2 cups household bleach.

MOSS PINK (*Phlox subulata*) will grow easily and well in any light, well-drained soil. In the eastern states they seem to do better in loose, rocky soil. *Phlox subulata* grows wild in the eastern, western, and southern parts of the United States on dry banks and in fields. They put on a beautiful "pink show" in the spring.

MOSS SANDWORT (*Arenaria verna caespitosa*) This low-growing, tufted grass substitute is one of the best plants available for planting between flagstones in a walk. They are deep-rooted, short, and not viney. Easy to care for and will stand lots of foot traffic.

MOUSE PLANT (*Arisarum proboscideum*) is a curious, rather than beautiful, tuberous-rooted dwarf herb from the Mediterranean region, belonging to the Arum family (*Araceae*). The name is that given by Dioscorides. It may be grown in open woodland or in a shady pocket in the rock garden, in cool leafy soil, and is easily increased by

Mouse plant

division in the early spring. Its spathes, produced among the leaves in spring, are whitish and olive-green, narrowing into tapering tails 4 or 5 inches long. It is hardy at least as far north as the vicinity of New York City. This is one of the fun-to-grow plants.

MOWING TIP   A "rule of thumb" for mowing home lawns is not to remove any more than one-third of the leaf surface at one time. If you follow this criteria for mowing frequency, you no longer need to "bag" your grass clippings. Grass clippings do not contribute to thatch, but instead return valuable nutrients to the soil. They usually contain about 4 percent nitrogen, ½ percent phosphorus, and 2 percent potassium, as well as the necessary minor elements plants need.

MULCH   As with composting, mulching is a basic practice of the organic gardening method. It is simply a layer of material, preferably organic, that is placed on the soil surface to conserve moisture, hold down weeds, and ultimately improve soil structure and fertility. Mulching also protects plants during winter, reducing the dangers of freezing and heaving.

Here are the advantages of mulching:

* Mulched plants are not subjected to the extremes of temperatures of an exposed plant.
* Many mulching materials contain rich minerals and these gradually break down and become incorporated into the garden soil.
* Mulching is an advantage for the busy gardener, saving many backbreaking hours of weeding and cultivating.
* Hot, drying sun and wind do not penetrate to the soil. Moisture is conserved and erosion prevented.
* Mulching keeps vegetables and fruits clean and dry. Unstaked tomatoes often become mildewed or moldy. They may even develop rot. A mulched garden has a tidy appearance, always looking clean and trim no matter what the season.

Less often considered are the *disadvantages* of mulching. In all fairness these need consideration as well.

* Seedlings planted in very moist soil should not be mulched immediately as it may cause the condition called "damping off." Attracted by the moist condition, sowbugs often attack small plants when they are mulched. Allow seedlings to become established before mulching.
* Crown-rot in perennials is a disease caused by a fungus. Do not permit mulches of peat moss, manure, compost, or ground corn cobs to touch the base of these plants, especially during times of heavy rain.
* Do not mulch a wet, low-lying soil. Leaves that mat down are particularly to be avoided.
* Don't mulch tomatoes until the first blossoms appear; they need the warmth of the sun on their roots to grow well. After flowers appear and first fruits form, mulching is helpful to conserve moisture, keep fruit clean, and prevent blossom-end rot.

MULCHING MATERIAL   Just about any organic waste material is useful for mulching. Here are some suggestions: grass clippings, corn stalks (preferably shredded), straw, shredded leaves, sawdust (mixed with straw or some other light material to prevent matting), cocoa bean hulls or shells, corn cobs, pine needles, peat moss, alfalfa hay, oak tow, rotted pine wood, packing materials, weeds and native grasses (shred and mix with grass clippings and use around trees or shrubs), buckwheat hulls, salt hay, grape or apple pomace, nut hulls. Inorganic mulches sometimes used are shredded paper, aluminum foil, black paper, or even dust or stones.

MULTIPLY BY DIVIDING   Plants may be propagated in two ways. The first and best-known way is by seed. The second is by vegetative propagation (also called cloning), when a part of an existing plant is used in growing a new plant. The main advantage of the vegetative method is that you get a new individual that is genetically the same as the parent plant. When seed or sexual propagation is used, the offspring of the two parents may not be like either one, a new combination of genetic material having occurred.

Some plants will multiply naturally in the vegetative or nonsexual manner by means of specialized structures. Examples of this are the strawberry by its runners, the tulips and garlics by their bulbs, and the iris by its rhizome. An easy, artificial way of reproducing plants is by means of cuttings. All you need do is cut off a small piece of the parent plant, root it in a suitable medium, and plant it. Cuttings may be made from different parts of the plant and are then referred to by that name: root cuttings, leaf cuttings, leaf bud cuttings, and stem cuttings. Such plants as ivy or philodendron root easily in a glass of water on a window sill. You can also root cuttings of chrysanthemums, yew, holly, crape myrtle, and almost all of our ornamental plants. In general, cuttings will grow better if made fairly early in the growing season but others, like the broad-leafed evergreens, will root from cuttings better in the fall.

Make a cutting by snipping off a 3- or 4-inch sprig of new growth, making a diagonal cut so as to expose as much of the growing tissue as possible. Strip leaves and buds off the bottom third of this stem and dip it in a rooting stimulant such as Rootone. Then set it about one-third deep into a rooting medium that will provide plenty of air and moisture, and also be disease-free. Try perlite, vermiculite, peat, or a combination, along with sand as a rooting medium.

MUNG BEANS (*Phaseolus mungo*) The mung bean is native to India where they are cooked, pureed, and eaten as part of the daily diet. The Chinese, however, cultivate them for their crisp, refreshing, delicately flavored young shoots. They're becoming increasingly popular in our own country. Growing the sprouts is easy, and they make a delicious vegetable for wintertime indoor growing. All you need is a warm place—about 70°F—the beans, and total darkness. Rinse beans and soak in a fruit jar for a day or two. When skins start to burst, spread beans on a piece of damp toweling and place them in a warm, dark cupboard. Keep constantly damp by watering several times a day. Don't keep them too wet, however, as they may mold. If all goes well, in a week to nine days you will have fat shoots about 2 inches long and ready to harvest with your scissors. Generally used in salads, they can be put into breads or muffins, adding their own nutty flavor.

MUSHROOM It is difficult to exaggerate the importance of mushrooms as food, for they contain ergosterol in large quantities—the raw material, so to speak, of vitamin D. Mushrooms also contain a large proportion of sulphur and calcium and they are the nearest approach to meat in the vegetable kingdom.

MUSTARD (*Sinapis alba* and *Brassica nigra*) Man was eating mustard seeds before 10,000 B.C. Tendergreens (mustard-spinach) is a new and delicious development, good cooked or in salads. Seeds germinate quickly. For a continuous crop, sow every two weeks and cut with scissors fifteen to twenty days later. Mustard greens are an excellent source of vitamins A and C, plus B vitamins, calcium, and iron. Burpee's Fordhook Fancy has deeply curled and fringed dark-green leaves, curving backward like ostrich plumes—handsome enough for the flower bed.

Mustard oil released from the roots of mustard family members will sweeten an acid soil, helping adjacent plants that suffer when the pH is too low. The secretion also inhibits the hatching of potato nematode cysts.

Nature ne'er deserts the wise and pure;
No plot so narrow, be but Nature there,
No waste so vacant, but may well employ
Each faculty of sense, and keep the heart
Awake to Love and Beauty!

SAMUEL TAYLOR COLERIDGE

NANDINA (*Nandina*)   If you live in the Southwest, as I do, nandina is the shrub for you. Mine has lived for over forty years without any care whatsoever—I don't even water it during our hot, dry, windy summers. Other easy-care plants are crape myrtle, Japanese quince, mock-orange, and Irish juniper.

NASTURTIUM (*Tropaeolum majus*)   These plants are another gardener's ally. The pungent essence they secrete is obnoxious to such plant pests as aphids and white flies, and the excretion from their roots into the surrounding soil not only frightens root lice but is actually taken up by other plants, making them also less attractive to pests. Try placing climbing nasturtium around apple trees to thwart woolly aphids, or grow them in your greenhouse to frustrate a variety of destructive pests. Nasturtiums are also good to sow with squash, broccoli, and cucumbers.

NATURAL CONTROLS   Hot weather has set in and so have the garden pests. If your garden is overrun with caterpillars,

hornworms, webworms, or cabbage loopers and there are not enough natural predators around, the answer to your dilemma is Bacillus thuringiensis (sold under various trade names). These microbes do not have harmful side effects and are generally nontoxic to animals. The insecticide works by entering the stomach of the insect and changing its digestive tract, causing the insect to starve to death. Beneficial insects such as ladybugs, honeybees, parasitic wasps, and the mantis, which do not eat leaves, are not affected. It may be used on edible plants as it has no poisonous residue.

NATURE'S MATH   There's a lot of emphasis on math these days, so it's interesting to note that nature herself is a diligent mathematician. Sunflower seeds, for instance, are arranged in two sets of logarithmic spirals outward from the center, one set running counterclockwise and the other set clockwise. The number of spirals also occurs in pine cones, pineapples, and daisy florets. No two snowflakes are ever alike but, though the pattern varies, all have six sides. Nature is beautiful, even in mathematical precision.

NEMATODES

Non-chemical controls of nematodes

- Move the garden every two to three years if sufficient land is available.
- Do not buy or use transplants that show tiny root swellings or knots on the roots.
- Keep vegetables watered during the hot months where there is not enough rainfall. Place some kind of mulch material around the base of plants to prevent rapid drying of the soil.
- Apply the correct amount of fertilizer to promote good growth. Add plenty of well-decomposed compost to the soil if available.
- Destroy the roots by pulling or plowing up and burning immediately after harvest is complete.
- Use resistant varieties where available.

Soil treatment for control of nematodes

The planting of marigolds is effective against certain types of nematodes. However, this is most beneficial over a period of time and results may not become apparent for several months.

Soil sterilization, while practical only on a small scale, is nevertheless useful under certain conditions such as for seed beds or greenhouse soil. Soil-filled flats can be dipped in water that is kept at the boiling point; pouring boiling water on soil doesn't seem to be effective. Steam heat and flame pasteurizers are also used by commercial growers. Tools can be disinfected in boiling water.

Crops for nematode-infested soil

Some crops are more resistant than others to root-knot nematodes. Broccoli, brussels sprouts, mustard, chives, cress, garlic, leek, groundcherry, and rutabagas are fairly resistant. Others possible, but less resistant, include globe artichoke, Jerusalem artichoke, asparagus, sweet corn, horseradish, some lima bean strains, onion, parsnip, rhubarb, spinach, sweet potato, and turnip.

NEMATODES AND SUGAR According to J.I. Rodale (*Control Garden Pests*), sugar will kill nematodes by drying them out. Here is the Department of Agriculture's description of what happens: Enough sugar is added to the soil to produce a greater amount of dissolved solids in the soil solution than in the cell fluid of the nematodes. Because liquid tends to move from a less concentrated solution to one more highly concentrated (osmosis), the body fluid moves out of the nematodes, and they die as a result of dehydration (exmosis).

NEMATODE TEST To find out if you have nematodes, plant two cucumber seeds in a styrofoam cup full of the soil in question. When true leaves appear, gently wash the soil from the roots. Small knotlike protrusions on the roots indicate nematodes.

NEWSPAPER MULCH Newspaper makes a good mulch for vegetables. Place several layers between plant rows, keeping them wet so they won't blow around and weighing here and there with a few clods of earth. Weeds won't sprout underneath, and when the papers finally decompose they'll enrich the soil.

NEW ZEALAND SPINACH (*Tetragonia expansa*) Not a true spinach, but when cooked the flavor is remarkably similar. Its great value lies in its adaptability to summer climates. It is heat-resistant, requires little

care, and produces abundantly throughout the summer. It's a tasty substitute to grow between your spring and fall spinach plantings. Set out young plants, or sow seed, when all danger of frost is passed. Give the plants, which take seventy days from seed to maturity, plenty of room, for they will spread 3 to 5 feet in every direction. The crop needs fertile soil and plenty of water.

Harvest either by pinching off the tender shoots at the top of the plant, which will allow new leaves to grow in their place, or by cutting off the entire plant a few inches from the ground. Cook as you would spinach or chard.

NO-DIG GARDENING Ruth Stout was the foremost exponent of this method. Here are the basic principles: **1.** To imitate nature closely by not inverting the soil. **2.** To economize on compost and other organic materials by using them as a surface mulch, just as nature keeps her fertility-promoting materials. **3.** To reduce weed growth by not bringing more and more weeds to the surface. **4.** And, by these practices, to maintain a balance of air, moisture, biological life, and plant foods.

Obviously, as with other gardening methods, there are some drawbacks. In some climates this method will work better than others. In the hot, dry Southwest the soil needs occasional stirring to permit penetration of rainfall or irrigation. Some proponents of no-digging have found that after a few years soil fertility seemed to decline, still others have been unable to get good yields of root crops, especially radishes.

If abundant organic materials are available to constantly replenish fertility I believe this method would work well for a small plot.

NORTHERN GARDENERS For early lettuce, in the cold parts of the country, try letting a few heads go to seed during the summer. By August these seeds will drop off and grow into small plants by fall, then get covered by snow. In the spring when the snow disappears, you will find hardy young plants for transplanting. Around the first of June

you will have fresh lettuce from your own garden again.

NO STRINGS ATTACHED Many new bean varieties are stringless, such as Burpee's Stringless Green Pod, Improved Tendergreen, Topcrop, Goldencrop Wax Bean, Surecrop Stringless Wax, Pencil Pod Wax, Royal Burgundy Purple Pod; and pole beans, Burpee Golden, Blue Lake White Seeded, and Romano (Italian Pole), to name but a few. Early riser is a great newcomer.

NOVICE GARDENER Hang in there and don't give up if heavy rain and/or cloudy weather cause loss of lower leaves, yellowing of leaves, and brown areas within leaves. If the rainy weather doesn't continue too long, the plants will soon recover with the sun's return.

Don't be too disturbed over small loss of leaf area due to insect feeding on plants such as beans. This is also a problem on cabbage or leafy crops. They can tolerate 20 percent leaf loss without greatly affecting yield.

Don't feel that you must kill all insects, beneficial or harmful. Try for identification. I recommend *Handbook of the Insect World*, published by the National 4-H Service Committee, Inc., 59 East Van Buren Street, Chicago, Illinois 60605. Your library may have a copy.

NUT PINES (*Pinus*) The seeds of the nut pines, rich, oily, and nutritious, with good keeping qualities, supply Indians and Mexicans of the Southwest with a store of food that permits hoarding for the winter. John Muir, explorer, naturalist, and writer, speaks of their qualities: "It is the commonest tree of the short mountain ranges of the Great Basin. Tens of thousands of acres are covered with it, forming bountiful orchards.... Being so low and accessible, the cones are easily beaten off with poles, and the nuts are procured by roasting until the scales open. To the tribes of the desert and sage plains these seeds are the staff of life. They are eaten either raw or parched, or in the form of mush, or cakes, after being pounded into meal. The time of nut harvest is the merriest time of the year. An industrious family can squirrel away fifty or sixty bushels in a single month before the snow comes, and then their bread for the winter is assured."

There are four types: The *Pinus cembroides* is the "piñon" that covers the upper slopes of Arizona mountains and the mountains of northern Mexico.

The pinon *P. edulis* ranges from the eastern foothills of the Colorado Rockies to western Texas and westward to the eastern borders of Utah, southwestern Wyoming, central Arizona, and on into Mexico, often forming extensive open forests and reaching an elevation of seven thousand feet.

The four-leaved *P. quadrifolia* is scattered over the mountains of southern and lower California. This is a desert tree. The cones are small with few scales but the nut is five-eighths of an inch long and very rich.

The one-leaved nut pine, *P. monophylla*, spreads like an old apple tree. The vigor of the tree is expressed in its abundant fruit, short, oblong, one to two inches in length, with rich plump brown seeds which have long been a staple in the diet of the Indians of Nevada and California. This tree is spread from the western slopes of the Wasatch Mountains of Utah, and ranges to the eastern slopes of the southern Sierra Nevada, that range's western slopes at the head waters of King's River, and southward to northern Arizona and the mountains of southern California.

One impulse from a vernal wood,
May teach you more of man,
Of moral evil and of good
Than all the sages can.

WILLIAM WORDSWORTH

OATS (*Avena sativa*)   A cover crop of oats, following sod before corn is planted, minimizes white grubs in the corn.

As food, oats have many benefits. In cases of indigestion and constipation, a drink may be made by taking a tablespoonful of oatmeal and stirring it slowly in a pint of boiling water for about five minutes, adding a little salt to suit the taste. Milk may be added as well as honey. One herbal recommends this drink for persons "who seek to retain their youth." It is also of value as a tonic to the general system and is stated as beneficial to the sexual system.

The presence of phosphorus in oats makes it valuable for the formation of brain and nerve tissue. In bygone times it was believed that ample use of oatmeal would help children become more adept in their studies. Because of its beneficial effects upon the nervous system, the consumption of oats in the form of oatmeal or as a fluid extract has been reported to facilitate sleep.

It is also believed that oats have a very beneficial action upon the heart muscle, oatmeal water being considered as a preventative for heart disease, as well as helping to remedy heart disease.

Oatmeal has many elements that have antiseptic properties, and when taken frequently as a food is believed to act as a natural preventative for contagious diseases.

Oats are composed of 67 percent carbohydrates, 14 percent albuminoids, amino acids, enzymes (amylase, protease, lipase), phytin, and vitamins A, B_1, B_2, and E and traces of other vitamins. A poultice of oatmeal is beneficial to the skin. It has been reported that boiling oats in vinegar and then applying the mash to the face and other parts of the body will remove freckles and other spots.

OKRA (*Hibiscus esculentus*), that beloved staple of Southern gardens, is an African native closely related to cotton. The large, attractive plants bear green-yellow flowers followed by edible pods which should be picked daily while young and tender. The pods are the prime ingredient in those delightful New Orleans gumbos which were first introduced into the United States from

Africa more than two hundred years ago by way of the slave trade.

Not only is okra good for you, the whole plant has medicinal qualities. The dried stems, leaves, and roots can be used as a substitute for mallow, another related plant. A Marquette University research team has also been able to turn okra into a cheap and plentiful substitute for life-giving blood plasma. The replacement is a product of okra pods. It is said that the new material has all the advantages of blood plasma and none of the disadvantages.

Okra is a heavy feeder, and it needs plenty of sunshine and a long growing season. It responds particularly well to well-rotted manure, but if this is not obtainable you will get good results with fish emulsion diluted with water. Okra grows best in the heat of summer, but likes plenty of water. I always plant a double row, digging a trench between the rows about a foot or two deep. This I fill with grass clippings, etc. which rise to the top when I lay the hose in the trench to water, then drop back to conserve moisture as the water soaks in. Although okra is

troubled by few insects, aphids will infest the flower buds and young pods. These are almost immediately followed by ladybugs—attracted to the aphids—and soon the situation is again under control. Okra will sprout quickly if boiling water is poured over the seeds and they are allowed to stand overnight.

ONION (*Allium cepa*) Without onions and all their relatives cooking many dishes just wouldn't be the same. We *need* onions in our diet for, according to Dr. Benjamin S. Frank, they are one of the best sources of ribonucleic acid (RNA) which, along with deoxyribonucleic acid (DNA), is fundamental to the life process itself.

Onions, which may be considered both food and medicine, are easy to grow. Take your choice for starting from seeds, sets, or plants—all will produce, in time, usable onions. Rather than one long narrow row I prefer to plant my onions in triple rows, staggering another row on each side of the first row planted. As onions grow straight up they take little space. As they grow I pull every other onion for table use, leaving space for the remaining onions to grow into large onions for drying.

Onions need plenty of humus and good drainage. The formation of the bulb is determined by the amount of daylight the plant receives and not because of the maturity of the plant. This explains why onions form bulbs in certain localities and not in others, Onions such as Yellow Bermuda or White Creole will form bulbs when receiving only twelve hours of daylight daily. Ebenezer and Yellow Danvers need thirteen hours and Red Wethersfield has to have as much as fourteen hours. So if you plan to grow from seed, get it in the ground just as early as possible, even before danger of frost is passed.

According to Dr. Hill, "A syrup made of the juices of onions and honey is an excellent medicine for asthmatic complaints." Others have found sliced onions, used for chest poultices, beneficial to influenza sufferers. In the garden it has been found that if you plant an onion in the center of hills of cucumbers, melons, or squash, worms and bugs are less likely to feed on these plants.

ONION FLOWERS YOU DON'T WANT Cool weather stimulates flower stalk production, and onions that flower are also likely to have woody centers and keep poorly. Avoid planting onions in the fall or early spring and snip off any flower stalks that appear. Cutting the flower stalks promptly will give you larger bulbs, but you should still use these up first.

OREGANO (*Origanum* spp.) is an herb you should get better acquainted with. Like its near relative, marjoram, it's a culinary herb, a companion plant, and a medicine. There are several species similar in appearance, one called wild oregano (*O. vulgare*), which is the better medicine and one called "true oregano," which is the better kitchen flavoring.

In the garden oregano is an excellent companion plant to repel squash bugs and cucumber beetles, as well as other pests of curcurbits. Plant liberally among the vines.

Herbal practitioners esteem it highly for various stomach complaints and skin ailments. The Nichols Garden Nursery lists a related species, *O. hortensis*; a tea made from its leaves can calm distraught nerves.

Oregano can be rooted quite easily from slips, with many of the creeping stems developing rootlets. Many seed houses also list one or another species. Give the plant a sunny, dry, well-drained location in full sun. Pick as needed, stripping the plants of the outermost stems and leaves. This allows what remains to help rejuvenate the plant. For the dried herb, pick leaves as flowers begin to blossom. Keep in a warm, dry place until leaves start to crumble between your fingers. Store in an airtight container.

ORIENTAL VEGETABLES Oriental vegetables are becoming very popular as they become better known. If you would have them do well in your garden remember that good, rich, loose soil does much to ensure

good, rich, firm veggies. To get a head start sow some of them in pots or flats and when they're a suitable size transplant to outside areas. Use clean containers, scrubbed to avoid fungi or insects, and be sure there is good drainage and an ample source of light. And good fertilization is a must.

The Good Earth Seed Company (Tsang & Ma), in *The Little Book About A Lot of Chinese Vegetables*, says to place planting rows in a north-south direction so plants will receive equal exposure to the sun. Also, "When plants are in seed or seeding phase overhead watering is fine. As plants mature watering moves down to trenches so that moisture does not touch or rot foliage." Many of the vining vegetables such as Chinese okra, snow peas, asparagus beans, etc. need poles or trellises to lift fruits from the soil to avoid rot. And you can also grow more plants in less space.

Bok Choy, rich in vitamins B and C, has just a gentle hint of mustard flavor, with tangy outer leaves and stalks and inner leaves that are tender and savory.

Garland Chrysanthemum (*Shinjuku*) is an edible chrysanthemum, also known as Chop Suey Green. The young leaves are tasty and have an aroma similar to chrysanthemum foliage. This is a cool weather crop, growing best in spring or fall. And it is rich in vitamin B and minerals.

Japanese Radish Daikon. A root crop in the same family as the Chinese radish. Daikon is mildly sweet and crisp and does well throughout the year in mild-weather areas. Daikon may grow up to 30 inches and several pounds and matures between 55 to 90 days. It contains vitamins B and C and many essential minerals.

Bunching Onion (*He-Shi-Ko*). This veggie has a green tubular stalk and slender long white base or head. They are used whole; not only the head but the foliage is mildly hot and sweet, and the head's flavor is more intensely sweet. In warm-weather areas this onion may be grown all year round. They may be eaten raw or cooked. Rich in vitamin C, they provide good fiber for the diet. The

Chinese have been using the bunching onion as herbal medicine for centuries. A good veggie to grow in containers.

Thai Basil is an unusual taste treat. The leaves are green with a purple base. The flower is described as having a hint of anise.

Japanese Turnip is mild and slightly sweet and may be used either steamed or fresh. Easy to culture, they grow to about the size of a ping-pong ball and are great to grow in fall gardens.

Yuen Shai (Chinese Parsley), also known as cilantro, and the seeds as coriander. Of delicious fragrance and flavor with no hint of bitterness. Use seeds as a condiment. A good container plant, growing best in potting mix of non-clay soil in cool weather.

Goat Horn Peppers. This is a fiery hot red pepper and a great favorite of those who want a pepper hotter than cayenne. It will make your eyelashes curl! The name comes from its curled and twisted shape. And it drys well.

Snow Pea This is the one with the edible pod that sells for fancy prices in the supermarket. Pods are crispy, sugary, and tiny, with a very delicate flavor. Grow in a cool climate, in a moist non-acid soil with good drainage. Pick pods when peas become visible, and snap off ends to remove stem and any strings along each side.

Thai Winged Bean (*Bin Dow*). Sometimes called Princess Pea, Asparagus Pea, or Koa Bean. It has been called a "Growing Grocery Store," as the leaves, shoots, roots, and of course the beans themselves (high in protein with an asparagus taste) are consumed. Needs cool weather and takes about 50 days to mature.

ORNAMENTAL GRASSES Pampas grass, fountain grass, feathertop, maiden grass, and other ornamental grasses need cutting back before new growth begins. In the lower South this should be done in February—don't delay, or you may damage the new foliage as you cut back the old. Cutting will promote new growth and give you a fresher look.

OVER EASY Progress in human nutrition may be measured best by the knowledge that many nutrition-related problems have been conquered. Life expectancy of the average American has increased significantly from about forty years of age at the turn of the century to approximately seventy years at the present time. Fresh vegetables unsprayed by chemicals and from your own garden not only give you better nutrition but exercise, fun, and longevity as well.

There is now proof that a properly fed heart will age more slowly. Doctors Emmanual Cheraskin and W. Marshall Ringdorf, Jr. were able to measure the aging effects of refined carbohydrates (starches and sugars) on the human heart. They tested "supposedly healthy" people both before and one year after they stopped eating potentially harmful "junk foods." By measuring the P-R interval (the time between the first and second parts of one's heartbeat), the doctors determined the effectiveness and the age of the hearts tested. Aging lengthens the P-R interval.

The results? All those tested had shorter—therefore "younger"—heartbeat responses. The improved diet enabled sixty-year-old hearts to become as much as fifteen years younger.

Gardening is preventive medicine you can prescribe for yourself.

OWLS Owls are more important than we may realize. The tiny screech owl, more often heard than seen, patrols moonlit yards for insects and mice. Lizards, salamanders, and worms may also be taken during their nightly forays. The barn owl is probably the most important predator of rats and mice in populated areas, rivaling the house cat in importance.

OYSTER PLANT (*Tragopogon porrifolius*), or Salsify. The oyster plant gets its name from the delicious flavor of its cooked roots. One of our most nutritious root crops, it is a biennial, growing 3 to 4 feet high with a white, deep taproot. A long-season crop, its seed should be sown as early in spring as possible. A sandy loam is best, with generous quantities of well-rotted manure incorporated into the soil. Frosts improve the flavor and texture. Part of the crop may be dug in the fall and stored like cabbage for winter use. A thick mulch will permit digging as needed all through the cold months. Make sure that the calcium supply is adequate.

To cook: Scrape roots; boil or steam until tender, then serve with cream cheese or Hollandaise sauce; braise in butter or run through food chopper, add seasoning, beaten egg, and bread crumbs, and form into small cakes and fry in butter.

The Spanish oyster plant, *Scolymus hispanicus*, is often called golden thistle and is similar to salsify. Even better in flavor, it is thought, is black salsify (*Scorzonera hispanica*), which has a black-skinned root. Its leaves are often used in salads.

What potent blood hath modest May.
RALPH WALDO EMERSON

PAINTING the trunks of fruit trees with Tabasco sauce helps deter rabbits and mice.

PAINT UP Paint the handles of your small tools a bright orange for greater ease in locating them if you put them down while gardening. Research has shown that this color is the one most easily seen and it is the color favored for hunter's caps and jackets as a safety measure. Use a magic marker to write your name on your hoes, rakes, shovels, etc.—if someone borrows them you will be more likely to have them returned.

PANSY (*Violaceae*) Pansy plants are small but durable. They begin blooming when plants are no larger than your fist and gradually increase in size to about 10 inches in height by midsummer. The blossoms are quite large in cool weather, up to 3 inches in diameter. Flower size decreases markedly in warm weather.

You can transplant pansies to the garden soon after the spring thaw. Here in Oklahoma, where winters are mild, mine are fall-planted for winter and spring bloom. Space plants 6 inches apart.

Try growing pansies from seeds. Buy seeds of the newer hybrids and plant them in your garden in late summer. Generally, with some protection, the small plants will live over winter and bloom early the following spring.

My Majestic hybrids from Burpee and Universals from Goldsmith give me breathtaking blooms every year. They blossom over a long season, but not "forever." When they begin to decline in vigor and flower size due to hot weather, I replace them with summer flowers.

PAPER CLIPS Keep a few handy in your pocket or garden basket and use to close opened seed packets while in the garden so seed will not spill. Or try clothespins.

PARSLEY—MORE THAN JUST A PRETTY GARNISH Parsley herb is a native of Sardinia and other parts of southern Europe, where it has long been hailed as a "miracle healer" because of its ability to relax "stiff fingers" or "gnarled joints." Parsley root has been found to contain ingredients that help produce an anodyne (pain-relieving) benefit and promote more youthful flexibility of the limbs. It is a rich source of vitamins A, B, and C as well as four vital minerals—calcium, copper, iron, and manganese—that work together in harmony. This meatless source of vitamin A is believed by many to be nature's major secret of youthful health.

Parsley is impervious to cold. I plant it in the autumn and have it all winter. It can even freeze solid, thaw out, and be as good as ever.

Parsley is best eaten raw for preservation of the food value. When prepared as a tea use about ¼ teaspoon of powdered parsley to the cup. If parsley flakes are used, about ½ teaspoon to a cup of boiling water is a suitable amount. Parsley may also be converted into a juice with the aid of a fruit and vegetable juicer.

PARSNIPS (*Peucedanum sativun*)   Love those parsnips . . . cooked till tender, lightly buttered, and sprinkled with cinnamon, they add a whole new flavor dimension to a meal. Even non-parsnip fanciers like them this way. The British have been eating them for some two thousand years. Unfortunately their sweetness is an acquired taste and in the last few decades fewer people have been acquiring it. Parsnips are outstandingly hardy but do need a depth of soil, especially for the long-rooted varieties, which many gardens lack. Try making cone pits (also good for carrots or other root crops in heavy or rocky soil). Drive a stake or piece of pipe 2 feet into the ground, then rotate it in a circle to create a cone-shaped hole with the top about 6 inches in diameter. Fill the hole with compost and plant 3 to 4 seeds in each hole.

Parsnip seeds germinate slowly and have a very short vitality. Secure fresh seed each year. Soaking seed overnight may help speed germination. Mulch the rows after planting so the soil will remain cool. Radish seed is useful in marking the row. Hollow Crown, the most popular variety, takes about 105 days to mature.

PASTEURIZING SOIL   Do not sterilize your soil—this means killing everything, the good organisms as well as the bad. What you should do to your soil is pasteurize it. This can be done by filling a baking pan with 3 or 4 inches of soil and putting a meat thermometer in the middle. Dampen the soil and put it in a preheated oven for a half hour, or until the temperature reaches 180°F. Any hotter than this and you run the risk of de-

stroying soil structure, organic matter, and all organisms in the soil. Here are the temperatures required to kill soil-inhabiting pests. The chart was prepared by the Ontario, Canada, Department of Agriculture and Foods.

Pests or Groups of of Pests	30 Minutes at Temperature:
Nematodes	120°F
Damping-off and soft-rot organisms	130°F
Most pathogenic bacteria and fungi	150°F
Soil insects and most plant viruses	160°F
Most weed seeds	175°F
A few resistant weeds	212°F

An alternate method to pasteurizing soil is to place it in a pressure cooker, cooking for 20 to 30 minutes at five pounds pressure.

Training is everything. The peach was once a bitter almond; cauliflower is nothing but cabbage with a college education.
                                        —Mark Twain

PEACHES   According to James Whitcomb Riley, "The ripest peach is highest on the tree." Peaches in the southern states have a lot of problems, one of them being our variable weather. Often the trusting peach is fooled into blooming early, thinking spring has arrived, only to have its lovely blossoms frost-bitten a few days later when the weather turns cold again. Smudge pots may help. If you have room for only one tree be sure it is self-fruitful, if not, you must plant a pollinator. Horsetail, made into a tea and used as a spray, is helpful against powdery fungus and peach leaf curl.

PEACOCK PLANT (*Calathea makoyana*) Sometimes called zebra plants. These tropical plants grow wild in South America. The flowers are insignificant but the large leaves form tufts of attractive rose, yellow, olive, white, or variegated foliage. *C. makoyana* is olive green with transparent "windows," red beneath. Grow as a houseplant and give it a spot near a north or east window, shading with a sheer curtain from direct sun. It needs a humid atmosphere; either mist foliage daily, group with other plants, or set the pot on a tray of pebbles and water. In December and January, water only when the soil is dry to the touch. Feed only two times a year; early spring and late summer.

PEAR PEELING   Pears can be peeled quickly and easily by dipping them into boiling water—just the same way as one does when preparing peaches for canning.

PEANUTS (*Arachis hypogaea*)   Peanuts, as warm weather plants, make a wonderful second crop. They are not only fun and easy to grow, but actually, as legumes, enrich the soil in the same way as peas and beans do. And one pound of roasted nuts or peanut butter contains more calories, protein, minerals, and vitamins than a pound of beefsteak. Lots of folks like to make their own peanut butter by roasting and grinding the nuts and adding honey.

Peanuts need a growing season of four to five frost-free months. Plant the seeds—in or out of shells—4 to 6 inches apart, 2 inches deep, in rows 3 feet apart. Well-drained sandy or loose soil is needed. Thin seedlings to 8 to 12 inches apart. Before frost, dig up entire plant and air-dry to cure before removing pods. Sometimes I hang mine on my clothesline.

There are three types of peanuts: Jumbo, Valencia, and Spanish. The Jumbo or "runner" type forms a sprawling plant 3 feet across, producing immense quantities of large peanuts. It needs a long growing season and lots of space.

The Valencia or "bunch" variety is more practical for small gardens. The plants, which don't form runners, have upright stems and form a tight clump of nuts under the base. The nuts are as large as the Jumbo type. While Valencias ripen faster they still require a growing season of 180 days or more. Park's Red Tennessee is a good Valencia type, useful also as a border for a flower bed or driveway with its attractive flowers.

Spanish peanuts are also a bunch variety, and they have the shortest growing season of all, making them suitable for Northern growers. In certain favorable areas they will even grow in southern Canada. The nuts, which are surprisingly low in starch, are much smaller than the other two varieties, but have more flavor, especially when eaten raw.

And do add your peanut hay to your compost heap, or use it as a mulch. It is as rich in nitrogen as the vines of peas or beans.

PEANUTS FOR THE NORTH   Good crops may be grown in most parts of Canada and the States if they are planted on warm, sandy soil with a southern exposure. Shell the nuts, sow May 15 to June 1, 3 inches apart and $1\frac{1}{2}$ inches deep. Keep well cultivated. The short flower stalks bend, touching the soil, after they are pollinated, and root themselves in the soft ground, developing the peanuts in clusters under the soil. Dig just before frost and hang to cure. Roast at 300°F for an hour, stirring often. Early Spanish is the earliest maturing variety of peanuts and the best kind for growing in Canada (Stokes).

PEAS (*Pisum sativum*, var. *hortense*)   Making the earth say "peas" can result in a lot of good eating. Garden peas are either wrinkled or smooth-seeded. The wrinkled have the best flavor but the smooth-seeded are hardier and will grow very early in the North, or in the fall in mild climates. The sweeter wrinkled types are sown from the beginning of March and are ready in 12 to 16 weeks.

Peas need a rich, loamy soil with plenty of compost or well-rotted manure incorporated in it. Don't give them fresh manure or you will have greener and fewer peas. Peas also need lime (pH 6.5).

By choosing varieties that mature at different times, spring and early-summer sowings will give you peas from the end of June to September. Peas need posts, wire, or plastic to cling to, if you are growing the taller varieties; the dwarf varieties can get along with small twigs. Mulch to keep down weeds and water in warm weather. A mild fungicide

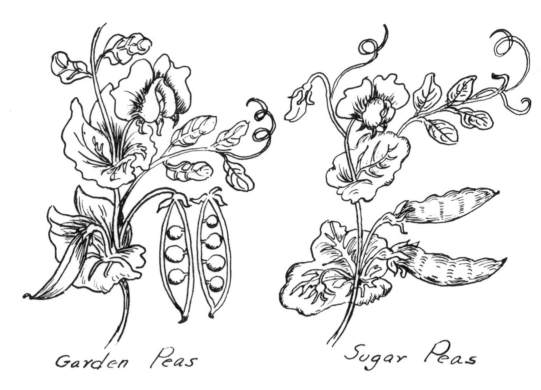

Garden Peas   Sugar Peas

like Captan will help to keep early sown peas from rotting. Nitrogen inoculation helps to insure an adequate supply of beneficial bacteria.

Sugar Peas (*P. sativum*, var. *saccharatum*), or "snow peas," are becoming deservedly popular. The delicious pods are eaten as one would beans.

Peas contain nicotinic acid, reportedly recommended for reducing cholesterol in the blood.

PEAS WITH A HINT OF MINT   To give your frozen peas fresh flavor add a sprig of fresh mint to the water used to steam the peas for one full minute. Not only do the peas stay bright and green, but the mint gives them added zing.

FOR PEAT'S SAKE   For many homeowners, building the fertility of a garden spot poses problems—it's difficult to know how to get a jump start. One way is to bring in bales of peat, several yards of sand, and rotted manure. Of course, in time, you will be adding compost to this from your own com-

post heap, but this way gives the land a quick boost. Each spring and fall, if a soil test shows it to be desirable, it's also good to add another bale of peat—especially good in dry soils for its water-holding capacity. Mulching between rows with straw, hay, or whatever other organic material is available also helps—all this will be incorporated into the soil at the next plowing.

PECANS   To grow and bear well, all pecan trees need zinc, and it is best applied by spraying the leaves. Pecan seed does not have a dormant period but will sprout anytime—you can grow your own pecan trees and later have them grafted to a desirable variety. Pecan trees are beautiful with their straight trunks and make fine shade trees. Even though they may not bear well they can be grown in the more northern and easterly sections of the country.

PEELING ONIONS THE NO TEAR WAY   Here's a trick: breathe through your mouth instead of your nose when you peel or slice onions. Or try peeling them in cold water, which prevents the onion chemical from becoming airborne. If you have a lot of small onions, soak them for a few seconds in boiling water, then in cold water, and skins will slip off easily.

PEPPERS (*Capsicum*)   Most gardeners simply grow peppers for food. But they're rapidly becoming one of our most ornamental vegetables, an extra bonus for gardeners who also want a feast for the eyes. The glossy green foliage and compact bushy growing habit, along with the lovely star-shaped flowers and developing fruit, make them handsome additions, even to the flower garden.

Peppers are also in step with today's eating habits. The ideal nibble for calorie-conscious eaters who want flavor and texture without fat, they're a perfect addition to *nouvelle cuisine*, today's lighter edition of the gourmet cooking of years past. And hot peppers are spicing their way into our diet with the increasing consumption of South-of-the-Border specialties. Sweet pepper use is limited only by imagination and taste: they're used for stuffing, can be cut up for snacks, alone or with dips, sliced and chopped for salads, stews, and soups.

Space plants 24 inches apart. Once the first blossoms open apply a light dose of fertil-

izer and water in well. Maintain adequate soil moisture; the lack at flowering time can cause blossoms to drop. Peppers set best in a temperature range of 60° to 75°F at night, and a daytime temperature above 90°F will also inhibit fruit set. Remember, peppers have a built-in load limit. Once the capacity of the plant is reached in number of fruit, they'll stop setting fruit until you pick some. Strangely, hot peppers become progressively less pungent the farther north they are grown.

PEPPING UP PEPPERS   When setting out pepper plants, try dropping three or four books of paper matches into the hole with each plant. The matches release phosphorus into the soil, which aids root development. After the peppers begin to grow, spraying the leaves with an Epsom salt solution (1 teaspoon of salts to 1 pint of water) will make the peppers grow larger. To protect the stems of young plants from cutworms, slip an empty toilet tissue spool over the plants and push spools into the ground 1 or 2 inches.

PERFUMING YOUR HOME NATURALLY   You, too, can make incense. For centuries fragrant gums, woods, and resins have been burned so that sweet odors might be enjoyed. Ancient civilizations of Egypt, Arabia, China, and many others record this practice. So how about letting the sweet smell of incense waft through your dwelling and evoke the mysteries of the East!

You may burn your incense in an open container or a special censer, but it should be in a well-ventilated room, as the fumes could be toxic in a tightly closed area. Place censer on a pad on the floor or table as there will be considerable base heat.

Making the same incense burned in ancient religious rites is a simple matter. A basic formula consists of equal proportions of powdered fragrant wood (sandalwood, cedar, star anise bark, balsam wood, etc.) and a resin such as gum benzoin, myrrh, or frankincense—about 1 ounce of each. To this base add 1 ounce of spices such as ground cinnamon or cloves, ground cardamon, mace, nutmeg, or allspice. Any of these excellent fragrances can be used separately or combined. Ground orange or lemon peel and bay or eucalyptus leaves are also good choices. Lavender, rosemary, and basil can be used for a delightfully different aroma. Blend your choices of materials together and place a small amount on a piece of burning charcoal. For hard-to-find supplies, try Indiana Botanic Gardens (See "Sources").

PHOTOPERIODICALLY SPEAKING
There are three types of plants: short-day, long-day, and intermediate. Experienced gardeners have found that flowering occurs when the vegetative growth has accumulated enough carbohydrates. To encourage flowering, some vegetable growers stop fertilizing—otherwise the plants would just keep on growing without blossom formation. For the same reason, growers of houseplants permit certain plants to get potbound.

Certain vegetables, such as broccoli, lettuce, and spinach, are a problem in the summer garden because they are long-day plants. In late June or early July they shoot up fast and become inedible. Heat, however, has nothing to do with it. If someone says, "spinach doesn't like heat," don't believe them. Just the opposite is true. It likes the summer so well it goes to flower and seed. And why not? That's what it's supposed to do.

PIECE OF THE ROCK The chemically produced fertilizer, superphosphate, has high levels of immediately available phosphorous and calcium. The pH of the area around the fertilizer is lowered to 1 or 2 when these high concentrations of minerals are released into the soil. The resulting acidic condition kills any microbes in the region but can also harm earthworms and beneficial insects. The high acidity also releases manganese and aluminum at levels that can burn root tips.

Rock phosphate, a naturally occurring substitute, is a better source of phosphorous for your garden; being released slowly, it does not have a drastic effect on pH. Follow the application rate recommended by your soil test.

PINCH YOUR PETUNIAS—THEY ADORE IT! Whether you buy petunias from the garden center or start your own, pinch out the first flower bud. This allows the side shoots to develop, forming a denser, more floriferous plant. Although this will delay first flowering by 7 to 10 days, the results all summer will be more than worth it.

Petunias have some other noble attributes often overlooked. They attract beautiful moths at night. And the fragrance of some kinds is very pleasing. Just because petunias can "take it," don't treat them like stepchildren. Give them a well-drained, light, sandy soil in full sun for best performance. The single varieties will tolerate heavier, more alkaline soils. Best spaced 12 inches apart in beds, but they don't mind closer planting with other plants in containers and hanging baskets.

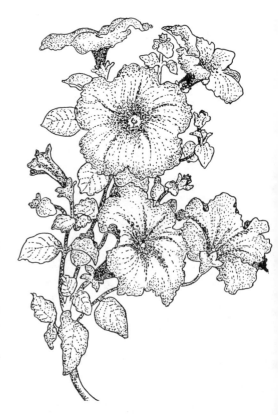

PLANTAGO (*Plantago psyllium*) is the working member of the Plantain family— and I do mean "working." This herb bears a seed that is used medicinally for its laxative qualities. When the seed is moistened, it looks like gelatin, swelling to provide bulk. Many bulk laxatives, such as Metamucil, basically contain the fiber hemicellulose, the same fiber as in bran cereal and whole wheat bread, with a gum added that comes from psyllium seeds.

P. psyllium is an annual herb and grows as high as 20 inches. Its leaves resemble grass and are from 1 to 2½ inches long. It has tiny flowers that are arranged in spikes, about half an inch long.

Plantagos are very easily cultivated in any well-drained soil in sunny places. They are readily raised from seeds. Garden varieties include: *P. argentes*, with silvery foliage; *P. cynopa*, a low evergreen shrub that is hardy in southern New England; *P. lanceolata marginata*, with white-variegated leaves; *P. major rosularia*, rose plantain, a very old garden plant that produces rosettes of green bracts in place of the usual taillike spikes of flowers, and reseeds freely. *P. nivalis* has leaves densely covered with silvery hairs and is suitable for rock gardens.

PLANT BANK Do your annual beds suffer from "tired blood," some expiring completely and others not flourishing well enough to be attractive? Does your perennial border get a moth-eaten look when some of the plants take a rest period after blooming?

Depositing both annuals and perennials in a plant bank may be your answer. Locate it in the cutting garden or in the empty rows where early vegetables have been harvested. Then, when you need a few plants, simply dig them up and set them in place. A little nursing will help them to recover from postoperative shock and become established sooner. Give them shade for the first few days—a shingle will often do nicely—and keep them moist for at least a week following transplanting.

When dividing perennials, put some in a special plant bank where they can remain until you need them. Chrysanthemums are particularly useful for filling vacant spots in the late summer garden, transplanting with almost no apparent shock. So start an account this year in your own bank. It will pay off handsomely in interest and the plants will come in handy on that "rainy day" in the garden.

PLANT PESTS TO AVOID Travelers are sometimes tempted to dig up plants and bring them home, thereby introducing them into areas where they have no natural enemies. Don't! One attractive nuisance is *Cortidera jubata*, a weedy pampas grass. Others are French broom (*Cytisus monspeculanus*), Scotch broom (*C. scoparius*), and Spanish broom (*Sparticum junceum*), all of which are aggressive spreaders. The related gorse or furze, rampant along the coasts of Oregon, Washington, and northern California, is spiny in addition to being a spreading nuisance. Four other plants to beware of: black acacia (*A. melanoxylon*), blue gum (*Eucalyptus globulus*), and tree-of-heaven (*Ailanthus altissima*). These three may start unexpectedly from wind- or bird-carried seeds. The fourth, fountain grass (*Pennisetum setaceum*, *P. ruppeli*), has recently extended its range and is becoming a potential fire hazard.

PLANT "PHEROMONES" Plants have developed many defenses to help them thrive and survive. This awesome arsenal of weaponry includes spines, thorns, and an array of defensive chemicals. But they must do more than repel their enemies. They must reproduce, and to do this they must have the assistance of go-betweens. Through the centuries, to enable them to attract allies, they developed not only bright-colored flowers but also irresistible aromas. Science is now finding that many plants emit scents identical to those of insect pheromones, the signal odors that lure male insects to the female for mating. By mimicking a specific scent, the plant's blossom can attract an insect which will then carry that plant's pollen to others of its own kind, thus increasing the chances for reproduction.

PLEASE DON'T EAT THE POINSETTIA! The three plants that play a special part in creating the mood and decorating the festivities of Christmas are poinsettia, holly, and mistletoe. Continue their use but do so with care. All parts of the mistletoe contain toxic amines (beta-phenethylamine and tramine), which can cause acute stomach and intestinal irritation with diarrhea and slow pulse rate. The berries are most frequently involved in poisoning. Hollies, both deciduous and evergreen, are not considered very poisonous but the red or black berries, when eaten, can cause vomiting, diarrhea, and stupor. Ingestion of the bright red berries of the poinsettia, which contain the bitter illicin, can poison small children. Poinsettia's reputation for being a very toxic plant is somewhat overstated, but frequently children who eat of it experience vomiting and diarrhea. When these symptoms are severe enough dehydration can occur and be very serious. If you suspect a child or a pet (cats like to nibble on houseplants) has been poisoned, call your nearest Poison Control Center for help.

POINSETTIA (*Euphorbia*) Gardeners who would like to carry their poinsettias over from one Christmas to the next can do so if the plants are treated with the right amount of *light* in the fall. This plant is sensitive to light and darkness, which means it should be put on a short-day, long-night schedule. If you want it to bloom for Christmas you must shut the plant off completely from light at night, starting in September. Place a black sheet (or box) over the plant, or put it in a dark room, starting at 6 to 7 p.m. Then bring it to light at 8 a.m. the next morning. Keep this up until Thanksgiving

Day. Remember, even a tiny shaft of light from a distant street lamp can delay flowering for Christmas. Once it was thought that temperature plus light decided whether a plant should produce flowers and seeds. Not so. It's successive rhythmic periods of both darkness and light which pull the trigger.

POLLINATION PUZZLERS Are your tomatoes failing to set fruit, the blossoms dropping off and nothing happening? Start thumping the bloom clusters every day or two. Tomatoes are not pollinated by insects but by *vibration*. If you have planted them close to a board fence there may not be enough wind agitation to spread the pollen around. Also, you should not mulch your tomatoes until they set blooms; they need the warmth of the sun on their roots to get blossoming started. If your area has a long growing season, plant your next tomato crop in late June or early July and you can enjoy tomatoes right up to frost. If you have trouble with sunscald, harvest tomatoes as soon as they start to turn pink and then ripen indoors on a bright windowsill.

Corn, too, is wind-pollinated, so you enhance your chances of success if it is closely planted in blocks rather than in widely spaced rows. Best to sow at least four rows within the block, with approximately 15 inches on all sides between the plants. Popcorn, being smaller, can be planted 10 inches apart. Germination will be speeded up if the seeds are soaked in warm water 24 hours before planting. A clear plastic mulch over the bed will also speed up germination. If crows pull up your corn, cut the top and bottom out of small cans and slip them over the corn as it sprouts.

POPCORN WITHOUT PAIN When you grow your own popcorn, you have to remove the kernels from the ear. This is easily done if you hold one ear in each hand and rub them against each other. The kernels quickly push each other off. No more sore thumbs!

Popcorn, like sweet corn, should be planted in blocks to ensure pollination. It will take longer to mature and ears should be allowed to dry on the stalks. After ears are shucked and shelled, store the kernels in jars with tight-fitting lids to keep out insects and hold in moisture. When corn doesn't pop satisfactorily you can put the "pop" back in by sprinkling a little water in the jar, and shaking up the corn so the moisture is evenly absorbed in a few hours. Even waistline-watchers can eat their fill of this wholesome "popular" snack because two cups of it *buttered* contain only 150 calories, yet it is rich in vitamins and minerals.

POTATO   It's not easy to think of the utilitarian potato as a "romantic" vegetable, but many varieties have a history that is downright fantastic. Take Shepherd's Caribe, for instance. According to Renee Shepherd this is a potato with a past! Caribes were widely grown in New England for export, largely to the Caribbean. They are handsome, deep violet-skinned potatoes with delicious creamy white flesh, wonderfully tender. I scan my Caribes and mark them as a diamond cutter does a fine stone, carefully marking out the sprouts. Early maturing, it's fine for the Southwest, being both heat- and drought-resistant.

Ruby Crescent (Shepherd's) is similar to the old-fashioned Lady or German Fingerlings, but produces much higher quality yields. The little tubers grow about 3 inches long and 1½ inches thick. Rosy tan on the outside, their waxy-yellow flesh holds together well when cooked, and they are a tasty first choice for potato salads. Yellow Finn (Shepherd's) has been called the "Dieter's Delight" because its tender flesh is a rich yellow that looks already buttered. And the flesh is sweet and moist.

Gurney's proudly boasts that their Lady Finger Potatoes have more natural sugar than most spuds. These little fellows measure 4 to 5 inches long by 1 inch wide—about the same size as a lady's finger. The sweet yellow flesh has a rich, robust flavor. They are good boiled, baked, roasted, or fried. Great in salads or casseroles, or for thickening soups.

For those who take their potatoes seriously, Gurney's also offers their new Beltville potato, free of nematode damage and scab or verticulium wilt, with no internal defects and of pleasing texture. I also like Henry Field's Red Pontiac for its fine texture. And for a real attention-getter try their All-Blue Potato.

The versatile potato can not only be grown in the garden, but in almost anything else from bushel baskets to stacks of old tires, bags, boxes, or bales of hay. But there are a few mistakes the unwary can avoid: Buy certified disease-free "seed" potatoes. Potatoes can host many diseases, so avoid bringing potato diseases to your garden. Good-sized pieces increase the chances of a good yield. Cut them about 1½ inches square, making sure that each has at least one good "eye." Some growers dip cut pieces in diluted bleach solution to prevent rot. Small potatoes, planted whole, avoid the risk altogether. Do not overfertilize before tubers are formed and do not ignore the best planting dates. Do not allow tubers to receive sunlight as this causes them to become green and inedible. Cultivate if needed to reduce weed competition, but never damage the shallow stems on which potatoes form. Often you can pick "new " potatoes as soon as the tips flower. These are small, tender, and delicious but they will not store. Potatoes for winter storage need to fully mature in the soil. Best not to use either horse or chicken manure for potatoes as they may cause scab, but they can be used if applied to your garden several months before planting, and applied sparingly.

You can grow wonderfully smooth potatoes in leaves. Dig a shallow trench, place your pieces of cut, sprouted potatoes in the trench and fill with leaves (which may often be gathered from curbsides in the fall), and continue mounding leaves. You can do this very early in the spring, even if a late frost nips the potato sprouts the plant will send up new ones. When harvest time arrives you may simply "scrabble" the large, smooth potatoes out by feeling for them under the plant.

Store your potatoes, if possible, in a very cool cellar, and piled or arranged so that a little air can circulate around them; otherwise they are likely to sweat. Loosely woven potato sacks or slat crates are satisfactory—much better than solid boxes or bins.

Seed potatoes do not differ from ordinary table potatoes (except that they are usually certified to be free from diseases). You can sprout ordinary potatoes in late summer or early fall and plant them for a fall crop if you cannot obtain seed potatoes.

Heavily tarnished silver may be cleaned by soaking for two hours in potato water. Any remaining tarnish can be removed with a soft brush and silver polish.

POTATO BEETLES   The Colorado potato beetle continues to be the number one potato pest, but there is hope. The pathogen, *Beauveria bassiana*, is a fungus which attacks the chitin in the hard outer covering of many beetles and moths. And a pin-sized wasp, *Edovum puttleri*, recently discovered in Columbia, parasitizes the eggs of the Colorado nuisance. Both are presently being researched and should be available in the near future. In my own small garden I hand pick the beetles and their nymphs and drop them into a can of old oil.

POWER TILLERS   A power tiller is a big investment. I always recommend renting a few models before deciding to buy one. What looks good in the store may not work well under your particular tutelage.

PRAYER PLANT(*Maranta leuconeura Kerchoviana*)   This is the plant for that low to medium light spot, perhaps near a north or east window. Shade it from any direct sun with a sheer curtain, otherwise the leaves may brown or pale at their edges. Folded upward at night to conserve moisture, the leaves of prayer plant look like praying hands. And it would seem as though nature took a paintbrush in hand to carefully pattern the striking foliage. The leaves of red-veined prayer plant are a dramatic combination of bright red, green, and light olive. Give your plant well-drained porous soil, uniformly moist most of the year, but in winter dry to the touch between waterings. They need repotting only once every year or two, as plants do best when slightly pot bound. Choose a pot no more than 2 inches larger than the old one.

PRIMROSES (*Primula acaulis* and *P. japonica*)   The seed of primroses must be frozen and thawed or it will not come up. An expert recommends sowing the seed outdoors, in a shaded bed prepared with good compost leaving the seed on top of the soil. She puts an old Dacron curtain over the bed and covers it with pine needles on top of the curtain until the seeds sprout. Then she takes the pine needles off, lifts the curtain and puts a little sand or compost on the seedlings, replacing the curtain. This is continued, adding sand or compost, a little at a time. The seedlings are kept moist and the curtain remains on until seedlings show a good green color.

PROPPING UP PEPPERS   The fruit of peppers such as bell can become quite heavy, and pepper plants are often very brittle. A good wind or rain can often uproot the plant or bend it over. Use protective cages about 18 inches across and 2 feet high to prevent damage in a storm, or even breakage of limbs when picking. Concrete reinforcing wire is best for this purpose.

PRUNE GRAPES   in late winter, leaving only a minimum of old wood. Newly planted grape vines should not be mulched. This encourages their roots, which should go deep, to stay close to the surface.

PRUNE SPRING-FLOWERING SHRUBS   right after the blossoms fade.

New flowerbuds form in late summer and early fall. Pruning delayed until then will remove next season's flowers. Cut off about one-third of the shrub's stems at ground level each year, selecting the oldest wood and any injured or misplaced stems. New shoots will appear from the shrub's base to replace those removed.

PSEUDO-PALMS—THE CYCADS

(*Cycadaceae*)   If you yearn for something dramatic and unusual for a real conversation piece, try one of the palmlike cycads. These plants are actually living fossils, representing the most primitive form of seed-bearing plants. They occupy a place between true flowering plants and flowerless plants such as ferns. They are not difficult to grow. In warm regions they do well outdoors, in colder climes use them as pot plants. Cycads require less water than most plants and also prefer a well-drained medium. Give them a mixture of equal parts of coarse sphagnum peat moss, coarse sand, and a loam-type soil. Feed with a water-soluble fertilizer according to directions three or four times year. Clay pots work well and the durable cycad can often remain in the same container for years.

Here are some possibilities for container culture of young cycads: Sago palm (*Cycas revoluta*). The shiny dark green foliage makes this Japanese native, a popular choice for decoration or for a bonsai specimen. Dioon (*Dioon edule*) is similar to the sago but has more of a bluish cast and is more feathery in appearance. Zamia (*Zamia furfuracae*), a Mexican native, has very thick leaflets, giving it the nickname of "cardboard palm." Coontie (*Zamia floridana*) is the smallest of the cycads and is a native of Florida. The shiny, dark-green leaves grow out of short trunks that are normally less than 2 feet tall. Partial shade is preferred for container plants.

PUMPKIN is not only a big fruit but big business! The new Burpee hybrid variety Prizewinner can grow to a weight of 300 pounds or more, is beautifully colored a lustrous reddish orange, and has smooth ribbed skin and the classic, deep round pumpkin shape. My own ambitions are somewhat more modest. I like to grow Small Sugar, which makes delightful pies. And, with the aid of a pantyhose sling, it may be grown on a fence or trellis, thereby taking little room. I also like Bushkin, which has edible seeds, or Triple Treat, a Burpee exclusive which is also great for Halloween carving, pies, and hull-less seeds.

"From where does the word 'pumpkin' stem?," asks Earl Aronson, AP news-features writer. It is derived from the Greek "pepon," which means "cooked by the sun." And the large-fruited varieties like Big Max, Big Tom, and, yes, Prizewinner, do require at least 110 to 120 days of warmth to mature. But Northern gardeners can extend the season a bit by covering with a tarpaulin on cold nights with daytime removal. Another helpful suggestion is to place your ripening pumpkin on a board or shingle to prevent insects from tunneling into the shell.

We know all about pumpkin pies, but have you ever heard of pumpkin soup? Those vigorous outdoor types, the Australians, regard a delicate appetite with suspicion, but are nevertheless fond of this soup, whose recipe comes to us from the *Round-the-World Cookbook*.

Pumpkin Soup

2 pounds pumpkin
1 teaspoon salt
1 cup light cream or "half and half"
2 onions chopped
½ teaspoon pepper
6 cups stock or 2 cans consomme and
   2½ cans water
1 tablespoon flour
¼ cup cold water

Peel pumpkin, discarding seeds and fiber, and cut into ½-inch cubes. Place in a deep saucepan with onions, stock, salt and pepper. Cook over low heat for 1 hour, or until pumpkin is very soft. Force pumpkin through a sieve and return to saucepan. Place flour and cold water in a cup and stir until very smooth. Add to the soup, stirring constantly until the boiling point is reached.

Add the cream, mixing well. Correct seasoning. Serve with toasted croutons.

PUMPKIN FLOWERS   Pick the young blossoms just before they open and before the bees and insects get to them. Wash and leave a 1-inch stem on the end of the blossom for a substitute when eating. Dip them in egg batter and drop into the deep fryer. Out they come, puffed up like big oysters. You can use squash, cucumber, and daylily blossoms the same way.

PUSSY WILLOW   The pussy willow is the familiar bog willow, whose gray (now you can get them in pink!) silky catkins appear in earliest spring. A walk in the woods in later February often brings us the charming surprise of a meeting with this little tree, just when its gray pussies are pushing out from their brown scales. We cut the twigs and bring them home and watch the wonderful color changes: turning them in the light, you can see under the sheen of silky hairs the varied and evanescent hues that glow in a Hungarian opal. Beauty is its own excuse for being and if you have a low wet spot, a natural or "sky" pool you may wish to grow pussy willow just because it is so lovely in early spring. Like all the willows it will root easily from a cutting if it has sufficient moisture.

Quietly Nature does her work,
Warming the earth where the violets lurk,
Bidding the crocus rise and glow,
Though the garden's still covered
With winter's snow;
Then she tells the birds to sing,
And green leaves usher in the spring.

LOUISE RIOTTE

QUAMOCLIT (*Quamoclit*), Star-glory. This genus of climbing herbaceous plants comes chiefly from Mexico. They are annuals and are best treated as annuals. They belong to the family *Convolvulceae*. Quamoclits are of easy cultivation. One of the best-known kinds is *Quamoclit lobata*, which bears crimson flowers that later turn to orange and yellow.

The lovely, lacy cypress vine (*Q. prennata*) is another popular kind for summer display. Under favorable conditions it attains a height of 20 feet. Both its fine, feathery green foliage and its funnel-shaped scarlet flowers are attractive. There is also a white-flowered variety of this plant named Alba.

The star impomoea (*Q. coccinea*) has scarlet flowers with a yellow throat. The cardinal climber (*Q. skiteru*) is a hybrid of crimson flowers with white throats. Plant quamoclit seedlings out of doors in a sunny position.

QUASSIA (*Quassia amara*) This tree, native to South America and the West Indies, has no odor, but contains a peculiar bitterness more intense and lasting than that of any other known substance. The bitterness, concentrated in the bark, extends to the roots, wood, leaves, and even the flowers, making it effective as an insecticide. Applied in water solution it may be used against a wide variety of insects, including greenfly, leafhopper, slug, mealybug, and thrip. According to *Organic Plant Protection* (Rodale Press), it is perhaps the safest protection of the group of lethal botanicals which work by paralyzing insects. It is also said to spare ladybugs and bees, while working against aphids, sawflies, and caterpillars. It may be purchased in the form of wood chips and

Quassia

shavings and the wood is simply steeped in water. Another very old recipe calls for quassia chips and larkspur seed boiled in water, the tea thus made being sprinkled on plants.

QUEEN VICTORIA'S WATER LILY

(*Victoria regia*)   Sometimes called "Royal Water Lily," according to the *New Illustrated Encyclopedia of Gardening*, *Victoria regia* is a remarkable water lily which was introduced into gardens from tropical America at about the middle of the nineteenth century. A native of the Amazon, it was first discovered in 1801. Several attempts were made to get it to grow in European greenhouses, but all were unsuccessful until seeds were sent in a bottle of fresh water. These seeds were collected and dispatched by two English physicians and arrived in England in February 1849.

The opening of the first flower was a dramatic event and it was sent to Queen Victoria from the conservatory at Chatsworth House in Derbyshire, England, where the plant was named in honor of the Queen. This spectacular plant belongs to the water lily family, *Nymphaceae*.

This aquatic giant can only be grown outdoors where tropical summers prevail; elsewhere it must be accommodated in a large greenhouse or conservatory such as is maintained in botanic gardens. It forms a number of round, floating leaves, averaging 6 feet in diameter, the margins of which are turned up at right angles to a height of 2 or 3 inches. A small child may sit in one.

The large fragrant flowers are 12 to 18 inches in diameter and open on two consecutive days. On the first day they are creamy white and the next day they change to rose-pink. The flowers have a delicious pineapplelike fragrance and are surrounded by large prickly sepals. After fertilization, they produce enormous prickly berries containing hard black seeds resembling peas.

QUICKER DECOMPOSITION   Compost will break down and decay faster if the heap is placed in a shady spot.

QUICK-TO-BEAR APPLES   Sometimes called the "old folks" apple, Anoka usually bears fruit the first year after planting. The large apples are red-striped with yellow. Good to eat and extra hardy. Ripens in late July but may be used for sauce and pies earlier. However, if you don't have more apple trees nearby you will need a cross-pollinator. Plant Haralson, which also usually bears the second or third year after planting. Haralson, of excellent quality, ripens in September and October, bearing large, crisp apples that will keep until the following spring. (Gurney's)

QUINCE (*Cydonia*)   It is a surprise to many that the fruit of the garden quince also contains medicinal properties. Containing vitamins A, B, and C, as well as calcium, iron, and phosphorus, it is beneficial in cases of sluggish liver, constipation, arthritis, and acidosis.

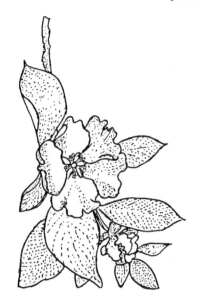

Quince Jelly
Here is my recipe for making quince jelly.
Wash, pare, and core 1½ pounds quinces.
Add 2½ cups water to parings and cook
for thirty minutes. Grate or grind quinces
or slice very thin. Weigh pulp and use
one pound. Add 2 tablespoons lemon
juice and strained liquid from parings.
Cook until tender, adding 3 cups sugar.
Cook until syrup gives test for jelly. Pour
into sterile glasses and seal with paraffin.

The fruit is not good eaten raw, but the
cooking changes it to a piquant flavor that is
quite pleasant. Added to other fruit preserves such as apple and pear, quince will
give a guavalike flavor. The beautiful flowering quince is a close relative but its fruit is
small and only occasionally used for preserves. Amylovora may severely blight
quince flowers. Since this bacterium is the
same one that causes fire blight, it is best to
seek out and destroy any diseased and neglected pear, quince, or apple trees that may
harbor this dread disease. Prune back the
branches of quince until healthy wood is uncovered, and break out any blighted fruit
spurs. A dormant oilspray has been found
effective in prevention of this disease. Dormant oilspray is also effective in the control
of scale.

The rolling river, the morning bird;—
Beauty through my senses stole;
I yielded myself to the perfect whole.
RALPH WALDO EMERSON

RABBIT MANURE In these days of automobile transportation, old-fashioned manure is not easy to come by. But a solution for the organic gardener is raising rabbits. Hutches do not require much space, and you can even raise something underneath the hutches—worms. Rabbits neither crow nor cackle, and the meat is delicious and nutritious eating. They will also eat much of your surplus garden produce, cutting down on the cost of feeding. Among common barnyard animals the rabbit is the most rewarding producer of high-grade fertilizer; its droppings are easily managed, and score well above all competitors in nutrients.

Rabbit manure is five times richer in nitrogen than a cow's and five and one-half times richer than swine's. Phosphorus content is seven times higher than horse manure, seven and one-half times higher than cow, and eight and one-half times higher than swine. A single doe with her litters kept to ten weeks will produce about 100 pounds of manure each year. And a rabbit can be kept for about one-third the cost of a laying hen. My personal preference is for New Zealand Whites—they are good eating and very docile.

RACCOONS Clever gardeners have devised many ways to foil this wily little bandit. Old screens and bushel baskets can be propped up against cornstalks to act as booby traps. Crumpled newspapers, placed between rows of corn and held down with stones, make crackling noises as raccoons step on them. Red pepper sprinkled in the silks of corn, or a small dab of hydrated lime painted on the cornstalk, repel raccoons. An ingenious gardener tried putting up a string of Christmas lights, and the blinking lights deterred the raccoons in their nightly foraging expeditions. Another ran an electric wire fence approximately one foot from the ground between the corn rows. Another

who was driven to the point of desperation even constructed a "corn cage" for the sole purpose of growing corn and keeping raccoons out. The cage was made of 14-gauge galvanized wire mesh with steel posts set in concrete.

RADISHES (*Raphanus sativus*) Radishes seldom have a patch of ground cultivated just for them. They are the catch crop above all catch crops and are planted with practically everything—carrots, beets, onions, lettuce, parsnips, cucumbers—but almost never by themselves. Why, I am sometimes asked, do radishes sometimes go to all tops, making leaves rather than roots? One authority says it is because they are not thinned early enough or severely enough, that radishes should be thinned as soon as seedlings produce their first true leaves. Another belief is that the right sign and quarter make the difference. Radishes should be planted in the third quarter of the moon and under the signs of Libra, Taurus, Pisces, Sagittarius, or Capricorn. Radishes, believed to have aphrodisiac qualities, were once served at Greek and Roman marriage feasts. However, the Romans also used to hurl radishes at politicians!

RAILROAD WORM These are apple maggots, slender white worms that feed within the pulp and carry with them germs of soft rot. Cleaning up every rotten, dropped apple is very important in preventing more maggot trouble for another year. These worms are different from the codling moth larvae, which are larger, ¾ inches long, and pinkish white with brown heads. The adult railroad worm is a small black-and-white fly. The larvae winter in cocoons in the crotches and under bark of trees. The moths emerge to lay their eggs in warm, dry weather about a week after the petals have fallen, and the newly hatched caterpillars enter through the calyx cup of the fruit.

Scraping the bark on the trunk up to 10 feet during the winter will be very helpful in reducing both railroad worm and codling moth infestation. Also, chemically treated bands on scraped trees will collect larvae and prevent damage.

RAISED BEDS—NOT WATERBEDS
If your garden is too wet, either in certain sections or all over, try the raised-bed method for your plants. Using stakes for guidelines, decide the width and length of the beds and walkways. Using a hoe, pull the soil from the walkways up onto the bed. You should have at least a four- to eight-inch difference between the height of the bed and the height of the walkways. After raising the soil and leveling off the beds, simply plant your transplants just as you would in a conventional bed. Raised beds drain faster because excess water doesn't just sit there; it runs off. Having the water run off means plant roots will receive the oxygen needed for good growth. And raised beds warm up faster in the spring and stay warmer all day. Particularly helpful for warm weather lovers such as peppers, eggplant, okra, and tomatoes.

RAPE (*Brassica Napus*) Recently a reader of my weekly column called to ask an interesting question regarding canola oil, believed to be the cooking oil lowest in dietary fat. Its use is now thought to be of great value in cases of high cholesterol. So where is canola oil obtained? From a plant with a strange name: rape. Charles S. Dorchester at Iowa State College, writing in *Forages*, states: "The agricultural varieties of *Brassica* fall into three groups, the cabbages, the swedes, and the turnips. The swede group, *B. napus*, includes, besides the swedes proper, the common rape and the colza, or oil-bearing rapes, the rapeseed being the source of the oil."

Rape has been known in England since the sixteenth century and is now distributed over much of Europe, northern Asia, Canada, and the United States. It is grown as a pasture crop and thrives on any fertile soil adapted to corn: it needs no cultivation and is an excellent winter forage in the South. The crop is an excellent source of vitamins A and C. *The Rodale Encyclopedia of*

Gardening tells us that the rapeseed meal from which the oil has been extracted has between 5 and 6 percent nitrogen and between 1 and 2 percent phosphoric acid and potash and is fine for compost activation.

Rape has a long history as a folk medicine. The powdered seed with salt is said to be a folk remedy for cancer. Rape oil is used in massage and oil baths, believed to strengthen the skin and keep it cool and healthy. With camphor it is applied for rheumatism and stiff joints.

RASPBERRIES (*Rubus spidaeus*)   Fresh raspberries are scarce. If you don't grow your own you probably won't have any because they are so fragile and tender, they can't be stored or shipped cross-country like tomatoes or strawberries. To pick red raspberries, take a half-peck basket and tie it to your waist. Place three plastic pint containers in the basket and pick with both hands. With small containers, the weight of the top berries won't crush those underneath. Pick only after the sun has dried the morning dew, for dew-moist berries don't keep as well as dried berries.

To freeze the berries, put the filled pint containers straight into the freezer. No need to wash them—the rain has done that. When they are frozen, pack them in plastic freezer bags. They will remain loose, and you can pour out a dishful for as many as you want. This method helps to keep the delicate berries whole. If washing is necessary place them in very cold water, and remove quickly. If the berries are very warm from the sun it might even be well to refrigerate them before washing. If whole berries are to be stored in the refrigerator overnight sweeten them with honey or sugar to prevent mold.

The berries I enjoy most are those I eat right off the canes when I'm picking!

RECYCLE LEMON AND ORANGE RINDS   Dry thoroughly and cut in strips. Use them to throw on a fire for terrific aroma.

RED SPIDER MITES   These little peskies seem to appear suddenly, especially on tomato leaves, when really hot weather hits. *Organic Plant Protection* (Rodale Press) states: "A spray of 2 percent oil of coriander will kill the red spider mite; a spray of anise oil should do as well." Frequent spraying with plain water will also help in control of red spider. Their natural controls are ladybugs, lacewings, and predacious mites.

RETURN OF THE NATIVE   Are you tired of plants (that you probably paid a high price for) shriveling in winter's cold or burning up in summer's heat? Why not try for the plants that grow naturally in your particular area of the country. Obviously every plant is native somewhere, and a garden that is beautiful and finished-looking, requiring little maintenance, can be a possibility just about anywhere—if we will search out the more attractive native plants. Look for plants like dogwood, spicebush, redbud, witch hazel, mountain laurel, low-bush blueberries, spirea, princess pine, wild asters, and native azaleas. Where these plants grow naturally, they will continue to look beautiful year after year in your own yard with almost no effort on your part.

RHUBARB (*Rheum rhaponticum*)   So many of our most popular plants have lost their native accent—so it is with rhubarb. While we may think of it as English, it is, in fact, a native of China and Tibet. As far back as 3000 B.C., the root of rhubarb was being used medicinally in the countries of its origin. When it arrived in Britain by way of the Volga region of Russia it was put to the same use. It then seems to have gone through a period of obscurity, turning up again in the early 1800s as a fruit. Rhubarb is not a halfway plant, most people either like or dislike it intensely.

I don't know much about its medicinal properties, although Dr. W.H. Graves states that it contains vitamin C and that it is helpful in cases of poor complexion, obesity, neuritis, and bronchitis. He also warns that it should not be eaten if suffering with rheumatism or arthritis as it is high in oxalic acid. Of course we also know that only stems should be used for pies or sauce because the leaves are considered poisonous.

Rhubarb does indeed have insecticidal properties and is protective to the roots of the cabbage family in preventing clubroot. When planting any of the *Brassicas*, put four or five 1-inch pieces of rhubarb stalks around the plant in a circle. This will keep those little white worms away. They are also helpful in growing worm-free carrots. Pulverize rhubarb, both stalks and leaves, add water and use this when planting carrot seeds.

To grow rhubarb well make sure the soil is rich and well drained. Barnyard manure (well decomposed) may be liberally spread and dug in. Set roots in holes 6 inches deep and 18 to 24 inches apart, with crowns just below the surface. Firm dirt around them. In autumn of the first year mulch the entire bed again and in spring dig this into the bed lightly, being careful not to cut the roots.

Rhubarb is propagated by dividing the older roots. This is best done in the early spring just as first buds appear. Don't let rhubarb flowers develop; they do so at the expense of the plant's stalks and will cause a poor crop the following year.

Remember, when you want to use rhubarb for pies or sauce, pull rather than cut the stalks, as the whole leaf-stalk (but not the leaves) is useable. Pull only a few stalks the first season, however, to give the plants a chance to become well established.

Rhubarb is a beautiful plant, and there are several outstanding varieties. McDonald is a brilliant red, with skin so tender that no peeling is required. Valentine, another dark-red type, grows high-quality, sweet stalks. Victoria, popular for growing from seed, has green stalks blushed red, and a delicious tart flavor when cooked.

Rhubarb has few problems but occasionally crown rot causes rotting of the leaves and stalks. Dig up and burn the affected plant.

RING AROUND THE MOON   Very likely this does mean that rain is imminent. Rain is generally caused by a collision of a warm front with cooler air. As a warm front approaches, fine cirrus clouds form in the upper atmosphere which contain tiny ice particles that scatter light from the moon in a circle or ring around it. Such a circle generally means rain within twenty-four hours.

RIPENING FRUIT   Fruit can be safely ripened by putting it in a paper bag on top of the refrigerator, according to a produce expert. It's warm up there, which helps stimulate ripening, and the paper bag helps concentrate the ethylene gas that ripening fruit gives off naturally, which further stimulates ripening. Just be sure to check the fruit frequently and refrigerate (or eat) the fruit as soon as it is ripe.

RIPENING TOMATOES   Place fairly mature but unripened tomatoes in a sealed plastic bag with a banana. The banana gives off ethylene gas, which will ripen the tomatoes in a day or two. Apples right off the tree can also be ripened this way.

ROBINS   Robins like to live in open areas near people. Few birds have more dignity and beauty, or a lovelier song. During the mating season, the males fill the air with joyful ringing notes that sound like "cheerily, cheerily, cheerily," warming our hearts, too. If you have the room, provide them with some wild fruit-bearing shrubs and trees nearby (which they actually prefer) so they will leave your garden crops alone.

ROCKET (*Hesperis matronalis*)   As members of the cruciferous order the rockets are edible and nonpoisonous. Pick the leaves before the plant comes into flower. Medicinally the plant is used while in flower, and many virtues have been attributed to the garden rocket. It is a gland stimulant and aphrodisiac. There is a double variety and the flowers of the sweet rocket give out their scent at night. (Park's Seeds)

ROOT-BOUND TRANSPLANTS need special care. First check for overcrowded roots by turning the container upside down and gently removing the plant. If there are just enough roots to fill the container and hold the soil together, nothing needs to be done. If the roots are heavily matted or growing out the drainage holes, the plant is root-bound.

To ensure proper growth you should untangle the matted roots, otherwise they often continue to grow in a circular pattern and may never spread out to properly anchor the plant. Such plants cannot take up water and nutrients well and are more susceptible to drought. Untangle by gently pulling the roots apart with your finger; then separate just enough to break up the mat. You may lose a few roots and some soil, but try to keep as much intact as possible. Set the transplants at the same depth they were growing in their container and keep well watered during periods of drought.

ROOTING CUTTINGS Sometimes difficult-to-root cuttings can be encouraged to do so by giving them a companion. Grape cuttings inserted in the same pot with the difficult-to-root cutting have been known to turn the trick. This method has been used successfully in rooting Dutchman's Pipe and other vines.

ROSE (*Rosa*) The rose is an ancient plant, apparently originating in central Asia and, from there, spreading over the northern hemisphere. Inexplicably it never crossed the equator, for no wild rose species has ever been discovered in the southern hemisphere. Historical records indicate that wild roses were brought under cultivation in China at least 5,000 years ago. They were grown in Egypt and Italy long before the Christian era.

It's a strange thing about many wild roses—their flowers don't look like roses at all. They look more like apple or strawberry, perhaps blackberry or plum blossoms, or maybe even those of the mountain ash or the hawthorne. That's really not so strange

after all, as all these species, plus about 2,500 more, are members of the huge rose family.

Centuries of cross-breeding have transformed the rose of antiquity into the vast assembly of modern roses of today. At present there are more than 13,000 identifiable varieties. The rose is our national flower, and the President signed the proclamation in the White House Rose Garden!

Keep those prize-winning roses perfect. Japanese beetles can be foiled. Take 5 or 6 clear plastic sandwich bags. Fold each into 1/2-inch-wide strips. Punch several holes along the length of each strip with a small hole puncher; then unfold the bags. Use each bag to enclose a rosebud just coming into bloom. While the holes are too small for beetles to crawl through, they keep the bags from blowing off the rosebuds.

Belles of old placed much trust in rose water and glycerine to keep them young and beautiful. Fresh rose petals, covered with water, placed in an enameled saucepan, were allowed to simmer gently for two or three hours. The water that remained became rose water after straining through a muslin bag. The rose water, combined with glycerine, was then bottled and stoppered. Japanese ladies, I am told, also make a skin lotion in a similar manner.

Ladies of yesteryear also favored cucumbers. A typical recipe called for short cooking and straining, flower petals sometimes being added for fragrance. Simmer two quarts of fragrant rose petals for an hour with enough water to cover, then add a finely minced cucumber and simmer another 10 minutes. Strain off and add a teaspoon of lemon juice. This lotion was used to smooth on face and neck for a few minutes before washing or bathing.

ROSE, ANTIQUE Fun-loving gardeners should consider growing "old" roses. Overlooked by gardeners for decades, old roses are making a comeback. Along with a legacy of history and romance, they offer beauty, fragrance, variety, vigor, and color. And they are so easy to grow—many times they can be found surviving on their own around an old homestead, rambling over a wall, enjoying themselves with no one to care for them but Mother Nature.

And, in comparison with modern roses they are for the most part almost unbelievably fragrant. Damask roses are the most fragrant roses of all, and they're still used today for making attar of roses and perfumes. These hardy, disease-resistant shrubs feature tall, thorny canes, and large clusters of soft pink or white flowers. Summer damasks bloom once each year, autumn damasks bloom both spring and fall.

China roses, in a warm climate, are almost always in bloom. Tea roses blend the beauty of the European types with the free-blooming habits of the Chinas. Hybrid Perpetuals were the toast of Europe when they were introduced in the mid-1800s. Species roses are unadulterated by hybridizing and come to us today just as they existed hundreds of years ago.

ROSE CUTTINGS   Roses, like most other woody shrubs, will root quite successfully from cuttings. Prepare a rooting mix of half peat and half sand, perlite, or vermiculite. Soak it so that it will be fairly moist, not wet, and put it in a pot or flat. Select a healthy, vigorous shoot and cut it to leave about four leaves. Break off the lower two leaves and snip part of the upper two off with scissors. Stick your cuttings into the rooting mix, cover with plastic to reduce evaporation, and place in the shade. Rooting should take two to four weeks. Long before plastic became readily available my mother used to root rose cuttings under glass fruit jars.

ROSE RESCUE   After pruning back branches, put a large thumbtack, stub tack, or upholstery tack into the cut end of the branch. This will keep borers from entering and damaging your roses. Works well with other woody shrubs, too.

RUTABAGAS (*Brassica campestris* var. *rutabaga*)   Sometimes called Swedish turnips, this vegetable was once confused with the turnips, but they are, in fact, larger and sweeter. They are also much hardier than turnips and are particularly good for storing. They have a fairly long growing season and grow best above the Mason-Dixon line. They need a fertile, adequately limed soil that does not dry out quickly in summer. It is good that they are harvested in September and October for, as with turnips, I do not particularly care for them in hot weather but love them when days are cool. Cook them as you would turnips. But I find them wonderfully tasty mashed, seasoned with butter, salt and pepper, and combined—half and half—with riced (mashed) potatoes.

R_x The next time you receive a prescription, look for the R_x in the corner. This is a modern form of an ancient astrological symbol, an invocation to Juniper to use his good offices to effect a cure. The Rx symbol is short for Latin "recipe"—take—and has this meaning in medical prescriptions.

Something attempted, something done,
Has earned a night's repose.
HENRY WADSWORTH LONGFELLOW

SALVIA—THE SULTRY SIRENS Discretely chosen varieties of salvia will give you a continuous display of blazing color from June until frost. These torrid charmers used to be tall, late to bloom, and therefore thought of only as a colorful addition to the late summer garden. Then the hybridizers went to work and gave us: 'Fireball' and 'Red Hot Sally' (8 to 10 inches), June 20; 'Carabiniere,' 'Caramba,' 'Red Hussar,' 'St. John's Fire' (12 inches), July 1; 'Blaze of Fire,' 'Red Pillar,' 'Violet Flame' (14 to 16 inches), July 10; 'America,' 'Firebrand' (18 to 20 inches), July 15; 'Bonfire,' 'Splendens Tall' (26 to 30 inches), August 1.

SASSAFRAS (*Sassafras albidum*) The sixteenth-century "Wonder Drug." According to *The Herbalist Almanac* there is an old story that the scent of sassafras carried out to sea by wind helped Columbus convince his mutinous crew that land was near. Early settlers of the New World found the native Americans using this bark of root for beverage, medicine, and flavoring. The new colonists were intrigued by sassafras' powerful flavor, different from cinnamon or any of the other highly prized spices yet known and it had a fascinating appeal. It soon became a very popular remedy in disease-ridden Europe as a

cure-all for many ills. According to Julia Ellen Rogers, writing in *Trees*, the first cargo of home products shipped back to England from Massachusetts contained a large consignment of sassafras roots. The wily Sir Walter Raleigh at one time controlled a monopoly of all the imports of the new botanical.

While the Spanish were futilely seeking gold, the English were busily scouring the eastern shores of the New World for sassafras, trying to meet the demand. Sassafras became a virtual "gold mine." The French got into the act, helping to fan the flames until no one felt secure from disease unless they had some sassafras.

Sassafras spreads by a multitude of fleshy root-stalks, and these natural root cuttings bear transplanting as easily as a poplar. Every garden border should have at least one tree to add its glorious flame of autumn foliage with the charming contrast of its blue berries on their coral stalks to the fall conflagration. Even in winter the sassafras tree is most picturesque because of the short, stout, twisted branches that spread almost at right angles from the central shaft.

Sassafras, which may be a shrub or tree, is usually found in large areas from Texas to Florida, thence northward to the Great

Lakes region. Indians used it first: later the Creoles adapted its delicate fragrant leaves to make filé for flavoring for soups and sauces. The strong-flavored and scented bark was very important to both the Indians and the early pioneers made as a spring tonic from the bark of the roots. Medicinally sassafras is used as an aromatic, mild stimulant, diaphoretic, and alterative. The white spongy pith is useful as a demulcent for inflammation of the eyes and makes a soothing drink for catarrhal affections. Derivatives of sassafras oil are used in the cosmetic and perfume industries.

In New England a decoction of sassafras bark was once used to give the housewife's homespun woolen cloth a permanent orange dye. Its name, the "Ague Tree," originated with the use of sassafras bark tea as a stimulant that warmed and brought out perspiration freely for victims of malarial "ague," or chills and fever.

The wood, described as dull orange-yellow, soft, weak, light, brittle and coarse-grained, is amazingly durable in contact with the soil, as the pioneers found when they used it to make posts and fence rails. Oil of sassafras distilled from the bark of the roots is used in perfuming soaps and flavoring medicines.

In spring the bare twigs are covered with a delicate green of opening leaves, brightened by many clusters of yellow flowers whose starry calyxes are alike on all the trees; but only on the fertile trees are the flowers succeeded by the blue berries, softening on their scarlet pedicels—and beloved of birds.

SAUNA BATH FOR SEEDS Homemade tunnels of clear plastic stretched over wire create a warm, moist greenhouse for sprouting seeds. In the spring use tunnels to collect solar heat and protect seedlings from cold temperatures and drying winds. Leave them in place until the weather warms up, closing the ends only during cold weather. In the summer you can use tunnels again for sprouting seeds during dry weather, leaving the ends open to reduce heat buildup and re-

moving the tunnel as soon as seeds sprout. Make the frame of either heavy gauge wire or lightweight wire doubled and twisted for rigidity.

SAW PALMETTO (*Serona serrulata* and *Sabal serrulata*) Native to South Texas, this palm will also grow in parts of Florida and California. With protection it will even grow in southern Oklahoma. The interesting leaves are fan-shaped and the scented, hermaphrodite flowers grow in inflorescences which are generally longer than the leaves, and greatly branched. They are followed by globose, blackish fruits. Propagation is by seed.

The berries, fresh or dried, are recommended by Jethro Kloss, in his book *Back to Eden*, in all diseases of the reproductive organs, ovaries, prostate, testes, etc. to give increased strength and tone of muscles. They are recommended for improving and increasing the function and size of the mammary glands. For men, this herb improves the functions of the glandular bodies in the scrotum.

If taken fresh, from three to five berries are sufficient for a dose, taken three times daily. If dried berries or powder is used, a solution must be prepared by steeping for several minutes in boiling water. Saw palmetto is especially valuable when used with damiana. (Indiana Botanic Gardens offers a tea blend.)

Saw palmetto is also of value in asthmatic conditions and all kinds of throat troubles, especially when there is excessive mucous discharge from the head and nose.

SCALLIONS BY THE JILLIONS Here's an easy way to have all the fresh green onions your heart desires. Deep-till a section to any length you like and fertilize with well-decomposed compost. Mound the section 3 to 4 inches high to make a raised bed and firm down with the back of your rake. Take newspapers and lay them down sheet by sheet along the row, overlapping as needed until they are 6 or 7 sheets thick. Rake soil on outside edges to hold down. Wet thoroughly with hose or watering can to soften paper. Push onion sets through wet newspaper, spacing about 2 inches each way. That's it. No watering, weeding, or cultivating, and you'll be surprised at how well the newspapers hold up.

SCARECROW You still see these comic devices with a purpose here and there—hopefully scaring birds or other animals from eating or otherwise disturbing seeds, shoots and fruit. The scarecrow of popular tradition is a mannequin stuffed with straw; free-hanging, and often decorated with reflective parts movable by the wind, believed to increase its effectiveness.

According to the *Barnhart Dictionary of Etymology*, we first meet the scarecrow in about 1553, at that time a real person employed to scare crows or other birds. By 1592 some thrifty soul had figured out that a mannequin dressed in old clothes, preferably those of a hunter who had fired on the flock, could be used instead at no cost. The word itself is said to derive from the English "sker", to terrify or frighten. The Old Icelandic word "skirra" also means to frighten and this, in turn, was derived from "skjarr"—meaning timid or shy.

Just because some of these are old ideas doesn't mean they can't still be useful. Beatrice Trum Hunter in her book *Gardening Without Poisons*, mentions a potato, stuck with many feathers to resemble a hawk being used to frighten away birds when fruit is ripening. "English gardeners have used brown-paper effigies of a death's-head moth to frighten bullfinches." Birds become accustomed to a still figure so it is wise to move it about. "Today", she says, "simple effigies are considered limited in their effectiveness. More elaborate, lifelike creations with moving parts improve their value, especially when combined with noise."

Even used aluminum pie plates, hung close enough together to bang against each other on a windy day and shining in the sunlight, can be effective.

SCATTER-PLANTING BUT NOT SCATTER-BRAINED This is an idea I give you for what it may be worth! I grant it is unorthodox but in some situations it not only works but works well. Consider that Mother Nature plants most of her seeds simply by scattering them far and wide, some travel by clinging to the fur of an animal's coat, others pass through the digestive tracts of birds and beasts. Here is the technique:

Instead of sowing seeds tediously in neat furrows and rows, just toss them on the ground in beds about 2 feet wide, then rake the soil lightly to cover most of the seeds and spread a half-inch layer of ground bark, peat moss, or compost over them to hold moisture. While this works well for such vegetables as carrots, onions, lettuce, and other small-seed vegetables, it is only fair to tell you that the larger seeds like corn, squash, and melon still have to go underground in hills or furrows. Often gardeners whose soil is gummy and untillable in the early spring find it useful to churn up the seed beds in the fall before the winter rains come, chopping in leaves and other organic materials. Then there is a semiprepared seed bed already for the scatter planting method.

Scatter planting works well in the flower beds too, and is fine for zinnias, marigolds, poppies, violas, and other small-seed flowers. It is also an excellent idea for garden clubs interested in roadside or vacant lot beautification.

SCENTED GERANIUMS (*Pelargonium* spp.) These useful copycats are fun to grow and complement any herbs or flowers that you grow them with, lending their myriad fragrances to countless projects. Flowers are inconspicuous, but the fragrance and the interesting leaf textures more than make up for this. Can you believe rose and peppermint geranium? And lemon, lime, ginger, apricot, strawberry, apple, nutmeg, oak, peppermint rose, and lemon rose? Though small, the exquisite flowers may be white, pink, or, sometimes, lavender. The varieties having rather spicy or pungent fragrances tend to have larger blossoms, some with striking black markings on fuchsia petals.

In general, scented geraniums can tolerate winter temperatures in the upper 30s without severe damage. To be safe lift them in the late fall, cut back hard, do not feed for a few weeks and let them winter in pots in a sunny area. Brush the leaves when you are nearby and you will be rewarded with a delightful, "live" room refresher.

Leaves can be placed in sugar, then the scented sugar can be used to sweeten tea or whipped cream. Lemon-scented varieties have long been used in finger bowls as well as in the teacup. Or, if you are into making butter try wrapping the butter patty in rose geranium leaves for a few hours to absorb the flavor.

SEAKALE (*Crambe maritima*)   This native of the coasts of Britain, and most of the coastal areas of western Europe, has given a bounty of spring greens to country dwellers for centuries. However, the cultivation of the forced white shoots, which are sweet and succulent, goes back to the nineteenth century. Once called "sea-colewort," it belongs to the *Cruciferae* family and is a relative of cabbage.

Easy to grow and to force, it is remarkably hardy and free of pests and diseases, and has a delicious nutty flavor. The curly green leaves of unforced seakale are delicious eaten raw in salads, and you can eat the stalks raw like celery. May be forced indoors or in the garden. Though outdoor forcing is said to give a better flavor, there is much to be said for having seakale in the middle of winter! Roots forced indoors are discarded after stems are used, but they also can be used as cuttings for the next season. Outdoor beds remain productive for 4 to 5 years but should not be forced until 18 months after planting. Shoots should be cut young, before leaves have fully developed.

SEA SHELL MULCH   Save those sea shells you collected at the beach and use them for a mulch, turned with the cups up, for houseplants that need high humidity. Each time you water, the cups will be filled with water that later evaporates into the air around the plant. And the top of the pot soil covered with small shells is also very attractive.

SEAWEED   Strictly speaking, any plant that grows in the sea can be called a seaweed. But when a botanist speaks of a seaweed he usually means one of the larger brown or red algae. On Columbus' first voyage to America, his ships passed through masses of seaweed. These weeds were brown algae known as *gulfweeds*. Irish moss and other red algae contain similar substances as *agar* and *carrageenin*, used in food and drugs.

The giant kelp, which may grow to 100 feet or more, belong to the phylum *Phaeophyta*, or brown algae. It is genus *Macrocystis*, species *pyrifera*.

If you live in a coastal area, or can obtain seaweed, it is one of the best possible sources of humus, containing 400 pounds of organic matter per ton. The chemical analysis of fresh seaweed is rather similar to barnyard manure; seaweed contains somewhat less nitrogen, half as much phosphorus, and twice as much potassium. Dried seaweed is 20 to 50 percent minerals, and contains such essential trace elements as boron, cobalt, copper, iron, manganese, molybdenum, and zinc. Because of its content of nitrogen and alginic acid, which stimulate bacterial growth, seaweed breaks down to form a rich, dark humus.

It is also possible that seaweed, growing in clean water, may be freer of pesticides and other poisonous residues than agricultural or industrial by-products.

SEED GERMINATION TIPS   We can learn much about ways of persuading seeds to germinate quickly from those excellent gardeners, the Japanese. Before a seed can sprout it must absorb moisture. When this happens, the outer skin or shell becomes soft, and the germ or kernel swells and bursts forth toward the surface seeking light.

Normally the seed will receive this needed moisture from the earth or seedbed, but the process takes time, no matter how damp the soil. Presoaking the seed in water before planting will speed up germination by as much as one to two days. This accelerated process also will reduce the chance of the shoot being attacked by chewing insects. In the garden it reduces the chore of keeping new seed beds constantly moist. Soak seeds in warm water in a wide-mouth thermos the day before planting. Drain them by placing a paper towel inside a sieve or colander and pour the seeds through it. Water will seep through but the seeds won't. Finally, place seeds on a dry paper towel for about thirty minutes, letting the skins dry, so the seeds won't stick to your fingers when planting.

Seed-soaking is particularly helpful with large, hard seeds such as corn, cucumber, melon, pumpkin, and squash, but it also may be used for carrots, turnips, and beets. Beans and lettuce are both strong sprouters so I never soak them, but just about everything else can benefit from the process. I'd like to suggest that you limit your seed soaking to no more than eight hours for your first try. In later soakings, change the water on the seeds at least every eight hours to discourage the growth of bacteria. Adding a little vinegar, about a teaspoon, to alternate soaking baths will lower the pH and eliminate many bacteria.

Hard-shelled seeds such as canna, okra, and sweet peas won't benefit much from presoaking unless the seed coating is notched or pierced. If you do this, be careful not to go deeper than the coat and stay away from the "eye" of the seed. Remember, too, that seeds so treated become very vulnerable to infection. It is best to soak them no more than eight hours after this operation and to plant them as soon as swelling becomes apparent.

Another important factor, in my opinion, in presoaking seeds is water. If possible, use rainwater instead of tapwater. I believe that seeds soaked in rainwater will grow healthier, sturdier plants.

Another hint: Place seed tray on top of the refrigerator after planting. Extra warmth radiating from the refrigerator will help the seeds germinate.

SEED SENSE   A seed is a little bundle of determination to grow. It has even been reported that seeds several thousand years old, found in Egyptian tombs, have sprouted and grown under proper conditions, though they did not mature.

Precise reasons for seed death are not clear. The most amazing thing is not that they degenerate with time, but that some of them degenerate so slowly. Paul Bequerel, a French botanist, has reported germination tests on about 500 species of old seeds from the storage room of a museum. Thirteen of the visible species were more than fifty years old, and of these eleven were legumes. One lot of cassia (legume family) seeds grew after 158 years; another after 115 years.

The quantity of seeds in a packet is something that puzzles the public. Usually the determination is based on the number needed to plant a certain length row. Seeds are measured by volume, and the amounts are checked by weight against packets that have been filled to an exact count. If you buy from a retail seed rack the packet will have a picture of the plant and description, plus cultural directions. If you buy by mail you often get only a packet with the name of the plant, since you presumably have bought from a description and picture in the catalog. Mail order dealers draw orders from large areas, so they can offer many special seed varieties not profitably handled by local dealers. Some mail catalogs specialize in seeds of unusual plants. If seeds are very valuable and expensive to produce, such as hybrid petunias, begonias, and other small-seeded hybrids, they are often put into a tiny inner packet for greater protection. Most seedsmen guarantee their seeds to be true to name. Mistakes are seldom made.

Like many people, I often overbuy on seeds. When spring planting time is over I find myself with partial or full packets of perfectly good seeds that I cannot use again for a full year. Will they keep until next spring?

My county agent, extension horticulturist, U.S.D.A., and some of the seedsmen provided responses to my questions—and I should quickly add that there is no complete answer, no hard and fast rule for how long a certain kind of seed will keep, because much depends on how good it was in the first place.

You can reasonably expect fresh seeds of different vegetable varieties to perform about as given in the table, and to retain their viability for the number of years shown—*provided* they are stored properly. The table comes from E.L. Whitehead, formerly extension horticulturist at the Oklahoma State University, Experiment Station, Stillwater.

Vegetable Seeds—
How Long and How Many

Vegetable	Percent Average Germination 1-year seed	Average Years of Germination	Number of Seeds per Ounce
Asparagus	90	3	1,000
Beans, dwarf	90	3	90–100
Beet, garden	80	4	1,750
Cabbage	85	4	5,000
Carrot	75	3	14,000
Cauliflower	85	4	14,000
Corn, sweet	85	3	125
Cucumber	85	5	1,000
Eggplant	75	4	5,000
Lettuce	90	6	12,000–16,000
Melon, musk	85	5	1,200
Mustard	85	3	18,000
Okra	85	1	425
Onion	80	2	12,500
Peas	90	3	50–150
Pepper	75	2	4,000
Pumpkin	90	4	100
Radish	90	4	5,000
Spinach	80	3	3,000
Tomato	85	3	6,000–7,500
Turnip	90	4	10,000

The storage methods are frequently where failures originate. I store seed by sealing the leftovers (still in packets) in small, dry, airtight jars and putting them in the refrigerator. The small baby food jars are perfect for small amounts, or if you have several packets use a pint fruit jar with tight lid. The seeds should be reasonably dry when stored, but not too dry. The ideal storage temperature is between 36°F and 45°F. I checked my refrigerator with a thermometer over several months and found it maintained a temperature of approximately 40°F (a happy medium) if kept on a medium setting.

Although it is practically impossible to tell the number of years the hundreds of thousands of different seeds might remain viable, there are certain characteristics by which you can judge whether or not a seed is good. A main one is the seed coat. The seed is more likely to be a long-lived kind if it has a hard and horny exterior, and often a smooth, polished appearance. The longest-lived seeds may not plump up readily when soaked in water—give them time.

Some seeds that do not keep well are delphinium, larkspur, and dwarf hybrid marigolds.

Seeds are still a great bargain but—like just about everything else—their prices have risen—so it's worthwhile to consider saving them for at least one year to the next.

SHADY STORY Many people living in mature neighborhoods have trouble with shade—there's just too much of it because trees planted generations ago are now casting their shadows on every inch of ground. If this is where you are don't despair—there's a wide range of summer-color flowers to pick up the dreariest aspect.

Impatiens are the premier plants for shade, blessed with exceptional flower production and a spreading growth habit that makes them look always tidy. The "Sherbet Mix" from Ball Seed Company is especially eye-catching with a range of delicious pastel colors. Begonias, too, bloom abundantly in shade—from large-flowered tuberous types in many flower forms to wax begonias with abundant flowers. Coleus have been spun into glowing colors and fanciful leaf shapes, fringed, notched, cut or solid. Achimines are hard to beat for porch boxes, giving abundant bloom in many colors right up to fall. And salvia 'Red Hot Sally' is great for hot color and not the least bit fussy—she will grow beautifully in shade or sun.

SHAKING THE SALT HABIT It is believed by many that salt causes water retention, thereby adding to the problems of dieters, and there are other problems believed to be caused by too much salt. Herbal salt substitutes are therefore timely and lovage is one of these, delicious on salads or in cheese biscuits. Celery, summer savory, thyme, and marjoram are also acceptable. Vegetable sources of salt also include beets, Swiss chard, beet greens, and carrots. Use lemon juice with garlic and oil for salad dressing, on cooked vegetables, in potato soup, and on fish. Use cayenne, Tabasco, or red and green chilies to enhance the taste of foods by adding just enough to dishes to make the peppery taste barely detectable— not "hot." Onion and garlic powder shaken lightly on grain and legume dishes will make salt forgettable! Kelp is an excellent seasoner containing not only common salt but also 20 to 25 percent potassium chloride, sodium carbonate, boron, iodine, and other trace elements.

If you feel you *must* salt your food, be sure to use sea salt (evaporated sea water), which contains all the trace minerals. Sea water is reported to have the same mineral content as our blood.

SHALLOTS (*Allium Cepa*), **THE GOURMET TOUCH** Shallots are the delight of the gourmet cook and are prized in French and other continental cuisines. Often outrageously expensive to buy and hard to find in most markets, they are one of the easiest vegetables to grow. They thrive on poor soil, need very little care and will divide and multiply year after year, producing clusters of small bulbs from the original bulb. These bulbs, dried and cured, lend a mild garlic-onion flavor to meats, sauces, and other dishes.

Plant shallots in a sunny area, 1 inch deep and 2 inches apart in moist soil. Keep soil slightly moist until plants appear and then irrigate on a weekly basis if there is no rain.

Shallot tops grow to about 28 inches tall, resembling chives and with similar flavor. You may snip a few and use as you would chives. Take only a few from each plant or bulb development will be retarded. When tops turn brown and topple over, shallots are ready to harvest. Pull bulbs, leaving on tops and cure by letting them dry in the sun for one week. Then remove tops and store bulbs in a dry area. They will usually keep a year without losing quality.

SHOCK ABSORBERS For even spacing I measure my garden rows, marking them at each end with a shock absorber. When planting I stretch my line between them so I will have straight rows. Later in the season when I must water I find the hose slips easily around the shock absorbers without whipping over and breaking the plants.

SHOOT FOR A TON AND HAVE SOME FUN As long as you're at it, why not shoot for a world champion vegetable? How? Here's a way to start:

- Genetics. Select a variety known to produce gigantic vegetables. Some examples are Delicious Tomato, Beefmaster, The Duke, Bragger, Park's Whopper, or Burpee's Supersteak, Big Max Pumpkin, Burgess Giant Pumpkin, Hungarian Mammoth Squash, Giant Banana Squash, Foot Long "Slim Jim" Chili pepper (Burgess), Jumbo Cabbage, or Lutz Green Leaf beets (Johnny's Selected Seeds), Mammoth Russian Sunflower.

- Soil conditions. Choose a well-drained, sunny spot where the soil is deep and fertile. Encourage growth of beneficial soil microbes by the addition of organic material to create humus.

- Water. This is vital. Vegetables are mostly water by weight, and a giant champion is going to need lots of the stuff. The water supply to the plant's roots should never be interrupted; on the other hand, there should never be a case of a plant standing in water.

- Fertilize. Fertilizer levels must be kept at an optimum level for the plant. You want to include all the plant nutrients, the trace minerals as well as the three major ones, a deficiency in any one is as bad as a deficiency in all of them. You can get trace minerals in liquid fish emulsions or other concentrated liquid fertilizers made from the sea.

- Hand pollination. To ensure an early fruit set you may want to try hand pollination. Cucurbits, especially, often benefit if you take the time to get them going.

- Prune. To grow really big vegetables, you must prune everything but one or two fruits off the plant. This will encourage it to concentrate all its energy into the growth of the ones you leave.

- Remember to give your giants plenty of room, about three times the area normally allotted for the variety you are growing. Also the soil should be well-prepared and worked to a depth of 2 feet or more. Compost, manure, and soil conditioners should be mixed in throughout the entire growing bed.

As for insects and predators, you must watch your giants like your very own babies. At no time should they be bothered by insects or disease. Remember, your plant must think that this is the best of all possible worlds, and getting better and better!

SLUDGE, BE SURE IT'S SAFE   Organic gardeners have for years been hauling off sewage sludge from digester plants to spread on their farms and gardens. Such sludge from small towns, well away from industrial developments should be safe, just do investigate. Analyses may reveal high percentages of heavy metals: cadmium, zinc, etc. in soluble or semisoluble forms. The National Garden Bureau advises gardeners to ask to see any analysis of any sludge before using it. If toxic heavy metals or PCB (polychlorianted biphenyls) show up don't use it and, if you have any sludge stockpiled on your place, return it.

SLUGGING IT OUT   One gardener solved his slug problem by purchasing some fiber glass insulation. He cut 10-inch squares and slit them through the center, filling the squares around the young tomato and pepper plants as he set them out, holding the squares down with a little soil at the corners. He found the slugs did not crawl very far in the fiberglass before retreating.

Slugs may also be discouraged with vinegar. Mix vinegar with water in equal parts in a plastic spray bottle. Working after dark, spray any you find on plants and give them another dose when they fall to the ground. You may also spray the soil around the base of your plants.

Oak leaves are a deterrent, providing a "bitter atmosphere" that slugs can't stand. You may line your garden paths with coal ashes, which provide a texture unacceptable to snails. When the ashes decompose they release sulfur, which combined with water, forms sulfuric acid—lethal to slugs. Powdered rock phosphate will enrich your soil at the same time it is deterring slugs.

SMILING FROM EAR TO EAR   Drip liquid mixture of Bacillus thurigienesis into the end or ears through the silks (after corn has been pollinated and silks begin to dry and darken) of varieties susceptible to corn earworm. Use on either sweet corn or popcorn.

SMOKE TREE (*Cotinus coggygria*)   Alluringly different, this fantastic shrub or small tree is perfect as your garden's exclamation point. 'Royal Purple' (Wayside gardens) has iridescent purple-black foliage and plumed inflorescences (the smoke) of the same color. The rich foliage becomes darker as it ages and the feathery plumes appear in July and August. Cotinus, a member of the Cashew family, thrives in any well-drained soil and succeeds remarkably well in land that is decidedly dry and rocky, preferring a sunny location. Care must be taken, however, at planting time to see that roots are disturbed as little as possible. Water thoroughly during dry spells the first summer. Once established the smoke tree is very hardy and requires little care.

SNAKES IN THE GARDEN   The harmless garden snake, when it isn't scaring you to death, can be very helpful, as it feasts on caterpillars and other slow-moving insects. But snakes do sometimes seek the warmth of a compost pile or shelter of a mulch. A mama snake once crawled up into my toy wagon I left overnight filled with weeds and gave birth, scaring me out of my wits the next morning when I started removing the weeds and picked up all those little wigglers. If you suspect your compost pile of harboring snakes give it a good hard whack with a board before you handle the mulch materials.

SOIL TEST TIP   Test your soil in spring or fall, not while some particular crop may be draining one element out of it. Rich-looking black soil is not necessarily better than faded red earth. The proof is in the growing. Garlic is a good indicator; if it grows like mad, your soil is rich.

SOW BUGS (*Oniscus asellus*)   The sow bug or wood louse is a small flat animal with seven pairs of legs. It is a crustacean, related to the crab and the lobster. It can and does roll itself up into a ball. Sow bugs are very destructive, taking great delight in feasting on roots and shoots of young plants. Plant refuse, boards and boxes provide hiding places, so keeping the area around the garden clean is a start toward their elimination. Some gardeners destroy them with boiling water; others let ducks or chickens loose to clean up the garden. Toads are another control for sow bugs and if you have these they must be given water and shade. Dry tobacco dust will repel the little nasties and, if all else fails, try pyrethrum spray which kills on direct contact.

SPACED-OUT SEEDS   Some seeds are so tiny that they are difficult to space by hand and you have to thin or transplant seedlings. Gadgets for spacing seeds are getting better all the time and it may pay you to invest in one. Some of them have adjustable gates that let seeds escape as you tap the container. Or, you can still mix tiny seeds with sand or dry coffee grounds. An old salt shaker (with large holes) is helpful in planting carrot seed.

SPIDER POWER   How well I remember one beautiful fall day when I took my small granddaughter Elizabeth, then aged three, by the hand and led her out to my garden to admire the webs the golden garden spider had spun on the okra plants. She took one look and screamed bloody murder!

The fear of spiders seems to be inherent in most of us. And perhaps that is the way it should be, for while most are harmless and often helpful—their diet consists mainly of insects and mites—there are some that should always be treated with respect such as the black widow and the fiddleback. The helpful spiders are legion, some working on the ground level and others like the golden garden species spinning their beautiful orb webs high in the air. The species seems to surface in the fall, just about the time the grasshoppers become more numerous—and help to hold down their populations.

It has been reported that in China farmers actually aid the spiders to overwinter by building little tepees out of straw to house and protect them so they will be there in the spring to feed on the insects that suck the life out of the young rice and cotton plants. This increases the yield and avoids the use of chemical insecticides.

Have you ever heard of the "banana spider"? This little brownish-gray fellow is a welcome house guest in Central America for it feeds on cockroaches and also eats other insects and some small lizards that crawl on the walls.

In Texas, according to Marvin Harris, a professor at Texas A & M University, spiders aid in the control of aphids in pecan orchards. Strangely, spiders can go for a long time without food, waiting patiently during a time of insect dearth, until they become active again and food arrives.

Scientists are becoming increasingly interested in the silk of the web-weaving spiders—some types of which are stronger than steel. Particularly though is "dragline" silk which supports the spider as it hangs in front of your face or rides the winds in search of greener pastures.

SPIDER LILIES (*Lycoris*) Exquisitely beautiful, despite their strange name, spider lilies bloom in summer and autumn when most other flowers are gone. A welcome addition to any garden, the handsome and unusual flowers appear on tall stems followed by grasslike foliage that remains green all winter. The variety *L. squamigera* has clusters of large but dainty pink trumpet-shaped flowers that perfume the air with their delightful fragrance. Sometimes called "Magic Lily" or "Resurrection Lily." *L. radiata* (spider lily) has airy rosy red blooms borne on 6-inch clusters of ten to twenty a stem in late summer and autumn.

SPINACH (*Spinacia oleracea*) Raw spinach is very high in vitamin A, as well as B, C, E, K, and very high in potassium. It's a good source of phosphorous, calcium, and iron. In addition it contains choline and inositol, the substances that help prevent arteriosclerosis, or hardening of the arteries.

Last fall I planted spinach and in my mild climate I had it for table use all winter. When it came time for spring plowing the spinach plants were so beautiful I dug up every last one of them and replanted them. And they all recovered and grew and I am still harvesting spinach while I wait for my new planting to grow large enough to use. In most climates it is best to plant spinach in fall and spring as it does not stand hot weather well. Of course you will want to cook some of your spinach, but eat it raw also, for cooking eliminates the calcium from the bloodstream.

"SPOONING" My love affair with my garden starts with the seedlings. When transplanting I use a long-handled ice tea spoon for the job, lifting each plant gently with as much earth around its roots as I can get without disturbing its nearby neighbor.

SPRAYER TIP If you have some spray left over put a piece of masking tape on the sprayer bottle to indicate what's in it. This way, there's no need to rinse it out before adding more of the same. But if you forget— you *can't* take a chance—you *have* to empty it and rinse it.

SPRITELY FLOWERS Here's a secret worth knowing! You can extend the life of cut flowers by placing them in a solution of one part Sprite to five parts of water. Clean the container thoroughly for the arrangement before adding the solution.

SPROUTING SUNFLOWER SEEDS As long as they have not been roasted, you can sprout your sunflower seeds, even if they've been hulled, just as you would sprout wheat and mung beans. Soak overnight, rinse and drain. For best flavor use them when the sprouts are the same length as the seeds—about one day in summer or two in winter.

Seeds in the shell are easy to sprout and also to hull. Soak a day's supply, about a third of a glassful, overnight. Pour off the water, taking just a few minutes to give the seeds a bath and a good shake-up, by holding the glass under the faucet and then turning it upside down on the hand or sieve to drain off excess water. By the time the sprouts are about as long as the seed, the glass is nearly full and the hulls are loose and flip off easily. If you can obtain them, black sunflower seeds (the seeds not the sunflower) are even tastier than the striped variety.

SQUASH BUGS GET A "CHEW" Give your squash bugs something to chew on. Soak a package of chewing tobacco in a gallon of water. To this add crushed garlic, a teaspoon of crushed red pepper, and some good sudsing detergent. Soak overnight, strain and use in a standard sprayer.

SQUASH, SUMMER (*Cucurbita pepo*) Summer squashes come in such infinite and delicious variety that it would be impossible to describe them all, but one in particular stands out for me, Park's Kuta. It's sweet,

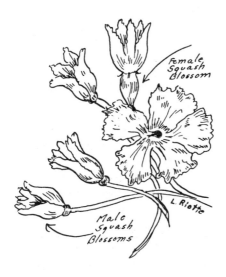

Female
Squash
Blossom

L. Riotte

Male
Squash
Blossoms

nutty flavor is indeed an entirely new experience and its versatility is almost unlimited. It may be used young as a summer squash or the larger fruits can be baked or stuffed like a winter squash. Other favorites include yellow squash, zucchini, and the patty pans, most of which are best eaten small.

Squash is best sown directly into the garden but may be started in small pots if great care is used in transplanting. In either case remember squash likes warm weather. Squash takes up a lot of room, so you may want to try some of the newer bush varieties. Squash are space-hogs and may cover their nearest neighbors if planted too close. Squash varieties will cross with each other but this only matters if you intend to save seed which I don't advise. And, in spite of what you may have heard, cucumbers and squash will not mix with each other.

Summer squash is an exceptionally good food for hot climates and has been found valuable for cases of high blood pressure, obesity, constipation, and bladder and kidney disorders. It is a very good source of potassium and the vitamins A, B, and C. After your summer squash has started to bear, mound dirt around the base of each plant so that all roots are covered . . . your plants will bear for a much longer time. Squash has shallow roots.

SQUASH, WINTER (*Cucurbita maxima*) Winter squash is a treasure trove of vitamin A, containing 4,950 I.U. per 100 gm. A rough or dry condition of the skin is often due to a deficiency of vitamin A, and winter squash tend to make the skin healthy, smooth and firm. Case histories also indicate that foods with high vitamin A content will improve eyesight and even make hair grow.

Again we have many varieties to choose from, including the acorn and butternut—baked with brown sugar, butter, and spices they are a gourmet's delight. Winter squash need a longer growing season, otherwise their culture is much the same as for summer squash. Pick winter squash for storage only when completely mature.

SQUIRRELS A tree squirrel is an energetic animal. Nuts have the right amount of fats and carbohydrates to take squirrels through a winter in good shape for producing more bushytails. The most choice seasonal foods would have to include the nuts of hickory and pecan. In fact, squirrels begin to cut on these crops even before they have fully ripened—and a squirrel requires about 100 pounds of food a year. Later, when these crops are gone, however, they will switch to other foods.

Small plantings of nut tree seed can be protected from squirrels by the "tin can" method. A number two size can (such as a soup can) is recommended. Remove the top and punch a hole about 1 inch in diameter in the bottom of the can. One inch of soil is placed in the can, followed by the seed nut and then the can is filled with soil. At planting the can is inverted and placed with the punched hole up and level with the ground surface. Iron cans will usually rust through before girdling the tree; aluminum cans should be cut away after the tree is established.

STOCKING-HEAD TRICK While cauliflower heads are one to two inches in diameter, enclose them with nylon and tie below the head. They remain worm-and-egg-free and grow surprisingly large.

STONED BEDS! Stones have most of the advantages of other types of mulch and a few of their own. They're particularly good for conserving moisture. They allow the soil to heat up quickly in the spring and, because they absorb heat, help to protect tender plants during cool nights. They also help keep weeds down. To be stone-mulched the bed must be cultivated deeply, just like any permanently mulched plot, and organic matter should be dug or tilled into the soil. If leaves are available, spread a thick layer over the soil and place the stones on top of the leaves. Set the stones in rows 2 feet wide, leaving a foot between stone paths for planting. Spaces between the stones can be filled with compost or garden loam and the rows mulched with compost, straw, or other mulches.

STRAWBERRY JAR HERB GARDENS

Strawberry jars can be miniature herb gardens, boasting a variety of foliage textures and fragrances, and they are very, very convenient for the cook. Use only one herb in each of the cut-outs in the jar, choosing training types for lower openings and more upright types for upper ones. Mix fine-textured herbs like santolina, rosemary, lavender, southernwood, tarragon, savory, and chives with the larger leaves of sage, basil, scented geraniums, parsley, and oregano. For color, add a sprig of purple basil, Tricolor sage, variegated thyme, or lavender. Of course I am not suggesting you plant all of these; choose five at the most, repeating the less vigorous plants in the extra cutouts.

SUCCESSION PLANTING

enables the gardener to make the utmost use of compost. Such heavy feeders as broccoli, brussel sprouts, cabbage, cauliflower, celeriac, celery, chard, cucumbers, endive, kohlrabi, leek, lettuce, spinach, squash, sweet corn, and tomato are best planted in soil newly fertilized with well-decomposed manure.

A second crop, using the same area, can be had if these heavy feeders are followed by such light feeders as beet, carrot, radish, ruta-

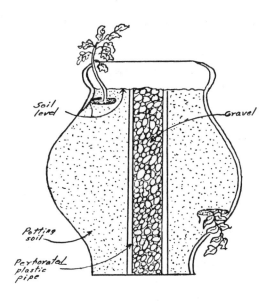

For even watering, put a watering column in center of jar: Use a length of plastic pipe an inch shorter than height of jar and about 2 inches less in diameter than jar mouth. Use a large nail and puncture the pipe every 2 inches all around. Position pipe in center of jar and fill with gravel. Then add enough potting soil to jar to fill to level of lowest cutout; insert first plant, firming soil. Fill jar to level of next opening and plant. Repeat procedure until pot is filled. Plant top of jar by setting herbs into soil around outside of pipe. When watering, pour into gravel. It will trickle down pipe and out through nail-punctured holes.

baga, and turnip which also like finely-pulverized raw rocks and compost.

The third crop in succession planting is the legumes, lima beans, bush and pole beans, peas, and soybeans. These are the soil improvers, collecting nitrogen on their roots and restoring it to the soil.

SUGAR CANE (*Saccharum officinarum*)

In recent years sugar has become almost a dirty word. But, Mrs. C.F. Leyel, an English herbal writer, has this to say: "Medicinally, sugar is a heart tonic of great value and is of such importance in the diet of the young and the aged that it cannot well be overrated. It strengthens the muscles, stokes the engine of the body, burns up acid, and makes food palatable." To this last observation, at least, we must certainly agree.

What many of us do not realize is that almost all plants make sugar though most of what we use comes from sugar cane and sugar beets. However, the maple tree is also an important source of sugar, and it is also made from corn, grapes, and milk. Sugar cane is actually a tall grass plant that grows in tropical and semitropical countries. It produces sturdy stalks 10 to 15 feet high, and about 2 inches in diameter. It is simply a plant, or herb, and is not evil in itself. It is the overuse of sugar that sometimes produces undesirable results.

SUMMER GARDEN No need to rush into planting the summer garden. Seeds and plants of many vegetables may be planted in the garden throughout May with good results. Warm soil is important for good seed germination. Corn is one of the first summer crops to be seeded. Snapbeans are often next in succession. Seeds that should not be planted until after soil is well warmed include lima beans, okra, cucumbers, squash, cantaloupes, and watermelon. Plants of tomatoes, peppers, eggplants, and sweet potato need warm temperatures to take off well.

Hardening plants is important to get them off to a fast, uninterrupted start. Those that are not adequately hardened may burn from wind and sun, or be more easily damaged by cool temperatures. Plants are hardened by placing them outdoors in a shady, protected spot for one to two weeks before planting. Gradually move them to a brighter more exposed location until they are exposed to conditions similar to those in the garden. Set out transplants with as little root disturbances as possible.

SUN-DRIED TOMATOES Preserving an abundant crop of tomatoes for winter use is fun when you try out different methods. Try cutting ripe tomatoes into 1/4-inch slices and laying them flat on large trays. Sprinkle them lightly with salt and place the trays in the sun. Protect from flies and bring them in at night. Every other day turn over each slice, until they are dried to about the same moisture content as soft prunes. Now is the time to put a thin coating of olive oil on all surfaces of each slice. Store in glass jars or crocks in a cool, dry place. These dried tomatoes are delicious fried with scrambled eggs, or broiled and served hot from the oven.

SUN WORSHIPPERS For real ability to take the heat there is just nothing like the warm-weather-loving gazanias. The daisylike flowers thrive in dry soil conditions, and one of the best new hybrids is 'Sundance' from Pan-American. You can even choose in this series from such "hot" colors as bronze, bright yellow, red, and bicolors. Another sun lover which also makes an excellent cut flower is the gerbera or African daisy. It has 3- to 4-inch flowers and long stems which can grow up to 12 inches. Groundcovers for sunny spots include vinca and the many-splendored portulaca which comes in a variety of bright colors. Many begonias, too, of the fibrous type can now take the sun. And never forget our old friends, tried and true sun-lovers, the zinnias—which now come in all sizes and colors and greatly improved types.

SUPPORT HOSE When planting young trees you can help steady them by carefully sliding a ring of auto radiator hose about an inch wide over the trunks. Then place stakes on either side of the tree and tie the rings to the stakes. The soft, but strong, hose avoids scratching the bark.

When there isn't much ground greenery for rabbits to nibble on they may decide to strip the bark from your small trees. Protect them with a section of old garden hose that has been spiral cut. Start cutting at one end at about a 45-degree angle going around the hose until you reach the other end. This allows for easy wrapping around the trunk and next spring, when it's safe, the hose comes off easily.

SURFACE PLANTING It may sound like heresy but not all seeds should be covered. There are quite a few that germinate much more easily if they are in the light. While they do need moisture, they do not need and should not have deep planting. This is logical, for many seeds in nature simply drop to the ground and remain there to spend their dormancy, develop as necessary, and take up water for germination when the time comes. The grasses are a good example of this but such seeds as lettuce and celery will come up better also if some light gets to the seeds. Such seeds should be merely pressed down in or gently watered down into the growing medium. Others liking this treatment include achimenes, African violet, ageratum, alpine strawberries, wax begonia, browallia, cape-primrose, coleus, conifers of most sorts, flowering tobacco, gloxinia, johnny-jump-up, kalanchoe, lobelia, painted tongue, petunia, scarlet sage, snapdragon, stock, temple-bells, and yarrow.

SWANS   being of a somewhat belligerent nature are not usually thought of as pets, but they are so beautiful floating about on a body of water that many people delight in having them on their premises. If you decide to accommodate them, construct a deep, rather than shallow, pond—one that possibly permits a fish crop to be harvested. A flat, shallow pond may turn into a swamp in summer as it loses water through evaporation. One of the advantages of a pond or small lake is that even temperature is maintained in the area near it—cooler in summer and warmer in winter.

If you have a fair-sized body of water you may find pleasure in keeping a pair of swans for their decorative effect. Since these birds mate for life you should endeavor to buy a mated pair.

Do not expect them to "buddy up" to you. They are not what you might call sociable. The male swan is called a *cob*, and the female, a *pen*. Don't ask me why, for diligent research has failed to give me the answer.

The young swans are called cygnets, and they are far from beautiful.

When the loving pair, and they do love each other if no one else, are ready they will put together a nest of twigs and other odds and ends available. You can help by providing such material—at a safe distance. Whistling swans make their nests out of water plants and line them with down from their bodies. And these nests sometimes stand two feet high and measure six feet across.

The female lays five to seven eggs, usually in June. The cygnets are covered with grayish down at first, becoming snow white by the end of their first year, thus effecting the famous transformation. The cygnets are delicate but if they survive their first season swans may live to 60 years of age. The graceful swan is—wouldn't you know it?—ruled by Libra under Venus.

The male swan takes his duties seriously. Apt to be ill-tempered at all times, he is extremely so during mating time, being tirelessly protective. He will fight anything that he deems to be a danger to the nest and his mate: dog, cat, you, or even a tractor, should one come along. If you must be around him at this time be exceedingly careful.

When they can, swans eat worms and shellfish and the seeds and roots of water plants. They dip their long curving necks into the water in search of food. Since these may not be available in sufficient quantity in the environment you provide, you will need to supplement their diet of water plants and insects and, in time, they will come regularly for feeding—but even then you should be very cautious during the mating season.

Waterside plants you might like to grow include the marsh marigold (*Caltha palustris*) and the globe flowers or trollius, this latter flourishing in either full sun or partial shade.

Other interesting plants for growing beside water are the cardinal flower (*Lobelia cardinalis*), the willow gentian (*Gentiana asclepiades*), and *Helonias bullata*, the swamp pink. Good groundcovers are the forget-me-nots, *Myosotis scorpioides* (palustris), and M. *scorpioides* var. *semperflorens*, which flowers all summer. Groundcovers help to keep the pool clear. *Ranunculus aconitifolius*, which flowers in May, blooms for a very long time. Astrantia is another moisture-loving plant that thrives by the waterside. The flowering rush (*Butomus umbellatus*) is also excellent for waterside planting. Often cattails, which may become a nuisance, and other water plants spring up "on their own" from seeds being carried by birds.

Japanese and Siberian iris are lovely in June. Some of the primulas are among the best waterside plants in regions where they thrive. Astilbes flower in late spring or summer. The musks or mimulus are useful for waterside planting with handsome flowers. Among plants with conspicuous foliage the most effective are *Arundo Donax*, the giant reed; and *Rheum palmatum*. Other useful plants include the *Rodgersias*, the *Ligularias*, and *Lysichium americanum*, especially recommended for small waterside gardens.

SWEET POTATOES (*Ipomoea Batatas*)
Sweet potatoes make a great second crop. Excessive nitrogen is not good for sweet potatoes so avoid heavy applications of fertilizer, especially manures. Set out started plants after the soil is warm using slips or cuttings. Plant each one on a slight rise or atop a long, 8-inch-high ridge, setting plants 12 inches apart. Sweet potatoes need lots of sun and warmth but can get along without heavy watering. Just before frost, harvest the tubers by digging them up with a garden fork. It is good to let them lie in the sun for several hours, or until quite dry. Store at 85°F. Once you place sweet potatoes in their storage container do not move or turn them again. The milk in the potato gets set, and if you turn it upside down, it will rot.

Sweet potatoes are vitamin-rich, containing both vitamins A and C, as well as small amounts of the B vitamins and minerals. One medium potato contains just 155 calories.

SWISS CHARD (*Beta vulgaris* var. *cicla*)
Swiss chard, which will even thrive during the hottest part of the summer, is handsome enough for the flower garden. And it is well suited to container growing, particularly if you use the selection known as Rhubarb, which has beautiful red stalks and rich-looking leaves with crinkled foliage, providing color that's both movable and edible. Chard is actually a variety of beet.

Start chard from transplants or seeds, planting two to four weeks before the last frost in spring and again in late summer—it will stand up to cold as well as heat. Give it a spot that receives full sun for three to six hours per day, and keep the soil moist to prevent bolting. Harvest by cutting off the leaves at ground level, using a sharp knife. They're best when less than 12 inches long. If you don't disturb the central leaves new foliage will continue to grow.

In cooking, the leaves may be substituted for spinach and the stems and midribs may be used instead of seakale. Chard is a powerhouse of vitamin A. When leaves and stalks are used together it contains 2,800 I.U. per 100 gm; leaves alone contain 8,720 I.U. per 100 gm. Also contains vitamins B and C, and calcium, iron, and phosphorous.

Throngs of insects in the shade
Try their thin wings and dance in the warm beam
That waked them into life.

WILLIAM CULLEN BRYANT

TALL IN THE SADDLE is our Western way of paying a compliment to something very important. Such as a really big houseplant to give special emphasis to a lucky room. This is a trend that is really catching on, particularly for larger rooms in houses or business buildings. Large plants are a good investment, have good staying qualities, and are less likely to die, given reasonably good care.

Plant possibilities include:

Bamboo palm *(Chamedora erumpens)*
Reed palm *(Chamaedorea seifrizii)*
Weeping fig *(Ficus benjamina)*
Indian laurel *(Ficus retusa nitida)*
India rubber plant *(Ficus elastica 'Decora')*
Red-margined dracaena *(Dracaena marginata)*
Janet Craig dracaena *(Dracaena dermensis 'Janet Craig')*
Corn plant *(Dracaena fragrans massangeana)*
Shefflera *(Brassaia actinophylla)*
Dragon tree *(Dracaena draco)*
Kentia palm *(Howeia belmoreana)*
Pony tail *(Beaucarnea recurvata)*

Saddle-leaf philodendron *(Philodendron selloum)*

Care for your friendly giant by giving it a regular monthly application of a water soluble, balanced fertilizer. With the exception of cacti, most plants like a regular, cleansing misting. Watering on a regular schedule is important and the use of a moisture meter is helpful in determining the condition of the soil. Inspect regularly for insects. Be certain your plants have good drainage. Place sphagnum moss over the top of the soil for a neat look and to slow down evaporation. Large plants need be watered less frequently.

Remember to consider your plants' lighting needs: rubber tree, good indirect light or morning sun; weeping fig, good indirect light or direct morning sun; red-margined dracaena, good indirect light; Janet Craig dracaena, good indirect light but no direct afternoon sun; areca palm, strong direct or indirect light; fishtail palm *(Caryota mitis)*, strong indirect or direct morning sun; schefflera, good indirect light or direct morning sun.

TATOO FOR AFRICAN VIOLETS To keep track of names of African violets you are rooting, just write the name on the underside of the leaf with a felt-tip marking pencil. This "tatoo" will stay legible until the new plant is ready for potting, does not hurt the leaf, and can't be lost. I also use this idea for iris I intend to divide—when it is no longer in bloom I know its name.

TEMPERAMENT TIPS It's good to know that failure to set fruit may not be the gardener's fault for lack of care. Plants like peppers and eggplants are just naturally fussy around blossoming time. They'll have a poor fruit set if temperatures at night are below 35°F or above 75°F while they are blossoming, and they'll also drop their blossoms if daytime temperatures are above 90°F. These temperatures will also delay the fruit that does manage to set. Eggplant and peppers, too, are likely to become stunted during cool weather and then not grow rapidly once warm weather comes back—and rapid growth is a must for quality fruit production. It's also worth noting that large-fruited eggplant are more demanding than the small-fruited varieties. If you've had a difficult time in the past growing eggplant it might be a good time to grow the more succulent, smaller varieties.

Okra, too, can make like a prima donna. Its blooms last only a day whether or not pollinated and constant rainy weather when they're blooming will often reduce yields since bees don't buzz around much in unsettled weather.

TENT CATERPILLAR As soon as webs form, while worms are still very small, wipe them out of the crotches of branches with a pointed stick or a swab dipped in kerosene. If webs must be destroyed after the caterpillars are well developed, do so in early morning or after sunset when they have returned to the web for warmth. A preventive control is to cut off and burn the twigs bearing egg masses which can be seen after the leaves have dropped in autumn or winter. Bacillus thuringiensis is a safe control. Tent caterpillars infest pecan, wild cherry, apple, and other trees in the spring and early summer.

TERRARIUM FUN Why not make a terrarium for yourself or a friend, perhaps someone who is confined to a wheelchair? They're fun to assemble and provide a friendly home to tender ferns, zebra plants, and other exotics that don't thrive in the dry air of most homes. You can add color and texture by nestling shells or pretty rocks among the greenery. Being a rockhound I often collect rounded pebbles of rose or white quartz and sometimes I am lucky enough to find quartz crystals as well.

You'll need a clear container with a lid (such containers are often available in garden centers, but a large pickle jar also can be used), charcoal, sphagnum moss, and sterile potting soil. Start with a 1- to 2-inch layer of sterile horticultural charcoal to provide drainage and keep the soil sweet. Soak the moss in hot water until it is soggy, then wring it out, pull it apart, and spread a layer over the charcoal. Add a layer of sterile packaged soil deep enough to plant ferns. Pat down the soil and clean the inside of the glass with a damp paper towel. Dig small holes to plant the ferns—the eraser end of a pencil is a handy tool.

Water the terrarium so that the soil is evenly moist but not soggy, and keep it in a good, well-lighted area, but not in direct sunlight. In winter be sure to move your terrarium out of a chilly window to a warmer spot.

Try planting delicate maidenhair fern, baby tears (for groundcover), glossy bird's nest fern, lacy pteris fern, holly fern, and Victoria fern (reportedly named for Queen Victoria, during whose era ferns were very popular).

Dwarf palm maranta and miniature fittonia also do well in terrariums. Blooming plants, such as African violets, grow well. Tiny violets—and there are now dwarf varieties—in an elegant glass container make lovely gifts. Just don't let water drop on violet leaves for it will cause ugly brown spots. It is helpful to make a collar with a hole in the center large enough for the stem, and a slit so it may be easily slipped over. Rotate terrariums every few days so plants will grow uniformly and occasionally pinch off old growth at a stem joint to keep your terrarium from becoming a jungle.

A terrarium can be practical as well as beautiful, being a perfect place to start new plants from seeds or cuttings.

Try using a lazy Susan or kitchen turntable (usually used for spice shelf or cupboard), as a platform for your terrarium. With a gentle turn you can rotate it towards the light for even growth, so it can be viewed from all sides. Not a bad idea either for a potted plant or flats for starting seeds.

THINK LITTLE   This is the story of a man who changed from a maxi- to a mini-home orchardist. When the little standard trees he planted began to grow he found he had to harvest precariously from a step ladder and even then the birds had tested nearly every peach or apple before it was ripe enough to eat.

A nurseryman suggested bending the new growth down in the fall and tying it to the lower limbs. This made sense to him, for in Japan he had seen orchards trained to grow like grape arbors. So he bought some rope and tried persuading his trees to make like vines. The following summer he says they looked like blackberry brambles but bore fruit he could reach from the ground. He could also toss nets over them to defeat feathered fruit samplers. He claims this tying method worked well for a while but eventually got so thick he could scarcely fight his way into the tangle to gather fruit.

By this time he was thinking little, so when some trees needed replacement he bought dwarfs, and found that they bore more quickly and gave him all the advantages of the tied-down trees with none of the entanglement. The moral of this story is that he thereupon steeled his heart, yanked out all the standard trees, replaced them with twice as many dwarfs and he and his orchard lived happily ever after.

THINNING—YOUR SECRET WEAPON   Most home gardeners and commercial growers wait until fruits reach marble size to thin by hand. However, early hand thinning of blossoms will also give good results. The sooner after flowering that excess fruit is removed, the more the remaining fruit will be improved in size and quality. A good general rule for apricots, plums, apples, Asian pears, nectarines, and peaches is to thin them twice as far apart as the diameter you want them to be at maturity.

TICKS (*Arachnids*)   This small animal is related to mites, spiders, and scorpions and can be very troublesome in some areas to gardeners and their pets. It is oval in shape, a parasite, and often a carrier of disease germs, which are transferred to the blood of its victims. Sometimes their bites are poisonous. Though not common, cases of paralysis have been known to follow their attacks. The head of the tick is a movable part at the front of the body; they draw the blood of their victims through a beak that has strong teeth which are bent backward. These teeth help the parasites cling tightly to their host. There are a number of kinds which have been given special names, such as chicken, cattle, dog, or sheep tick. Many that attack animals also annoy man. Spotted-fever ticks transmit a disease of man called Rocky Mountain spotted fever. Pennyroyal and eucalyptus oil are good against ticks.

If you find a tick on your body, do not try to dislodge it forcibly, the toothed beak will often break off and remain inside the flesh causing a festering sore. Instead, drop gasoline, kerosene, or chloroform on it. It will then loosen its hold and come out easily. I have also found that coating the tick with fingernail polish will cause it to let go.

TICKBIRD (*Cuculidae sulcirostris*)   When nature hands us a pest, like the tick, she usually provides control. The tickbird is a black bird belonging to the cuckoo family. It is also called the groove-billed ani. It gets its name from the fact that it eats ticks. The tickbird perches on cattle and picks off their ticks. It is about twelve inches long, dull black in color, with a touch of violet on its wings. The tickbird usually lays about four eggs, pale blue in color, and sometimes several female tickbirds lay their eggs in the same nest.

TIMING YOUR HARVESTING   The time of day when certain garden activities are undertaken is more important than is often realized. The vital life forces, or mitogenic properties, of all plants gradually return to the roots during the course of the late afternoon and evening. And, having returned, these vital forces remain in the roots during the hours of the night, the roots storing up what they have gained during the day's photosynthesis.

As day breaks, these forces again start their gradual rise back into the aboveground portion of the plant. This has been proven to be a fact and is scientifically measurable. In harmony with this it becomes apparent that we should harvest all root crops late in the afternoon, when the energies gathered that day are in the plant in their most concentrated form.

Further, to obtain the best results from utilizing this knowledge of roots, it is well to plan all root divisions, root feedings (such as side dressings of compost or fish fertilizer), and root prunings (often necessary when transplanting) to take place when root vitality is highest. These hours being late afternoon and evening or shortly before daybreak. These are, of course, the late afternoon and evening hours, or very early in the morning, shortly before daybreak.

Top crops, on the other hand, should be harvested between ten in the morning and not later than three in the afternoon to obtain maximum quality.

These rules also apply to flowers. Roses generally last longer if cut between two and three in the afternoon, as they generally have more stored food available than those cut in the early morning. As soon as you finish gathering your roses, recut the stems, making a slanting cut. This will expose the largest possible surface area for taking up water. Immerse stems in a container of *warm* water and place in a cool dark room. Once the water cools to room temperature, the roses are ready to arrange.

TIME-SAVING TRIMMING TIP
When trimming a hedge, or any large shrub, use a large cloth or plastic dropcloth underneath the shrub you are trimming. When work is complete all you have to do is fold the cloth and take away the trimmings to trash can or compost heap. No need to rake, sweep, or pick up.

TINE CLEANING MADE EASY   If you have ever tilled an overgrown field or garden you know how aggravating weeds and vines can be when they get wrapped around the tines of your tiller. An ingenious solution is to use a hoof knife (the type to trim and clean out horses' hooves). You can cut and clean out the vines and weeds in short order because of the sharp hook at the end of the blade.

TIRED HOSE   To quickly store 100 feet of garden hose lay an old auto tire flat on the ground and coil the hose inside. Tire is easily rolled to store in shed or garage and hose will come right out again when you need it without snarling.

TOAD   His chief weapon of defense is his rough and warty skin. The warts are really glands containing a poisonous fluid. Two of the largest lie just behind his eyes. When attacked, the poisonous fluid oozes from the glands and warts and makes the attacking animal sick. If the toad is a large one, the poison may kill his enemy. While the substance helps to protect the toad from other animals, it cannot cause warts on a person. Invite this fellow to your garden for he will catch many insects and small animals with his tongue which he extends full length when he is hungry.

TOMATILLO (*Physalis ixocarpa*)   This fruit, so important in Mexican cooking, can be difficult to obtain in most parts of the United States unless you grow it yourself. The tomatillo is the tart green husk tomato used in *salsa verde*, or green taco sauce. The tomatillo (*Physalis ixocarpa*) should not be confused with the more commonly grown cherry (*Physalis pruinosa*), which is smaller and sweeter and used for desserts and preserves. A member of the nightshade family, they were known and used centuries ago by the Aztecs.

The tomatillo, swelling to about 2 inches in diameter, will completely fill its papery husk with solid flesh. There are no juice cavities and it cooks down to a thick, smooth sauce; green chilies are added for zip.

The fruit is easy to grow and seed is obtainable from Horticultural Enterprises, Box 34082, Dallas, Texas 75234. You can save seeds from your first planting for the following year. You may even find fruits in your supermarket which you can use for seed. Cover seed thinly and mulch lightly to preserve ground moisture. Pinch out excess plants, leaving one plant every 13 inches. Fruit are ready for harvest about September. The plants form yellow blossoms which give way to balloonlike husks. Best flavored while fruits are still deep green, and when the husk has changed from green to tan. If left on the plant to ripen the fruits become rather sweet and bland. Since plants are very rangy it is wise to stake or cage them to support their prolific vine and heavy harvests.

To can: Remove husks and wash well. Drop into boiling water in a covered pan. When tender (about 10 minutes) pack into hot jars and fill with boiling water to within a ½ inch of the rim. To each pint add ½ teaspoon salt and 1 teaspoon vinegar or lemon juice. Seal and cook in boiling water bath for 30 minutes.

> The tomatillo is a prize,
> A small tomato in disguise.
> Lemon-flavored, crisp, and tart,
> It sets a salsa sauce apart!
> —Louise Riotte, 1991

Tomatillo Salsa

8 tomatillos, roasted and peeled
1 or 2 scallions, coarsely chopped
1 serrano chile, char/roasted, peeled, seeded and chopped
1 tablespoon lime juice
¼ teaspoon or 1 small clove garlic
1 tablespoon chopped fresh cilantro
Salt and pepper to taste

In a blender or food processor, combine all ingredients except cilantro. Chop very coarsely; do not overprocess. Add cilantro and salt and pepper to taste. Makes about 1¼ cups.

(Recipe by permission of Shepherd's Garden Seeds. Seeds for serrano chiles and cilantro may also be obtained from Shepherd's Garden Seeds. See "Sources.")

TOMATOES BY MOON SIGN For centuries, growers have consulted the phases of the moon and zodiac signs in divining the best planting times for their crops. Researchers have recently found that the traditional practice of planting crops during a new moon is more than superstition; chances for heavy rain in the week following both the new moon and full moon are far greater than for the week preceding the new moon. Tomato seeds, for example, will benefit by being planted in the moon's second quarter, under the signs Cancer (for fruitfulness), Scorpio (for sturdiness), or Pisces (for good root growth). Each year, you can determine which days fall under these signs by availing yourself of an ephemeris, a booklet telling what the planets and moon are up to.

TOMATO CAGES Put tomato cages to good use during cold weather by letting them protect tender or marginally hardy shrubs. Stake the cages over the plants and fill them with shredded and/or whole leaves (shredded are better as whole leaves tend to pack). Or you can attach burlap to the framework to protect shrubs from the wind. Roses benefit greatly from this protection. Improve on the idea by putting down (inside the cage) a 4-inch layer of well-rotted manure, a layer of leaves, and a 4-inch layer of soil. Then when spring comes, your roses will already have compost around them.

TOMATO DEFECTS?   Sometimes your tomatoes escape insect and disease damage but are still less than perfect. The weather could be the culprit, or maybe the way the fruit develops, or a combination of both.

- Fruit crack is often a puzzler. This happens with tomatoes (and sometimes with cabbage and other plants) when a heavy rain or excessive watering follows a period of drought; the tomato simply takes up too much water so rapidly that it splits open. Cracking often happens when the temperature is above 90°F. To help reduce this, water regularly during periods of drought so the plant is not subject to a fluctuating water supply. Also limit pruning in order to keep a good foliage cover that will shade the fruit. Resistant varieties include Burpee Big Girl VF, Burpee VF, Early Cascade VF, Florida MH-1, Hasty Boy VF, Heinz 1350, Manalucie, Marglobe, Terrific VFN, and Walter.
- Zipperlike scar: A tomato occasionally develops a brown, zipperlike band down the side of the fruit. This is more likely to happen when wet, cool weather prevails during flowering and fruit development. The scar is caused when the yellow part of the flower (corolla) sticks to the ovary (immature fruit). As the ovary expands, the corolla breaks loose, tearing away a small amount of tissue. The tomato suffers cosmetically but the flavor is not harmed.
- Navellike scar: This usually happens at the blossom end of large fruited tomatoes such as the beefsteak types. It looks a bit like the navel on an orange. The scar is actually present on all tomatoes but it's only a dot on the smaller varieties and quite unnoticeable. Beefsteak and other older, large-fruited selections are more likely to show this than the newer ones like Burpee Supersteak Hybrid VFN and Beefmaster VFN. Though such tomatoes look a bit strange the defect does not affect taste or texture.
- Double tomatoes: I've had double tomatoes develop on my vines from what was apparently a double blossom. I usually work up my less-than-beautiful tomatoes into barbecue sauce, catsup, or tomato juice—the taste is still delicious.

TOMATOES DETERMINATE AND IN-DETERMINATE   Tomatoes fall into two different types of growth—and harvest. Look for this when you read their description in nursery catalogs. Determinate varieties, or bush types, bloom and set fruit nearly all at once, so that ripening of all fruit can occur within days . . . and the harvest from one plant will be over in a short time. Self-topping plants, they seldom need staking. Indeterminate varieties continue blooming and setting fruit so that harvest is over a long period. Because they keep growing they need staking or caging.

Many favorite old standard varieties are now best replaced by newer hybrids.

Old	New
Beefsteak	Beefmaster VFN
Bonny Best (John Baer)	Super Fantastic VFN or Champion VFNT
Earliana	Early Girl V
Glamour	Better Boy VFN or Champion VFNT
Heinz 1350	Sunripe VFN
Homestead 24	Sunripe VFN
Jubilee	Golden Boy
Marglobe	Floramerica
Roma	La Roma
Rutgers	Floramerica
Super Sioux	Better Boy VFN or Champion VFNT

TOMATO SUCKERS TO TRANS-PLANTS   Choose suckers 3 to 5 inches long with several leaves. Gently pinch from plant and insert about 2 inches deep into rooting medium (sterile potting soil, vermiculite or sand). Label by name. Keep suckers indoors; place by a bright window but away from direct sunlight. Keep moist but not wet. Roots start to form in about two weeks and plants may be moved outdoors to partial shade two to three weeks later. When 2 to 4 new leaves have developed, transplants are ready to be set out in the garden. For deep planting set transplants so that only the top two leaves are above ground level. This method not only gives a supply of transplants throughout the season, saves money, but also gives plants at a time when they may not be available from local nurseries.

TOMATO TIP   When transplanting tomatoes and other vegetables, dig a hole a few inches deeper than usual. Place several layers of black-and-white newspaper in the bottom of the hole; then cover with a layer of soil. Plant the tomato seedling as usual, and water well. The paper helps to keep the soil moist longer and will eventually decompose, forming more fertilizer.

TOOL CARE   Sometimes when you finish a gardening chore you do not have time to clean your tools. Keep a bucket of oily sand handy and stick them into this until a more favorable time.

Get the grass, weeds, or other debris off of the blades of your garden plow before using it again. Washing off the mud also helps. Be sure to clean and oil it well before storing it for winter.

TOPPING THINGS OFF   Top dressing is the application of compost, lime, manure, and fertilizers to the surface of the soil. Usually the material is lightly raked into the ground around growing plants and along rows and is intended to give an extra boost during the growing season when earlier elements incorporated into the soil may have been depleted.

TOXOPLASMA GONDII   Because gardeners often keep house cats and have a need for disposing of the contents of litter boxes, it may be well to touch on this subject. It is best to keep this material out of the compost heap because cats may carry diseases that can infect man. *Toxoplasma gondii*, a protozoan, seldom causes symptoms in man and therefore remains unnoticed. However, infection of pregnant women can lead to severe birth defects, and infection of newborns may cause blindness or mental retardation. The cysts of *Toxocara cati*, nematode, can infect the digestive tract of man, leading to migraine headaches and visual impairment.

While such diseases are not very common, maintaining good sanitation, having your cat checked for worms regularly, keeping cats out of gardens, and not using sandbox material will minimize chances of any problems. One additional caution: **Pregnant women should never clean litter boxes**.

TRANSPLANTING TOMATOES,   peppers, eggplant, cabbage, broccoli, brussels sprouts, and cauliflower. These vegetables grow better when transplanted as small plants rather than planted as seed. Always remove plastic, paper, or clay pots from transplants and crack peat pots so that roots can grow easily and unrestricted into the soil. Depth of planting is also very important. Always place a container-grown plant slightly deeper than the level of its container. Tall or "leggy" plants may even be planted deeper. "Trenching in" very large tomato plants will avoid breakage from wind and encourage more roots.

TRANSPLANTING TREES   In the fall, before frost, dig a trench around the tree and cut the roots, being careful not to cut too near the tree. When the ground has frozen remove the tree, raising it up with the frozen earth adhering to its roots. Transport to new location where hole has been previously dug. Stake trees until well established. Even quite large shade trees and bushes moved by this method will grow in the spring.

TRAPPING THE APPLE WORM   To reduce worm-damaged apples try putting blackstrap molasses in paper cups and hanging them in your apple trees. It has been noted that the highest placed cups trap the most codling moths.

TRAVELING FRUIT DRYER   If you don't happen to have a dryer handy try using the back of your car. Cut your fruit in slices, place it in pans and set these in the trunk of your car. Cover with cheesecloth if you are going to travel on dusty roads; around town you don't need this. Go about your usual business but if the weather is cool park your car in the sun. With this method you don't have to bring in the trays at night or if it rains.

TRAVEL TIME   Mount a rural mailbox on a post and place it in your garden. Use it for storing small garden tools . . . saves you many a trip back to the tool shed when you have a few minutes to give to weeding and other gardening chores.

TREASURE FLOWER (*Gazania ringens*) An excellent flower choice for full sun areas where the climate is dry and hot. Simply sow seeds outdoors in a sunny, well-prepared bed where you want them to grow. Cover lightly with soil, keep the seedbed moist and germination will occur in about two weeks. Thin seedlings to 8 inches apart. These are very bright, showy flowers, orange in color and

will give a brilliant display of bloom in July and August when the garden needs color.

TREE TOMATO (*Cyphomandra betacea*) An unusual fruit. Even centuries ago the agriculturally minded Incas of ancient Peru were planting this little tree for its fruit, and planting it on the mountainsides up to an altitude of 8,000 feet. Not a true tomato, it is in the *Solanaceae* family, and is a cousin of the potato and the ordinary tomato. The tree tomato grows readily from seed or may be propagated from cuttings. It is suitable for pot cultivation or in a greenhouse or conservatory in colder climates.

Growing 8 to 12 feet, this soft-wooded, evergreen miniature tree or shrub has large soft leaves and has ornamental value as well as bearing fruit. The compost in which it is grown should be a rich loam—add leaf mold or well-rotten manure.

Fragrant purple and green flowers appear in spring, but under ideal conditions the plant flowers continuously and is a prolific bearer. Flowers are followed by red or orange-red, smooth-skinned, egg-shaped fruit, pointed at the ends. The fruit has a sweeter taste than the ordinary tomato, subacid and refreshing. May be eaten raw for dessert or used for jams and preserves.

TRIPLOID MARIGOLDS   Pity the poor triploid marigold—it will never have offspring—no sons or daughters to call its own. But cheers for home gardeners who reap the benefits of this situation—causing the marigolds to turn all their energies to producing flowers instead of bearing seeds. Triploids are the latest advance in the world of marigold breeding. They are crosses between tall American (formerly African) and the more compact French marigolds. Marigolds can be grown from seed or purchased as started plants from greenhouses or garden centers. If you want enduring bloom all summer long these are for you.

TRIUMPHANT SPRING   When spring arrives we gardeners learn all over again that our work is governed by principles as inflexible as the laws of gravity and inertia. The more beautiful the plant, the more difficult it is to keep alive while the most despicable species resist all attempts at destruction or control. The exotic lovely, no matter how petted and protected, suddenly shrivels, swoons, and dies. Yet only a few feet away the holy war fought against crab grass is totally ineffective.

But hope springs eternal and when a neighbor gave me a yellow-blossomed vine called Carolina jasmine (*Gelsemium*), I planted the delicate beauty, promising myself I would not mourn if it turned into a botanical basket case in the heat of summer. Even after it survived August's heat and the first ungracious autumn norther I was still cynical. The following spring it emerged triumphant, complete with green shoots and trumpet-shaped flowers, promising generous growth. At last, a hardy beauty, with strength to survive.

TRUE COLORS Chlorosis is a term used to describe the insufficient development of chlorophyll (the green coloring matter in leaves) that occurs as a result of deficiency of one or more essential nutrient elements or of some other unfavorable circumstance. In chlorotic plants the foliage is yellowish in parts or all over, and has a generally unhealthy appearance. One of the most common causes of chlorosis is iron deficiency and the correction lies in applying chelated iron and in decreasing the alkalinity of the soil by the use of organic manures. Rhododendrons, mountain laurels, and other plants belonging in the botanical family *Ericaceae* often suffer from iron deficiency when grown in soil that is not sufficiently acid for their needs. Their leaves become yellow, with the veins typically remaining green. Poor drainage may also be the cause of chlorosis. If chlorosis occurs and you are not certain of the cause, send soil samples to your State Agricultural Experiment Station for diagnosis and recommendations.

The major elements needed for healthy plant growth are nitrogen, phosphorous, potassium, calcium, magnesium, and sulphur; the trace elements are manganese, boron, copper, zinc, molybdenum. Abnormalities in leaf coloring are sometimes a clue to a mineral deficiency.

TRUMPET HONEYSUCKLE (*Lonicera sempervirens*) This honeysuckle comes to us from gardens of long ago. Different from the white, it has orange-scarlet flowers with long tubes, yellow inside, produced from May to August. A delicately lovely plant, it deserves to be more widely planted.

TUFA ROCK This is one of the secrets of success in planning a rock garden. No rock is more acceptable to a wide diversity of plants than a soft, porous grade of tufa. But because of its glaring, bony color in sunny places it is not an attractive-looking material. In shade, and moisture, it quickly accumulates mosses and then becomes very beautiful. You can, of course, use any porous, weathered rock that will look natural in place. All the better if it's deeply fissured. Use only one kind of rock throughout the garden.

TUPELO (*Nyssa*) If you haven't tasted tupelo honey you haven't really lived! Its tiny, greenish white flowers provide not only a feast for the bees but a feast for us as well. The fruit of the tree is either blue, red, or purple and the wood is known as "gum." The "gums" are handsome trees, sometimes growing as much as 60 feet tall. The sour or black gum of the South has a wide range, being hardy to southern Ontario and Maine. To the New Englander this is the "Pepperridge;" the Indians called it "tupleo," but woodsmen, Northern and Southern, call it the gum tree as a rule. "Sour gum" refers to the acid, blue-black berries, one to three in a cluster, ripe in October, and greatly beloved by birds.

We may know this tree by its tall, slender trunk, clothed with short, ridged, full-twigged, horizontal branches. With little claim to symmetry, the black gum is a striking and picturesque figure in winter. It is beautiful in summer, covered with dark polished leaves, two to four inches long. In autumn patches of red appear as the leaves begin to drop. This is the tupelo's signal that winter is coming. Soon the tree is a pillar of fire against yellowing ashes and hickories. The reds of the swamp maple and scarlet oak are brighter, but no tree has a richer color than the gum tree.

A spray brought in to decorate the mantelpiece lasts till Christmas holly displaces it. The leaves, being leathery, do not curl and dry, as do thin maple leaves, in the warm air of the house, but give pleasure to the beholder over a period of time.

TURNIPS (*Brassica campestris* var. *rapa*) To grow large, yet tender turnips plant seed in late July or early August in a well-limed soil that is thoroughly serrated. Don't use too much nitrogen, but plenty of potash. Dig turnips at any time they are ready and you feel like eating them. They are best when no smaller than a golf ball and no larger than a tennis ball. For storage twist off the tops and store the roots in sand-filled or peat-filled boxes in a cool, frostproof place. Do not try to store any damaged or diseased roots.

Turnips will grow "corky" if they have too much nitrogen or hot weather. Hot weather is also responsible for neck elongation. Plant late enough so turnips will develop during cool nights. Hot weather is also responsible for bitterness or they may have been left in the ground too long.

TWIN ONIONS   Not long ago one of my readers wrote asking me what caused twinning—two bulbs in one outer casting. Twinning is undesirable for many reasons, one being poor keeping quality. Prevent it if possible. Splits are formed when the soil is allowed to dry out. When the tops get about ten inches tall, put a good mulch around them and check periodically to see that the area doesn't go completely dry. Usually this will take care of the problem.

TWO PLANTS FOR ONE That striped dracaena (*Dracaena dermensis Warneckei*) was beautiful when you bought it, but now it has aged, gradually dropped its lower leaves, leaving an unattractive bare stem. You can restore its youthful charm.

You will need a pair of sharp pruners, some rooting powder, a small stick or pencil, and a pot filled with a mixture of 2 parts potting soil and one part perlite or vermiculite.

Now, decide where on the bare stem you want new leaves to emerge; then cut through the stem at that point with pruning shears. The cut should be about a quarter inch above a leaf joint (called a node). The cutting is now ready for potting.

Strip off leaves from the bottom of the cutting, dust cut end with rooting powder. Using a small stick or pencil, make a hole in the potting soil about 1 inch deep and insert the cutting. Firm soil and water thoroughly.

Enclose the cutting in a clear plastic bag and secure the bag to the pot—this will keep humidity around the cutting while it's growing new roots. Place cutting in bright, indirect light (no direct sun) and keep potting soil evenly moist. If cutting is given a temperature between 70°F and 75°F the rooting process will be speeded up, and it should root in about a month.

Now, what has happened to the plant from which the cutting was taken? In a short time, buds will form at the tip of the stem and then sprout into new shoots and leaves. Before you know it you've got two beautiful plants instead of a single leggy one.

You can use this gardening tip on broad-leaved rubber plant (*Ficus elastica Decora*), variegated croton (*Codiaeum variegatum Pictum*), ti plant (*Cordyline terminalis*), and many other plants with woody stems.

Stripes on dracaena become wider under low light levels. 'Florida Beauty' and 'Gold Dust' dracaena are dramatically beautiful plants—start increasing them early and you will have Christmas gifts for your friends, or plants for exchange.

Under the greenwood tree
Who loves to lie with me,
And turn his merry note
Unto the sweet bird's throat,
Come hither, come hither, come hither:
Here shall he see
No enemy
But winter and rough weather.

WILLIAM SHAKESPEARE

UMBEL ONES Umbel simply means the kind of blossom a certain group of plants produces, "umbel" meaning umbrellalike in shape. Included in this group (*Umbelliferae*) are such good actors as carrots, parsnip, parsley, coriander, dill, caraway, anise, fennel, angelica, and chervil. On the other hand, we find bad actors having poisonous roots, such as hemlock (*Onium maculatum*)—remember Socrates and hemlock?—and wild parsley or fool's parsley of the open meadows. Leave these alone.

Most plants of the umbel family will tolerate cold weather and grow beautifully for you, even surviving temperatures in the low 20s with small evidence of damage. But summer's soaring temperatures and muggy, showery weather often do them in.

Plant umbels in moist, rich soil where they'll enjoy much shade during the hot

An "umbel one" you don't want: poison hemlock (*Conium maculatum*).

months of summer. To gain a little time seeds of *Umbelliferae* can be planted in a flat or box of good soil. Transplant when first true leaves are formed. Since all umbels have very long taproots they must be transplanted at a very young and tender age to be successful. Umbels are also good plants for baskets or containers if they have sufficient space.

Southernwood (*Artemisia abrotanum*) is most effective when planted around parsley, fennel, and other members of the *Umbelliferae* family to repel their most common predator, the larvae of the black or anise swallowtail butterfly. This beautiful striped yellow and black wormlike pest has a tremendous appetite. Pick them off by hand if you don't have southernwood.

UTILITY AND PLAY LAWNS Lawns in utility and play areas need not be so perfectly groomed. Screened by good landscaping, the distant corners of the home ground might be more or less "let go," as places where children can dig, seasonal equipment can be stored, and the dog can be fenced in. The quality grasses prove quite satisfactory here, but there is also a place for the coarse, clumpy grasses such as tall fescue.

Mowed high, tall fescue is an endearing grass in the face of little care and no watering.

Higher mowing will increase resistance to abuse. Practice fertilization, however, though frequency of application can be reduced and except in times of extreme drought watering will not be necessary.

Picnic and barbecue areas, although informal, are usually upgraded a notch from the utility lawn. And, in these frequently used areas it is helpful if portable equipment can be switched from place to place to avoid building pathways or unduly wearing limited patches of sod.

UTILITY AREA LANDSCAPING is often a problem and screening seems to be the most effective and practical solution. By planting a tight hedge of narrow evergreens, by a split sapling, woven-plat, or tightly rustic fence, or simply by a tall board fence over which roam interesting vines like English ivy, Dutchman's-pipe, honeysuckle, or climbing hydrangea, they can be screened or at least made less conspicuous. Another way is to erect a tight-fitting red-cedar sapling fence, which in itself is interesting, and on the outside train a few espaliered yews, pyracanthas, or a pear tree.

Variable watering causes trouble—
A LOT!
It's the reason tomatoes,
Get that awful BLACK SPOT.
LOUISE RIOTTE

VACATION CARE Vacation time often proposes a problem for gardeners. For your flower beds and vegetable garden you might try swapping with a fellow gardener for watering, weeding, and picking while you are away, and do the same for him when he vacations.

If you have pot plants in clay pots, water them thoroughly. Then in a shady location, dig holes large enough to bury each pot completely; fill the holes with water, and let it soak in. Place the clay pots in the holes, fill in around them, making sure the pots are completely covered with soil. Rewater each plant. When you come back from your vacation, remove the pots from the soil, hose them off, and return them to porch or terrace.

Thoroughly water your lawn, garden, and plants before leaving. Apply mulches to flower beds and vegetable gardens. Cut back annuals and perennials to encourage new growth, and you'll have flowers to enjoy when you return.

Apartment dwellers can also keep potted plants happy during vacation by careful prep-

aration. Line the bottom of the bathtub with several heavy terry bath towels and run just enough water to soak them thoroughly. Place already watered plants on plant saucers turned upside down so as to keep the base of the pot away from the wet towels. This method is a good way to maintain a microclimate for ferns and other plants needing a high humidity.

Save some of those big plastic bags you get when your clothes come back from the dry cleaners. When you go on vacation water your houseplants well and enclose each one in a cleaner bag to help them retain moisture until you return. Covering should be loose, so plant can breathe. If it seems airtight, poke a little hole or two into the plastic. *Do not* let the plastic touch the plant, or the leaves will be damaged.

Several plants may be watered by using heavy cotton clothesline cut into lengths long enough to reach the bottom of a large container of water (such as a small tub or dishpan), placed at a lower level than the plants. Weigh down one end of each line to hold it in the container and stick the other end in a hole (made with a dowel or pencil) in the pot of plant to be watered. Be sure to soak the line first to prime it, the idea being to start a siphoning action through the clothesline for continuous watering of the plant.

One or more plants may be watered at the same time by inserting strips of pantyhose (presoaked) into the drainage hole of a potted plant and placing the pot over a container of water with the pantyhose dangling in the water. Be sure pantyhose wick has started its siphoning action. In all cases plants should be watered well before leaving.

VANILLA (*Vanilla fragrans*) The vanilla flavoring you use comes from a climbing orchid and is obtained from the prepared seed capsules which are 6 inches or more long and beanlike in shape. You can grow the vanilla orchid in a greenhouse with a tropical atmosphere, but the complicated process of making vanilla flavoring is best left to commercial manufacturers. Most people don't realize that vanilla extract is also a burn remedy and will quickly soothe the pain should you burn yourself jockeying cookie sheets in and out of the oven.

'VARIEGATA' IRIS This is an answer to an iris lover's dream. Iris foliage is attractive even when the plants are not in bloom, but it is all the same color. *Iris pallida* 'Variegata' stands out fully nine months of the year as a striking accent. The handsome foliage is boldly streaked with white and cream against a glaucous green background, and the variegation never fades. Deliciously fragrant flowers of light lavender blue appear in early summer. It loves sun but tolerates shade.

VEGESCAPING The home landscape that is partly edible but entirely ornamental is an idea whose time has come. Small space, high food costs, and less disposable time is attracting gardeners to food in the flower border, edibles overhead, and even fruit and nut trees in the lawn.

Fruit trees blossom as beautifully as those that are simply ornamental, so why not grow a cherry tree that bears fruit, too, instead of

merely flowering? Flowering vines were never so wonderful as when dangling peas and beans. Few things could be more decorative on a patch of sunny ground than lush strawberries ripening amid their starry white flowers and fluted foliage.

Intermix cabbage with the coleus. Plan to border a flower bed with parsley. Tie up tomatoes against an unattractive wall. Cover the fence with a cucumber trellis. Plant peppers of a good stuffing type for their crisp green foliage and lovely, yellow-eyed white flowers. Eggplants, such as Dusky, have even prettier lavender flowers and silvery green foliage . . . and the black-purple fruit has a high gloss.

Florida Basket is a new tomato from Pan-American Seed with a cascading habit, an ideal premise for its name and its growing container. Strawberries, too, are ideal for baskets, barrels, or doorside beds. For aphid protection, plant marigolds, with nasturtium here and there. Other insect deterring flowers are asters, calendula, chrysanthemum, geranium, petunia, pot marigold, peppermint, rue, sage, southernwood, summer savory, tansy, and thyme . . . and these can also serve you well in salads or as seasoning.

Grow lettuce and zinnias together; they are both lovely. Let sweet peas and sugar snap peas climb the same trellis, or Kentucky Wonder beans and morning glories.

And don't stop with vegetation; blueberries make handsome shrubs. Currants and gooseberries are nice for borders. Almost all varieties of fruit trees come now in manageable and docile little dwarfs. Who said you can't have your landscape and eat it too?

VEGETABLE POWER   Like most peoples, the Romans saw the connection between their agriculture-sex god and the value of fruits and vegetables in their amatory diet. Our word vegetable, for example, comes from the Latin *vegetus,* "active or lively," and both slave and patrician thought all food from the fertile earth was spur to love. Indeed, many aristocratic Roman families took their names from vegetables: the Fabii from the *faba,* or bean, the Piso clan from the *pisa,* or pea, the Lentuli from the *lente,* or lentil, and the great house of Cicero took its name from the *cicer,* or chickpea. These are only a few noble families whose patronyms honored widely hailed aphrodisiac vegetables.

Among the Hindus, as a rule vegetarians who rarely drink stimulants, vegetables and fruits were infinitely more venerated as love foods than in Rome. The same holds true for the Chinese, who have particularly extolled the value of garlic, leeks, onions, celery, yams, carrots, and chives. The Chinese who lived on the water even went to the trouble of growing vegetables on their boats, so strongly did they believe in "green power." In France, there was a widespread belief in the virile power of rocket, tarragon, cresses, parsley, rampions, celery, etc. And it is said that Madame Pompadour kept an extensive vegetable garden, arranging it as beautifully as she arranged herself for her royal lover, the King.

Among the famous vegetarians of history, who include such immortals as Plato, Milton, Voltaire, Tolstoy, Gandhi, and George Bernard Shaw, a number were spirited lovers. Medically, in fact, raw or properly cooked vegetables are held in such high esteem because they really do contain ingredients that keep us in prime condition.

VENTURING WITH VINES   There is often a problem in getting a vine to climb up from the planting bed and guiding it where you want it to grow. Try giving it a wire support; two of the best choices are chain link fencing or chicken wire. A wire-supported vine also means easier maintenance of the structure it's growing on. For example, when painting becomes necessary, the vine-covered wire can be detached and simply folded back temporarily, then reattached when work is completed. Twining vines, such as wisteria and yellow jessamine are especially suitable. Other likely candidates that climb by tendrils (tiny, octopuslike arms) that wrap around objects to hold the plant firmly in place, are smilax, coral vine, and clematis.

VETCH (*Vicia*)   Vetches are used for hay, green manure, pasture crops, silage, and as a cover crop for orchards. They are also valuable for renewing soil fertility. Vetches require a cool growing season. The bacteria left in the soil from vetch roots serves as an inoculant and will help the growth of peas.

A VICTORIAN BOUQUET   That the little Princess Victoria loved flowers as well as animals there seems to be no doubt, for Lord Albermarle, writing in his recollections, has this to say, "One of my occupations of a morning was to watch from the window the movements of a bright pretty little girl, seven years of age. It was amusing to see how impartially she divided the contents of the watering pot between the flowers and her own little feet." Just what flowers the little princess was watering the record does not say but I think we may safely assume that some of them might have been plants of the justly famous English roses. Perhaps there was also Queen's gilliflower, sometimes called dame's violet, old names for the sweet rocket, a night-scenting flower "that does not lose its looks or its figure by day but appears always comely and fresh," according to Louise Beebe Wilder.

There must surely have been foxglove (*Digitalis*). The auricula might have been there. In *A Dictionary of English Plant Names* it has the strange name "Reckless." Other old names are bear's ears and tanner's apron. We know it by dusty miller.

In Sweet's *English Flower Garden* there is a figure of *Hesperis fragrans*, which is said to have purple night-scented flowers and hairy leaves. He recommends for pot plants to be brought indoors to scent the house agreeably. The author of *The Book of Old Fashioned Flowers* mentions *Silene mutans*, a catchfly found on limestone rocks in parts of England, which bears many large white flowers during June and July, "scented by hyacinths and lasting but three nights."

And surely there must have been some sweet-scented English violets for the pleasure of the little princess to both gather and enjoy their fragrance.

VICTORIA'S PETS   Have you ever wondered if the little Princess Victoria, later to become queen of England, had any pets? As a matter of recorded history, Cecil Woodham-Smith, in *Queen Victoria*, tells of a little horse named Rose "which she dearly loved to ride as fast as she was allowed." And a spaniel, "dear sweet little Dashy." She treated "dear Dashy" as a doll, dressing him "in a scarlet coat and blue trousers." She also had various birds, including a canary and a parakeet.

Presumably even the "royal" Dash had fleas, and just as presumably they would not have been tolerated, so what did the Victorians do about such problems? A decoction found effective was one teaspoonful of eucalyptus oil and two teaspoonfuls of ammonia mixed into a half-pint of tepid water, the lotion being well rubbed into the fur with

the neck area being given special attention, the ear-flaps and base, the brisket, the back and the base of the tail, according to Juliette de Bairacli Levy.

Chamomile flowers may be used in the dog's bed against fleas, walnut leaves are also good, and rue, according to Schola Salernitans, "putteth fleas to flight." But use it only for dog pillows for cats abhor it—in fact it will often stop them from clawing furniture if rubbed on upholstered chairs. It is reported that fleas on cats and dogs may be dislodged with a bath of wormwood tea.

I don't know if Dash had access to couch grass (*Agropyrum repens*), also known as dog grass, but this herb is considered one of the best for the urinary system, increasing the flow. Dogs eat couch to promote cleansing vomiting.

Did you know that dogs like anise (*Pimpinella anise*) so much that dog thieves once used it as a bait? Castor bean (*Ricinus communis*) produces the oil we know as castor oil. Levy calls it a "speedy and powerful purge" useful for expelling worms, even tapeworm. She recommends for a dog "such as a spaniel, two dessert spoons."

VINCA (*Vinca*)   Commonly known as periwinkle. This group of some ten kinds of tender and hardy herbaceous plants and subshrubs is widely distributed and belongs to the family *Apocynaceae*, the dogbane family. They are useful trailing plants for covering banks and other rough places, quickly clothing them with glossy green foliage and long, green shoots which root as they grow. The large round flowers of clear lavender blue open in spring.

Now science has found another use for the periwinkle. According to a report from the Office of Technology Assessment, the plant has provided chemicals valuable in anticancer treatments.

VINEGAR   Because it's acid in nature, vinegar helps cuts flowers to keep longer by preventing spoilage caused by bacteria and fungi.

VINE PEACH (*Cucumis chito*), sometimes called the mango melon, grows on a vine and yields yellow fruit the size of a peach. After the danger of frost is past, plant in hills about 3 feet apart. The fruits, resembling large limes, turn lemon-yellow when ripe. Delicious eaten raw as a melon, or cubed into fruit salad after peeling off the thin, leatherlike skin. Peeled fruit has the color and texture of a ripe pear and may be made into preserves, pies, and marmalades.

As a member of the cucurbit family the vine peach has the same insect enemies, such as cucumber beetles, which may be controlled with rotenone.

VINES FOR CAMOUFLAGE Do you have a garden eyesore—maybe a wire fence, an old tree trunk, or a cement block wall you'd like to hide? Here are four excellent ideas:

Climbing hydrangea (*Hydrangea anomala petiolaris*). This vine climbs up large expanses of brick or stone, rock piles, stumps, or dead trees. The green leaves and midsummer blooming white flower clusters will be decorative for months, while the branches grow out from the support giving the multilayered textural effect. Initially slow growing, once established (within two to three years), it will grow sixty to eighty feet tall. Plant in full sun or partial shade and water thoroughly until mature, when it can take dry conditions and withstand cold, wind, and even seaside weather. Mulch young plants in the fall.

Silver lace vine (*Polygonum*). There's a good reason this vine is called the "mile-a-minute" vine; 20 feet in one season is a common occurrence. Its masses of lacy, fragrant flowers bloom profusely from July to the first frost. Silver lace vine tolerates wind, drought, city conditions and, in general, is ignored by pests.

Plant in well-drained, rich soil and full sun. Cut it back drastically in fall and winter, because it flowers on new wood. It may die back to ground level in severe winters, but will produce ample new growth in the spring.

Wintercreeper (*Euonymus fortunei*). Plant this evergreen climbing form of euonymus for foliage all year long. It makes a good wall cover because it clings to any support with a rough surface and will grow as tall as thirty feet up old trees.

Plant in moist, well-drained garden soil in either spring or fall, setting seedlings 1 to 2 feet apart. Will grow well in full sun or partial shade. Come late fall it's covered with orange berries. *Coloratus* has deep green foliage turning plum purple in winter.

Moonflower (*Calonyction*), quick-growing and deliciously lemon-scented, may fill a need for a night-flowering vine. The pure white, fragrant flowers 5 to 6 inches across open from evening until the following moon. In mild areas it is perennial. I have enjoyed this one for many years, especially watching the flowers open with a quick motion like pinwheels. It also attracts the lovely sphinx moths.

VINING VIGILANCE Here's a tip for increasing fruit on your vine crops, especially melons. When the vines really start to grow, pick off the fuzzy vine ends. This will concentrate the plant's energy into producing flowers and fruit, rather than more vine. Enjoy your melons all summer, but when nearing the end of the fruiting season, remove the little green melons you know won't have a chance to ripen before frost. The larger fruit remaining will ripen faster and better.

VIOLETS (*Violaceae*) Violets have always been among our most beloved flowers—to early gardeners the violet was chief flower of delight and usefulness. Tusser (1580) includes it in his list of "Seeds and Herbs for the Kitchen," his "Herbs and Roots for Salads," his "Strewing Herbs," and "Herbs for Windows and Pots." Dozens of recipes appear in old cookery books and medical treatises in which violets have a part—potages, wines, sweetmeats, plates, liqueurs,

VOLCANIC MULCH The gritty ash that fell when Mount St. Helens in Washington erupted messed up a lot of farm machinery but proved an unexpected benefit to the land. Wheat farmers whose fields were coated by the ash reaped a bumper crop, due chiefly to the effect of the ash as mulch. Not only did it prevent erosion during the heavy rains that followed the eruption, but it prevented evaporation of moisture from the soil and hindered the growth of weeds. The mulching lesson is clear: a layer of loose, porous material on the ground equalizes soil temperature, conserves moisture, and never fails to benefit whatever plants you may be growing.

V'S HAVE IT Varieties of vegetables which permit the short-season gardener to make a crop are very important to those living in the northeastern and north central regions of the United States and Canada. Now, to the rescue, comes Dr. Ernest A. Kerr, who has joined Stokes Seeds to direct their vegetable breeding research program, which develops new vegetables specifically adapted to these areas. Dr. Kerr, formerly with the Horticultural Experiment Station, Ontario Ministry of Agriculture and Food, has published some seventy-five articles dealing with plant genetics, and has received the Award of Merit from the Ontario Fruit and Vegetable Growers Association.

Dr. Kerr developed Earlivee corn, which matures in just 55 days with a seven-inch cob and twelve to fourteen rows of sweet, juicy kernels. Of outstanding quality, Earlivee matures just five days after Polar Vee (53 days), and is followed by Butter Vee (58 days) and Sunny Vee (60 days).

many cosmetics and sweet waters also, and remedies for disorders, chiefly of the spirit.

A characteristically optimistic Gaelic recommendation runs: "Rub thy face with Violets and goat's milk and there is not a prince in the world who will not follow thee."

Even so, there is something strange about violets not generally known. Certain plants, flowers, and fruit give off exhalations, that is, the scents of their volatile substances. It is these usually subtle odors that make them acceptable or repellent to other types. An instance of the reality of these substances is the particular breath of violets. Violet exhalations numb the nerves that control the sense of smell in human beings. As a result, gardeners who grow a lot of these flowers are often unable to enjoy their fragrance.

What wondrous life is this I lead!
Ripe apples drop about my head;
The luscious clusters of the vine
Upon my mouth do crush their wine . . .
"The Garden"
ANDREW MARVELL

WARTS Warts are one the most common afflictions mankind has to suffer. . . . So just what the heck are they anyway? They are infections caused by viruses, and if a wart is scratched open, the virus may spread by contact to another part of the body, or even another person. The viruses that cause warts, according to the *World Book Encyclopedia,* live in cells of the surface layer of the skin and do not infect the deep layer. The thickened surface layer forms folds into which little blood vessels grow. Sometimes warts go away without treatment as mysteriously as they appeared.

But while you are waiting for this minor miracle to happen there are a number of vegetative remedies you can try. John Heinerman, a medical anthropologist, suggests treating plantar warts by cutting a piece of ripe banana skin and applying the inside white mushy part against the warts, taping it down with adhesive tape. It is to be removed only when bathing or showering, after which another ripe peel is to be applied. Plantar warts are the most painful kind and are usually surgically removed.

For the more common, less painful type, Heinerman cites the experience of a Lubbock, Texas, woman who cured her wart by soaking a piece of cotton in aloe gel and taping it over the wart, adding more gel every three hours with an eyedropper.

It has been reported that the milky sap contained in the stems of dandelions is effective when rubbed on warts. This is also purported to help erase age spots, sometimes called liver spots, which often plague the elderly.

A slice of pineapple gently rubbed on a wart, making several applications, is said to remove it. In Jamaica the milky latex of the green papaya fruit is slowly dripped onto warts several times each day for about a week.

Mai Thomas, in her book *Grannie's Remedies,* says to rub the wart daily with a cut radish or with the juice of marigold flowers.

Other remedies: Fig *(Ficus Carica).* Before the fruit is ripe, when it is broken from the branch, a milk escapes that may be dropped upon warts and allowed to soak for several hours before ultimate removal.

Houseleek *(Sempervivum tectorum).* The fresh leaves of this plant are bruised and placed directly on burns, stings, and other affections of the skin, including warts and corns. The leaves serve as an astringent, reducing discharge and drawing the tissues together.

Jewel weed *(Impatiens aurea, I. biflora).* The juice of the plant is reported to be effective for removal of warts, corns, and similar growths on the skin. It is said to relieve cases of ringworm on the skin, and also to be effective against poison ivy.

WATCH FOR A CLOUDY DAY Bright sun can hurt newly planted seedlings, so always try to transplant on an overcast day, in late afternoon or in the evening. Shading transplants the first day or two is also helpful if the sun comes out.

WATERCRESS *(Nasturium offinale)* If you don't have running water, you can still raise watercress. Plant seeds or seedlings in a trench 1 foot deep and 2 feet wide that is lined with 8 inches of well-decomposed manure and 4 inches of fine soil. Don't let soil dry out.

WATERING HOUSEPLANTS with soft or distilled water will avoid toxic salt buildup. You must be particularly careful with carnivorous plants. Rubber plants prefer partial shade but react poorly to overwatering. Wash leaves frequently with a damp sponge to remove dust that will otherwise clog their pores.

WATERING TIP Don't stun your plants with cold water. Ice water can act like frost on a young plant. And plants that sit near the radiator or air vent need water more frequently than plants that sit in a "green-house" effect. Don't leave water droplets on the leaves in the hot sun; the droplet can act like focusing lenses, actually burning spots into the leaves.

WATERING YOUR HANGING BASKET Wire hanging baskets, often lined with sphagnum moss, sometimes have the water pour through so quickly that the plant doesn't get enough moisture. A solution is to immerse the basket in a tub of water to just above the soil surface and let it stand for about 5 minutes, or until the soil is thoroughly soaked. Let it drain well before rehanging.

WATERING YOUR GARDEN If watering is necessary, the best time is in the morning or early afternoon, giving ample time for plants to dry before sundown. If plants are wet overnight, fungus troubles may develop. Water enough to soak the root area, but no more than once or twice a week. While this rule applies to most of the country, I find it necessary to water more often here in the dry and windy Southwest.

WATERMELONS *(Citrullus lanatus)* Wouldn't it be fun to try some of the new seedless watermelons such as Jack of Hearts, King of Hearts, Nova Seedless Hybrid, Sweetheart Hybrid, Honey Red, and Honey Yellow? These are insect-pollinated and must be planted near seed-producing varieties. Pollinator seeds, such as Bush Jubilee, usually come with an order for the seedless variety. Insects such as honeybees carry the pollen from flower to flower, so avoid using pesticides. You can grow the seedless variety by sowing in mid-March in small peat pots. Maintain them for forty-eight hours after sowing in as near 85°F as possible, then move to an area of 72°F to 75°F. In about three weeks transplant them to the garden. The soil should be free draining and well-prepared. Try inverting a milk jar over them until weather is consistently warm. Melons usually ripen in 85 to 100 days. Any seeds are usually small and very soft.

HAPPINESS IS A VINE-RIPE WATER-MELON But how will you know? Actually the popular "thump test" may not be accurate because overripe melons make the same sound. One of the best signs of ripeness is when the typically shiny surface becomes dull and the bottom of the melon turns from a whitish color to a creamy yellow. The skin should be soft enough to pierce with a fingernail. In most varieties, the curled stem that attaches the melon to the vine turns brown and crisp when the fruit is ripe. Placing a sheet of waxed paper under watermelons, cantaloupes, etc. will often prevent insect damage.

WATER RATIONING If water rationing hits your community, don't panic. Most established lawns, trees, and shrubs can survive with a watering once every five to seven days, if soaked thoroughly. Following repeated waterings, soil often becomes compacted. Cultivate lightly, being careful not to damage shallow root systems. Work in organic matter to increase the soil's water-holding capacity, and mulch regularly. If you cannot water as often as recommended, be sure to mulch heavily around trees and shrubs. Newly planted turf, trees, and shrubs will, in most cases, need to be watered more often than established plants.

Sometimes you can hold your vegetable garden plants such as tomatoes, okra, eggplant, and peppers over a longer period of time by mulching them heavily with grass clippings. Just keep putting on successive light layers. Many times these can be picked up at the curb where homeowners have set them out for the sanitation department or street department to pick them up.

WATER WISDOM Vine crops are nature's camels, containing up to 95 percent water at maturity, yet they don't need any more watering than other vegetables. What is necessary is that the moisture supply be steady, about an inch a week, a bit more in really hot weather. If they don't get enough, this is the reason cucumbers and melons become bitter or bland if they're under stress

from dryness or lack of soil nutrients. The best way to grow curcubits is on top of organic matter which holds moisture. Many people grow them around or on their compost heap. In the garden mulching helps also to conserve moisture.

WEATHERPROOF FLOWERS Have you ever walked outside in the morning after one of those spring thunderstorms and found, once again, that the flower garden has taken it on the chin? Soon it will recover, but for a few days it may look as if an army had marched through your beds! Cheer up! Now there's a weather-resistant petunia called "Summer Madness" which stands up to wind, rain, and harsh weather. An F_1 hybrid, this prize from the Ball Seed Company is a vigorous, full-flowering petunia with the strength to withstand the beating that storms heap on flowers. It also has a unique hot-pink color set off by a dark red throat. It practically shouts, "Look at me!"

WEATHER-WISE GARDENING In few other occupations is weather of such importance as it is to gardeners and farmers. And it is interesting to note how much centuries-old weather-lore still holds true. Farmers and other weather watchers have sworn by certain signs, conditions, and feelings through the years to predict natural phenomena. The reactions of birds, insects, animals, and plants to changing atmospheric conditions have long been used to forecast the weather and much of this lore is still valid today.

Crickets are amazingly accurate weather instruments, responding to temperature changes faster than a thermometer by chirping faster when warm than cold. The number of chirps in 14 seconds, plus 40, gives the temperatures in their locations.

Birds are also indicators, roosting more during a low pressure period preceding a storm because thinner air makes flying more difficult than in the dense air of a high. High pressure also raises the altitude levels of migrating flights and indicates fair weather, while a lower flight means low pressure.

Swallows and bats fly close to the ground before rain because of their delicate hearing mechanisms. They also fly low because the insects they eat descend when the barometer falls. As the barometer begins to drop about twelve hours before a storm, such behavior can be a first indication of bad weather.

On spring and fall evenings vapor rising from a river is a precursor of frost. This is because the warm moist air at the river's surface is mixing with cooler air from the land, which is releasing daytime heat. The result is likely to be frost.

A mackerel sky indicates rain. These high cirrocumulus and/or lower altocumulus clouds resembling fish scales are the forerunner of an approaching warm front. Riding over cooler ground air, it forms thicker clouds and produces rain, usually within twenty-four hours.

Rain is on the way if there is a morning rainbow in the west. Rainbows are created when the sun shines through raindrops, creating prisms. Since they must always be opposite the sun, in the morning they must be in the west. As most of our weather comes from the west, rain from the airborne moisture is probably very close.

Frogs do croak more before a rain. This is because they cannot tolerate much evaporation of their skin's moisture. Thus low-humidity days find them in water most of the time. But before a storm, when humidity is higher, they are more likely to emerge . . . croaking.

Weather patterns usually move from west to east, so take a glance at the westward horizon at sunset to get a good indication of coming weather. That red sky means the sun is setting through dry air likely to reach you the next day and bring fair weather. If the garden is drying out, water the crops. A gray night sky and you may take it that the sun is setting through lots of moisture, alerting you that poor weather is brewing in the west and probably soon to arrive.

Another clue you can follow as you go about your gardening activities is plant behavior. There are signs to watch for when it comes to predicting the weather. Plants are programmed to react to the weather in ways that assure their survival. These signs can help you to know when it is safe to plant various vegetables in the garden. When lilac leaves first appear, put in cool season crops such as lettuce, peas, spinach, and beets. After the lilac blooms it's generally safe to plant tender, or warm-season crops such as corn, eggplant, peppers, and tomatoes. When dogwood trees are in full bloom, plant broccoli, brussels sprouts, cabbage, cauliflower, collards, kale, and kohlrabi. When dogwood blossoms are fading, plant squash, beans, okra, and cucumbers. A sunflower raising its head indicates rain.

WEEDING   To most gardeners this is the most disagreeable part of gardening. While it may be difficult to eliminate the problem entirely, for the home gardener at least, there are ways to make things easier. If you have sufficient material, mulching will go a long way in keeping most weeds from getting started, and making it easy to pull those hardy ones that break through. Use whatever is cheapest and most readily available—a hay mulch, newspapers covered with leaves, peanut shells, lawn clippings. Hay spoiled for animal feed may sometimes be had for a small price, or even given away. Stable cleanings of hay and manure are excellent.

Groundcovers help to smother weeds; pachysandra, myrtle, and vinca are good choices. Many kinds of large ferns will crowd out weeds. So will Siberian iris, day lilies, violets, feverfew, and catnip—all perennials. Lilies-of-the-valley are good plants for a shady spot. If you prefer annuals as groundcovers, try marigolds, nasturtiums, snapdragons, petunias, and some of the herbs. Plant by scattering the seeds. Or use a vegetable, like lettuce, producing a garden that is handsome and weed-free as soon as the leaves get large enough to overshadow the whole plot.

Squash grown among corn controls weeds and protects the soil. If you let tomatoes

spread instead of staking them, they will discourage weeds, and some clean hay under
the plants as a mulch will keep the fruits
clean and free of pests.

Get out there and cultivate to make sure
the plants get the goodies and not the weeds.
Whether you cultivate with a hoe, tiller, or
whatever, it's important to remember that it
should be shallow—not more than an inch
below the soil surface. Most weed seeds are
close to the surface, and deep cultivation
will just bring more of them up near the surface where they can germinate. Also deep
cultivation may injure the roots of your
plants. Try to weed after a rain when the
plants have dried off, but before the soil becomes too dry. Weeds pull easily from loose,
moist soil if weeding is done before they get
a good start.

WEEDS GET THE POINT One of my favorite tools is a tooth-edged grapefruit knife
ground to a point. I use it to extract deep-
rooted pests such as dandelions and for
twitching out tiny weeds in a row of seedlings where there isn't room for a finger. In a
close planting, I can snick off weeds just
below ground without disturbing roots of
nearby plants, or pick them out of close
clumps such as phlox. Any well-equipped
hardware store can grind the knife's rounded
tip to a point.

WEEDS IN YOUR MULCH? If you have
problems with weeds coming up through the
mulch you spread around flowers and shrubs,
try this trick. Instead of spreading plastic
sheets under the mulch, use sections of gray
nylon screening. Besides providing perfect
drainage this is also excellent weed control.

**WEEDS MAKE WONDERFUL WILD
GREENS** There are many wild foods you
can pick from your garden, or possibly from
nearby vacant lots, but do make sure they
have not been sprayed with any pesticides if
you gather along a roadway. These weeds are
actually "good to eat," free, vitamin-packed
edibles that are usually gathered and thrown
away.

Lamb's-Quarters (*Chenopodium album*),
also known as goosefoot, pigweed and wild
spinach, is actually a spinach cousin. It has
also been cultivated in years past for its abundant yield of seeds which contain an average
of 16 percent protein, compared to 14 percent in wheat. As a green it is both
nutritious and delicious, the uncooked
plants being richer in iron, protein, and vitamin B2 than either raw cabbage or raw
spinach. Standing from two to seven feet tall
at maturity, lamb's-quarters can be identified
by their jagged-edged, diamond-shaped
leaves. These leaves are powdered on the undersides with coarse, whitish particles (*album*
is Latin for white). Short leafstalks are either
plain green or slightly streaked with red. Use
only the tender, mild growing tips and cook
like spinach. Cooked *with* spinach they give
it more "body," and enhance the flavor.

Curled Dock (*Rumex crispus*). The deep-
rooted docks are hardy and persistent
weeds—widespread, they are found almost
everywhere that you would expect a weed to
grow; alongside streams and roads and drive-
ways, in pastures and vacant lots and
gardens. The plant has slender, lance-shaped
leaves, most of which sprout directly from
the ground. The leaves, reaching two or
more feet in length, have wavy edges. The
leaves, if more than a foot long, may taste
slightly bitter. One way of overcoming this is
to boil them through two waters. Another
way to rid them of astringency is to cream
them. Mix a tablespoon of flour with a tablespoon of butter, add two cups of chopped
dock leaves and a half cup of milk. Cook,
stirring constantly, until the sauce thickens.

Pokeweed (*Phytolacca americana*) is beloved of Southerners who delight to serve it
with cornbread. The pink-green shoots
which come up in the early spring are good
cooked like asparagus. I like the "bite" but
many people prefer to boil them through
several waters. The roots and berries are
considered poisonous weeds, but are used in
medicines that treat skin and blood disease,
and relieve pain and inflammation of rheumatism.

Purslane

Purslane (*Portulaca oleracea*). The despised purslane, sometimes called "pussley," is a weed that can actually be eaten raw with perfect safety. This small, ground-hugging plant is very persistent and in no time at all will spread its fleshy, reddish-purple stems and paddle-shaped leaves over your entire garden if not checked. Actually all above-ground parts of this iron- and calcium-rich semisucculent are edible. If you want to keep it alive all summer harvest only the tender, growing tips. Raw purslane lends a slightly acidic flavor to salads. Or, dip the plant in beaten egg, roll it in a mixture of breadcrumbs and flour, and fry in fat until it is brown. You may also use it as an okra substitute in any recipe calling for a thickener.

Green Amaranth (*Amaranthus retroflexus*). This milder-tasting relative of lamb's-quarters can be prepared in the same manner. It is also known as redroot and wild beet. You can recognize green amaranth by its stout, hairy stem, rough-to-the-touch, pointed oval leaves borne on stalks almost as long as the leaves themselves, and its crimson-colored root. The height of the plant varies but is generally about three feet. Brief cooking will drive the saponin out of the plant's leaves and create a vitamin-rich vege-

table. The plants have a delicate flavor, and are good served with a cheese sauce.

Any of these wild greens, as well as dandelion leaves and buds, may be safely eaten. They may even be blanched and frozen. Just be sure that you have correctly identified them—if in doubt take the plant to your county agricultural agent. Eating the weeds will add nutrition to your menu and at the same time subtract from your grocery bill.

WICK WATER   If you're going to be gone here's a way to "wick water" your African violets. Take a piece of No. 12, 100% nylon twine (about 6 inches long) and push about half of it into the bottom of a potted plant. Start the capillary action by placing the potted plant in a saucer of water, or water from the top until it drains from the bottom. Cut a small hole in the lid of an empty butter tub, fill with water and replace lid. At once set plant on lid, letting twine dangle through hole into tub of water. Depending on size of tub, your plant won't need watering for two to three weeks.

WIDTH   is more important than length if you want an attractive perennial garden. Some of our loveliest plants have a short blooming season, so use a selection so later flowers will grow up around bare spots and hide the dying foliage of earlier bloomers.

WILDFLOWERS   In some situations a lush growth of wildflowers is very desirable. To plant a field, turn the soil under until all growth is removed. Broadcast seed as though you were feeding it to chickens; for a large area mix four parts of sand to one part seed. Seed sown in the fall should be watered once; in the summer water until germination. Several seed companies have wildflower seed mixes—many especially formulated for particular regions.

WILDFLOWERS WORTHY OF THE GARDEN   Wildflowers are some of the hardiest perennials you can grow—just plant them in an area similar to their native habitat and they will thrive. For the fun-loving gardener who wants to keep things simple they are hard to beat.

Purple coneflowers (*Echinacea purpurea*) are native to the South and their flowers are so large and showy they appear to be the work of a hybridizer, but are solely nature's creation. Looking like rosy purple daisies, they open into a flat flower that is 3 to 4 inches across. As they open the cone enlarges and the petals droop around it. Plant them where they will receive full sun.

The first time you notice sundrops (*Oenothera fruticosa*) you'll wonder how you could have missed them. The blossoms are pure sunshine yellow, clustered on 2-foot stems. Plant sundrops in full sun to light shade. The plant will spread but will not become invasive—the crown just grows into a generous clump which you can divide.

Another old favorite is common bleeding-heart (*Dicentra spectabilis*) but you will probably like fringed bleeding-heart (*D. eximia*) even better. Planted lovingly in the shade garden, this native perennial will give you a burst of bloom each spring.

WILD LETTUCE (*Lactuca virosa*)   Traditionally wild lettuce has been dried and smoked like opium. A vegetable tranquilizer, it is considered milder than opium but just as "dreamy." It has been used for nervousness and as a sedative. It looks like opium, smells like opium, and even tastes a bit like raw opium, according to Euell Gibbons. Lettuce opium was often used by the North American Indians by smoking the dried resin or sap obtained from the plant by cutting the flower heads off, gathering the sap that drained off and letting it air dry. This process could be repeated over a two-week period by cutting just a tiny slice off the top each time.

The active ingredient in wild lettuce has been identified as *lactucarine*, now known as lettuce opium. All lettuces contain opium, even the domestic, but it is present in greater concentration in the wild type. Lettuce should not be eaten by anyone who has any form of stomach disorders, especially ulcers, as the lettuce opium will coat the

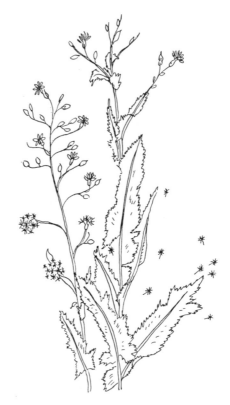

Prickly Lettuce (*Lactua serriola*)

stomach wall and impair the digestive processes. It also represses sex drives.

"WILD SWEET PEA" (*Lathyrus latifolius*) This perennial is an excellent and easy-care choice for a lattice fence, provided the slats are not too large for the tendrils to grasp. Sow seeds in autumn, preferably where they are to grow as they resent disturbance.

WILLOW (*Salix* spp.)   A friend of mine had me rocking with laughter a few days ago as he described his childhood punishment. It seems his father believed in "spare the rod and spoil the child"—none of this new-fangled nonsense had filtered through yet about moral persuasion. When he perpetrated a naughty deed he was sent out to select his own willow switch as an added humiliation. He described his quandary: if he selected one too small his father went out and made the decision, so it had to be just right—and not too large either because a big one would HURT! Since he has grown to be a fine young man he seems to be none the worse for his childhood experience. And he and his father are the best of friends.

Willow is the name given to a group of trees and shrubs which grow in almost all parts of the world. Willows less than an inch tall grow in the Arctic regions on high mountains. Other willows in temperate regions of North America sometimes reach a height of 140 feet.

Willows usually grow near water and most of them have flowers borne in small furry catkins, which appear on the branches before the leaves come out. When the catkins split open the white, silky hairs on the seeds allow them to ride on the wind. Since willows are both male and female they must be pollinated, work usually performed by honeybees. The roots of willows interlace underneath the ground and form a strong network. Willows planted on a riverbank are good protection against soil erosion. Even a twig lying upon the ground strikes root at every joint if the soil it falls on is sufficiently moist.

Willow is a somewhat mystic wood, a favorite for dowsing. My father was a "dowser," I am a dowser, my son is a dowser, and now my granddaughter has also shown the ability. That's how *dowsing*, or "water witching," travels its mysterious path—from male to female and then back again to male. And water witching is a lot of fun, and lots of people have this ability and do not realize it.

Few trees have more uses than the willow. Salicin is a drug made from its bark, formerly used to relieve pain. Newer drugs have now replaced it and scientists now use salicin primarily in biochemical analysis. The bark also contains tannin.

Willow is used as a hedge and shade tree because of its rapid growth. The Indians depended on the inner bark of the withy willow for material for their fish nets and lines and for making willow baskets. Farmers in pioneer days took the tough, supple stems, when spring made the sap run freely, for the binding together of the rails of their fences. Knotted tight and seasoned, these twigs hardened and lasted for years. Willow wood makes the finest charcoal for gunpowder. The heartwood of willows is used for cabinet work, cricket bats, artificial limbs, and in the manufacture of paper pulp. Willow wares and willow furniture are as old as civilization.

WINDOWBOX GARDENING   An old book, *Watkins Household Hints*, published in 1941 by the J.R. Watkins Co., has the best "recipe"—and the easiest—I've ever run across for preparing a window box: "A window box should be eight to ten inches deep as well as wide. The box should contain six holes in the bottom for drainage. Put in a two-inch layer of gravel or cinders—not ashes. Next, a two-inch layer of well-soaked peat moss to hold the moisture, then fill with a mixture of equal parts of peat moss, garden soil and sand. . . ."

If possible select south or southeast exposure for flowering plants and for indoor spring bulbs. For a north window, plant ivy, ferns or foliage plants. Fresh air without a draft, a temperature about 65°F, and moisture are important.

For sunny boxes, use balcony-type petunias and geraniums with ageratum and a few trailing vines such as vinca or grape ivy. For shady window boxes, use English daisies, ageratum, ferns, ivy, and wandering Jew. Other vines include the philodendron; English, Kenilworth, and ground ivies; Hall's honeysuckle, and Chinese evergreen.

It is a mistake to water plants too frequently. Probably more plants have been "killed by kindness" than any other way. Frequent cultivation is advisable. A fine mist spray for several hours is better than ordinary sprinkling. Watering is best done in the evening. For plants in pots, tap the pot with the knuckles. If the sound rings, water is needed, if dull, there is sufficient water.

Use your window boxes for herbs as well as flowers. Both chives and parsley are popular candidates. Lemon verbena (*Aloysia triphylla*) is seldom more than 5 inches tall grown as a pot plant, and may be used to flavor fruit drinks, fruit salad, and jelly. Roman chamomile (*C. nobile*) is a mat-forming perennial 2 inches to 4 inches tall. The dried flowers are used to make a tea which is taken as a sedative and for feverish colds. Give it full sun. Corsican mint (*M. requienii*) is a low, creeping perennial ¾ inch tall used as a flavoring for iced drinks and fruit cups. Reportedly used to flavor liqueurs, it likes full sun or light shade, moist, well-drained soil. An unusual mosslike mat is formed with a surprisingly strong fragrance. Sweet marjoram, which is 12 inches to 18 inches tall, has a host of flavoring uses: vegetables, poultry stuffing, sauces, soups, and as a garnish for salad. Its leaves and flowering tops make a fine tea.

WINDOWSILL GREENS All you need is a sunny window, a container, seeds, a little soil, and presto! Window greens. And they can be unusual. Wheatgrass, buckwheat lettuce, sunflower greens, radish greens, comfrey, and nasturtium are but a few. Easy to grow they can be ready for salads in seven to ten days.

For a first crop I suggest wheat. It helps purify the air and a bunch of wheatgrass in your bath or drinking water will neutralize the chemical content of the water. Wheatgrass is also an excellent salad staple.

Growing Directions

1. Use shallow containers (about 1 inch deep), such as cake-baking pans or trays. You can often pick these up at garage sales. It's best to make several drainage holes at bottom or sides but not absolutely necessary if you water carefully.
2. Fill pans with the best soil available, first covering the bottom of container with small gravel, vermiculite, cat litter, or calcined clay. Add earthworm castings if available. Fill container to within ¼ inch of the top rim.
3. Soak seeds overnight and they will germinate faster. Save the water as it contains many nutrients and can be applied to other plants.

4. Wet soil thoroughly with rainwater or tap water. Spread a thick layer of seeds over the top of the soil. Be sure seeds are moist.
5. Cover seeds with seven thicknesses of wet newspaper, precut to fit inside container.
6. Place a plastic sheet over the newspapers to prevent drying. Place container in the windowsill. After two or three days the seeds will sprout. Remove the sheet and place container in good sunlight.
7. Water young plants regularly, and morning and evening misting will be beneficial. Maintain adequate moisture but never allow plants to stand in pools of water.
8. Depending on variety, the plants will reach 6 to 12 inches in height after several days. Using scissors or a sharp knife, cut the blades back to about ½ inch from the base. Under ideal conditions many of the plants (wheat for example) will come up again for a second crop.

WINTER WISDOM In the northern hemisphere, you're always better off having your indoor plants on the south side of the house, because for most of the year the sun is south of you. Sun *never* shines from the north. This also prevents plants from being exposed to strong winter winds if you occasionally open the window, since cold winds blow from the north and warm winds from the south. If you can't face your plants south, west is next best, then east. North exposure will have light, of course, but no direct sunlight.

WISHBONE FLOWER (*Torenia fournieri*) This attractive little plant resembles miniature snapdragons with its purple, lavender and gold flowers. A bushy plant, wishbone makes a good substitute for pansies in late summer. As an added attraction, the foliage turns plum in late autumn. Start the seeds in May in a seed bed as they are very tender. Grows well in sun or shade.

WISTERIA (*Wisteria*) This lovely plant increases in beauty with the years, and is particularly lovely when trained to a wall, or allowed to climb onto a large tree. A wisteria in full bloom produces a magnificent display in the spring. Wisteria is one of the flowers that fades gently as the blossoms mature, signifying that the blossoms have been visited.

Propagation is carried out by grafting dormant shoots on sections of roots in a warm greenhouse, by layering the lower branches in spring, by root cuttings and by seeds. High nitrogen fertilizers should be avoided as they will produce excessive vegetative growth at the expense of flowering. Root pruning often encourages bloom on reluctant plants.

WIZARDRY WITH WITCH HAZEL

(*Hammelia*)   Long preferred by "water witches" for witching up underground water, this odd little shrub prefers to bloom about the end of October when witches fly and jack-o'-lanterns leer, waving its gay yellow petals and smelling like spring. But it has other, perhaps more practical uses, and around the turn of the century was often incorporated in perfumes and after-shave lotions. Also widely favored as a multipurpose liniment applied to a variety of bumps, bruises, bug bites, aching muscles, and itchy rashes. We can still buy witch hazel but you may, if you wish, make your own. Start with a good-sized kettle with a domed lid, either stainless steel or flameproof crockery. Gather your hazel leaves, dry them in the sun, put them in the bottom of the kettle, and add a half gallon of water. Place a stainless steel rack on the bottom of the pot and put a small bowl on it. Invert the kettle lid and place it over the mouth of the kettle—the knob or handle should hang above the bowl inside.

Fill the inverted lid with cold water and replenish the liquid whenever it begins to warm. Heat kettle slowly; it should steam but not boil. The volatile oils of witch hazel will evaporate before the water does. Hitting the cold lid they condense, run down the dome, and drip into the bowl. A two-cup batch of leaves should produce about two cups of witch-hazel distillate. Mix distillate with ½ cup of rubbing alcohol and you will have a first class liniment just like the one your grandmother used to make and keep on hand for many family ills.

WOOD ASHES   Burning natural wood is again becoming popular, so how can the ashes be used? Wood ashes are very alkaline so should never be used around azaleas or other acid-loving plants. Also they are too light to be used as an effective mulch. However, because they contain potassium, phosphorus, and other minerals, they can be beneficial when added to the soil in rose beds, flower beds, perennial borders, and vegetable gardens. Spread them on the soil surface at the rate of about 10 pounds per 100 square feet; then cultivate lightly to work in. Ashes are also useful as insect repellents and, mixed with fresh sawdust and spread around your plants, will repel armadillos.

WORK SAVER—STOVE SAVER
When canning, preserving, or jelly-making, cut aluminum foil to fit the well around the stove burner; it will catch the drips and save much time in cleaning up.

WRAP SESSION   Protect your plants when fall frost threatens and you can probably enjoy vine-ripened tomatoes during the Indian summer weather that often follows the first threat of frost. Look around the house for old sheets, bedspreads, tablecloths, shower curtains, ponchos, pieces of burlap or anything else you can drape over the plants in early evening to fend off frost during the night. Even newspapers may work. Pin or otherwise fasten the covering tight enough around the foliage and fruits to keep out the cold night air. As soon as the temperature rises above 50°F in the morning, remove the coverings. Put them back in the evening if frost is still in the weather forecast. Sweet peppers, squash, and even cantaloupes that are almost ripe can often be saved from an early frost as well by wrapping up the plants.

WRINKLES
- Comfrey (*Symphytum officinale*)
  Combining comfrey with a good face or hand lotion produces a product that has

been found valuable for removing various imperfections on the skin. Where wrinkles are due to a lack of nutritive elements in the skin, the composition of comfrey is such that wrinkles will tend to disappear. However, there can be no assurance that comfrey will always remove wrinkles in all types of skin conditions.

- Quince (*Cydonia oblonga, Pyrus Cydonia*). A mixture of the seeds (crushed), using two parts seeds to one hundred parts of water, results in a lotion that is excellent for the skin. When allowed to remain on the skin overnight, the skin will tend to contract and, temporarily at least, lessen wrinkles.
- Kelp (*Fucus vesiculosus*) The presence of silicon in kelp is reported to keep the skin from wrinkling and sagging. Silicon is also an important food for the roots of the hair and an ample supply of kelp will usually prevent hair from falling out. The fingernails are also aided by the presence of kelp, which not only contains silicon but also calcium and sulphur, which are all needed for healthy fingernails.
- Sesame seeds have uses other than decorating the tops of hamburger buns. Once known as bene, benne, or benny, their oil was used as a cosmetic to soften and whiten the skin. Sesame can be grown anywhere that you can grow cotton. You may start the plants indoors and replant outdoors when danger of frost is past. Extract the oil by bruising seeds in a mortar, pouring hot water over them, and skimming off the oil that rises to the top. This oil keeps well.
- Cucumbers also provide a fine skin lotion. Simmer two quarts of rose petals for an hour in enough water to cover, then add a finely minced cucumber and simmer for another ten minutes. Strain off liquid and add a tablespoon of lemon juice. Smooth on face and neck for a few minutes before washing or bathing. Keep mixture chilled in refrigerator when not in use.

Xanadu may not exist,
But we can dream with Kubla Khan
Of gardens of exotic beauty
Touched by light of glorious dawn.

LOUISE RIOTTE

XANTHISMA TEXANUM An annual, found wild in Texas, suitable for naturalizing. A daisylike flower with yellow blossoms and narrow, linear leaves, belonging to the *Compositae* family. The name comes from *xanthos*, "yellow." This dainty plant is sometimes called the Star of Texas.

Sow the seeds in March or April in a pan, pot, or flat of sandy soil, and place in a greenhouse with a temperature of 45°F to 50°F (night). Lift the seedlings when one inch high and set 1½ inches apart in flats of light soil. When established, harden them off and plant outdoors in May. Or seeds may be sown directly out of doors, where they are to bloom, when weather is warm.

XERANTHEMUM, Immortelle. Pretty annual flowering plants from southern Europe. The flowers are "everlasting" and are cut and dried for winter decoration. The plants, 2 to 3 feet high, bear terminal heads of rose, pink, or purple, single or double flowers in summer. Seeds may be sown directly outdoors in early spring where plants are to bloom. Flowers wanted for winter decoration should be gathered on a dry day when fully

expanded and hung in an airy shed or attic for a week or two.

XEROPHYTES Plants especially adapted to withstand long periods of drought or to grow where supplies of water are scarce are called xerophytes. Most are natives of desert and semidesert regions but some grow in windswept places or along seashores. Included among these plants are cacti and such succulents as aloes, cotyledons, crassulas, echeverias, haworthias, sedums, and sempervivums. Many of these store water in their fleshy leaves and stems.

XTOMATL (*Lycopersicum esculentum*) The Mayans, whose seafaring traders brought seed to Yucatan, called the then tiny fruit *tomatl*, or *xtomatl*. And they so prized *L. esculentum* (even its scientific patronym sounds delicious) that they traced its form along with more erotic scenes on their pottery. When Cortez and his band escaped the first Aztec uprising in Mexico, they managed to buy tomato seeds in the great market of Chichen Itza to bring back with their plunder to Europe, where the plant was initially called both *pomi del peru* and *mala peruviane*.

An ingenious Spanish chef is credited with combining the fruit with olive oil, spices, and onions, thus creating the world's first tomato sauce, which became widely popular. In time, and no one really knows why, tomatoes were dubbed "love apples." At any rate, the tomato quickly gained a reputation as a wicked aphrodisiac, and justly or unjustly, it has held this distinction ever since. Quite probably also, the tomato's scarlet past contributed in part to its notoriety as a poisonous plant: *L. esculentum* was reputedly a *deadly* aphrodisiac.

If any one man liberated *L. esculentum* it was Colonel Robert Gibbon Johnson, an eccentric gentleman of Salem, New Jersey. In 1808, after a trip abroad, Johnson introduced the tomato to the farmers of Salem, and each year thereafter offered a prize for the largest locally grown fruit. But the Colonel wanted his introduction to be regarded as more than an ornamental bush. On September 26, 1820 (or 1830), he announced that he would appear on the Salem Court House steps and eat not one but a whole basket of tomatoes. His personal physician, Dr. James Van Meeter, and 2000 other curious people from miles around, arrived to watch him commit what they believed was certain suicide. Colonel Johnson bit and bit again and the amazed crowd beheld the Colonel still on his feet as he ate tomato after tomato. With the basket empty, Dr. Van Meeker slipped away, and the crowd struck up a victory march, beginning to chant a cheer that eventually led to Johnson's election as mayor when Salem was first incorporated as a township.

Tomatoes are wonderfully sympathetic to the cabbage tribe. On the other hand, their root excretions have been shown to cause the eradication of a very persistent weed—couch grass.

Yellow dandelions alas
Are often viewed as Nature's brass,
But I see them through rosy glass
As gold doubloons tossed on the grass.
LOUISE RIOTTE

YARROW (*Achillea millefolium*)   Yarrow has long been acclaimed for its invaluable qualities in companion planting, adding strength to herbs and assisting in the battle against insect pests. It is also of benefit to people; yarrow in the medicine chest is a good home cure for an oncoming cold or

cough. To make yarrow tea steep the leaves in a teapot for about fifteen minutes; it tastes terrible but does the job. You will find cultivated yarrow in the seed catalogs, the most common type being the two-foot perennial called 'Pearl' (Burpee, Parks). The closest to the wild variety are millefolium cultivars called 'Cerise Beauty,' 'Crimson Beauty,' 'Fire King,' and 'Rose Beauty.' These four are selected, improved plants that came from the same stock as the wild plant, so you can expect that precious little of the medicinal qualities have been bred out.

Plant yarrow in the same beds with mint, chives, thyme, parsley, basil, oregano, or any other culinary or tea herbs. Or plant it in your flower beds to add beauty and protection.

YELLOW ROSE OF TEXAS   When is a rose not a rose? When it is a beautiful woman! Here is what David G. McComb, writing in *Texas, A Modern History*, has to say about the "Yellow Rose of Texas," fabled in song and story: "According to folklore, the reason that Santa Ana did not respond quickly to the Texas charge at San Jacinto was because he was being entertained by a

The antique yellow rose 'Mermaid'

beautiful slave woman in his tent during siesta time. The twenty-year-old Emily Morgan, a Texas patriot, was a mulatto, and thus referred to as a 'high yella gal' in the slang of the time. Since then, in song and fable she has been called 'the Yellow Rose of Texas.' There is little historical evidence to support this story, but there is also no other explanation except arrogance for Santa Ana's incredible carelessness at San Jacinto."

Like many others I always thought the "yellow rose of Texas" was a *real* rose, but upon researching I found out some surprising facts about yellow roses as well. I did not know, for instance, that while roses in white, pink, and red have been with us for centuries, yellow is a relatively new color.

The catalog for "Roses of Yesterday" describes the tea rose 'Safrano,' which flowers repeatedly, as "sensation when it made its appearance in the early 1800s for there were very few remontant [repeat flowering] yellow roses at the time." And then there was 'Harrison's Yellow' (1830), with but one annual flowering, but nevertheless beloved: "Widely planted in pioneer days and one

may practically follow the trail of the Forty-niners by plants of it." Since the pioneers planted slips they have spread all over the place and one may see great thickets of them in ghost towns of California. Hugonis, variously referred to as "Father Hugo's Rose" and "Golden Rose of China," was discovered growing wild in China and brought into cultivation in 1899. Early to bloom it has small, dainty, bright yellow flowers.

Will Tillotson, founder of "Roses of Yesterday" was fond of quoting, "The new roses are for admiring, the old ones are for loving." I love yellow roses and they are the only color I have ever planted in my own yard.

YELLOW-WOOD (*Cladrastis*) Want something different? Yellow-wood has white flowers resembling wisteria and, as an added bonus, a sweet perfume. It is especially beautiful on a moonlight night. But place your tree in a sheltered place where it will not have to resist high winds as the wood is inclined to be brittle.

YES-YOU-CAN-VEGETABLES! Join the Bod Squad. Whether you are on the generally approved 1200 calorie per day reducing diet, or the low-carbohydrate diet, it's great to know that you can grow many of the vegetables which are a dieter's delight right in your own garden. Here are some suggestions giving both "cals" and "carbs."

Vegetable	Calories	Carbohydrates
Asparagus, cuts and tips, ½ cup	16	2
Beans, green, ½ cup	20	4
Bean sprouts, mung, ½ cup	16	3
Soy sprouts, ½ cup	25	3
Beets, sliced, ½ cup	25	6
Beets, greens, ½ cup	13	2
Broccoli, chopped, ½ cup	27	4
Brussels sprouts, chopped, ½ cup	27	4
Cabbage, raw, ½ cup	10	2.5
Carrots, cooked, ½ cup	24	5
Cauliflower, fresh, ½ cup	14	2
Celery, raw, 3- to 5-inch stalks	10	2
Chard, cooked, ½ cup	15	5

Collard greens, cooked, ½ cup	30	5
Cucumbers, raw, average slice	1	0.2
Eggplant, cooked, ½ cup	20	4
Kale, cooked, ½ cup	20	3
Mushrooms, raw sliced, ½ cup	10	2
Okra, cooked, sliced, ½ cup	25	5
Onion, raw, ½ cup	30	7
Pepper, sweet, raw, green, 1 medium	13	3
Poke shoots, boiled, 4 ounces	23	4
Radish, sliced, ½ cup	12	3
Rhubarb, cooked, ½ cup	10	2
Rutabaga, boiled and diced, ½ cup	30	9
Sauerkraut, ½ cup	20	5
Spinach, leaf, ½ cup	25	4
Squash, summer, ½ cup	15	3
Tomato, fresh, 1 medium	24	5

Turnip, ½ cup	20	4
Turnip greens, boiled, ½ cup	15	3
Zucchini, ½ cup	15	3
The usual seasonings stack up like this:		
Margarine, 1 tablespoon	100	0.1
Butter, stick, 1 tablespoon	100	0.1
Butter, whipped, 1 tablespoon	68	0.1
Salt, ½ teaspoon	0	0
Pepper, ⅛ teaspoon	Tr.	Tr.

YEW Here's a time-saver for the fun-loving gardener. Hick's yew will keep a neat shape without shearing. It will eventually grow to 6 feet but will take several years to grow that high if small plants are purchased. Farther south the Irish yew would be a good choice.

Zephyrs are light, soft winds they say,
I bless them when they come my way
When tending my garden
On a warm summer's day.
LOUISE RIOTTE

ZEPHER LILY The "Flowers of the West Wind" that belong to the *Amaryllidaceae* family, these delicately beautiful flowers are natives of the Americas, including the southern United States. Plant them in fall in mild climates placing the bulbs in light, well-drained soil and a sunny location. The plants produce offsets freely, and these, separated in early fall, give a ready means of increasing your stock.

ZIGGING AND ZAGGING Togetherness is one way to practice companion planting—get the neighbors right in there next to each other. Plant zig-zag rows with the onions and beets or carrots and tomatoes tucked into one another. Or use the techniques of intercropping, and plant several companions in the same row, one of which might be a protective herb or flower.

ZINNIA (*Zinnia elgans*) A flower for the fearless green thumb! Practically insect- and disease-proof, zinnia is a flower for the gardener who likes to take things easy, especially during the heat of summer. The new hybrid zinnias of today need take a back

seat to nobody! There are mammoth dahlia types, giant cactus types, and the new Ruffles hybrids. And the more you cut, the bushier the plants will be—and the more they will bloom. And there is an unbelievable riot of brilliant color. Plus the dignified 'Carved Ivory,' a rich cream with 5-inch flowers so precisely fitted that the flower seems to have been fashioned by an artist. The nearest to a white zinnia so far produced.

All in all zinnias are a fun-loving gardener's dream!

ZOO OF FERNS Ferns make a fine background for flowering plants but they also have some very interesting qualities of their own. These "old men" of the plant kingdom were here long before the appearance of man. Once great forests of giant ferns covered the earth. Ferns are ideal for damp, low spots by fences, shady areas under trees, and on the north side of houses. They are undemanding as container plants—given dim light, for too-strong illumination yellows the fronds of many species. Most do best in a north window with about two hours of sun a day, plus rich organic soil with good drainage, with a temperature range of 50°F to 70°F, and most ferns will thrive indoors beautifully.

For various reasons of mimicry ferns have been given unusual names, such as:

Rabbit's-foot fern (*Polypodium aureaum*). Sometimes called hare's-foot fern. Its interesting rhizomes rest on the ground and are densely covered with long, coarse, yellow hairs. Sooner or later these hang over the edge of the pot and bear a strong resemblance to a rabbit's foot.

Spider ferns (*Pteris*). These are excellent small ferns for the home. The fronds are once divided, the divisions being long and narrow and pointed.

Bird's nest ferns (*Asplenium nidusavis*). The upright growing smooth fronds attain a height of 3 feet and form a neatly shaped plant.

Ostrich fern (*Matteuccia struthiopteris*). The tall fronds, growing to 5 feet in height, resemble ostrich feathers. Does well in sun or shade.

Lady fern (*Athyrium filix-femina*). Fronds of delicate texture grow to 3 feet.

Hayscented fern (*Dennstaedtia punctilobula*). Sword-shaped blades are fragrant when crushed.

Other ferns with strange names include **squirrel's-foot** (*Davallia bullata*); **staghorn** (*Platycerium*); **strawberry** (*Hemionitis palmata*); **sword** (*Nephrolepis*); **tongue** (*Cyclophorus lingua*); **walking** (*Camptosorus*) . . . and this by no means exhausts the list.

A fun-loving gardener can have a "field day" with ferns. Many found in the woods will thrive under similar conditions.

ZOYSIA (*Zoysia*) These eastern Asiatic, perennial creeping grasses are particularly valuable for planting on sandy soils, especially in the South. Forming a dense turf, they are propagated vegetatively by means of small pieces of turf called plugs.

ZUCCHINI (*Cucurbita Pepo* var. *Melopepo*) "Beware the curse of an answered prayer" must have been uttered by the gardener growing his first patch of zucchini. Be brave, all you first-time gardeners who may have overplanted this enthusiastic squash—zucchini production isn't all bad. In fact, there are so many ways you can use zucchini that we may decide that it is a real garden treasure and stop making bad jokes about it.

Having grown zucchini myself year after year I fully realize its frightening productivity. It starts in spring, a little sun, a little water, and the plants flourish and our hearts are filled with anticipation.

And then, usually after a rain, the first fruits of our labor appear. We have fresh zucchini in salad, then in ratatouille, then the young zukes like pickles. You imagine garden-fresh vitamins and minerals coursing in your veins—and then comes the deluge. Zucchini is growing faster than you can find uses for it. Moreover, the zukes are hiding everywhere. Heeding the cries of all those who have been terrorized by finding an overlooked zucchini big enough to make Hiawatha a canoe, the hybridizers have come up with a solution.

One hundred thirty-one years after its first gold rush, California brings in another. This time it is gardeners, across the country, not miners, who are stampeding. A golden squash is shining in their pans rather than elusive gold nuggets. Gold Rush hybrid squash is creating the new bonanza: a bright waxy golden yellow squash that you can find with no trouble at all. You won't have to dig for gold when you harvest Gold Rush, the plants are open, easily seen and the golden fruit highly visible. And it is just as easy to grow as the green variety . . . plant 2 or 3 seeds to the hill and thin to the strongest, give them plenty of room, pick at about 6 inches and enjoy. Raw or cooked the flavor is delicious.

As with other squash the male blossoms arrive first, followed in a week or ten days by the female, distinguished by a little knob back of the flower. Bees visit and a happy marriage results.

> Oh, Adam was a gardener, and God
> who made him sees
> That half a proper gardener's work is
> down upon his knees.
> RUDYARD KIPLING

> You can't win 'em all
> But it's fun to try;
> Let's laugh and live,
> As the years go by
> It's very important to survive
> And a garden helps us to stay alive . . .
> LOUISE RIOTTE

APPENDICES

LAYERING:
A HEALTHY WAY TO GROW

Cuttings, or "slips," sometimes referred to today as "clones," will produce a plant exactly like the parent plant. But there is always the possibility that the cutting may not live. So it is good to know about another method of plant propagation that is practically a sure thing—layering. The shoots remain attached to the parent plant while new roots are forming, there is no shock of separation and the layered plant derives sustenance from the parent plant.

Many of our common fruits, herbs, ornamentals, and even vegetables can be reproduced, true-to-type, by layering. Every gardener should know how to practice this method of extending his garden with new plants and replacing older plants with vigorous offspring.

Organic gardeners look to nature for much of what they do—and in nature many of the creeping plants layer themselves, gradually enlarging their "territory." The banyan tree of India is often cited as an example. One banyan tree may reach the size of a grove or a small forest. The herb spearmint will creep along the ground and, every few inches at a node of the prostrate stem, send down roots. By this means of growing a few inches, sending down roots, and growing out in several directions from each new root system, the original mother plant will extend out to the

area of several feet in just one growing season.

This same ability is also inherent with certain garden vegetables such as squash and tomatoes. With squash it is particularly valuable in cases where the squash borer gets into the main stem. New plants are readily formed at nodes and keep the crop going.

But, while much layering takes place naturally, we can give certain plants, especially berries, a nudge. Let us say that you have a very fine black raspberry plant. The simplest method for propagation is "tip" layering and very often, as the canes lengthen, the plant will do this on its own initiative. This works well but with an outstanding plant you may wish to propagate more new plants quickly.

So take the cane, bend it over so the tip is brought into a little dugout trough prepared for it. Make a slight cut, about 1/2 inch long, but not too deep, on the underside of the cane just below the tip. Then bury the end in the dirt. As soon as the tip is well rooted, sever it from the mother plant.

Let the plant grow the first season where it is, transplanting it to its permanent location just before growth starts early the next spring. This system is so easy and natural that even fruit-laden canes sometimes bend over to the ground by themselves and form roots.

Another variation is the simple layer. However, this method, like tip layering, has one disadvantage as it can be used to produce only one new plant from each vine or cane at a time. But it is so easy that even new gardeners can use it and be very successful.

Take a spade and open up a slit in the ground about 6 to 8 inches deep. Now, take the cane, bend it into the slit several inches deep, but make sure to turn the tip upward. Close the slit, making sure that 3 to 4 inches of the tip remain above ground. The cane, so placed in the ground, has been made to do a sharp U-turn. Rooting will take place more quickly if a shallow cut, just at the place where the cane begins the upward bend, is made. Be sure not to cut through the cane, just slice off a bit on the bottom side.

Berries are usually very flexible, but if you are working with a plant that does not bend easily, like a shrub, it helps to bend the stem in the opposite direction from which it grew. Twist it slightly as you anchor it into position with a U-shaped wire. Try to select year-old wood for your layering project as it is both more vigorous and more flexible. Exceptions, however, are certain plants like azaleas which *must* be started from old wood.

There is a third method that will give you even more rapid propagation. These systems are called "continuous" and "serpentine" layering and they may also be used with various ornamentals such as ivy or clematis.

Continuous Layering

In continuous layering, the entire shoot is laid down flat in a shallow trench, which runs directly out from the center of the plant. You must take care to anchor vines or they will not remain in place. To do this take a piece of heavy wire (such as an old coat-hanger), bend it into U-shaped pieces and push it over the stems.

Again you must make a shallow cut at each node on the underside. As the shoots (or lateral buds) grow to 4 or 5 inches, you should gradually fill the trench, using a mixture of one part each of peat moss, compost, rotted sawdust, and good garden soil.

After a strong root system has been established, sever the stem from the mother plant. Then you can divide each rooted shoot (or node) from the others. With some strong growing vines, like ivy, it is not necessary to dig a trench, just bring the vine in contact with the soil and anchor it down.

Serpentine Layering

This is a variation on the same theme but is very useful with just about any plant which will readily root at the stem nodes. It's also useful in some situations where continuous layering may not be successful, as may be the case with wisteria or honeysuckle.

As an alternative to laying the entire plant in a trench and then burying the prostrate stem as it starts to root, you make the shallow cut at the first node, then that node is buried in the ground. The next node is above the surface (or possibly the next two if the distance between them is short and bending is difficult). The node after that one is buried, and again the next after that is allowed to remain above the surface. Repeat until you have buried the entire cane or vine.

This method has some amusing overtones and may be somewhat reminiscent of the Loch Ness monster as the effect in general is a bit like the classic drawing of a sea serpent swimming through the water—hence the name "Serpentine."

Mound Layering

If you want to produce many shoots all at once from a bushy plant, try using the mound layer. In early spring, decide on the shrub you want to propagate. When growth starts cover the entire plant with a peat moss-compost-garden soil mixture. Depending on the size of the plant cover to a depth of 4 to 5 inches. As the shoots penetrate the soil mix, throw on another 4 inches, repeating this a third time. By the end of the last application the plant will have passed through the growing season and you should have a whole bush full of well-rooted shoots which may then be cut from the parent and placed in a nursery bed. A good mulch covering will help to see them safely though the winter. Further rooting will take place in the fall and by spring they can be planted out in their permanent location. Flowering almonds and Japanese quinces are good subjects for mound rooting as well as currants and gooseberries.

A variation that may be tried with huckleberries, blueberries, and certain of their cousins is to cut the bush down to the ground, cover it with a mixture of sand and peat moss in early spring, and you may expect shoots to root that season.

Layering has so many possibilities for increasing plants, particularly those that are expensive and valuable, without disturbing the parent plant that it is good to know all the different and enjoyable ways for "how to."

HARVEST WHEN THE TIME IS RIGHT!

Gardening books and articles are just chock-full of good advice about plant vegetables but first-time gardeners and even some of us oldtimers are often puzzled about when to pick. Weather has a lot to do with this. For instance:

"Pick **okra** when it is 2 to 4 inches long and snaps easily." With plenty of moisture okra will "snap easily" when it is even longer, depending on the variety, yet in a dry spell may start to harden when it is just a few inches long. But you must keep okra well picked every day, even if you don't use it, or it will not continue to produce.

Of course by now some of your crops have already been harvested, but the fall harvest is yet to come. Even so, no matter how well your fruits and vegetables have been grown, if they are not picked at the right time some of your effort is wasted. Can, dry or freeze what you can't use immediately.

Let's start with **beans**. Pick snap beans when the pods snap but tips are still pliable. Leave shell beans until the pods are well filled and limas until the ends of the pods are spongy.

Beets give you a double crop, tops and roots. For tops, harvest when roots are 1 to 1½ inches across. For roots, 2 to 3 inches in diameter. A second sowing in early July will give you a crop for fall use and winter storage. Harvest after 30°F nights. When harvest- ing avoid those with growth cracks or rough ridges.

For **broccoli** harvest when the flower cluster is in the tight bud stage, leaving about 6 to 8 inches of the stem. Some say broccoli cut in early morning has a better flavor—and I am inclined to agree. Cut before the heat wilts it. But then others like to cut just before cooking. Harvest lateral flower clusters in the same way—whichever method you think gives you the best quality.

Brussels sprouts should be hard and compact. **Cabbage** should be firm and heavy for its size. Early cabbage may be three-fourths headed, late ones fully matured. Harvest when heads feel hard and solid by cutting head off at the base with a sharp knife. Sometimes tasty "mini" heads will form on the base if you leave a little of the stem at cutting time. You can use them like brussels sprouts, or shred them and cook them lightly in olive oil.

I never have much luck with **cauliflower** in the spring, and as we go into warm summer weather it just doesn't do well. But if the fall is not too hot and dry it is often possible to grow cauliflower successfully. I start my plants from seed about August and set them out in September if I get a cool, rainy spell. I harvest the edible curds before they open and become "ricey"—if the flowers break and spread they lose quality. Unlike cabbage, cauliflower will not stand cold weather. Heads, however, will keep for several weeks if the whole plant is pulled and hung upside down in a cool, dark place. .

Carrots, like beets, contain the most sugar when fully matured but they are better eating when small, firm, and well-colored. Large leaf bases indicate thick cores. When the ground is dry a handy-dandy tool for harvesting carrot and parsnip crops is a dandelion weeder—otherwise all you get is a fistful of tops when you try to pull them, especially if weather is hot. Carrots need not be harvested all at one time, they can stay in the ground until just before a hard frost and, in some areas, over winter. Cover them with a foot of leaves or straw before the ground has frozen to make digging easier.

Corn is ready to harvest when silks begin to turn dark brown. Corn doesn't store well so it is best to cook at once right after picking. It tastes wonderful from plant to plate in a matter of just how long it is necessary to boil the water and drop it in. If you must hold it for a short time husk and refrigerate. The silks will slip off easily if you have put a little mineral oil on them, which will also help to keep out the corn ear worm. Corn freezes well but be sure to let it thaw out before cooking—the cob as well as the kernels. When harvesting corn the kernels should be nicely filled out and squirt a milky juice when dented with your fingernail. At one time I happened to be present at the home of a friend who had a large corn field. It seems that his mother was an expert at telling just when the corn was perfect for harvest. Grandmother was escorted to the corn field and placed on a comfortable chair. Father, mother, the kids and I all gathered 'round. Every few minutes our "expert" would check a few ears. Finally, she shouted "It's right, go to it." We all sprang into action and began harvesting as quickly as possible and it was, indeed, at the peak of perfection—the experience of many years had paid off.

Cucumbers should be picked when they are deep green before they turn yellow. And keep them picked to encourage the plant to keep producing. Don't harvest when the plants are wet, it may spread disease. Pulling weeds after the plants are mature disturbs their roots and causes wilting. Moderate-sized cucumbers are best, especially when the spines are just softening. Cucumbers allowed to vine on a fence or trellis, so the cucumbers depend, will produce straighter fruits.

Pick loose-leaf **lettuce** as soon as leaves are large enough to use; and other types as soon as they have headed. Lettuce transplants well so pop in lettuce plants that have come up too thickly here and there and you will prolong your harvesting time.

Onions should be dug when all the tops have withered and turned brown. Cut the stem, leaving 2 to 3 inches attached. Place in filtered sunlight for a day or two to dry and toughen the skin. I store my onions on old window screens propped up on bricks so they have air circulation both above and below. I place the onions so the stem end slants downward; this helps them to dry and prevents rot. Be sure to use your thick-necked onions first as they don't keep well. Flowering stalks should always be broken off but even so these are the onions most likely to be thick-necked and poor keepers whether they are red, yellow, or white. Don't throw away any onions after they sprout. Plant them instead. If the winter is mild they will give you mild-tasting table onions early in the spring. Onions grown from seed are thought to have the best keeping qualities.

Garlic, as with onions, is ready when the tops die down. Store the bulbs in open trays in an airy, dry place to cure until the husks are paper dry. Don't allow garlic, after it is out of the ground, to freeze. My garlic, sometimes called "serpent garlic," has a multitude of tiny bulbs at the top of the stalk instead of flowers. Every one of these is a miniature garlic plant that will grow and, in time, make a full-sized garlic bulb. But you will get quicker production if you will separate and plant the garlic "cloves" which make up your garlic bulbs.

Pick **peas** when pods are well filled but still bright green.

Pick **black-eyed peas**, or field peas, when the pods and seeds are mature but do not let them become dry. There may be mature pods and blossoms on the same vine as they have a long season of production. Pick early in the morning while the wasps, which pollinate the blossoms, are still lethargic and not working on the pea blossoms.

Peppers may be picked when the skin is green, red, purple, or yellow, depending on the variety. Gather regularly to keep the plant producing—they are fine for soups and stews during the winter months when peppers become very high priced. I cut off the tops, take out the seeds and "nest" them. Then I place them in bags and store in the freezer. I cut jalapeño peppers in two, rinse out the seeds and also store them in freezer bags for winter use.

Potatoes should never be dug when the tops are green: they won't keep well. Best time to harvest late potatoes is before a killing frost but never allow them to freeze in the ground. Try not to dig when the soil is wet. Protect from sun and wind and avoid bruising. I like to dig with a garden fork. Usually late potatoes keep well but if they start to sprout in early spring sprinkle them with ordinary table salt.

Sweet potatoes may be dug when large enough for use, usually when foliage begins to yellow. Harvest full crop as soon as touched by frost. Cut vine tops from roots early in the day to prevent bitter juices from going back into the tubers. If there are lots of vines it will help you to find the potatoes if you will cut the vines with a lawnmower. Lift roots carefully with a fork to avoid damage (injured sweet potatoes rot easily in storage). Leave a good stem on each sweet potato. Store your sweet potatoes and when you get ready to use them, take what you need, disturbing the rest as little as possible. The juices tend to work their way down to the lowest point, and if the sweet potato's position is reversed they tend to rot.

Asparagus is best if harvested just before it is cooked. Snapping spears off at the surface rather than cutting below the surface increases the yield. Keep the spears picked or they will shoot up into ferns and end the harvest. Spears should be from 6 to 8 inches above the ground. In my area asparagus tends to go into summer dormancy. For this reason I do not cut it back until November or December. If I do it will start sprouting in the fall and I will not get a crop of spears the following spring.

In my opinion **celeriac** is easier to grow than celery. It may be harvested early when the roots are only 2 inches around, the roots being 4 inches across when fully mature. Pull up by the tops, clean off side roots, twist off tops.

For me **celery** is a problem plant, but if you can grow it in your area a few stalks can be harvested early, as soon as sufficient growth has taken place. Once a tight head has formed, cut plants at base (just beneath crown). Celery also may be cut about 2 inches below ground. Trim away outer stalks. Celery will withstand light frosts if hilled. Some gardeners report that celery will grow best in a tight circle (about two feet in diameter) rather than in a row. Water from inside the circle.

Eggplant "tells" you when it's ready for harvesting so watch it carefully. Black Beauty is the type most frequently grown and fruits are usually best when 4 to 5 inches in diameter (about two thirds grown), and a glossy purple black. The fruit is too old when the skin starts to dull. Snip off the fruit with kitchen shears or a sharp knife (never twist off) and allow a short stem to remain on each fruit. Don't grow eggplant where tomatoes, potatoes, or eggplant have been grown in the last three years; it is a crop that should be rotated.

The outer leaves of **endive**, often used as a lettuce substitute, may be harvested without cutting the plant. Or, the entire plant can be used for salads. The flavor improves with cool weather. For milder flavor gather outer leaves and tie loosely. Hearts thus blanched are mild and tender.

Horseradish should be dug in early fall. Trim off the rootlets growing on the large root and wash and dry. Grated horseradish is a real pepper-upper.

Kale may be harvested by using the entire plant. Or you can twist off the outer leaves as needed. The leaves should be bright green and crisp with firm texture. Dark green "heavy" leaves are overmature and likely to be tough and bitter.

Kohlrabi, delicious if harvested at the right time, is not a popular plant because most gardeners tend to let it overmature. The thickened base of the stem should be no larger than 2 to 3 inches. Cut off the plant just below the "bulb" and dispose of the rest of the plant. Young kohlrabi is excellent eaten raw or steamed without peeling. More mature kohlrabi should be peeled, sliced or diced and boiled in very little salted water. Margarine and seasonings provide a simple way of serving.

I like **leeks** and harvest them early in the spring. I gather a lot of dandelion buds and cook them with the sliced leeks, serving them with margarine, salt and pepper, and a dash of nutmeg. You can sow seeds in late spring or early summer for winter use.

Watermelons should be cut, not pulled from the vine. Always leave a short stem. Check *all* melons in the morning for ripeness, before they get warm. Ripe watermelons have a dull thudding sound rather than a sharp sound when thumped. Other ripeness indicators: brown tendrils on stem near fruit; yellowish rather than white color where melon touches the ground; rough, slightly ridged feel to surface. Watermelons and other melons will benefit if a piece of waxed paper is placed under them; this often prevents insect damage.

Honeydew and **casaba melons**, when ripe, have a sweet odor and a creamy-yellow surface color. Smell the blossom ends of your Persian melons. If the smell is sweet and fruity, the melon is probably ripe.

Mustard greens are especially great for the fall garden. Sow them where something else has been removed and enjoy them right up to really cold weather. Don't pull your plants, just snip off the outer leaves and the growing tip will produce more leaves. Leaves should be picked just before they mature. Plants should be kept cut back to prevent flowering as the leaves become tough and bitter if plants flower.

Parsley, chock-full of vitamin E, is more than just a pretty face. I have a bed of parsley going all season long in a protected place. Parsley will freeze and thaw out and still be good. For best time to pick choose early morning before the delicate oils have evaporated. Pinch off older outer stems and discard.

Dig (never pull up by tops) your **parsnips** as needed from late summer through the fall. In warm climates dig as soon as the roots are mature. In colder areas cover row with organic mulch or newspapers if hard frost is predicted. Root flavor is improved by frost and freezing. When harvesting always cut off tops immediately.

Pumpkins should have a board slipped underneath as they ripen to keep them from turning white or rotting where they touch the ground. Once the orange skin color begins to darken, the skin becomes tough, the vines dry up, and they're ready. When harvesting for storage, cut (don't pull) pumpkins from the vines and leave a 3-to 4-inch stem or they won't store well. Handle very carefully to prevent bruises or scratches. Don't wash fruits before storing.

Harvest your **summer radishes** regularly, when the shoulders first appear through the soil. Left in the ground they get tough and woody. If kept well watered they won't be "hot."

Don't let your **summer squash** get too big. Harvested regularly and small it will continue to produce over a long period. Ideally harvest cylindrical types when 6 to 8 inches long (3 inches across for patty pans) before rind hardens. Depending on variety, skins should be dark, glossy green or yellow. Fruits are usable even if giant size, as long as your fingernail can easily penetrate the skin. Keep close check as zucchini and other summer squash develop quickly.

Winter squash should be picked only when ripe and mature. Acorn squash should have a dark green color, be hard, and have an orange or yellow spot where it touches the ground. Butternut will have a hard skin and will be a buff or tan color when mature.

Leave the butternut on the vine until the stem shrivels. Pick after vines have dried out but before frosts. For storage leave a 4-inch stem on each fruit.

Harvest **tomatoes** at ripeness state most appealing to you, up to dead ripe. This is one of the great things about growing your own—you can leave them to sun-ripen on the vine and enjoy their really delicious flavor. So many of the tomatoes in the supermarkets only "look" ripe, but they have been artificially colored and are actually still green.

Keep your tomatoes picked for continued production but don't pick when plants are wet. Protecting plants with burlap bags in fall will help prolong their fruiting season. If a really cold spell threatens, harvest entire

plant and hang by the roots in a cool, dark place for slow ripening of fruits.

Some years, depending on season, you have overproduction of such things as squash, okra, tomatoes, or even eggplant. There comes a day when family, friends and neighbors have all been gifted to the point of saturation. This is when I take some of my produce to the nearby Adventist hospital. Knowing I am an organic gardener and use no poisonous sprays they are delighted to receive my vegetables. I also give vegetables and fruits to the Salvation Army, which makes up food baskets for the needy. They, too, are happy to have the extra vegetables and give me a receipt for their value that comes in mighty handy at income tax time.

USE YOUR GARDEN FENCE

It always surprises me to see an idle fence surrounding a garden. Of course the fence is, in itself, beneficial. It provides a boundary, gives privacy, keeps children and pets in bounds, or screens an eyesore. But a fence can do so much more. Clothed with blossoming vines, a fence becomes a beautiful backdrop for your garden, your flower border, or a colorful focal point to view from picture windows or patio.

If vegetables are your cup of tea, your fence can be more than a pleasant green divider along property lines. Sugar snap and

other tall-growing peas, pole snap beans, pole limas, cucumbers, and tall tomatoes all can be grown vertically, supported on a *strong* fence four or more feet high. Prizetaker pole lima, the new Early Pride Hybrid cucumber, Burpee's Ambrosia Hybrid cantaloupe, the heat-resistant, vining Malabar "spinach" that supplies greens all summer, and Supersteak Hybrid VFN tomato are excellent varieties to grow "in the air" in a sunny location. With a little assistance Small Sugar pumpkin and some varieties of vining squash will also take to the vertical.

Make sure that the soil is well prepared, fertile, and well drained.

Follow directions on seed packets for planting, thinning, and care. Peas thrive in cool weather, and still can be planted toward late summer for a fall crop, except in areas where severe freezing weather comes in early fall. Of course, they can be planted again early next spring.

If the fence is a backdrop for your garden, be sure to allow easy access. You'll need room to tend the vegetables climbing the fence and to harvest their bounty. You probably will want to prune the tomatoes to a couple of main stems to control excessive growth. Keep cucumbers picked to encourage bearing. As pumpkins and melons enlarge, you may need to support their weight with cloth slings (such as old pantyhose) or mesh bags tied to the fence. Sometimes potatoes or fruits come in mesh bags useful for supporting the heavier vining fruits.

Flowering Vines From Seed

For quick-growing vines you simply can't beat morning glories. Heavenly Blue (bright sky blue), Pearly Gates (shiny-white), and Scarlett O'Hara are excellent choices. Introduced in recent years, the Early Call series of morning glories in blue, rose, and a mixture of colors, extend the season of bloom. They start flowering earlier than most other varieties, yet keep right on blossoming until frost.

Morning glories greet the day, whereas moonflowers open at dusk, with a shimmering display of large, pure white, fragrant flowers, which are very attractive to sphinx moths. If you must enjoy your garden during the evening hours these are for you. Plant some of each along your fence for a morning and evening show of bloom. Invite your friends and neighbors for a moonflower party. It's fun and exciting to watch the moonflower buds spring wide open like little parasols before your eyes, as if by some magic command from Mother Nature.

For variety, there are other easily grown climbers. Canary creeper is dainty and grace-

Nasturium

ful, with beautifully cut and finely fringed, rich canary yellow, nasturtiumlike flowers. There are also tall, single climbing nasturtiums in a riot of colors. They are excellent for scaling fences or trailing over a compost pile or bank.

Cobaea scandens, the cup-and-saucer vine, is a very strong grower, and can quickly reach 20 feet. Use it where there's a large area to cover. The bell-shaped blooms open clear green, then turn rich purple-blue. Plum-shaped fruits follow for added interest.

Dutchman's pipe (*Aristolochia durior*) is an unequaled foliage vine that creates dense, cooling shade or opaque screens for complete privacy. The glossy, dark-green leaves are large, handsome, and heart-shaped. It will make a rapid growth and is ideal for porch, trellis, pergola, or archway. It reaches up to 30 feet in height and adapts well to practically any situation. It receives its name from its somewhat inconspicuous flowers—a rare mahogany, intriguingly odd-shaped bloom that resembles a miniature Dutch pipe. The vine will grow in sun or shade.

For a more refined effect, there's the cypress vine. This climber has rich green, fernlike foliage—a perfect foil for the trumpet-shaped flowers in white, rose, and red shades.

If you need a dainty little climber or trailer, you'll enjoy *Thunbergia,* the black-eyed Susan vine. This winsome beauty climbs or trails about 5 feet and blooms mostly in shades of orange, sometimes with dark eyes. One type is pristine white.

Lathyrus, the perennial sweet pea, is a vigorous trailer or climber, with pink, white and purplish red flowers from June to September. It may take a year to get *Lathyrus* established and blooming. After that it's a tough, rampant grower and endures difficult conditions. Be sure to locate it where it won't crowd out other plants.

Climbing types of annual sweet peas include the Galaxies, Giant Spencers, and early Multiflora Giganteas. They bloom in lovely colors and are delightfully fragrant. Nothing is prettier than sweet peas to curtain a fence in early summer, or throughout the season where the weather stays cool. Sweet peas thrive in moderate temperatures ranging from 50°F to 75°F, but decline fast in hot weather. In nearly frost-free areas, sweet peas planted from early fall into winter bloom beautifully in late winter to early summer. In all other climates, sweet peas must be planted in early spring to beat the heat.

Although not grown for their flowers, gourds are also attractive vines. Their foliage makes a nice green background in summer and their fruits are interesting to watch as they develop many shapes and color patterns. The mature gourds are ready to harvest just before frost and great to use for decorations or craft projects.

How To Grow

All the flowering vines just mentioned thrive in well-prepared, average soil, free from long-standing puddles after heavy rain. Nasturtiums even grow well in poor soil. Canary creeper and *Thunbergia* like partial shade, the rest full sun most of the day. Dutchman's pipe will grow in sun or shade.

Sow seeds in spring, according to directions on seed packets. Be sure to wait until all danger of frost is over and weather and soil are warm before planting morning glories, moonflower, and *Thunbergia.* They sprout poorly (maybe not at all) in cold ground. It is helpful to soak seeds of morning glories and moonflower in room-temperature water for about 8 hours (or overnight) before planting. This softens the seedcoats and speeds germination.

In addition to beautifying fences, climbers are also attractive scaling lamp or sign posts, trellises, arbors, and open pergolas. If you don't have any permanent structures like these, you can easily erect trellis netting to support climbers.

CONSERVING ENERGY—YOURS!

Someone once said, "There's no such thing as a free lunch!" Right. And I don't believe there's any such thing as a "no work" garden either. But that doesn't mean we have to be gluttons for punishment. There are ways— and gadgets you can make for yourself—that will definitely make gardening easier and more enjoyable. And I'm all for that.

First there is the matter of hoeing. Hoes comes in many shapes and sizes. Besides the usual flat-blade sort there is also a pointed hoe that is particularly useful in the very small garden. With this one you can make a furrow of the required depth when planting. A little neighbor boy used to call this one his "grubbin' hoe, for to grub out the hard to grub places." And he was right, you can use this one to get closer to plants, while still being careful not to disturb the roots.

The flat-bladed hoe, however, is used for most cultivating jobs, so select with care. A big, heavy hoe is tiring to swing (especially for a lady or an elderly person), so the lighter the better. Also consider the thickness of the handle in relation to the size of your own hands. It should be comfortable to hold with or without gloves. These matters are important to consider also with other tools such as spades or rakes.

Make the most of what you have by placing it directly in the garden row where you will plant your seed, rather than scattering it broadcast. Open the row, put in your compost and then mix more with the soil you will use to cover. Or, better still, cover the seed with peat moss, which will help to ration moisture and keep the soil "open" so the seed will have an easier time emerging.

Speaking further about compost. If you don't have a shredder, here is a way you can use your own (and your neighbor's) leaves and lawn clippings. Raise your rotary lawn mower about four inches on a platform built of 2-by-4's. The frame should be solid, the mower wheels blocked, and care taken in starting the machine. Pile leaves near the outside of the propped-up mower, start it and sweep up a rakeful of leaves. As they are sucked through the blades and ejected through the chute, they will make a heap about one-tenth the size of the original pile. This is a fine mulch and is just right for composting as it will break down far more rapidly.

Of course you aren't lazy, no indeed, but it's very nice to get through those garden chores easily and rapidly so you can have the fun of going swimming, picnicking, or just lying around in a hammock and reading a book.

Hoe length is important, too. It should be just long enough for you to grasp almost at the end and still be able to stand nearly straight and chop. For someone not too tall this is especially important. Cut the hoe handle to fit your size and round it off a bit by sanding. You see, the longer the handle, the less your leverage on the blade. Have the handle come to just about the middle of your chest and it will be just about right.

How you use your hoe when weeding also will make a great difference in conserving your strength. You must destroy the weeds' root system to be effective, as well as the part seen on the surface. You can do this without getting tired (well, not *quite* as tired) if you tip your hoe blade to one side. This means that (starting on the right side of your row) you will tip the blade so that the right corner strikes the ground first. Then, chopping in an arc from one side of the row to the other and with short easy strokes, you bring your blade in contact with the ground as close to flat as possible.

With each stroke your blade edge should stop about two inches under the surface and should travel about six inches through the soil. On your way back down the row you should reverse the process with the left corner of your blade hitting the ground first. Tipping your blade will cause it to slide under the ground easier and you will save a surprising amount of energy. It is much more effective, too, than hitting the weeds head on. The triangular or pointed hoe is particularly adapted for working close to the rows and also is handy for raised beds where vegetables are planted very close together.

Weeds . . . and Weeding

Now, I'm going to tell you something about weeds that sounds like absolute heresy. Weeds are not always enemies (lots of our garden plants were originally weeds and there are many, such as wild carrot, still growing as weeds). Sometimes, if not allowed to grow too thickly, weeds are friends. Many weeds send down roots very deeply, bringing up minerals from the subsoil that benefit garden plants. Weeds, again if not allowed to grow too thickly, provide shade for young plants. Weeds, thoroughly composted so their seeds will not sprout, make good organic fertilizer.

I've learned something about weeds, myself, the last few years that may help the "gardening morale" of others who, like myself, have limited time and energy. You can let a few weeds grow and still have a very productive garden anyhow—clean cultivation is not absolutely necessary.

The trick, I've discovered, is to keep your vegetable garden as weed-free as your strength and time will allow while the plants are small. They also must not be crowded and must have sunshine to grow well. This is in early spring when the sun is not so strong. All vegetable plants must have sunshine while they are little, otherwise they will not make good growth and will fall easy prey to insects, as well as lacking vigor and having spindly growth.

But, once your plants are well up, and the ol' sun is getting hotter, a few weeds will help to shade the ground, especially for tall-growing plants such as corn, pole beans, cucumbers, melons, and other plants trained to vine on a fence or sprawling on the ground. Spend your energy on keeping the not-so-tall-growing plants weed-free. Most of us have just so much time and energy for gardening, so let's make it as easy as possible. Hoe, hoe, hoe!

Digging . . . or Tilling

Digging a garden, unless it is a very tiny one, can be quite a chore, yet the price of a tiller may stop you. I would suggest that you rent a tiller the first year (and maybe each year in the spring for the initial plowing) to get the ground started and the soil mixed.

SOURCES OF SUPPLY

These sources were viable at the time this book was written.
The author cannot be responsible for discontinued companies, changes of
address, or variety changes.

Aphrodisia
282 Bleeker Street
New York, NY 10014

Applewood Seed Company
333 Parfet Street
Lakewood, CO 80215

Armstrong Nurseries
Dept. MN
P.O. Box 473
Ontario, CA 91764

Ball Corporation
Consumer Products Division
345 South High Street
Muncie, IN 47305-2326

Bedding Plants, Inc.
P.O. Box 286
Okemos, MI 48864

Bluestone Perennials
Dept. 47
7247, OH 44057

Bountiful Ridge Nurseries
Dept. MN, P.O. Box 250
Princess Anne, MD 21853

Breck's
Dept. MN
6523 North Galena Road
Peoria, IL 61601

Bunting's Nurseries, Inc.
Dept. MN, Duke's Street
Selbyville, DE 19975

Burgess Seed & Plant Co.
Dept. 39-50
905 Four Seasons Road
Bloomington, IL 61701

W. Atlee Burpee Seed Co.
Warminster, PA 18974

DeJager Bulbs
Dept. MA-1, 188 Asbury Street
South Hamilton, MA 01982

Dutch Gardens, Inc.
Dept. MN, P.O. 168
Montvale, NJ 07645

Dutch Mountain Nursery
Dept. MN, 7984 North 48th
Street
B-1
Augusta, MI 49012

Farmer Seed & Nursery Co.
Dept. MN
818 Northwest 4th Street
Faribault, MN 55021

Henry Field Seed & Nursery
Dept. MN
407 Sycamore Street
Shenandoah, IA 51602

Flower Essence Services
P.O. Box 1769
Nevada City, CA 95959

Dean Foster Nurseries
Dept. MN, Route 2
Hartford, MI 49057

Gardens Alive
Highway 48
P.O. Box 149
Sunman, IN 47041

Goldsmith Seeds, Inc.
P.O. Box 1349
Gilroy, CA 95020

Gurney Seed & Nursery Co.
Dept. MN
Yankton, SD 57078

Joseph Harris Co.
Moreton Farm
Rochester, NY 14624

Hastings
1036 White Street, S.W.
P.O. Box 115535
Atlanta, GA 30310-8535

Hastings
434 Marietta Street N.W.
Atlanta, GA 30302

Herbst Brothers Seedsmen
Dept. MN
1000 North Main Street
Brewster, NY 10509

Hilltop Herb Farm
P.O. Box 1784
Cleveland, TX 77327

Horticultural Enterprises
Box 34082
Dallas, TX 75234

House of Wesley
Bloomington, IL 61701

J.L. Hudson Seedsmen
World Seed Service
Box 1058
Redwood City, CA 94064

Indiana Botanic Gardens
Hammond, IN 46325

Jackson & Perkins
Dept. MAN, P.O. Box 1028
Center
Medford, OR 97501

Johnny's Selected Seeds
North Dixmont, ME 04932

J.W. Jung Seed Co.
Dept. MN, 333 South High Street
Randolph, WI 53956

Kelly Bros., Nurseries, Inc.
Dept. MN, Maple Street
Dansville, NY 14437

Kitazawa Seed Co.
356 West Taylor Street
San Jose, CA 95110

Krider Nurseries, Inc.
Dept. MAN, P.O. Box 29
Middlebury, IN 46540

Lakeland Nurseries Sales
Dept. MN, 340 Poplar Street
Hanover, PA 17331

Lewis Strawberry Nursery
Dept. MN
Rocky Point, NC 28457

Lilypons Water Gardens
Dept. MN, 6885 Lilypons Road
Lilypons, MD 21717

Earl May Seed & Nursery Co.
Dept. MN 208 North Elm Street
Shenandoah, IA 51603

Michigan Bulb Co.
Dept. MN, 1950 Waldorf NW
Grand Rapids, MI 49550

Musser Forests, Inc.
Dept. MN, P.O. Box 340
Indiana, PA 15701

Natural Gardening Research
Center
Highway 48
P.O. Box 149
Sunman, IN 47041

Nichols Garden Nursery
1190 North Pacific Highway
Albany, OR 97321

Northrup King Co.
Consumer Products Division
Minneapolis, MN 55440

Oklahoma Peanut Commission
P.O. Box D
Madill, OK 73442

L.L. Olds Seed Co.
P.O. Box 7790
Madison, MI 53791

Geo. W. Park Seed Co.
Dept. MN, P.O. Box 31
Greenwood, SC 29640

Plants of the Southwest
1570 Pachaco Street
Santa Fe, MN 87501

Rayner Bros. Inc.
P.O. Box 1617-M
Salisbury, MD 21801

Roses of Yesterday & Today
802 Brown's Valley Road
Dept. M
Watsonville, CA 95076

Seed Savers Exchange
Kent Whealy
203 Rural Avenue
Decorah, IA 52101

Shepherd's Garden Seeds
30 Irene Street
Torrington, CT 06790

R.H. Shumway Seedsmen
Dept. MN, 628 Cedar Street
Rockford, IL 61101

Spring Hill Nurseries
Dept. MN
6523 North Galena Road
Peoria, IL 61601

Stark Bro's Nurseries
Box B2968A
Louisiana, MD 63353-0010

Stern's Nurseries, Inc.
Dept. M
607 West Washington Street
Geneva, NY 14456

Fred A. Stewart, Inc.
Dept. MN
1212 East Las Junas Drive
San Gabriel, CA 91778

Stokes Seeds, Inc.
737 Main Street
Buffalo, NY 14240

Survival Shop
P.O. Box 42216
Los Angeles, CA 90042

Suter's Apple Nursery
3220 Silverado Trail
St. Helena, CA 94574
(old apple varieties)

Tropexotic Growers, Inc.
708 60th Street
Dept. MN
Bradentown, FL 33529

Tsang & Ma
The Good Earth Seed Company
P.O. Box 5644
Redwood City, CA 94063

Van Bourgondian Bros.
Dept. MN
245 Farmingdale Road
P.O. Box A
Babylon, NY 11702

Van Ness Water Gardens
Dept. MAN
2460 North Euclid
Upland, CA 91786

Vermont Bean Seed Co.
Garden Lane
Bomoseen, VT 05732

Wayside Gardens, Inc.
Dept. WG
Hodges, SC 29695

White Flower Farm
Dept. MN
Litchfield, CT 06759

*Statuary, Gazebos, Garden
Ornaments, Supplies, Tools,
Furniture, etc.*

David Kay
4509 Taylor Lane
Cleveland OH 44128

Gardener's Supply
128 Intervale Road
Burlington, VT 05401

Burpee Ornamental Gardens
(Special catalog)
W. Atlee Burpee & Co.
Warminster, PA 18974

Smith & Hawken
25 Corte Madera
Mill Valley, CA 94941

The Vermont Country Store
P.O. Box 3000
Manchester CTR, Vt 05255-3000

BIBLIOGRAPHY

Arkins, Frieda. *The Essential Kitchen Gardener* (New York: Henry Holt & Co., 1990).

Ascher, Amalie Adler. *The Complete Flower Arranger* (New York: Simon & Schuster, 1974).

Bailey, Ralph, ed. *House & Garden's Gardener's Day Book* (New York, M. Evans Co., 1965).

Baily, Emma. *Country Gardeners Cookbook* (Emmaus, Pennsylvania: Rodale Press,1974).

Blanchard, Marjorie Page. *The Sprouter's Cookbook* (Pownal, Vermont: Garden Way Publishing, 1975).

Brimer, John Burton. *Growing Herbs in Pots* (New York: Simon & Schuster, 1976).

Carson, Rachel. *Silent Spring* (Greenwich, Connecticut: Fawcett Publishers, 1962).

Chalmers, Irene and Glaser, Milton. *Great American Food Almanac* (New York: Harper & Row, 1986).

Clarkson, Rosetta E. *Herbs, Their Culture and Uses* (New York: Macmillan, 1970).

Coon, Nelson. *Gardening for Fragrance* (New York: Hearthside Press, 1970).

Coon, Nelson. *Using Plants for Healing* (New York: Hearthside Press, 1963).

Coon, Nelson and Gissen, Georgiane. *The Complete Book of Violets* (S. Brunswick, N.J.: A.S. Barnes, 1977).

Creasy, Rosalind. *Edible Landscaping* (San Francisco: Sierra Club, 1982).

Crockett, James Underwood. *Vegetables and Fruits* (New York: Time-Life Books, 1972).

Duff, Gail. *Natural Fragrances* (Pownal, Vermont: Storey/Garden Way, 1989).

Encyclopedia of Organic Gardening (Emmaus, Pennsylvania: Rodale Press, 1974).

Firth, Grace. *A Natural Year* (New York: Simon & Schuster, 1972).

Forsdyke, A.G. *Weather and Weather Forecasting* (New York: Bantam Books, 1970).

Franz, Dorothy and Olds, Jerome, eds. *How to Grow Vegetables & Fruits by the Organic Method* (Emmaus, Pennsylvania: Rodale Press, 1977).

Fulder, Stephen. *An End to Aging? Remedies for Life Extension* (New York: Destiny Books, 1983).

Gibbons, Euell. *Stalking the Healthful Herbs* (New York: McKay Pub. Co., 1967).

Goodman, Linda. *Star Signs* (New York: St. Martin's Press, 1987).

Gordon, Jean. *Rose Recipes* (Woodstock, Vermont: Red Rose Pubs., 1959).

Graves, W.H. *Medicinal Value of Natural Foods* (Santa Barbara, California: 1972).

Greer, Anne Lindsay. *Cuisine of the American Southwest* (New York: Harper & Row, 1983).

Harris, Ben Charles. *Eat the Weeds* (Barre, Massachusetts: Barre Publishing Co., 1968).

Hatfield, Audrey Wynne. *How To Enjoy Your Weeds* (New York: Macmillian Pub. Co., 1971).

Hunter, Beatrice Trum. *Gardening Without Poisons* (Boston: Houghton Mifflin Co., 1964).

Hunter, Beatrice Trum. *How Safe Is Food In Your Kitchen?* (New York: Scribner's, 1981).

Jacobs, Betty. *Profitable Herb Growing at Home* (Pownal, Vermont: Garden Way Publishing Co., 1976).

Jarvis, D.C. *Folk Medicine* (New York: Holt, Rinehart & Winston, 1960).

Kadans, N.D. *Encyclopedia of Medicinal Herbs* (Richmond, Virginia: Macoy Publishing & Masonic Supply Co., 1973).

Kloss, Jethro. *Back to Eden* (Santa Barbara, California: Lifeline Books, 1974).

Kraft, Ken and Pat. *The Best of American Gardening* (New York: Walker and Company, 1975).

Levy, Juliette De Bairacli. *Herbal Handbook for Everyone* (Newton, Massachusetts: Charles T. Branford Co., 1967).

Levy, Juliette De Bairacli. *Herbal Handbook for Farm and Stable* (London: Faber and Faber, 1963).

Lowenfeld, Claire and Back, Philippa. *Herbs, Health & Cookery* (New York: Award Books, 1977).

Meyer, Clarence. *50 Years of the Herbalist Almanac* (Glenwood, Illinois: Meyerbooks, 1977).

Millspaugh, Charles E. *American Medicinal Plants* (New York: Dover, 1974).

Mittleider, J.F. *More Food From Your Garden* (Santa Barbara, California: Woodbridge Press, 1975).

Nichol, John. *Bites & Stings* (New York: Facts on File, 1989).

Percival, Julia and Burgen Pixie. *Household Ecology* (New York: Prentice Hall, 1971).

Philbrick, Helen and John. *The Bug Book, Harmless Insect Controls* (Pownal, Vermont: Garden Way Pub. Co., 1974).

Rabkin, Richard & Jacob. *Nature In The West* (New York: Holt, Rinehart & Winston, 1981).

Raymond, Dick. *The Joy of Gardening* (Pownal, Vermont: Garden Way Pub. Co., 1983).

Raymond, Dick. *Vegetable Gardening Know-How* (Pownal, Vermont: Garden Way Pub. Co., 1975).

Riotte, Louise. *Carrots Love Tomatoes* (Pownal, Vermont: Garden Way Pub. Co., 1975).

————*The Complete Guide to Growing Berries and Grapes* (Pownal, Vermont: Garden Way Pub. Co., 1974).

————*Nuts for the Food Gardener* (Pownal, Vermont: Garden Way Pub. Co., 1975).

————*Planetary Planting* (San Diego, California: Astro Computing Services, 1975).

————*Roses Love Garlic* (Pownal, Vermont: Garden Way Pub. Co., 1983).

————*Sleeping With A Sunflower* (Pownal, Vermont: Garden Way Pub. Co., 1987).

————*Astrological Gardening* (Pownal, Vermont: Garden Way Pub. Co., 1989).

Rockwell, F.F. and Grayson, Esther C. *The Rockwell's Complete Book of Roses* (Garden City, New York: Doubleday & Co., 1958).

Root, A.I. and E.R. *The ABC and XYZ of Bee Culture* (Medina, Ohio: A.I. Root Co., 1935).

Rose, Jeanne. *Modern Herbal* (New York: Perigee Books, 1987).

Sanders, Robert E. *A to Z Hints for the Vegetable Gardener* (Pownal, Vermont: Garden Way Pub., 1976).

Scully, Virginia. *A Treasury of American Indian Herbs* (New York: Bonanza Books, 1970).

Seddon, George and Radbecka, Helena. *Your Kitchen Garden* (New York: Simon & Schuster, 1978).

Shepherd, Renee. *Recipes From A Kitchen Garden* (Shepherd's Garden Seeds).

Southwick, Lawrence. *Dwarf Fruit Trees for the Home* (Pownal, Vermont: Garden Way Pub., 1972).

Sunset New Western Garden Book (Menlo Park, CA: Lane Publishing Co., 1988).

Tillona, Francesca and Strowbridge, Cynthia. *A Feast of Flowers* (New York: Funk & Wagnalls, 1969).

Tilgner. *Tips for the Lazy Gardener* (Pownal, Vermont: Garden Way Publishing, 1985).

Tompkins, Peter and Bird, Christopher. *Secrets of the Soil* (New York: Harper & Row, 1989).

Tompkins, Peter and Bird, Christopher. *Secret Life of Plants* (New York: Avon Books, 1973).

Tisserand, Robert B. *The Art of Aromatherapy* (New York: Inner Traditions, 1979).

Valnet, Jean, *Organic Gardening Medicine* (New Paltz, N.Y.: Erbonia Books, 1975)

Valnet, Jean. *The Practice of Aromatherapy* (New York: Destiny Books, 1980).

Waters, Patricia. *A Guide to Bringing Flowers Into Your Daily Life* (New York: William Morrow & Co., 1982).

Wilder, Louise Beebe. *The Fragrant Garden* (New York: Dover Publishing, 1932).

Woodham-Smith, Cecil. *Queen Victoria* (New York: Alfred A. Knopf, 1972).

Yepsen, Robert B. *Organic Plant Protection* (Emmaus, Pennsylvania: Rodale Press, 1966).

INDEX

A

Acacia, 20
Achimines, 153, 160
Acid soil, 23, 57, 106, 117, 171, 190
Adder's tongue, medicinal ointment of, 5
A-Frames, 5
  see also Climbing vegetables; Support
African daisy, 160
African violet (*Saintpaulia* sp.), 5–6
  culture and seeds, 6, 160
  tatoos for, 163–164
  for terrariums, 164
  watering tips, 6, 186
Agave (*Agave*), uses of, 49
Ageratum, culture and seeds, 160
Air conditioning, with plants, 101
Air layering, 6–7, 200–202
  see also Propagation
Air pollution, plant sensitivity to, 52
Alder (red), chemical defenses of, 34
Alfalfa, and walnuts, 38
Alfalfa meal, as compost activator, 41
Algae, bleach for, 41
Allergies, to chocolate, 29
Aloe gel, for warts, 181
Aluminum foil, 30, 190
Amaranth, 7, 37
American goldfinch, 12
Ammonia, as sting treatment, 76
Ammonium nitrate, composted with bark, 21
Anchusa, 20
Anemone, 26
Anise hyssop, 84
Anise (*Pimpinella anise*), attracting fish with, 65
  companion plants for, 39
  and coriander, 38
  culture, 66
  and dogs, 178
Antibiotics, from corn cobs, 41
Antique Roses, 146–147
  see also Roses
Ants,
  in aphid proliferation, 8
  and bees, 19
  deterred by tansy, 40
  eaten by armadillos, 9–10
  repelled by mint, 39
Aphids, 7

and ants, 7–8
and daddy longlegs, 46
deterred by nasturtiums, 39
and elderberries, 58
and fire ants, 64
on jasmine, 71
and lacewings, 103
and lady bugs, 22
and milkweed, 39
and okra, 123
and quassia, 139
repelled by coriander, 39
Ryania speciosa for, 9
woolly apple, 7, 9
Aphrodisiacs, 8–9, 29–30, 46, 78, 99, 101–102, 145
Apple maggot, non-toxic control for, 9
Apple (*Malus pumila*), 9, 20
  and aphid control, 7, 9
  attracting songbirds with, 12
  blackthorn revives, 38
  blight resistant varieties, 64
  codling moth and bats, 16
  quick bearing varieties, 140
  and railroad worm, 143
  for skin care, 60
  see also Aphids; Fruit trees
Apple scab, carrot spray for, 39
Apple worm, and molasses, 170
Apricot (*Prunus armenica*), 9
Aquatic plants,
  for ponds, 161–162
  to attract songbirds, 12
  willows, 188
Armadillos, 9–10, 190
Armyworm, citrus spray for, 108
Arteriosclerosis, and spinach, 157
Arthritis, evening primrose for, 49
Ashes,
  for cabbage worms, 28
  for cucumber beetles, 44
  as soil conditioner, 52
  uses for, 190
  see also Insecticides, natural; Pests
Asparagus (*Asparagus officinalis*), 10
  companion plants for, 39, 40
  harvesting tips, 203
  and Japanese beetles, 98
  with tomatoes, 38
  varieties, 37

Asparagus beans (*Phaseolus multiflorus*), 10–11
  see also Beans
Asparagus beetle, repelled by marigold, 40
Aspirin, for cut flowers, 44
Asters, 176
Astilbes, 162
Astrological signs,
  in bamboo culture, 15
  and planting, 73–74
Auricula, 178
Autumn-olive, 12, 13
Autumn sage (*Salvia greggii*), 11
Avocadoes, grown by Aztecs, 13
Azaleas, 106, 201
Aztec lily (*Sprekelia formoissima*), 13–14
Aztec marigold (*Tagetes erecta*), 14
Aztecs, 7, 13, 42

B

Bacillus thuringiensis,
  for cabbage worm, 25, 27
  and corn, 155
  insects controlled by, 118
  qualities of, 118
  for tent caterpillars, 164
  see also Insecticides, natural
Baking soda, 21
Baldness, 15
Baltimore oriole, 12
Bamboo, 15–16
Bamboo (edible), 57
Bamboo palm (*Chamedora erumpens*), 163
Bananas, 16, 60, 181
Banyan tree, 200
Bargains,
  bottle greenhouses, 24
  from the dump, 21
  inexpensive seeds, 16
  used berry baskets, 22
Bark,
  aphid eggs in, 7
  composted, 21
  disease reduction with, 21
  as soil conditioner, 52
Barrel cactus (*Ferocactus*), candy from, 49
Basil, 19, 85, 159
  with asparagus, 38
  companion plants for, 40
  as natural insecticide, 38
  with tomatoes, 38
Bat house, plans for, 17
Baths, herbal, 20–21
Bats, 16–18, 184

Bean beetles,
  controls for, 112
  deterred by rosemary, 40
  deterred by summer savory, 40
  and marigolds, 39, 112
  and wasps, 112
Beans, 160
  as aphrodisiacs, 8
  and buttercups, 26
  in companion planting, 38, 39, 40
  with corn and squash, 92
  green, 18
  grown by Aztecs, 13
  harvesting, 18–19, 202
  historical claims for, 18
  hot weather varieties; 55
  and Japanese beetles, 98
  for landscaping, 176
  nutritional value, 18
  partial shade and, 38
  with potatoes, 38
  seeds from packaged food, 16
  varieties, 18, 120
  and walnuts, 38
Beans (bush), 18, 37, 159
  companion plants for, 38, 39
Beans (Lima), 37, 40
Beans (pole), 18, 159
  companion plants for, 38
  on fences, 206
  Purple Pod var., 37
Beans (runner), Red Knight var., 37
Beans (shell), 18
Beargrass (*Nolina*), as food, 48
Beauty aids,
  apricots, 9
  bromeliads, 25
  chamomile, 20
  herbal baths, 20–21
  honey, 20
  nucleic acids, 21
  plants for, 82–83, 190–191
  rose water, 146
Bedstraw (*Galium* spp.), 20, 82
Bee balm, 19, 38
Beer, 20, 88
Bees,
  beekeeping techniques, 19
  and fire blight, 64
  and insecticides, 86
  killer, 19
  plants for attracting, 19–20, 37, 51
  as pollinators, 20

and quassia, 139
sting treatment, 76
and watermelons, 182
Beetles, 22, 24, 108
Beets, 159
  in companion planting, 38
  companion plants for, 38, 39
  growing, 21
  harvesting tips, 202
  hot weather varieties, 54
  and kohlrabi, 102
  nutritional properties, 21
  salt for, 21
  varieties, 37
Begonias, 153, 160
Bells-of-Ireland (*Molucella laevis*), 21
Bergamot, essential oil of, 59
Berries, 12, 122
Biological control,
  of aphids, 7
  bluejays, 24
  for cabbage worms, 25
  insects for, 21–22
  predators for, 7
  see also Insecticides, natural
Birds,
  and blueberries, 23
  and gardens, 22
  and leaf growth, 22
  and plant pest seeds, 133
  plants for attracting, 12–13, 37
  shelter for, 12, 13
  as weather instruments, 183
  see also specific kinds
Bird's nest fern (*Asplenium nidusavis*), description, 198
Black acacia (*Acacia melanoxylon*), 133
Blackberries, 19, 38
Blackbirds, protecting corn from, 22–23
Black-eyed pea, varieties, 37, 202–203
Black-eyed susan vine (*Thunbergia* sp.), for fences, 208
Black flea beetles, repelled by mint, 39
Blackthorn, apple and, 38
Black walnut, and companion plants, 38
Blanching, 33, 71
Bleach,
  for algae control, 41
  for iris root rot, 94
  used in pruning, 64
Bleeding heart (*Dicentra spectabilis*), 187
  see also Dutchman's-breeches
Blight, on tomatoes and potatoes, 40
Blood,
  in amaranth cakes, 7
  celery for, 33–34
  and okra, 123
Blood meal, 41, 57
Blood purifiers, 23
Blossom-end rot, 23, 116
Blueberries, 23, 202

Bluebonnets (*Lupinus texensis*), germination, 23–24
Blue gum (*Eucalyptus globulus*), 133
Bluejays, 12, 24
Bobolinks, 13
Boiling, to prevent botulism, 24
Bok choy, qualities of, 124
Bolting,
  in cabbages, 28
  in Chinese cabbage, 35
  and day length, 132
  in lettuce, 106
Boneset, healthful benefits, 82
Borage, 19, 24, 37
Border plants,
  catnip, 39
  landscaping with, 176–177
  lemon thyme, 105
  marigolds, 14
  milkweed, 113
  monkey grass, 114
  wormwood, 40
  yarrow, 40
Borers, 16, 20
Botulism, from home canning, 24
Box elder (*Acer negundo*), maple syrup from, 111
Box turtle, 25
Brain function,
  beets for, 21
  chocolate in, 29
Broccoli (*Brassica oleracea*), 25, 27, 132, 159, 169
  in fall planting, 61
  grown at altitude, 86
  harvesting tips, 202
  hot weather varieties, 54
Broconid wasp, in aphid control, 7
Bromelain, 25
Bromeliads (*Bromeliaceae*), 25
Brooms, from broomcorn, 111
Broomsedge, 36
Brown thrashers, 13
Brush clearing,
  for chigger control, 35
  for fire control, 62
Brussels sprouts (*Brassica oleracea*), 25, 27, 159, 169
  in fall planting, 61
  grown at altitude, 86
  harvesting, 25, 202
  hot weather tips, 54
  varieties, 37
Buckwheat, 189
Budding, and dormant oil spray, 7
Bud moth, and frost, 71
Buds, and pinching, 132
Bulbs,
  delayed planting tips, 95
  of desert lily ajo, 48
  insecticidal properties of, 9
  and mulches, 25
  for naturalizing, 68

Bunching Onion (*He-Shi-Ko*), qualities of, 124–125
Burbank, Luther, 28
Burdock, healthful benefits, 82
Burnet (*Poterium sanguisorba*), 25–26, 82
Burns,
  houseleek for, 182
  lavender oil for, 59
Buttercups (*Ranunculus*), 26, 38
Butterflies, 26–27
  and milkweed, 113
  as pollinators, 20
Butterfly bush (*Buddleia davidii*), 26
Butterfly gardening, 26–27
Butterfly weed (*Asclepias tuberosa*), 26

C
Cabbage (*Brassica oleracea*), 27, 159, 169
  bolting, 28
  companion plants for, 38, 39, 40
  in fall planting, 61
  harvesting, 28, 202
  history, 28
  hot weather tips, 54
  for landscaping, 176
  splitting, 28
  in succession planting, 2
  varieties, 37
Cabbage moth, 38, 39, 40
Cabbage worm, 25, 28, 38, 40
Cabbage worm butterfly, 27, 39
Cactus, 28–29
Cages, for tomatoes, 167–168
Caladium, 101
Calcium deficiency, lime for, 23
Calcium oxalate, in houseplants, 101
Calendula, 176
Camellias, vinegar for, 106
Camphor creeper, for fences, 207
Cancer,
  and rape, 143
  and sunlight, 53
  and vinca, 178
Canes, propagation of, 200–201
Canna (*Canna × generalis*), 30
Canning, 202
  botulism poisoning from, 24
  fruits and vegetables, 2
  tips for, 195
Canola oil, and rape, 143
Cantaloupes (*Cucumis melo*), 30, 160, 206
Caraway, 16, 38
Carbohydrates, and flowering, 132
Cardamoms, in cooking, 8
Cardinal, 12, 13
Cardinal flower (*Lobelia cardinalis*), 161

Cardoon (*Cynara cardunculus*), 30
Carnation, 20, 21, 70, 74
Carob (*Ceratonia siliqua*), 20, 29–30
Carolina jasmine (*Gelsemium* sp.), 171
Carpenter Bees (*Xylocopa*), 30–31
Carrageenan, in irish moss, 94
Carrot fly, deterred by rosemary, 40
Carrots (*Carota*), 159
  as aphrodisiac, 8
  with beans, 38
  carotinemia from, 31
  in companion planting, 38, 39, 40
  cooking, 31
  culture, 31
  grown at altitude, 86
  harvesting, 31, 202
  insect control with, 39
  juice, 31
  for skin care, 60
  storage, 31–32
  varieties, 37
Castor beans, 48, 113–114
Catalogs, understanding, 32
Catchfly (*Silene mutans*), 178
Catclaw acacia (*Acacia greggii*), as food, 49
Caterpillars, 27, 90, 108, 139, 156
Catnip (*Nepeta cataria*), 32, 39, 83 184
Catnip, lemon, 105
Cats,
  diseases from, 169
  and flea control, 69
  and pregnant women, 169
  and rue, 83
  and toxic plants, 101
Cattails, 36
Cauliflower (*Brassica oleracea*), 159, 169
  blanching, 33
  companion plants for, 38, 39
  culture, 32–33, 158
  grown at altitude, 86
  harvesting tips, 202
Cecropia moth (*Hyalophora cecropia*), 33
Celeriac (*Apium graveolens*), 33, 54, 159, 204
Celery (*Apium graveolens*), 159
  as aphrodisiac, 8
  blanching, 33
  companion plants for, 38, 39
  culture, 33
  growing from starts, 34
  harvesting tips, 204
  hot weather varieties, 54
  light for seeds, 160
  nutritional qualities, 33
Chamise (*Adenostoma fasiculatum*), in fire control, 62
Chamomile, 84, 189

companion plants for, 38, 39
essential oil of, 59
and fleas, 178
healthful benefits, 82
medicinal properties, 20
revives sick plants, 39
for skin care, 60
Chaparral (soft), chemical defenses of, 34
Chard, 54, 159
Chemical defenses, of plants, 34, 38, 134
Chemotherapy, natural substances for, 9
Cherry, 12, 20, 87
Chervil, companion plants for, 39
Chickens, 34–35, 45
Chickweed, healthful benefits, 82
Chicory, 37
  see also Endive
Chigger (*Trombidiidae alfreddugesi*), 35
Chinampas, 13
Chinch-bug, and floratam grass, 66
Chinese cabbage, 35
Chinese parsley (Yuen shai), qualities of, 125
Chive (*Allium Schoenoprasum*), 84, 159, 188
  companion plants for, 38, 39
  culture, 35
  earthworms for, 35
  varieties, 37
Chlorosis, and iron, 171
Chocolate flower (*Berlandiera lyrata*), 30
Chocolate (*Theobroma*), 29–30
Cholesterol, 18, 29, 104, 143
Christmas trees, living, 108
Christmas wreathes, 35–36, 172
Chrysanthemums, 36, 70, 133, 176
Cigarette ash, for compost, 88
Cigarette smoke, as insecticide, 88
Cilantro (Chinese parsley), 125
Cinnamon, in cooking, 8
Cinnamon basil, 84
City water, and houseplants, 6
Clay soil, 31, 52
Cleavers, *see* Bedstraw
Clematis, 26, 177, 201
Climate, 10, 13
Climbing hydrangea, *see* Hydrangea, climbing
Climbing plants, 206–208
  landscaping with, 176–177
  tips for supports, 177
  varieties, 177, 206–208
Climbing support,
  A-Frames, 5
  for asparagus beans, 11
  cornstalks for peas, 23
  for cucumbers, 43

fences, 206–208
  for hops, 87
  old bed springs, 21
  plastic can holders, 20
Cloches (row covers), 42
Clones, alternatives to, 200
Clothes, for gardening, 53
Clouds, 182, 184
Cloudy weather, problems from, 120
Clover, companion plants for, 38, 39
Codling moth, 16, 20, 170
  see also Apples; Insecticides, natural
Coffee,
  for compost, 88
  dandelion substitute for, 47
  as soil conditioner, 52
Cold frames, 41, 42, 44
Coleus (*Coleus*), 36, 153, 176
Colewort, 36
Collard greens, 36
Collodium, 42
Colorado potato beetles, *see* Potato beetles
Columbine, companion plants for, 38
Comfrey (*Symphytum officinale*), 82, 189, 191
Common reed (*Phragmites communis*), uses for, 48
Companion planting, 38–40, 113
  corn and peas, 23
  and cuttings, 146
  doubling up, 52
  Indian methods, 92
  and landscaping, 176–177
  and mulch, 2, 52
  on trellises, 40
  with zig-zag rows, 197
Compost, 130
  activators for, 41
  air and water for, 94
  applying, 56–57
  for asparagus, 10
  for broccoli, 25
  and cats, 169
  and crop rotation, 43
  and crown rot, 116
  for desert gardens, 48
  efficient use of, 3
  in fall, 61
  from bark, 21
  and humus, 89
  for indoor gardeners, 88–89
  and lawn mowers, 209
  and leaf mold, 104
  materials for, 52–53
  and no-dig gardening, 120
  placement of compost piles, 140
  preparing, 56–57
  in raised bed gardens, 50
  and snakes, 156
  and succession planting, 159
  see also Manure; Mulch; Organic matter
Conifers, 12, 36
Container plants,
  chinese parsley, 125
  Christmas trees, 108

composted bark for, 21
culture, large varieties, 163
devil's-backbone, 49
fatsia, 61
hanging baskets, 81
ice cubes for, 90
most fragrant, 70–71
ponderosa lemon, 20
pseudo-palms, 137
rhododendron, 21
swiss chard, 162
and transplants, 169–170
and vacations, 175
and windowboxes, 189
Contour planting, for sloping ground, 10
Cooking, 8–9, 84, 85
  see also Recipes
Cool weather crops,
  and aphid control, 7
  fall planting, 61
  and fog, 68
  and fruit set, 164
  garland chrysanthemum, 124
  grown on A-Frames, 5
  spinach, 157
  turnips, 172
Coral vine, 177
Coriander (Chinese parsley), 38, 39, 125
Corn, 160
  attracting songbirds with, 12, 37
  and Bacillus thurigienesis, 155
  with beans and squash, 18, 92
  brooms from, 111
  in companion planting, 38, 39, 40
  and crows, 22, 134
  growing, 41
  grown at altitude, 86
  grown by Aztecs, 13
  harvesting and cooking, 41, 160
  hot weather tips, 54
  Indian, 92
  and Japanese beetles, 98
  medicinal properties, 41
  for northern climates, 41, 129
  nutritional qualities, 41
  pollination by wind, 134
  popcorn, 37, 134–135
  preparation for freezing, 71
  protecting from blackbirds, 22–23
  and raccoons, 142–143
  and squash, 184
  sweet, 159
  and tomatoes, 24–25, 39
  varieties, 41
Corn earworm, 39, 41, 108, 155
Cornfield ant, 7–8
Corn leaf aphids, predators for, 7
Corn plant (*Dracaena fragrans massangeana*), 163
Corn root aphid, control of, 7–8

Corn salad (*Valerianella olitoria*), 41
Corn smut, 41, 42
Cosmetics, 60
  see also Beauty aids; Skin care
Cosmos, 39, 98
Cotton (*Gossypium herbaceum*), 42, 109
Couch grass (*Agropyrum repens*), 178, 193
Cowpeas (*Vigna siensis* cvs.), 42–43
Coyote bush (*Baccharis pilularis*), in fire control, 62
Crabgrass, edible seeds of, 42
Cream peas, *see* Cowpeas
Cress, culture, 43
Crested pricklepoppy (*Argemone platyceras*), narcotic in, 48
Crickets, as weather instruments, 183
Crop rotation, 7–8, 43, 50
Crown rot, 116, 145
  and mulch, 116
  and rhubarb, 145
Crows, and corn, 134
Cucumber beetles, 40, 44, 179
Cucumbers, 34, 159, 160
  in companion planting, 38, 39, 40
  culture, 43
  on fences, 206, 207
  flowers, cooking, 138
  grown at altitude, 86
  gynoecious varieties, 80
  harvesting tips, 202
  hot weather varieties, 54
  for landscaping, 176
  restoring bitter cukes, 43–44
  for skin care, 60, 191
  straight growing, 5
  trained on A-Frames, 5
  varieties, 43
Cultivation,
  for aphid control, 7
  of celery, 33
  for cornfield ant, 7–8
  and mulch, 48
  and rain, 185
  and roots, 51
  and weeds, 185
  and wet soil, 51
Cup-and-saucer-vine (*Cobaea scandens*), 207
Curculios, and horseradish, 39
Curled dock (*Rumex crispus*), 185
Cut flowers, 44, 157, 166, 178
Cuttings,
  and air layering, 200
  chrysanthemum, 36
  and companion plants, 146
  from roses, 147
  for geraniums, 76
  for propagation, 44
  techniques for, 44
  tips for rooting, 146

Cutworms, 22, 44–45, 58, 67
Cyanide, in apricot seeds, 9
Cycads, *see* Pseudo-Palms

D

Daddy Longlegs (*Arachnida*), 46
Daffodils, and walnuts, 38
Damiana (*Damiana aphrodisiaca*), 46
Damping off, 39, 46, 116, 128
Dandelion (*Taraxacum officinale*), 47, 181
Datura (*Datura stramonium*), 39, 40, 47
Daylily, 38, 70, 138, 184
Deer, controls and deterrents, 48
Deer's tongue, properties of, 48
Deet, in mosquito repellents, 115
Delphiniums, 26, 38
Desert gardening, 48
  plants for, 48–49, 79–80, 121, 149
  see also Hot climate plants
Desert lily ajo (*Hesperocallis undulata*), bulbs of, 48
Desert sage (*Salvia*), as food, 49
Devil's-backbone (*Pedilanthus tithymaloides*), 49
Devil's claws (*Proboscidea*), as food, 49
Diatomaceous earth, 35, 64
Diffenbachia, 101
Dill (*Anethum graveolens*), 16, 49, 84
  companion plants for, 38, 39, 40
Dioon (*Dioon edule*), 137
Disabled gardeners, *see* Housebound
Disease,
  from chiggers, 35
  prevention of, 50
Diseases,
  and crop rotation, 50
  crown-rot, 116
  fall plowing for, 61
  fire blight, 64
  red stele, 21
  reduced by bark, 21
  root-knot, 21
  and ticks, 165
Dittany, American (*Cunila mariana*), 50–51
Dog food, as compost activator, 41
Dogs,
  and anise, 178
  control for, 50
  and couch grass, 178
  and flea control, 69
  garden damage from, 50
  and garlic, 76
  and hush puppies, 89
  manure from, 111
Dogwood, 12, 13
Dolomite, properties of, 51
Dormancy, plants and, 51–52
Dormant oil, 7, 33, 140

Dowsing, 188, 190
Dracaena (*Dracaena dermensis Warneckei*), 172
Dragonfly (*Odonata*), 52
Dragon tree (*Dracaena draco*), 163
Drainage,
  and chlorosis, 171
  "good" vs."bad," 52–53
Drip irrigation, 53
Drought,
  blossom-end rot and, 23
  vegetables resistant to, 53–55
  and xerophytes, 192
  see also Desert gardening; Mulch; Water
Dutchman's-breeches (*Dicentra Cucullaria*), 55
Dutchman's pipe (*Aristolochia durior*), 207
Dwarf varieties, 9, 32, 55

E

Earthworms, 35, 57
Eastern bluebird, 12
Eastern states, cecropia moth and, 33
Edelweiss (*Leontopodium*), 57
Eggplant (*Solanum Melongena*), 160, 164, 169
  companion plants for, 39, 40
  culture, 57–58
  and flour of sulfur, 67
  harvesting tips, 204
  history, 57
  hot weather varieties, 54
  for landscaping, 176
  varieties, 37
Eggs, for skin care, 60
Eggshells, for compost, 88
Egyptian onion (*Allium cepa*), 58
Elderberry (*Sambucus nigra*), 58, 82
Elder flowers, in herbal baths, 21
Electroculture, for gardens, 107
Endive (*Cichorium Endivia*), 58, 159, 204
Epsom salt, for growing peppers, 131
Escarole, *see* Endive
Essential oils, 21, 39, 40, 58–59
Ethylene gas, and fruit ripening, 145
Eucalyptus, 21, 62
Eupatorium, Japanese beetles and, 98
Evening primrose (*Oenothers*), 49
Evergreens, 34, 59, 61, 179
Eyebright, 82
Eyes,
  fennel for, 66–67
  remedies for, 59, 82

F

Facial masks, 60

see also Beauty aids; Skin care
Fall,
  flowers of, 11
  gardening in, 61
  kale, 100
  predator inactivity in, 7
  for tree transplants, 170
Fatsia (*Fatsia japonica*), culture, 61
Feeders, for butterflies, 27
Feet, tired, remedies for, 61–62
Fences,
  of corn, 37
  for deer, 48
  for dogs, 50
  good uses for, 206–208
  for increased productivity, 2
  plants for, 174
  for pole beans, 18
  and tomatoes, 134
  for turtles, 25
  for utility areas, 174
  vegetables for, 206–208
Fennel, 38, 39, 59
Ferns, 62–63, 164–165, 198
  and weeds, 184
Fertilizer,
  amounts to use, 51
  banana peels as, 16
  and blueberry hybrids, 23
  and cabbages, 28
  for cauliflower, 33
  from rabbits, 142
  for giant vegetables, 155
  rock phosphate, 132
  superphosphate, 132
Feverfew, 184
Figs (*Ficus* spp.), 63
  to remove warts, 182
Fire,
  defenses against, 62
  from lightning, 107
  pine cones for, 65
Fire ants (*Solenopsis invicta*), 63–64, 108
Fire blight, 64, 140
Fireflies (*Lampyridae*), 45, 65
Fish, 65–66
Fishtail palm (*Caryota mitis*), 163
Flame bottle tree (*Brachychiton acerifolius*), 66
Flats, sterilizing, 119
Flax, companion plants for, 39
Flea beetles, on eggplant, 58
Fleas, 69, 76, 178
Flies, 22
Floral oils, 21
  see also Essential oils
Floratam grass, and chinch-bug, 66
Florence Fennel (*Foeniculum vulgare*), 66–67
Flour of sulfur, and potatoes, 67
Flowering,
  and carbohydrates, 132
  and day length, 132
  and light color, 60
  and pinching, 132

warmth for, 23
Flowering rush (*Butomus umbellatus*), 162
Flowers,
  artificial pollination of, 20
  for attracting songbirds, 12
  best times for, 166
  for the blind, 69–70
  bulbs, 9, 25, 48, 68, 95
  for butterflies, 26
  candied, 24
  edible, 37, 74, 78, 138
  fragrant, 69–71
  in herbal baths, 20–21
  and herbs, 85
  for hummingbirds, 11
  for insect control, 176–177
  language of bouquets, 67–68
  male and female, 51
  night blooming, 109
  purple and red, 37–38
  and Queen Victoria, 177–178
  and scatter-planting, 150
  and vinegar, 178
  see also specific kinds, i.e., African violet
Fog, vegetables for, 68
Foliage, iron sulfate for, 68–69
Forget-me-not (*Myosotis scorpioides*), 162
Forsythia, nematodes and, 21
Foundation plantings, 93–94
Fountain grass (*Pennisetum setaceum*), 133
Four-leaf pine (*Pinus quadrifolia*), 121
Four-O'Clock (*Mirabilis Jalapa*), 69
Foxglove (*Digitalis*), 9, 48, 178
Fragrance, best flowers for, 69–71
Freezing, 71, 202
  herbs, 83
  for primrose seeds, 136
French broom (*Cytisus monspeculanus*), 133
Frogs, indicating rain, 184
Frost,
  Brassicas hardy in, 25
  and bud moth, 71
  and corn, 41
  curtails blooming, 11
  and fresh greens, 42
  and garden huckleberries, 75
  and geraniums, 76
  guarding for, 71–72
  mulching bulbs for, 25
  protection against, 190
  and river vapor, 184
  salt remedy for, 72
  and tomatoes, 61
Frost protection, in covered A-Frames, 5
Fructose, 72
Fruit,
  aids to ripening, 145
  and boiling water, 129
  drying in cars, 170
  failure to set, 164

and flour of sulfur, 67
freezing and preserving, 71
from artificial pollination,
20
fructose in, 72
gathered wild for jam, 97
improved by pruning, 9
and mulch, 48, 116
propagation by air layering,
200–202
thinning, 165
to remove warts, 181
on vines, 179
see also specific kinds, i.e.,
Apple
Fruit drop, 72
Fruit fly, 20
Fruit trees,
and carrots, 39
chives for, 39
dormant oil for aphids, 7
dwarf varieties, 55, 165
espaliered, 72
garlic plantings for, 16
ground oystershell for, 9
and horseradish, 39
insect barriers for, 93
insect control for, 9
landscaping with, 176–177
and mice, 112
and nasturtiums, 39, 118
pollination of, 51
and tansy, 40
and tent caterpillars, 164
thinning, 165
tips for, 72
see also Apple; Apricot;
Peach; Pear
Fuchsia (*Fuchsia*), varieties,
72
Fungicides, 7, 39
Fungus, 41, 136

G

Garbage, for compost, 75
Garden huckleberries
(*Solanum
melanocerasum*), 75–76
Gardenias, 70, 74
Gardens,
arrangements for, 10
benefits of weeds in,
209–210
best watering times, 182
and birds, 22
and butterflies, 26–27
and cats, 169
choosing site for, 51
crop rotation in, 50
in deserts, 48–49
determining profile of, 32
for herbs, 85
improving fertility of, 130
and lightning, 107
raised bed, 143
and scatter-planting, 150
size of, 186
and snakes, 156
in summer, 160
sunlight maps, 111
and vacations, 175
and water rationing, 183
Garland chrysanthemum
(*Shinjuku*), 124

Garlic,
as baldness remedy, 15
in companion planting, 38
companion plants for, 38,
39
for cucumber diseases, 44
for gophers, 78
harvesting tips, 202
healthful benefits, 82
hot weather tips, 54
and pets, 76
as soil test, 156
starts from supermarkets, 16
for tired feet, 61–62
Gazania, *see* Treasure flower
Genetic diversity, and gene
banks, 109
Geranium (*Pelargonium*
spp.), 84, 159, 177
and frost, 76
lemon, 105
lifting in fall, 151
overwintering, 76
qualities of, 69
Geraniums, scented
(*Pelargonium* spp.),
150–151
Gerbera, 160
Germination,
days to maturity and, 32
and light for seeds, 160
and lunar cycles, 114
for lupines, 23–24
and seed storage, 153
tips for, 151–152
Giant Onion (*Allium
giganteum*), 76, 77
Giant reed (*Arundo Donax*),
162
Gibbons, Euell, 187
Ginger (*Zingiberaceae
officinale*), 8, 16, 77
Gladiolus, 38, 39, 77
Glaucoma, coleus for, 36
Globe thistle (*Echinops* spp.),
26
Gloxinia (*Sinningia speciosa*),
77–78
Goat horn peppers, qualities
of, 125
Gobernadora (*Larrea
mexicana*), 78
Goldfinches, 13
Good Housewife's Jewelle
(book), 66
Goosefoot, *see*
Lamb's-quarters
Gophers, repellents for, 78
Gorse, 133
Gourds (*Lagenaria leucantha*),
73
Gow choy, 37
Grafting, for fruit trees, 72
Grains, 7, 12, 13, 18
Grapes (*Vitis aestivalis*), 71,
78, 136
Grass, 36
floratam grass, 66
indicating soil quality, 51
and lawns, 103
light for seeds, 160
ornamental, 125
substitutes, moss sandwort,
115

sugar cane, 159–160
varieties, 37, 125
zoysia, 198
Grass clippings, 116
Grass cutting, for chigger
control, 35
Grasshopper, 22
Grassland, chaparral and, 34
Gray water, cautions for
using, 78–79
Green Amaranth
(*Amaranthus
retroflexus*), 186
Greenaway, Kate, 66
Greenbelt, for fire control, 62
Greenfly, 40, 139
Greenhouses,
aspects of, 79
bottles and jugs as, 24
for corn, 41
and cuttings, 44
of plastic bags, 87
plastic baskets as, 22
for seedlings, 149
soil sterilization for, 119
Green manure, varieties, 79
Greens,
cloches for, 42
fall planting, 61
from windowboxes, 189
using weeds for, 185–186
see also specific kinds
Ground cherry (*Physalis
pruinosa*), 79, 167
Groundcovers,
and fire control, 62
for hot weather, 160
ivy, 95
lamb's-quarters, 39
monkey grass, 114
for ponds, 162
purslane, 40
vinca, 178
and weeds, 184
Ground layering, alternatives
to, 6–7
Growth hormone, wheat
used as, 79
Growth, of plants, and light,
60
Grubworms, and june
beetles, 99
Guayule (*Parthenium
argentatum*), 79–80
Gypsies, 5, 9

H

Hail, seedling covers for, 22
Hair conditioner, 20, 48
Hanging baskets,
impatiens for, 90
strawberries for, 176
tips for, 81
tomatoes for, 176
watering tips, 175–176, 182
Hardening off, suggestions
for, 160
Harvesting, 51
spray intervals and, 7
timing for, 166
tips for, 202–206
Harvest mite, *see* Chigger
Hawthorn, 19
Hay, 52, 81–82, 184

Hayfever, and honey, 86
Hayscented fern
(*Dennstaedtia
punctilobula*), 198
Headache remedy, 20, 32
Heart,
foods for, 125
oatmeal for, 122–123
and sugar, 159–160
Heartsease, 82
Heath, for bees, 20
Heather, 20, 106
Hedges, 104, 166, 174
Heeling in, 82
Hemp, grown by Aztecs, 13
Henbane, companion plants
for, 39
Herbal baths, 20–21
Herbal oil, preparation and
use, 85
Herbal tea, preparation, 84
Herb gardens, and strawberry
jars, 159
Herbs,
for bees, 19–20
for cooking, 84
and flowers, 85
freezing, 83
gifts of, 83
growing from seed, 84
in homemade incense,
131–132
light for seeds, 160
most fragrant, 69–70
preserving in oil, 85
propagation by air layering,
200–202
purple and red, 37–38
as salt substitutes, 154
for sunscreen, 83–84
for tea, 84
and weeds, 184
see also specific kinds, i.e.,
Anise
High altitude gardening,
85–86
Hoes, 208–209
Hogs, for cutworm control,
45
Holly, male and female, 51
Honey, 7, 8, 19, 20, 27, 60,
72, 86, 93, 171
Honeydew, and aphids, 8
Honeysuckle (*Lonicera* spp.),
12, 13, 86, 201
Hops (*Humulus*), culture, 87
Hormones,
in essential oils, 58–59
insect, and trees, 34
for plant growth, 79
Hornets, and bees, 19
Horseradish, 39, 40, 87, 204
Horsetail, as fungicide, 39
Hose, 160, 166
Hose, garden, uses for, 75
Hot climate plants,
annual flowers, 88
canna, 30
carob, 29–30
for fire control, 62
gazanias, 160
groundcovers, 160
guayule, 79–80
malabar spinach, 111

nandina, 118
New Zealand spinach, 119–120
okra, 122–123
pine, 121
saw palmetto, 149
summer squash, 158
swiss chard, 162
treasure flower, 170
see also Desert gardening; Southwestern
Hot peppers, preparation, 87–88
Housebound,
bee and butterfly feeders for, 19
butterfly gardens for, 26
hummingbirds for, 11
raised beds for, 50
terrariums for, 164–165
Houseleek (*Sempervivum tectorum*), 182
Houseplants,
benefits of, 94
culture, large varieties, 163
and day length, 132
distilled water for, 182
growing from seed, 6
ice cubes for, 90
important points for, 100–101
most fragrant, 70–71
and music, 88–89
and pollution, 88
preparation for winter, 88
tips for, 175–176, 182
and vacations, 175
and windowboxes, 188–189
in winter, 189
Hoyas, culture, 71
Huckleberries, and air layering, 202
Humidity, 6, 7, 101
Hummingbirds, 11–12
Hummingbird trumpet (*Zauschneria latifolia*), 11
Humus, 23, 31, 57, 89
Hunzas, and apricot oil, 9
Hush puppies, recipes for, 89
Husk tomatoes, *see* Ground cherry
Hydrangea, climbing (*Hydrangea anomala*), 179
Hyssop, companion plants for, 40

I
Iceland moss (*Cetraria islandica*), 90
Immortelle, 192
Impatiens (*Impatiens*), 90, 153
Impetigo plant, *see* Four-O'Clock
Incense, recipes for, 131–132
Incienso (*Encelia jarinosa*), uses of, 49
Indian corn, 92
Indian laurel (*Ficus retusa nitida*), 163
Indian paintbrush (*Castilleja integra*), 11
Indian recipes, 91–92

Indians,
datura and, 47
and milkweed, 113
native plants and, 48–49
and nut pine, 120
and wild lettuce, 187
India rubber plant (*Ficus elastica 'Decora'*), 163
Indoor plants, *see* Houseplants
Industrial wastes, garden sites and, 51
Infusions, 20, 32, 49, 83
Insecticides, 7, 86
see also Pesticides
Insecticides, natural,
Bacillus thuringiensis, 118
bay leaves, 43
for cabbage worms, 28
citrus limonoids, 107
cucumbers, 43
elderberry, 58
fermented carbohydrates, 20
garlic, 16, 39
ground oystershell, 9
herbal repellents, 83
Iceland moss, 90
Irish moss, 94
jalapeño peppers, 97
marigolds, 34, 39
milkweed, 113
molasses, 170
oregano, 124
primrose, 9
quassia, 139
soap and water, 36
sumac leaves, 9
wood ashes, 190
Insects,
ants, 7–10, 19, 39, 40
aphids, 7–9, 22, 39, 46, 58, 64, 71, 103, 123, 139
apple scab, 39
apple worm, 170
armyworm, 108
asparagus beetle, 40
bean beetles, 39, 40, 112
bees, 19–20, 37, 51, 64, 76, 86, 139, 182
beetles, 22, 64, 108
in biological control, 21–22
and biological control of, 7, 9
black flea beetles, 39
bluejays and, 24
borers, 16, 20
bud moth, 71
butterflies, 20, 26–27, 113
cabbage worm, 25, 28, 38, 40
cabbage worm butterfly, 27, 39
carpenter bees, 30–31
carrot fly, 40
caterpillars, 27, 90, 105, 108, 139, 156
cecropia moth, 33
chiggers, 35
chinch-bug, 66
clothes for, 53
codling moth, 16, 20, 170
corn earworm, 39, 41, 108, 155

cutworms, 22, 44–45, 58, 67
daddy longlegs, 46
destroyed by bats, 16
eaten by armadillos, 9–10
evaluating damage from, 120
fall plowing for, 61
fire ants, 63–64, 108
fireflies, 45, 65
and flour of sulfur, 67
and giant vegetables, 155
grease barriers for, 93
herbal repellents for, 83
and hummingbirds, 11
inhibited by herbs, 38
inspecting for, 36
June beetles, 99
life cycles of, 9
and lizards, 108
mealy bugs, 36, 139
mites, 46
nematodes, 21, 34, 119, 128
overwintering, 7
and plant defenses, 34
and plant pheromones, 133–134
as pollinators, 20
predatory, 7
red-banded leaf roller, 9
repelled by garlic, 16
and soil pasteurization, 128
and songbirds, 12
sting treatment, 76
trap crops for, 25
traps for, 27
and turtles, 25
wasps, 7, 20, 22, 112, 136
see also specific insects, i.e., Aphids
Insomnia, 32, 93
Intercropping, zig-zag, 197
Interplanting, 2–3
see also Companion planting
Irish moss, healthful benefits, 94
Iris (*Iris*), 38, 94, 184
Iris, Variegata (*Iris pallida*), 176
Iron, 23
in apricot, 9
in cantaloupes, 30
in celery, 34
and chlorosis, 171
in figs, 63
from beans, 18
in peas, 18
in spinach, 8
Iron sulfate, as soil conditioner, 68–69
Ivy, 95, 201

J
Jalapeño (*Capsicum annuum*), 96–97
Jam, from wild fruit, 97
Japanese beetles, 39, 40
controls for, 97
flowers immune to, 97
and vegetables, 97–98
Japanese black pine, 98
Japanese iris, 162
Japanese radish (daikon), 124

Japanese river fever, from chiggers, 35
Japanese turnip, 125
Jasmine, essential oil of, 59
Jasmine, Night Blooming, 70–71
Jasmine, yellow, 177
Jekyll, Gertrude, 62
Jerusalem artichokes, 16, 55
Jewel weed (*Impatiens aurea*), 182
see also Impatiens
Jicama, 37
culture, 98
hot weather tips, 54–55
toxicity of seeds, 98
Jimson weed, *see* Datura
John the Baptist, and carob, 29
Jojoba (*Simmondsia Chinensis*), 98–99
Joshua tree (*Yucca brevifolia*), 48
Junco, 12, 13
June beetles, 99
June drop, 72
Juniper berry (*Juniperus communis*), 59, 99

K
Kale, 36, 37, 100, 205
Kava-kava (*Piper methysticum*), 100
Kawain, 100
Kelp (*Fucus vesiculosus*), 15, 71–72,191
Kenaf (*Hibiscus cannabinus*), 101–102
Kenilworth ivy (*Cymbalaria muralis*), 102
Kentia palm (*Howeia belmoreana*), 163
Kerosene, for tent caterpillars, 164
Killer bees, benefits of, 19
Kiwi fruit (*Actinidia chinensis*), 102
Kohlrabi (*Brassica oleracea caulorapa*), 159
and beets, 102
and celeriac, 33
companion plants for, 40
cooking, 102, 205
culture, 102
description, 102
and fennel, 38
harvesting tips, 205
varieties, 37

L
Labor saving tips, 13, 208–210
Lacewing larva, 22
Lacewings, 7, 35, 103, 144
Lady bugs, 7, 22 123, 139, 144
Lady fern (*Athyrium filix-femina*), 198
Lady's mantle, healthful benefits of, 82
Laetrile (vitamin B-17), from apricot, 9
Lamb's lettuce, *see* Corn salad

Lamb's-quarters
(*Chenopodium album*),
39, 103, 185
Land, idle, 51
Landscaping,
to attract songbirds, 12–13
for utility areas, 174
with vegetables, 176–177
Language of Flowers, 66
Larkspur, and Japanese
beetle, 39
Lasers, and plant growth,
60–61
Laurel, vinegar for, 106
Laurel, common (*Kalmia
latifolia*), 50
Lavender, 20, 21, 84, 159
for bees, 19
companion plants for, 38
essential oil of, 59
qualities of, 70
Lavender Vera, 37
Lawn mowers, and compost,
209
Lawns,
characteristics of, 174
grass seed varieties, 103
and june beetles, 99
mowing tips, 116
and plugs, 103
preparation and care,
103–104
and sod, 104
and sprigs, 103
terms and definitions,
103–104
and vacations, 175
Layering, techniques for,
200–202
Lead, in garden vegetables,
104
Leaf bud, cuttings from, 117
Leaf-cutter bees, *see*
Carpenter bees
Leafhopper, and quassia, 139
Leafing, dormant oil spray
before, 7
Leaf miners, and
lamb's-quarters, 103
Leaf mold, and compost, 104
Leaves,
in compost, 41, 56
cuttings from, 117
and insect damage, 120
and slugs, 155
Lecithin, 104
Leeks (*Allium porrum*), 159
companion plants for, 38,
39
culture, 104
harvesting tips, 205
qualities of, 104
using supermarket starts, 16
Lemon balm, 84, 105
Lemon basil, 105
Lemon catnip, 105
Lemon fragrance, plants
with, 105
Lemon juice, for skin care, 20
Lemon verbena (*Aloysia
triphylla*), 188
Lentils (*Lens esculenta*),
105–106

Lettuce (*Lactuca sativa*), 132,
159, 177, 184, 189
in companion planting, 38,
39, 40
companion to *Brassicas*, 2
companion to onions, 2–3
culture, 106
grown at altitude, 85–86
healthful benefits, 106
hot weather varieties, 54
and northern states, 120
seeds need light, 160
starting seeds, 106
in succession planting, 2
tips for bolting, 106
varieties, 37, 106
Lettuce, wild, *see* Wild
lettuce
Licorice (*Glycyrrhiza glabra*),
106–107
Life-everlasting (*Anaphalis
margaritaceae*), 83
Light,
at night, 52
for houseplants, 100
improving fruit quality, 9
and plant growth, 60,
60–61
for seed germination, 160
Lightning, as farm hazard,
107
Lily family (*Amaryllidaceae*),
13
Lima beans, 40, 159, 160, 206
Lime, 20, 23, 51, 58
Lime (hydrated), for
cucumber beetles, 44
Linden blossom, 20
Linnaeus, 13, 29
Living stones (*Lithops*), 108
Lizards, 108, 125
Loganberries (*Rubus
loganobaccus*), 108
Lollipop plant (*Pachystachys
lutea*), 108–109
Long-light days, plant
growth and, 52
Loosestrife, healthful
benefits, 82
Lovage, 39, 66, 82
Luffa (*Luffa cylindrica*), 109
Luna moth, as pollinator, 109
Lunar cycles, 15, 18, 114
see also Moon
Lunar signs, and tomatoes,
167
Lupines, bluebonnets, 23–24

M
Magnolia (*Magnoliaceae*), 110
Magnolia, Southern, 105
Maidenhair fern (*Adiantum
pedatum*), 62, 110–111,
164
Malabar spinach (*Basella
alba*), 111
Mallow, and okra, 123
Manure,
for asparagus, 10
as compost activator, 41
and crown rot, 116
from dogs, 111
for heavy feeders, 159
and plant contact, 51

rabbit, 142
as soil conditioner, 52
Maple, big tooth (*Acer
grandidentatum*), 111
Maple syrup, 72, 111
Marigolds, 176, 184
and bean beetles, 112
companion plants for, 39,
40
growing, 14
and Japanese beetles, 98
for nematode control, 34,
119
origins of, 14
qualities of, 70
triploid, 170
varieties and uses, 14
Marjoram, 19, 20, 84
companion plants for, 39
sweet, 189
Markers, garden, 111–112
Marsh mallow (*Althaea
officinalis*), 112
Marsh marigold (*Caltha
paulustris*), 161
Marvel-of-Peru, *see*
Four-O'Clock
Mathematical relationships,
in nature, 118
Meadowlarks, 13
Mealy bugs, 36, 139
Medicinal plants,
adder's tongue, 5
apricot, 9
blueberries, 23
burnet, 25–26
carob, 29–30
catnip, 32
chamomile, 20
coleus, 36
corn, 41
crested pricklepoppy, 48
damiana, 46
dill, 49
evening primrose, 49
Mormon tea, 49
Melons, 179
companion plants for, 39
culture, 112
on fences, 206, 207
harvesting tips, 205
trained on A-Frames, 5
Mescal, from agave, 49
Mesquite (*Prosopis juliflora*),
49
Methoxychlor, 7
Mexico, 7, 13–14, 42, 48
Mice, 39, 112
see also Rodents
Midget vegetables, varieties,
112
Mildew, and flour of sulfur,
67
Mildew, powdery (downy),
carrot spray for, 39
Milk cartons, for seedlings,
112–113
Milkweed (*Asclepias
speciosa*), 26, 36, 39, 113
Millet, inhibited by
cucumber, 34
Mineral oil, for corn ear
worm, 41

Mint (*Mentha* spp.), 19, 38,
39, 70, 84, 105, 113,
130, 189
Miscible oil, in aphid
control, 7
Mites, and daddy longlegs, 46
Mitogenic properties, of
plants, 166
Mockingbird, 12, 13
Molasses, 9, 20, 72, 170
Mole plant, deters moles and
mice, 39, 113
Moles, 58, 113–114
Monarch butterfly, 26
Monkey grass (*Liriope*), 114
Monoculture, hazards of, 113
Monstera Deliciosa,
description, 101, 114
Moon,
and frost, 71
and rain, 145
see also Lunar cycles
Moonflower (*Calonyction
sp.*), 105, 179
Mormon tea (*Ephedra
nevadensis*), 49, 114–115
Morning glories, 39, 97, 177,
207
Moso (*Phyllostachys moso*),
edible bamboo, 57
Mosquitos (*Culex pipiens*),
16, 52, 115
Moss, control for, 115
Moss pink (*Phlox subulata*),
115
Moss sandwort (*Arenaria
verna caespitosa*), 115
Moths, 22
Cecropia, 33
destroyed by bats, 16
harmful varieties, 109
and moonflowers, 179
repelled by lavender, 39
Mound layering, 201–202
Mouse plant (*Arisarum
proboscideum*), 115–116
Mowing lawns, 116
Mugwort, 82, 84
Muir, John, 120
Mulch, 184
advantages, 48, 116
for air layering, 201–202
in aphid control, 7
and blossom-end rot, 23
and bulbs, 25
and companion planting,
2, 52
and crown rot, 116
for cucumbers, 43
and cultivation, 48
and damping off, 116
disadvantages, 116
for disease prevention, 50
in fall, 61
from leaf mold, 104
from newspaper, 119
from volcanoes, 180
in garden rows, 2
materials for, 116
and no-dig gardening, 120
and peanuts, 129
and rodents, 25
of seashells, 151
and seedlings, 116

for squash, 55
for tomatoes, 23
and tomatoes, 116
and water rationing, 183
and weeds, 184, 185
of wood ashes, 190
see also Compost
Mung beans (*Phaseolus
mungo*), 117
Mushrooms, nutritional
qualities, 117
Music, and houseplants,
88–89
Mustard oil, for acid soil, 117
Mustard (*Sinapis alba* and
Brassica nigra), 16, 25,
37, 61, 117

N
Nandina (*Nandina*), 118
Nankininsis perilla, 37
Narcotics,
Datura, 47
Wild lettuce, 187
Nasturtiums (*Tropaeolum
majus*), 176, 184, 189
companion plants for, 39,
40, 118
for fences, 207
qualities of, 70, 118
as trap crop, 25
Nausea, dill for, 49
Nematodes,
as disease vectors, 21
and marigolds, 34
non-chemical controls for,
119
soil pasteurization for, 128
and sugar, 119
tests for, 119
Nervousness, catnip for, 32
Netting, for bird protection,
22
Nettles, 38, 39
Newspapers, .
for carrot storage, 31–32
as mulch, 119, 184
New Zealand spinach
(*Tetragonia expansa*),
119–120
Nicotine (pesticide), 7
Nitrogen,
for cauliflower, 33
and eggshells, 58
from peas, 40
in legumes, 104
and lightning, 107
in peanuts, 129
for tomatoes, 23
Nitrogen fixers, poisoned by
buttercups, 26
No-dig gardening, 120
Nopales (cactus pads), 29
Nut pines (*Pinus*), 120–121
Nuts,
with beans, 18
as chicken feed, 34–35
fat from, 5
pecan trees, 130
and squirrels, 158

O
Oatmeal, as chicken feed, 34
Oats (*Avena sativa*), 122

Oil, 21, 98
Ointment, from adder's
tongue, 5
Okra (*Hibiscus esculentus*),
22, 37, 160
boiling water for seeds, 123
culture, 123
description, 122–123
and fruit set, 164
harvesting, 202
hot weather tips, 53–54
and mallow, 123
medicinal properties, 123
Olive, 20
Olive oil, 15, 60
One-leaf pine (*Pinus
monophylla*), 121
Onions (*Allium cepa*),
as aphrodisiac, 8
in companion planting, 38,
39, 40, 123–124
companion to lettuce, 2–3
culture, 123
in fall planting, 61
flowers of, 124
harvesting tips, 202
hot weather tips, 54
medicinal properties, 123
parsley for odor, 36
preparation for freezing, 71
slugs repelled by, 39
tips for peeling, 131
twinning in, 172
varieties, 37, 123
Onions, giant, *see* Giant
Onion
Opium, in wild lettuce, 187
Orange flowers, in herbal
baths, 21
Oregano (*Origanum* spp.),
37, 39, 124, 159
Organic matter,
and compost, 56
and earthworms, 57
and humus, 89
to attract worms, 22
see also Mulch
Organic pesticides, *see*
Pesticides, organic
Oriental fruit moth, 20
Oriental vegetables, 124–125
Ostrich fern (*Matteuccia
struthiopteris*), 198
Overwintering, and heeling
in, 82
Overwintering insects, sprays
for, 7
Owls, 125
Oyster Plant (*Trapopogon
porrifolius*), 125–126
Oystershell (ground), for
insect control, 9

P
Pak choy, 37
Pampas grass (*Cortidera
jubata*), 133
Pansy (*Violaceae*), 69, 74, 127
Papago Indians, desert lily
ajo and, 48
Papaya, 25, 60
Parasites, 9, 21, 22
Parasite wasp, in aphid
control, 7

Parsley, 8, 85, 159, 188
with asparagus, 38
companion plants for, 39
culture, 127–128
eating, 128
harvesting tips, 205
for landscaping, 176
as nutritious aphrodisiac, 8
for onion odor, 36
qualities of, 127–128
Parsnips (*Peucedanum
sativun*), 128, 205
Pasteurization, for soil, 128
Peaches, 128–129
Peacock plant (*Calathea
makoyana*), 128–129
Peanuts (*Arachis hypogaea*),
129
hot weather tips, 54
Peanut shells, for compost, 88
Pears, 20, 64, 129
see also Fruit trees
Peas (*Pisum* spp.), 159
and asparagus beans, 11
and beans, 18
Black-eyed, 23
and buttercups, 26
in companion planting, 38,
39, 40
culture, 129
fungicides for, 129–130
grown at altitude, 86
harvesting tips, 202
hot weather tips, 54
for landscaping, 176
medicinal properties, 130
and mint, 130
and potatoes, 52
seeds from packaged food,
16
varieties, 129–130
and vetch, 177
and walnuts, 38
Peas, sugar-snap, on fences,
206
Peat moss, 21, 61, 116, 130
Pecans, culture, 130
Pennyroyal, companion
plants for, 38
Penstemons, and
hummingbirds, 11
Peonies, 26, 38
Peppermint, 19, 177
Peppers (*Capsicum* spp.),
160, 164, 169
culture, 131
and flour of sulfur, 67
growing tips, 131
grown by Aztecs, 13
harvesting tips, 203
for landscaping, 176
qualities of, 131
supports for, 136
and walnuts, 38
Peppers (green), banana
peels for, 16
Peppers (hot), 37, 131
Peppers (jalapeño), hot
weather tips, 54
Peppers (sweet), varieties, 37
Perennials,
for butterfly gardens, 27
for fire control, 62
garden size for, 186

for naturalizing, 68
and plant bank, 133
and weeds, 184
Perfume, recipes for incense,
131–132
Periwinkle, *see* Vinca
Pesticides, 2, 7
Pests,
armadillos, 9–10
biological control for, 22
butterflies, 27
carpenter bees, 30–31
chigger, 35
controlled by companion
planting, 2
deterred by garlic, 39
fire ants, 63–64
mealy bugs, 36
railroad worm, 143
red spider mites, 144
repelled by marigold, 40
rodents, 25
and soil pasteurization, 128
sow bugs, 156
tomato worm, 38
see also Insects
Pets,
and garlic, 76
and Queen Victoria, 178
Petunias, 177, 184
companion plants for, 40
culture, 132
pinching buds on, 132
and rain, 183
Pheromones, 59, 92–93,
133–134
Philodendron, 101
Phlox, 97
Phytophora, 21
Pieris, vinegar for, 106
Pigweed, 40
see also Lamb's-quarters
Pinching, and flowering, 132
Pineapple, 25
Pink bollworm, 108, 109
Pinks, 20
Piñon pine (*Pinus
cembroides*), 121
Plantago (*Plantago psyllium*),
133
Plantar warts, 181
Plant bank, procedures for,
133
Planting, by astrological
signs, 73–74
Plant lice, *see* Aphids
Plant nutrition, and
dolomite, 51
Plant pests, varieties to
avoid, 133
Plastic bags, for greenhouses,
87
Plastic cups, for seed starts, 24
Plowing, in fall, 61
Plugs, and lawns, 103
Plums, 37, 39
Poinsettia (*Euphorbia*), 134
Poisoning, from home
canning, 24
Poison ivy, 16, 90, 182
Poisonous plants,
castor bean, 48, 113–114
and children, 134
datura, 39

henbane, 39
holly, 134
laurel, 50
mistletoe, 134
poinsettia, 134
wormwood, 40
Pokeweed (*Phytolacca americana*), 185
Pollination,
of corn, 41
for giant vegetables, 155
for houseplants, 20
and insects, 20
and pheromones, 59
and tomatoes, 134
varieties and, 51
Pollinators, luna moth, 109
Pollution,
and houseplants, 88
and plants, 101
Ponds, 161–162
Pony tail (*Beaucarnea recurvata*), 163
Popcorn, 134–135
Potato beetles, 39, 40, 58, 136
Potatoes,
apples stored with, 9
with beans, 38
cleaning silver with, 136
in companion planting, 38, 39, 40
culture, 135
as eye remedy, 59
fertilizing, 135
and flour of sulfur, 67
growing in leaves, 135–136
harvesting tips, 203
healthful benefits, 82
history, 135
and peas, 52
as sting treatment, 76
storage, 135
for tired feet, 61–62
varieties, 37, 76, 135
and walnuts, 38
Potato nematodes, mustard oil for, 117
Potting mixes, with bark, 21
Poultice, of banana peel, 16
Prayer plant (*Maranta leuconeura Kerchoviana*), 136
Praying mantis, in biological control, 22
Precautions, for pesticide use, 7
Pregnant women, and cats, 169
Prescriptions, history of, 147
Preserving fruit, 71
Preserving vegetables, 2
botulism poisoning and, 24
Prickly Pear (*Opuntia*), 28–29, 35, 49
Primrose (*Cyclamen elegans*), 9
Primroses (*Primula acaulis* and *japonica*), 136, 162
Propagation,
bare root techniques, 76
by air layering, 6–7, 200–202
cuttings for, 116–117

Pruning,
for fire blight, 64
for giant vegetables, 155
grapes, 136
shrubs, 136–137
tips for, 147
wisteria, 190
Pseudo-Palms: Cycads (*Cycadaceae*), 137
Pulque, from agave, 49
Pulverized rock, in compost, 43
Pumpkins, 137
companion plants for, 39, 40
edible flowers, 138
on fences, 206
harvesting tips, 205
Pumpkin seeds, promoting virility, 9
Pumpkins (small), trained on A-Frames, 5
Purple coneflower (*Echinacea purpurea*), 187
Purslane (*Portulaca oleracea*), 40, 186
Pussy Willow, 138
Pyrethrum, 7, 156

Q
Quamoclit (*Quamoclit*), 139
Quassia (*Quassia amara*), 139–140
Queen Anne's lace, 36
Queen Victoria, 177–178
Queen Victoria's Water Lily (*Victoria regia*), 140
Quince (*Cydonia oblonga*), 140, 191

R
Rabbits, 127, 142, 160
Rabbit's-foot fern (*Polypodium aureaum*), 198
Raccoons, 40, 142–143
Radishes (*Raphanus sativus*), 159, 189
as aphrodisiac, 8
in companion planting, 38, 39
companion plants for, 40
culture, 143
harvesting tips, 205
lunar planting for, 143
and parsnips, 128
to remove warts, 182
varieties, 37
Railroad worm, and apples, 143
Rain,
and contour planting, 10
and cultivation, 185
effect on bush beans, 18
and lunar cycles, 145
and petunias, 183
problems from, 120
seedling covers for, 22
Rainbows, indicating rain, 184
Rainwater, for houseplants, 6
Raised beds, 50, 143
Rape (*Brassica Napus*), 143–144

Raspberries (*Rubus spidaeus*), 39, 144, 200–201
Recipes,
Al's bean soup, 18
asparagus, 10
with carob, 29
compost, 56
cosmetics, 60
erotological, 8
herbal bath, 20–21
hush-puppies, 89
Indian, 91–92
infant infusions, 49
jalapeño peppers, 96–97
lentils, 106
marigolds, 70
medicinal hay, 82
pumpkin soup, 137
quince jelly, 140
rose water, 146
skin care, 20, 21
tomatillos, 167
wild fruit, 97
Red-banded leaf roller, on apple, 9
Red columbine (*Aquilegia elegantula*), 11
Red-leaved perilla, 37
Red-margined dracaena (*Dracaena marginata*), 163
Red spider mites, controls for, 144
Red stele disease, 21
Reed palm (*Chamaedorea seifrizii*), 163
Rhododendrons, vinegar for, 106
Rhubarb (*Rheum rhaponticum*), 40, 98, 144–145
Rinds, citrus, 144
Ringworm, and jewel weed, 182
Robins, 12, 145
Rocket (*Hesperis matronalis*), 145
Rock gardens, 57, 108, 115–116
Rock phosphate, and superphosphate, 132
Rocks, 159, 171
Rodents,
and bees, 19
and catnip, 83
deterred by Tabasco sauce, 127
and mulch, 25
and owls, 125
repelled by wormwood, 83
see also Pests; Predators
Romans, favorite vegetables of, 8
Root-knot, in tomato, 21
Root rot, control with bark, 21
Roots,
and air layering, 201–202
aphid control in, 7–8
appearance in air layering, 7
black walnut, toxins in, 38
of cardoon, 30
of carob trees, 30

and cultivation, 51
cuttings from, 117
edible, 37
good drainage for, 52–53
ground oystershell for, 9
harvesting, 166
and june beetles, 99
of marigolds, 34
planting depths for, 51
root-bound plants, 146
warmth for, 23
water systems for, 53
Rosemary (*Rosmarinus officinalis*), 19, 20, 21, 38, 84, 159
companion plants for, 38, 40
in fire control, 62
healthful benefits, 82
Roses, Old (*Rosa*), 146–147, 195
Roses (*Rosa*), 19, 20
banana peels for, 16
birth control pills for, 22
and carpenter bees, 30–31
and companion plants, 39
essential oil of, 59
history, 146
insect control for, 146
and Japanese beetles, 98
old names for, 178
qualities of, 69–70
rhubarb spray for, 40
and rose cuttings, 147
rose water, 146
for skin care, 21, 60
tips for pruning, 147
varieties, 70
yellow, 194–195
Rot, blossom-end, 23
Rotation, in aphid control, 7–8
Rotenone, 7, 58, 69, 179
Rototillers, *see* tillers
Royal Water Lily, *see* Queen Victoria's Water Lily
Rubber, in guayule, 79–80
Rue, 19, 38, 40, 83, 177
Runoff, plants for controlling, 13
Rutabagas (*Brassica campestris* var. *rutababa*), 147, 159
Ryania speciosa, 9, 10
Rye, as green manure, 79

S
Saddle-leaf philodendron (*Philodendron selloum*), 163
Safety lights, and plant vigor, 52
Sage, 19, 84, 159, 177
companion plants for, 38, 39, 40
healthful benefits, 82
Sago palm (*Cycas revoluta*), 137
Salsify, 125–126
Salt,
for beets, 21
for flea control, 69
for frosted plants, 72
herbal substitutes for, 154

in houseplants, 100
in natural insecticides, 28
for sprouting potatoes, 203
Salt bush (*Atriplex* spp.), in
 fire control, 62
Salt (coarse), in herbal
 baths, 20
Salvia, 148, 153–154
Sand, 21, 31
Santolina, 19, 159
Sassafras (*Sassafras albidum*),
 148–149
Savory, 159
Sawdust, as soil conditioner,
 52
Saw Palmetto (*Serenoa
 repens*), 46, 149
Scabious, 20
Scallions, 8, 37, 149–150
Scarecrow, 150
Scarlet bugler (*Penstemon
 barbatus*), 11
Scarlet hedge-nettle (*Stachys
 coccinea*), 11
Scotch broom (*Cytisus
 scoparius*), 133
Seakale (*Crambe maritima*),
 83, 151
Seaweed, 151
 spray applications, 71–72
 see also Kelp
Seed beds, soil sterilization
 for, 119
Seedlings,
 covers for, 22
 and eggshells, 58
 fall planting, 61
 handling with spoons, 157
 and mulch, 116
 protection for, 22, 112–113
Seeds,
 for attracting songbirds, 12
 bean, 18
 beet, 21
 crested pricklepoppy, 48
 and disease prevention, 50
 edible, 42
 from packaged spices, 16
 germination and storage,
 24, 151–152, 153, 160
 information about, 152–153
 and lunar cycles, 114
 nut pine, 120–121
 in packaged food, 16
 planting, 156
 planting depths for, 51
 prickly pear cactus, 29
 promoting health, 9
 scatter-planting, 150
 starting in plastic cups, 24
Seepwillow baccharis
 (*Baccharis*), 48
Serpentine layering, 201
Sesame seeds, for skin care,
 191
Sex, in plant kingdom, 51
Shade,
 of *Brassicas* for lettuce, 2–3
 in companion planting, 2
 for ferns, 63
 for hardwood cuttings, 44
 helpful for transplants, 182
 ivies for, 95
 plants for, 13, 153

for seedlings, 61
unsuitable for gardens, 51
and weeds, 184
and willows, 188
Shallots (*Allium Cepa*), 8,
 38, 154
Sheep, poisoned by laurel,
 50–51
Shefflera (*Brassaia
 actinophylla*), 163
Shoots, and air layering,
 201–202
Short-day plants, 52, 132
Short-season crops, for
 mountain gardens, 86
Shrubs,
 and air layering, 201
 for fire control, 62
 for foundation plantings, 93
 pruning, 136–137
Side dressing, 25, 33
Silver lace vine (*Polygonum*),
 179
Skin care,
 and apricots, 9
 and bedstraw, 20
 and bromeliads, 25
 and chamomile, 20
 essential oils for, 58–59
 facial masks, 60
 for hands, 111
 and Irish moss, 94
 and lemon juice, 20
 and oats, 122
 plants for, 60, 82–83,
 190–191
 and rose water, 146
Skullcap, and catnip, 32
Skunk cabbage, repels
 raccoons, 40
Skyrocket (*Ipomopsis
 aggregata*), 11
Sludge, hazards of, 155
Slugs, 25, 39, 139, 155
Smilax, 177
Smoke tree (*Cotinus
 coggygria*), 155
Snails, 25
Snakes, 10, 156
Snapdragons, 184
Snow,
 and evergreens, 59
 and kale, 100
 for watering houseplants, 6
Snow Pea, 125
Soap, from Spanish bayonet,
 48
Sod, and lawns, 104
Soil,
 as compost activator, 41
 conditioned with bark, 21
 and disease prevention, 50
 from lake bottoms, 13
 for giant vegetables, 154
 good drainage for, 52–53
 for herb growing, 84–85
 improved by sunflowers, 40
 loamy, 13
 and mulch, 116
 and no-dig gardening, 120
 pasteurizing procedures, 128
 peat moss for, 21
 preserved by contour
 planting, 10

protected by grasses, 13
protected by plantings, 13
in raised bed gardens, 50
for songbird trees, 13
sterilizing, 119
tests for, 156
tips for protecting, 51
treatment for nematode
 control, 119
warmth in, 23
weeds indicating quality, 51
Soil conditioner, compost,
 56–57
Soil-conditioning, from
 companion planting, 2
Soil (heavy), 52
 improved by chamomile, 39
 organic matter for, 52
 and raised beds, 50
Soil tests, for gardens, 130
Soil (wet), unsuitable for
 gardens, 51
Songbirds,
 list of, 12
 plants for attracting, 12–13
 shelter for, 12, 13
Songs, of birds, 22
Sotol, from spoonplant, 48
Soul food, 36–37, 42–43
Southern peas, *see* Cowpeas
Southernwood (*Artemisia
 abrotanum*), 19, 40,
 159, 174, 177
Sow Bugs (*Oniscus asellus*),
 156
Soybeans, 40, 90–91, 98, 159
Spanish bayonet (*Yucca
 arizonica*), 48
Spanish broom (*Sparticum
 junceum*), 133
Sparrows, 13
Spearmint, 200
Sphagnum moss, 6–7, 77
Spices,
 in homemade incense,
 131–132
 seeds from markets, 16
Spider fern (*Pteris* sp.),
 description, 198
Spider lilies (*Lycoris*), 157
Spiders, 22, 156–157
Spinach (*Spinacia oleracea*),
 22, 132, 159
 as aphrodisiac, 8
 companion plants for, 40
 culture, 157
 on fences, 206
 hot weather varieties, 54,
 206
 nutritional qualities, 8–9,
 157
 varieties, 38
Spined soldier bugs, and
 bean beetles, 112
Splitting, in cabbages, 28
Spoonplant (*Dasylirion*),
 beverages of, 48
Sprays,
 and bees, 86
 best times for, 7
 and biological control, 9
 carrot, 39
 for caterpillars, 107
 for cecropia moth, 33

chamomile, 39
for cucumber beetles, 44
marigold, 39
Octagon soap, 112
for peach leaf curl, 128
soap and water, 36
tips for, 157
see also Insecticides;
 Pesticides
Sprekelsen, J.H. Von, 13
Sprigs, and lawns, 103
Spring,
 fire blight in, 64
 flowers of, 11
 gardens in, 170
 and long-light days, 52
 predator inactivity in, 7
 use of dormant oil in, 7, 33
Sprinklers, coverage with, 86
Sprouts,
 of mung beans, 117
 of sunflower seeds, 157–158
Spurge (mole plant), 39, 113
Squash bugs, 40, 158
Squash (*Cucurbita* sp.), 159,
 160, 200
 with beans, 18
 companion plants for, 38,
 39, 40
 with corn and beans, 92,
 184
 edible flowers, 138
 grown by Aztecs, 13
 harvesting tips, 205
 hot weather tips, 55
 and squash borer, 200
 trained on A-Frames, 5
Squash, Summer (*Cucurbita
 pepo*), 158, 205–206
Squash, Winter (*Cucurbita
 maxima*), 158, 206
Squirrels, 158
Squirrel's-foot fern (*Davallia
 bullata*), 198
Staghorn fern (*Platycerium
 sp.*), 198
Star-glory, 139
Star of Texas, 192
Steam, for sterilizing, 119
Stems,
 banana peels for, 16
 cuttings from, 117
Sterilization of soil, for
 nematode control, 119
Stinging nettles, butterflies
 and, 26
Stings, treatment for, 76
Stock peas, *see* Cowpeas
Stolons,
 of lawn grass, 103
 of mint, 113
Storage,
 carrots, 31–32
 celeriac, 33
 and harvesting tips,
 202–206
 and seed germination, 153
Stout, Ruth, no-dig
 gardening, 120
Stratification, for primrose
 seeds, 136
Straw, as soil conditioner, 52
Strawberries, 38
 benefits of bark in, 21

and buttercup, 26
companion plants for, 38, 39, 40
healthful benefits, 83
landscaping with, 176
for skin care, 60
Strawberry cactus (*Echinocereus*), as food, 49
Strawberry fern (*Hemionitis palmata*), 198
Strawberry jars, 85, 159
St. Augustine grass, decline of, 66
St. Catherine's lace (*Eriogonum giganteum*), 62
St. John's Bread (carob), 29
St. John's Wort, for sunscreen, 84
Streptomycin, for fire blight, 64
Subsoil,
pigweed and, 40
unsuitable for gardens, 51
Succession planting, 159
Succotash, 43
Succulents,
for fire control, 62
living stones, 108
Sugar,
in butterfly nectar, 27
in carob, 29
and fructose, 72
as insecticide, 20
and nematodes, 119
in spoonplant, 48
Sugar cane (*Saccharum officinarum*), 159–160
Sulfur, and bees, 86
Sulfuric acid, for seed germination, 24
Sumac leaves, in aphid control, 9
Summer,
flowers of, 11
gardens for, 160
pruning in, 9
survival tips for, 101
Summer savory, 177
companion plants for, 38, 40
deters bean beetles, 40
healthful benefits, 82
Sundrops (*Oenothera fruticosa*), 187
Sunflowers, 189
attracting songbirds, 12
companion plants for, 38, 39, 40
sprouting the seeds, 158
Sunflower seeds, 9, 158
Sunscreen, herbal, 83–84
Sun tea, 84
Swamp pink (*Helonias bullata*), 161–162
Swans, 161
Sweat, benefits of, 20
Sweet olive, culture, 70
Sweet pea (*Lathyrus* sp.), varieties for fences, 208
Sweet potatoes (*Ipomoea Batatas*), 160
culture, 162

harvesting tips, 162, 203
hot weather varieties, 54
nutritional qualities, 162
storage, 162, 204
Sweet-shoot (*Phyllostachys dulcis*), edible bamboo, 57
Swiss chard (*Beta vulgaris* var. *cicla*), 38, 162
Sword fern (*Nephrolepis* sp.), 198
Syrphus flies, in aphid control, 7

T
Tabasco sauce, and fruit trees, 127
Tannin, 9, 34, 49
Tansy, 40, 45, 82, 177
Tarragon, 40, 84, 159
Tatoos, for African violets, 163–164
Tea,
chamomile, 20, 189
dandelion, 47
dittany, 50–51
herbal, 84
Mormon tea, 49
saw palmetto, 149
Tea bags, 59, 88
Teasel, 36
Temperature, and fruit set, 164.
Tendrils, in climbing plants, 177
Tent caterpillar, control for, 164
Tents, for frost protection, 5
Tequila, from agave, 49
Terpene, 34, 58
Terrariums, 164–165
Texas,
armadillos in, 9–10
and yellow roses, 194–195
Thai basil, 125
Thai winged bean (Bin Dow), 125
Thinning, 51, 165
Thiophene, and marigolds, 34
Thistle (*Cirsium*), medicines from, 49
Three Sisters, 92
Thrips, and quassia, 139
Thyme, 19, 20, 84, 177
companion plants for, 38, 40
lemon, 105
Tickbird (*Cuculidae sulcirostris*), 165–166
Ticks (*Arachnids*), 39, 165
Tillers, 136, 166, 210
Ti plant (*Cordyline terminalis*), 172
Tip layering, 200–201
see also Air layering; Propagation
Tires, and hoses, 166
Toads, 156, 166
Tobacco, and squash bugs, 158
Tobacco budworm, citrus spray for, 108

Tomatillo (*Physalis ixocarpa*), 166–167
Tomatoes, 37, 159, 160, 169, 200
analyzing defects in, 168
as aphrodisiac, 8
banana peels for, 16
barksoil for root-knot, 21
and blossom-end rot, 23, 116
cages for, 167–168
in companion planting, 38, 39, 40
corncobs for, 24–25
and couch grass, 193
determinate vs. indeterminate, 168
on fences, 206, 207
and flour of sulfur, 67
and frost, 61
grown at altitude, 85–86
harvesting tips, 206
hot weather varieties, 54
for landscaping, 176
and lunar signs, 167
and mulch, 23, 116, 134
nutrients for, 23
and pollination, 134
soil preparation for, 23
starts and transplants, 168–169
sun-dried, 160
tips for ripening, 145
transplanting, 24–25, 169
varieties, 168
watering, 23
and weeds, 184
and wind, 134
see also Xtomatl
Tomato worm, 38, 40
Tongue fern (*Cyclophorus lingua*), 198
Tools,
care for, 169
hoe, flat blade, 208–209
hoe, pointed, 208
hoe, using, 208–209
mailboxes for, 170
orange paint for, 127
post-hole digger, 25
sterilizing, 119
for transplanting, 25
for weeding, 185
Tools (wheeled), for long rows, 10
Toothache remedy, seepwillow baccharis, 48
Top dressing, 10, 169
Topsoil, and pigweed, 40
Toxicity,
of animals to pesticides, 7
from car exhaust, 104
Toxic plants, 101, 134
Trace minerals, and kelp, 71–72
Transplants,
and air layering, 200–201
banana peels for, 16
corn, 41
and days to maturity, 32
and flour of sulfur, 67
root-bound, 146
and shade, 182
for summer garden, 160

of tomatoes, 168–169
tools for, 25
trees, 170
vegetables requiring, 169–170
Trap crops,
for *Brassicas*, 25
for deer, 48
eggplant, 40
for Japanese beetles, 97
Traps, for butterflies, 27
Treasure flower (*Gazania ringens*), 160, 170
Tree-of-heaven (*Ailanthus altissima*), 133
Trees,
acacia, 20
alder, 34
bark, 7, 21, 52
for bees, 20
black acacia, 133
black walnut, 38
blue gum, 133
box elder, 111
chemical defenses of, 34
conifers, 12, 36
for fire control, 62
insects in bark, 7
and lightning, 107
and squirrels, 158
supports for young, 160
to attract songbirds, 13
to reduce noise, 13
transplanting, 170
walnut, toxins in, 38
Tree tobacco (*Nicotiana glauca*), 49
Tree tomato (*Cyphomandra betacea*), 170
Tree wrap, for rodents, 112
Trenches, for carrots, 31
Trichogramma wasps, 22, 35
Trollius, 161
Trumpet honeysuckle (*Lonicera sempervirens*), 171
Tubers, planting depths for, 51
Tupelo (*Nyssa* sp.), 20, 171
Turnips (*Brassica campestris* var. *rapa*), 159
fall planting, 61
growing, 172
and hot weather, 54
storage, 172
varieties, 38
Turtle, Box (*Testudinidea*), as garden predator, 25
Tussie-mussies, 67–68

U
Ulcer, corn smut for, 41
Umbelliferae (family), 173–174

V
Vacations, and gardens, 175
Valerian, companion plants for, 40
Valerian root, catnip and, 32
Vanilla (*Vanilla fragrans*), 176
Varieties, of plants, choosing, 32

Vegetables,
  as aphrodisiacs, 8–9
  bamboo as, 15
  bolting, 28, 35, 106, 132
  canning, 2, 24, 195, 202
  choosing, 32
  companion plants for,
    38–40
  and day length, 132
  etymology, 177
  fall planting, 61
  freezing, 71
  fructose in, 72
  history, 177
  and insect damage, 120
  and Japanese beetles, 97–98
  landscaping with, 176–177
  and mulch, 116
  planting market produce,
    16
  propagation by air layering,
    200–202
  purple and red, 37–38
  resistant to nematodes, 119
  and scatter-planting, 150
  tips for canning, 195
  varieties for fences,
    206–208
  warmth for, 190
  and weeds, 209–210
  see also Gardens; Insects;
    specific kinds, i.e.,
    Asparagus
Vegetables, baby, see Midget
  vegetables
Vegetable seeds, information
  about, 152–153
Vegetables, giant, 154–155
Vegetables, oriental, 124–125
Vegetative propagation,
  by air layering, 6, 201–202
  techniques for, 116–117
Verbena (Verbena), 26, 105
Vetch (Vicia), 39, 177
Vinca (Vinca) (periwinkle),
  160, 178, 184
Vinegar,
  for acid soil, 106
  burnet in, 26
  in fire ant control, 64
  and flowers, 178
  in herbal baths, 21
  and slugs, 155
  as sting treatment, 76
  storage of, 21
Vine peach (Cucumis chito)
  (mango melon), 179
Vines,
  and continuous air
    layering, 201
  for fences, 207
  for fire control, 62
  and mulch, 183
  supported on bed springs,
    21
  tips for growing, 208

  trained on A-Frames, 5
  varieties for camouflage,
    179
  watering tips, 183
  see also Climbing plants;
    Climbing support
Violets (Violaceae), 69, 74,
  178, 179, 180, 184
Viper's bugloss, 20
Virility, vegetables
  promoting, 8–9
Virus (granulosis), for insect
  control, 9
Vitamins,
  in apricots, 9
  in broccoli, 25
  and bromeliads, 25
  in cactus, 29
  in cantaloupes, 30
  in corn, 41
  in figs, 63
  in parsley, 8
  in spinach, 8
Volcanoes, mulch from, 180
Voodoo, and datura, 47

W
Walking fern (Camptosorus
  sp.), 198
Walkways, plants for, 115
Walnut, black, see Black
  walnut
Warmth,
  for black-eyed peas, 23
  for melons, 112
  methods for determining,
    61
  providing for vegetables,
    190
  stones in garden for, 159
  in summer garden, 160
  and tomatoes, 23
Warts, 16, 18, 181
Wasps, 7, 20, 22, 112, 136
Wastes (industrial), in
  garden sites, 51
Wastes (organic), as soil
  conditioners, 52
Water,
  and blossom-end rot, 23
  and cabbages, 28
  for cucumbers, 43
  for desert gardens, 48
  and disease prevention, 50
  efficient systems for, 53
  and giant vegetables, 154
  and good drainage, 52–53
  and gray water, 78–79
  methods for applying, 51
  to attract songbirds, 12–13
  for windowboxes, 188
Watercress (Nasturtium
  offinale), 182
Watering,
  African violets, 6
  in air layering, 6–7

  best times for, 182
  drip irrigation, 53
  for houseplants, 100,
    175–176
  and mulch, 116
  with pipes, 94
  with sprinklers, 86
  for vines, 183
Watermelons (Citrullus
  lanatus), 160
  growing, 182
  harvesting, 205
  and pollinators, 182
  ripeness test, 183
  varieties, 182
Watermelon (small), trained
  on A-Frames, 5
Water rationing, and mulch,
  183
Water witching, see Dowsing
Weather lore, for gardeners,
  183–184
Weeding, 184, 185
Weeds, 51
  for attracting songbirds, 12
  beneficial, 5, 209–210
  bleach for, 41
  bluejays and, 24
  buttercups, 26
  controlled by companion
    planting, 2
  and cultivation, 48, 185
  and dolomite, 51
  edible, 39
  and ferns, 184
  and groundcovers, 184
  indicating soil condition,
    51
  inhibited by cucumber, 34
  and mulch, 116, 185
  and no-dig gardening, 120
  as soil conditioner, 52
  see also Companion
    planting; Gardens
Weeping fig (Ficus
  benjamina), 163
Wheat, as growth hormone,
  79
Wheatgrass, 189
White vinegar, for herbal
  baths, 21
Wilder, Louise Beebe, 62,
  69, 178
Wildflowers, 186–187
  see also specific kinds
Wild game, and juniper
  berries, 99
Wild ginger (Asarum
  canadense), 77
Wild lettuce (Lactuca virosa),
  187
Wild rose, 19
Wild spinach, see
  Lamb's-quarters
Wild sweet pea (Lathyrus
  latifolius), 187

Willow gentian (Gentiana
  ascelepiades), 161
Willow (Salix spp.), 34,
  187–188
Wilting, and carpenter bees,
  30–31
Wind, 133, 134
Windbreaks, trees for, 13
Windowboxes, greens
  varieties for, 189
Windowbox gardening,
  choosing plants for, 188
Wine, and elderberries, 58
Winter,
  attracting birds in, 13
  chickens in, 34
  houseplants in, 189
Wintercreeper (Euonymus
  fortunei), 179
Wishbone flower (Torenia
  fournieri), 189
Wisteria (Wisteria), 177,
  189–190, 201
Witchcraft, and datura, 47
Witch hazel (Hammelia sp.),
  190
Woolly apple aphid, 7, 9, 118
Worms, 22, 25, 125
Wormwood, 19, 40, 83

X
Xanthisma texanum (Star of
  Texas), 192
Xeranthemum (Immortelle),
  192
Xerophytes, description, 192
Xtomatl (Lycopersicum
  esculentum), 192–193
  see also Tomatoes
Y
Yarrow (Achillea millefolium),
  194
  in Christmas wreaths, 35
  companion plants for, 40
Yeast, in insecticides, 9, 20
Yellow rose of Texas, history,
  194–195
Yellow-wood (Cladrastis sp.),
  195
Yew, 195
Yields, 76, 120
Yoghurt, for skin care, 60
Yuen shai (Chinese parsley),
  125

Z
Zamia (Zamia furfuracae), 137
Zebra plant, see Peacock
  plant
Zepher lily, 197
Zinnia (Zinnia elegans), 160,
  177, 197–198
Zoysia (Zoysia), description,
  198
Zucchini (Cucurbita Pepo
  var. Melopepo), 198–199